Before and After the Fall

Before and After the Fall

CONTRASTING MODES IN

Paradise Lost

KATHLEEN M. SWAIM

THE UNIVERSITY OF MASSACHUSETTS PRESS

AMHERST 1986

Printed in the United States of America

Designed by Barbara Werden

Set in Linotron Garamond #3 at G & S Typesetters

Printed by Cushing-Malloy and bound by John Dekker & Sons

Library of Congress Cataloging-in-Publication Data

Swaim, Kathleen M.

Before and after the fall.

Bibliography: p.

Includes index.

1. Milton, John, 1608–1674.   Paradise lost.

2. Fall of man in literature.   3. Angels in literature.

4. Theology in literature.   I. Title.

PR3562.S93   1986   821'.4   85-28925

ISBN 0-87023-504-4

This publication has been supported by the
National Endowment for the Humanities, a federal agency which
supports the study of such fields as
history, philosophy, literature, and language.

FOR MY PARENTS

Contents

Preface

My starting point is a proposition about which there can be no disagreement: that *Paradise Lost* is about the fall and its antecedents and consequences and that the fall in Milton's epic makes a radical difference to humanity, to the physical universe, to human perception and communication, and to the relationship of humanity and God. Although enormous amounts of illuminating theological and literary analysis have been targeted on Milton's backgrounds, contexts, and literary art in *Paradise Lost*, some portions of the epic have received less than due attention. My present purpose is to examine two such large blocks of the text, the record of Raphael's visit to Adam and Eve in Books 5–8 and the record of Michael's visit in Books 11–12. This body of material, amounting to nearly half of the twelve books of *Paradise Lost*, presents the dichotomy of the prelapsarian and the postlapsarian in amplified and telling form. I shall attend particularly to the lapsarian contrasts between Raphael and Michael as angelic ambassadors, as teachers, reasoners, and explicators of the radically different principles and epistemologies that govern the unfallen and fallen universes and the alterations in the conduct of human life and relationship to deity. Because Milton deliberately deployed Raphael and Michael for purposes of such a contrast, a thorough examination of the content and intent of these major characters in the epic and these major blocks of text will provide new perspectives on the whole epic's design and themes and on some heretofore unexplored ways in which *Paradise Lost* fulfills an epic's generic responsibility to include (all) the learning of the culture it represents. This study will also put in perspective what have been the least appreciated and the most severely criticized sections of the epic, Raphael's Battle in Heaven and Michael's review of biblical history.

The following study is organized as follows: An introductory chapter reviews backgrounds, characteristics, and the divinely assigned missions of the two angels and looks at some lapsarian issues and thematic dichotomies in Milton's thought and prose works. Chapter 1 explores primarily structural evidence from *Paradise Lost* to call attention to lapsarian contrasts in the pedagogical procedures of Raphael and Michael and to some notable occasions on which Michael's postlapsarian materials recapitulate Raphael's prelapsarian analogues. Chapter 2 pursues the distinction between Raphael's use of the book of God's works and Michael's use of the book of God's word, especially as these are available in contrasting patterns of vegetative and solar imagery and diction. Chapter 3 provides a detailed consideration of the ways in which the lapsarian angels' procedures are informed by Ramistic logic, suggesting that the first half of Ramistic logic, Invention, illuminates Raphael's province in the epic and that the second half of Ramistic logic, Disposition or Judgment, illuminates Michael's. Chapter 4 seeks to define several bases of contrasting lapsarian poetics, especially Raphael's characteristic use of analogy and Michael's characteristic use of typology. The concluding chapter suggests some widening perspectives on the lapsarian contrasts in Milton's epic. Measured against the background of Renaissance faculty psychology, for example, Raphael's prelapsarian materials and presentation align with the faculty of the fantasy or the imagination, and Michael's postlapsarian materials and presentation align with the faculty of the memory.

Although no full-scale contrasts of Raphael and Michael and the prelapsarian and postlapsarian in *Paradise Lost* exist, many commentators either directly or indirectly shed light on these issues. A review of a few of these will outline some of the directions of the following study. Lapsarian contrasts are implicit in George Whiting's phrases "the pendant world" and "this transient World" (*Paradise Lost* 2.1052 and 12.554), and in John Spencer Hill's distinction between "self-regulating generation" and "divinely directed *re*generation," and in Virginia R. Mollenkott's contrast of "Hellenic questioning" and "Hebraic sense of duty to God," and in William G. Riggs's distinction between the "Homeric epic" of the "Orphic poet" Raphael and "Michael's biblical redaction," and in Robert L. Entzminger's examination of divine revelations in the creation and the Scriptures, on the one hand external and indicative and on the other hand internal and commemorative.[1] Northrop Frye's recognition of shifts in metaphors from the eye to the ear also underlies the inquiry:

> The visual image is centripetal: it holds the body immobile in a pose of static obedience, and sets the sign of authority before it. The revelation by the word

is centrifugal: it is primarily a command, the starting-point of a course of action.[2]

A more precisely developed and expansive contrast between the two angels and their procedures and intentions occurs in Sherman Hawkins's concise introduction to a discussion of *Samson Agonistes*:

> The contrast amounts almost to a difference of genre, with Raphael's narrative as epic and Michael's as tragedy. The action of Raphael's epic is cosmic and mythical, a war between superhuman forces of good and evil. In this direct confrontation, evil is defeated and good triumphant; the destruction of Book VI and the creation of Book VII are separate and sequential actions. The world of epic affirms the good; Abdiel, the exemplar of solitary virtue, the epic hero proposed for Adam's imitation, is finally with the majority, the side that wins. In contrast, the action of Michael's prophecy is historic and human: the conflict of God and Satan takes place in this world and in the heart of man. Creation and destruction are strangely interwoven throughout human history, in the tragic paradox that good is produced from evil. For the world of tragedy is "To good malignant, to bad man benign" (XII 538) and Christ, the one just man alive, the tragic hero proposed to Adam's faith, is on the side that loses—at least in this world and time. [3]

Finally, and suggestively, in a chapter entitled "The Two Instructions," Irene Samuel illuminates the contrast between Raphael and Michael, aligning Raphael's materials and teaching with Dante's *Paradiso* and Michael's with *Purgatorio*. For Raphael and Beatrice, who function in the relation of more or less equals with their pupils, the atmosphere is of leisure, effortless ascent, and expansion of tone and of universe. For Virgil and Michael, however, who function in the relation of superiors to their inferior pupils, the atmosphere is of urgency, difficult progress, and compression. Here, following contrition the goal is cure or reeducation and is necessarily stressful.[4] Hawkins, too, draws a distinction between prelapsarian nourishment and postlapsarian cure.

Although they are not generally recognized as lapsarian dichotomies, as many commentators on his work have pointed out, Milton tends to deal in dichotomous structures of art and thought. We may note as examples some of the philosophical issues that have most exercised human reason throughout its recorded history: the relationship of physics and metaphysics, Pla-

tonic synthesis and Aristotelian analysis, the ontological and the tele-
ological, noetic and dianoetic address to the world, and the deity's creative
or generative capacity and his redemptive or providential office. In his
discussion of Milton's typology, William G. Madsen has outlined a set of
wide-ranging philosophical, theological, and psychological distinctions
that provide a context for my present inquiry. Madsen aligns Milton with
the Hebraic categories in this survey:

> *Paradise Lost* brings into dramatic and symbolic confrontation two modes of
> thought that appear in varying proportions in the Christian tradition. On the
> one hand there is the Greek, and especially the Platonic and Neoplatonic,
> emphasis on ontology, on the universe as a harmonious and proportioned
> structure, on the regularity of nature as the visible manifestation of the logos
> that is immanent in the world; on the other hand there is the Hebrew
> emphasis on psychology, on the primacy of individual encounters with God
> and of particular covenants with Him, and on nature as the setting in which
> these encounters take place. In Greek thought the emphasis is on the
> present, the Eternal Now which bodies forth the rational structure of the
> universe. In Hebrew thought the emphasis is on history as the embodiment
> of God's purpose, and history is especially the record of those specific times
> when God communicated with man in a special way. The past and the future
> thus assume an importance they do not have in classicism.

In the discussion that follows Madsen finds the Middle Ages embracing the
Greek view in its liturgical and sacramental emphasis and in its preference
for being over becoming and for the visual over the aural. Its elaborate
system of static correspondences between the earthly and the heavenly
bespeaks a primary but not exclusive interest "in the timeless structure of
eternity as physically manifested in the natural world and in the forms and
symbols of daily life." For Madsen the Hebraic view, on the other hand, is
embraced by the Reformation with its emphasis upon history and personal
encounters with the deity. Although he contrasts the Neoplatonic and
typological in chronological terms, Madsen prefers the latter as the ex-
clusive explanation for Milton's literary practice; he does not, that is, take
into account the lapsarian contrast within Milton's epic.[5]

One of the most fundamental systems of dichotomies in sixteenth- and
seventeenth-century England is to be found in Ramistic logic, a reforma-
tion of Aristotelian logic which flourished in Protestant countries of Europe
and especially among Puritans in England and America. Milton's *Fuller
Institution of the Art of Logic Arranged after the Method of Peter Ramus* (1672) is

one of many contemporary revisions of Ramus's basic logical textbook. To the twentieth-century eye, the most prominent features of Ramistic logic are its inexorable oversimplifications and bifurcations, and indeed, according to its modern expositor, Ramism was a system "of pedagogic exigency, rather than intellectual integrity."[6] In chapter 3 of the present study I borrow the logical categories and vocabulary of this radically dichotomized textbook to establish some binary bases for examining the values, pedagogy, and poetics of Raphael and Michael in *Paradise Lost*. I apply, that is, Milton's logical text to the content and processes of these angelic teachers' instruction of their prelapsarian and postlapsarian pupils. Like the two angels Milton was himself a teacher, and as his pamphlet *Of Education* makes clear, in Milton's view education is a radically lapsarian matter, as famously in the pronouncement: "The end then of learning is to repair the ruins of our first parents by regaining to know God aright." Milton's prose works frequently call attention to his judgment of how poorly logic was taught in the schools of his time, but close examination of the uses of logic in *Paradise Lost* shows that it can be truly an organic art, as it is labeled in *Of Education*, one worthy of alignment with "the sublime art" of poetry. Because Milton's aims in *Paradise Lost* are variously didactic and because two of the major characters in the epic are explicitly teachers, close attention to the author's educational theory and logical textbook, as well as to the angels' pedagogical practice as it derives from these, promises to illuminate the thematic and artistic issues of the epic in expected and unexpected ways.

Although the following discussion focuses constantly on contrasts and dichotomies within *Paradise Lost*, it must be stressed that these do not function as exclusive or excluding alternatives, as either/or's. I am dealing with oppositions here in the way in which *L'Allegro* and *Il Penseroso* are opposites; that is, although the two lapsarian conditions and the two angelic messengers, like the two halves of Milton's youthful twinned poems, articulate directly oppositional complexes of imagery and thought, they also participate in a cumulative design that reflects the complex reality of the human condition, both in its diurnal vicissitudes and in its processes of maturing. The contrasts are between the halves that make up the complete whole that is a human individual.

. . .

Unless otherwise indicated, citations of Milton's works are drawn from *John Milton: Complete Poems and Major Prose*, ed. Merritt Y. Hughes (New York: Odyssey Press, 1957). Citations of prose works not available in Hughes's edition are drawn from the Columbia edition of *The Works of John Milton*, ed. Frank A. Patterson et al. (New York: Columbia University Press, 1931–42), identified when necessary within my text as CE. The numerous citations of Milton's *Art of Logic* are also referenced within the text to the Yale edition: *Complete Prose Works of John Milton*, ed. Don M. Wolfe (New Haven: Yale University Press, 1953–82), vol. 8, ed. Maurice Kelley. Introductions and other apparatus in this edition have often been consulted. Unless otherwise indicated, biblical citations are from the King James version.

A portion of chapter 2 is a revised form of "Flower, Fruit, and Seed: A Reading of *Paradise Lost*," published in *Milton Studies*, vol. V, ed. James D. Simmonds (Pittsburgh: University of Pittsburgh Press, 1973), pp. 155–76; and chapter 4 shares a half-dozen paragraphs with "The Mimesis of Accommodation in *Paradise Lost* Book III," published in *Philological Quarterly* 63 (1984): 461–75. Both are reused by permission.

For their helpful readings of the present manuscript, I wish to thank Mary Ann Radzinowicz, Lee Jacobus, Vincent DiMarco, and Dan Collins, and for similar and additional assistance on this project my thanks are due to Suzie D. Beans, Elizabeth Ann Swaim, and Margo Culley.

Before and After the Fall

Introduction

BROADENING understanding of the range of meanings of *fall* will emerge as our study progresses, but we may begin with some foundational Miltonic categories. In *At a Solemn Music* Milton looks forward to a return to the prelapsarian condition, contrasting it with present fallen realities in these terms:

> That we on Earth with undiscording voice
> May rightly answer that melodious noise;
> As once we did, till disproportion'd sin
> Jarr'd against nature's chime, and with harsh din
> Broke the fair music that all creatures made
> To their great Lord, whose love their motion sway'd
> In perfect Diapason, whilst they stood
> In first obedience and their state of good. (17 – 24)

The terms *fall* and *lapse* presuppose a standard from which one has been separated downward, and in this early lyric Milton identifies that standard as perfectly unified, harmonious, and naturally continuous and celebratory of the divine toward which the creation aspires. The original lapse into disobedience and sin intrudes disproportion and disharmony upon such divine and natural order and unity. The consequences of the radical breach are all-inclusive, but much of the range is captured in Michael's explanation to Adam of the loss of "Rational Liberty":

> yet know withal,
> Since thy original lapse, true Liberty
> Is lost, which always with right Reason dwells

> Twinn'd, and from her hath no dividual being:
> Reason in man obscur'd, or not obey'd,
> Immediately inordinate desires
> And upstart Passions catch the Government
> From Reason, and to servitude reduce
> Man till then free. (12. 82–90)

In Book 1 of *Christian Doctrine*, chapters 10 and 11, Milton examines "the Providence of God" as it relates to man "in his state of rectitude" (CE 15 : 113) and as it is observable in his sin "and the misery consequent upon it, as well as in his restoration" (179). In man's first state of obedience, goodness, and freedom, God "furnished him with whatever was calculated to make life happy" (113). In Eden "it was the disposition of man to do what was right, as a being naturally good and holy" (115). Made in the image of God, man there had "implanted and innate in him" "the whole law of nature," "which is sufficient of itself to teach whatever is agreeable to right reason, that is to say, whatever is intrinsically good" (115–17). Such "perfect Diapason" is jarred by sin, disobedience to divine command, and transgression of the law and conscience. As Milton explains, "The sin which is common to all men is that which our first parents, and in them all their posterity committed, when, casting off their obedience to God, they tasted the fruit of the forbidden tree" (181). That heinous offense comprehended transgression of the whole law (181). In a later definition, original sin is "the loss of original righteousness, and the corruption of the whole mind" (197), and, of course, "After sin came death, as the calamity or punishment consequent upon it" (203).

In the tradition Milton inherited, Raphael and Michael, along with Gabriel and Uriel, are the four angels of the presence of God. Etymologically, *Raphael* is "medicine of God" or "God has healed," and *Michael* is "godlike" or "strength of God" or "who is as God." Traditionally, Raphael is also the angel of prayer, love, joy, light, and the guardian of the Tree of Life in the garden of Eden, and most importantly for our purposes he is the angel of science and knowledge, the preceptor angel. Michael, on the other hand, is the angel of repentance, righteousness, mercy, and sanctification; most importantly for our purposes, he is the deliverer of the faithful and the angel of the final reckoning and the weigher of souls, the benevolent angel of death and the mighty warrior of God.[1] In Pico's *On the Dignity of Man*, Raphael is invoked as the "celestial physician" who may "set us free by moral philosophy" and Michael as the "high priest" "who will distinguish those who have completed their term in the service of philosophy with the holy office of theology as if with a crown of precious stones." [2] In general and in Milton's *Christian Doctrine* Michael is considered the greatest of the angels, often (though not explicitly by Milton) equated with Christ.

In Book 1, chapter 9, of *Christian Doctrine*, "Of the Special Government of Angels," Milton finds that good angels are "dispersed around the throne of God in the capacity of ministering agents"; that their principal office is praising God to whom they are "obedient in all respects"; that they preside over particular areas and are sometimes divine messengers; and that although they have remarkable intelligence, they are not omniscient (Hughes, pp. 990–92; CE 15 : 105–11). In his study of Milton's angelology, Robert H. West judges that Milton "does not care exactly how angels control the fancy, or what the orders are, or what precisely the substance— once it is conceded to be inferior to God's, superior to ours, hence immortal, invisible, swift, yet in some senses bodily, best described as like that of highest heaven." West summarizes that generally Milton's angelology shares "the Puritan indifference to speculation more detailed than piety calls for." [3]

Milton's angelic messengers are not merely theological givens or epic machinery; more importantly, they are characters and agents in the justification of God's ways to men and in the exploration of the causes and effects of the fall. In his definitive study of angelic visits in the epic tradition, Thomas M. Greene summarizes the features of the celestial descent in these terms:

> It constitutes typically a crucial nexus of the narrative; it represents the intersection of time and the timeless; it points to the human realm of paramount concern to the gods; and it brings divine authority to the unfolding heroic action. [4]

An introductory consideration of the arrivals, natures, and missions of Milton's heavenly messengers will highlight the divine's paramount concerns in *Paradise Lost* and this epic's various intersections of the human and the divine, time and the timeless. In incidental detail as well as in its largest shapes, the evidence also outlines the contrast between the prelapsarian and the postlapsarian. It quickly becomes clear that Milton intends these contrasts to be significant.

The descents from heaven of Adam's two angelic visitors in *Paradise Lost* evidence the contrast between the prelapsarian and the postlapsarian both in largest outlines and in small details. Raphael visits and explicates for his pupil Adam a prelapsarian universe that is unified, harmonious, continuous, and hierarchical; Michael visits and addresses a world that is divided and contradictory. As Raphael presents hierarchies of nature, meaning, and understanding, Michael offers arrays that are horizontal rather than vertical, temporal rather than spatial, methodical rather than organic, teleological rather than ontological. In contrast to Raphael's lessons in the book of nature, Michael presents lessons in Scripture and conduct. Both angels affect human vision, but Raphael takes up the simpler process of guiding Adam to full awareness of external reality manifesting itself and its creator. Michael's is theological revelation, the divine manifesting himself and his will throughout history and by means of signs, types, and covenants. Raphael presents Adam with an open-ended world and ascent, and Michael defines a contained structure of time and truth, sequence and consequence, in which one collects fragments and then re-collects them. Re-collection translated into psychology becomes the process of memory, and memory is central to Michael's instruction as immediate perception, or what the poem calls "sudden apprehension," is central to Raphael's. As Raphael's instruction aims at synthesis, so Michael's proceeds through analysis. If Raphael provides the model of the poet, Michael provides the model of the literary critic, a role which the Protestant Reformation enjoined upon every believer.

This series of contrasts will be explored in the following pages; for the present we may begin with the evidence of Raphael's and Michael's missions and arrivals. Both messengers are sent in the wake of a Satanic temptation, a failed and a successful one, and as a kind of reply to human acts of worship. In Book 5 Raphael's assignment follows the extended hymn of praise in which the first couple affirm the interrelated units of the hierarchical cosmos whose lyric celebration they share in perfect diapason in their state of good. After the close examination of Eve's temptation dream, the threat and residue of evil evaporate: "All was clear'd" (5.136). "So pray'd they innocent," the narrator informs us, "and to thir thoughts / Firm peace recover'd soon and wonted calm" (209–10). The morning hymn and the contexts it epitomizes reflect the prelapsarian condition as defined above: all is perfectly unified, harmonious, and naturally continuous and celebratory of the divine toward which the creation aspires.

The analogous postlapsarian scene follows the remorseful couple's prostration, confession, and contrition with which Book 10 ends and the regeneration and intercession of Christ with which Book 11 begins. As in *Christian Doctrine* 1.11, the providence of God is now observable in man's sin and its miseries but also, and more importantly, in mankind's restoration (CE 15.179). Prevenient grace descends (11.3) to the first couple who, upon ending their orisons,

> found
> Strength added from above, new hope to spring
> Out of despair, joy, but with fear yet linkt. (11.137–39)

As Adam describes the paradoxical influx of grace, it is both a novelty and a restoration, New Dispensation and *re*demption.

> persuasion in me grew
> That I was heard with favor; peace return'd
> Home to my Breast, and to my memory
> His promise. (152–55)

Prelapsarian stasis, hierarchy, and unity have given way to postlapsarian dynamism and the new possibilities for height as well as depth in the spirits and psychologies of the fallen humans. As emissary to this complex and contradictory condition, Michael is singled out from the Synod of the Blest to present divine justice and represent divine mercy and promise.

Raphael's assignment is thus formulated by the deity:

> *Raphael*, said hee, thou hear'st what stir on Earth
> *Satan* from Hell scap't through the darksome Gulf
> Hath rais'd in Paradise, and how disturb'd
> This night the human pair, how he designs
> In them at once to ruin all mankind.
> Go therefore, half this day as friend with friend
> Converse with *Adam*, in what Bow'r or shade
> Thou find'st him from the heat of Noon retir'd,
> To respite his day-labor with repast,
> Or with repose; and such discourse bring on,
> As may advise him of his happy state,
> Happiness in his power left free to will,
> Left to his own free Will, his Will though free,
> Yet mutable; whence warn him to beware
> He swerve not too secure: tell him withal

His danger, and from whom, what enemy
Late fall'n himself from Heaven, is plotting now
The fall of others from like state of bliss;
By violence, no, for that shall be withstood,
But by deceit and lies; this let him know,
Lest wilfully transgressing he pretend
Surprisal, unadmonisht, unforewarn'd.

So spake th' Eternal Father, and fulfill'd
All Justice. (5.224—47)

The speech begins with a recapitulation of the poem's immediately preced-
ing action and of the Satanic intent from Books 1 and 2 as made operative in
Satan's toad-inspired dream and of the first couple's garden context and
diurnal rhythms. The motives are paternal, just, and compassionate. The
imperative verbs of Raphael's assignment—"Converse," "such discourse
bring on," "advise," "warn," "tell him," and "this let him know"—dictate
his "medicinable" sociability and allow Raphael considerable creative free-
dom in communicating his message of past history, instructive example,
and future danger. Raphael highlights the danger in his war story and man's
happy state in his creation story.

The sociable spirit is asked to reinforce Adam's understanding of his
earthly situation with its definitive condition of obedience, his future chal-
lenge, and his spiritual prospects. The warning is a double one: against a
particular agent whose powerful enmity is to be analogously offered and
against Adam's overconfidence in the security of his situation and will.
Because the enemy will proceed through deception, Adam's grasp of truth or
Truth must be strengthened. In New Testament terms that Truth is repre-
sented in Christ, who is presented both to post-Christian readers of the
poem and to the pre-Christian Adam through the Son's role in the Battle in
Heaven. In the Old Testament or pre-Christian terms that obtain chrono-
logically, the truth against which Satanic lies can be measured is available
through the unity, order, justice, creativity, wisdom, and love of the Cre-
ator. Adam's not yet tainted experiential world harmonizes with faith,
unity, truth. As the warning "to beware / He swerve not too secure"
indicates, Raphael must provide certain securities while removing others.
Raphael must keep Adam's world of images and Adam's mental processes
open to spiritual and poetic or noetic awareness and modes of awareness.

Raphael's strategy of presenting analogies between Heaven and earth, here recommended by the deity himself, fulfills this mission and becomes the most characteristic feature of his content and expression.

The verbs of Michael's assignment, the divine imperatives—"Haste thee," "drive out," "denounce," "all terror hide," and "reveal"—define a quite different mood and chronology:

> *Michael*, this my behest have thou in charge,
> Take to thee from among the Cherubim
> Thy choice of flaming Warriors, lest the Fiend
> Or in behalf of Man, or to invade
> Vacant possession some new trouble raise:
> Haste thee, and from the Paradise of God
> Without remorse drive out the sinful Pair,
> From hallow'd ground th' unholy, and denounce
> To them and to thir Progeny from thence
> Perpetual banishment. Yet lest they faint
> At the sad Sentence rigorously urg'd,
> For I behold them soft'nd and with tears
> Bewailing thir excess, all terror hide.
> If patiently thy bidding they obey,
> Dismiss them not disconsolate; reveal
> To *Adam* what shall come in future days,
> As I shall thee enlighten, intermix
> My Cov'nant in the woman's seed renew'd;
> So send them forth, though sorrowing, yet in peace. (11.99–117)

God's tone is now saddened and muted; he is an Old Testament jealous God concerned to defend sanctity and exclude the fallen as justice seems to demand. The earthly context has widened in space and time. Temporal and moral categories recur throughout Michael's assignment, as do suggestions of the "mysterious terms" to be revealed more fully in the future. The "If" of line 112 shows that contingencies now operate. Haste, banishment, qualified rigor, and consolation are the terms of the postlapsarian assignment. But the content of the message is also to be revelation, prophetic history, inspired enlightenment, an intermixture of divine covenant and human historical renewal, a mixture of sorrow and peace. Michael's assignment is contingent, as Raphael's was not, upon the receptivity of his audience and upon the illuminations the messenger will himself be given in the process of fulfilling his errand. Insofar as he is the military angel, Michael is assigned to establish clear battle lines and solid fortification against an enemy whose attack has already been mobilized.

The epithets applied to the two visiting angels reinforce these distinctions and purposes. Raphael's introductory epithet is "the sociable Spirit" (5.221), and he is sent by a foreseeing and pitying deity to converse with Adam "as friend with friend" (5.229). In Adam's phrases Raphael is "Our Heav'nly stranger" (316, 397) and "Native of Heav'n" (361); in the narrator's he is "the Angelic Virtue" (371). The sociable spirit is socially received and socially entertained; he invokes from Adam and Eve what of his own sociability they share. Additional epithets clarify Raphael's presence and function: In Adam's direct address Raphael is "Inhabitant with God" (461), "favorable Spirit, propitious guest" (507), "Divine instructor" (546), "Divine Interpreter" (7.72), "Divine / Historian"(8.6–7), "pure / Intelligence of Heav'n, Angel serene" (180–81), and "heavenly Guest, Ethereal Messenger" (646). To the narrator Raphael is "th' Empyreal Minister" (5.460), "the winged Hierarch" (468), "his illustrious Guest" (7.109), "the Godlike Angel" (110), and "the Godlike Power" (8.249).⁵ Adam addresses neither Raphael nor Michael directly by name, but Book 11, line 235, shows that he is aware of the name of his first angelic visitor.

Similarly, the epithets applied to Michael clarify his presence and his relationship to Adam. The initial address shows Adam's uncertainty:

> Celestial, whether among the Thrones, or nam'd
> Of them the Highest, for such shape may seem
> Prince above Princes. (9.296–98)

In other of Adam's epithets Michael is "safe Guide" (11.371), "O Teacher" (450), "True opener of mine eyes, prime Angel blest" (598), "Heav'nly instructor" (871), "O sent from Heav'n, / Enlight'ner of my darkness" (12.270–71), "O Prophet of glad tidings, finisher / Of utmost hope" (375–76), and "Seer blest" (553). The narrator refers to Michael as "the gentle Angel" (11.421) and "the hast'ning Angel" (12.637), but otherwise the narrator uses Michael's name without adjective or epithet, consistently calling him only "th' Angel" or "th' Archangel." An index of the sequential and formulaic quality of Michael's books of the epic may be seen in the eight recurrences of the phrase "To [or T'] whom thus *Michael*" (11.334, 466, 603, 683, 787; 12.79, 285, 386), plus the similar "To whom *Michael* thus" (11.453). Adam never indicates an awareness of Michael's name or a recollection that his interlocutor is the angel whose martial exploits in the Battle in Heaven Adam has heard of from Raphael, the "Prince" of "Celestial Armies," the first "in Military prowess," and "the Prince of Angels" (6.44–45, 281).

Adam explicitly contrasts the second angel's visit with Raphael's in Book 11. Raphael is described as "sociably mild . . . that I should much confide," and Michael is "not terrible / That I should fear . . . But solemn and sublime" (11.233–36). Eve takes an active part in the hospitality for Raphael but must retire from the majestic Michael's arrival. Raphael inspires confidence in the Adam who goes to meet him clad only in "his own complete / Perfections" (5.352–53); Michael inspires awe in the Adam whose eyes have been dimmed by "doubt / And carnal fear" (11.211–12). Although, like Raphael, Michael approaches Adam without escort, unlike the solitary Raphael, Michael is sent to earth attended by "flaming Warriors" (11.101) and "the Cohort bright / Of watchful Cherubim" (127–28).

Raphael's "glorious shape"(5.362) is that of a Seraph with three pairs of wings. His presence is signaled by "Heav'nly fragrance," and his appearance is marked by wondrous colors and textures: "With regal Ornament," "with downy Gold / And colors dipt in Heav'n," "with feather'd mail / Sky-tinctur'd grain" (280–85). A series of similes (which we shall return to in a moment) describes his approach: to the birds he resembles a phoenix; the narrator compares him to Maia's son Mercury; and Adam tells Eve he "seems another Morn / Ris'n on mid-noon" (310–11). The angels guarding Eden honor the "message high" (5.289) he brings, and Adam expects from him "some great behest from Heav'n" (311). The "glorious Apparition" Michael, too, brings "Heav'n's high behest" (11.251), but the unprefaced suddenness of its delivery contrasts with Raphael's gradual graciousness. Adam bows to both visitors, but of Michael we are told: "Hee Kingly from his State / Inclin'd not" in response (11.249–50). Michael comes to the fallen Adam "Not in his shape Celestial, but as Man / Clad to meet Man" (239–40). He comes as a wondrous sight, but in human regalia: clad in a military vest and armed with sword, spear, and helmet. Even so small a detail as the specification of a particular age for Michael— "prime / In Manhood where Youth ended" (245–46)—reflects the intrusion of temporal categories into the fallen world. The Prince of Angels fulfills the pattern of a prince among men. The majestic military angel has come to militarize humanity for the battle ahead, the only battle that matters, the exercise of "the better fortitude / Of Patience and Heroic

Martyrdom" (9.31–32), a battle to be waged by those who put on the whole armor of God as in Ephesians 6 and the first book of *The Faerie Queene*. Adam advises Eve to "expect great tidings" (11.226) from the approaching Michael, and these are the good news of the Matthew Gospel. Adam anticipates "New Laws to be observ'd" (228), and they are the laws of love and grace and of the New Dispensation which Michael's prophecy looks forward to the occasion and fulfillment of.

Contrasting solar phenomena are invoked to describe the arrivals of these angelic ministers of light. Raphael comes through air that is perfectly clarified: "no cloud or, to obstruct his sight, / Star interpos'd" (5.257–58). Raphael is perceived by Adam as "another Morn / Ris'n on mid-noon" in an enhancement of light that exactly models the prelapsarian vision he mediates. Raphael arrives at noon, Michael just with and after the dawn, which *re*salutes "the World with sacred Light" (11.134). The complex solar phenomena of Michael's arrival require interpretation and application. Adam asks Eve:

> why in the East
> Darkness ere Day's mid-course, and Morning light
> More orient in yon Western Cloud that draws
> O'er the blue Firmament a radiant white,
> And slow descends, with something heav'nly fraught. (11.203–7)

The juxtaposition of eclipse with angelic radiance nicely models Michael's postlapsarian target and mode.

As we shall see in various later evidence, generally speaking the classical attaches to the prelapsarian and to Raphael, and the biblical attaches to Michael. Thus, the arriving Raphael is "Like *Maia's* son" (5.285), and the arriving Michael recalls the angels who approached Jacob in Mahanaim and Elisha in Dothan (11.213–20). Even so small a detail as that *Raphael* does not appear in the canonical Scriptures but that Michael appears several times reinforces the point.

As Thomas Greene has pointed out, the conventions of angelic descent have involved bird similes ever since *The Odyssey* and *The Aeneid*.[6] The attachment of the phoenix, then, to the descent of the Hellenic Raphael into the perfections of Eden is thoroughly appropriate, although this bird image also provides Milton with an opportunity for suggesting Christian transformation of epic convention. Raphael's approaching light introduces an epic simile with classical provenance:

within soar
Of Tow'ring Eagles, to all the Fowls he seems
A *Phoenix*, gaz'd by all, as that sole Bird
When to enshrine his reliques in the Sun's
Bright Temple, to *Egyptian Thebes* he flies. (5.270–74)

Kester Svendsen examines the image and its implications for Raphael's mission in *Milton and Science*:

Raphael descends like a great legendary solar bird . . . to instruct mankind, flying a long while before he reaches the low level of the towering eagle, a natural bird also sacred to the sun. Out of that creative center— God and the sun—comes supernatural grace, conveyed now as instruction, later by Christ, who like the phoenix dies and is resurrected. There are undercurrents in the pagan-Christian connotations of the solar bird, the god of sun and of healing Apollo, and Raphael, literally the divine healer, who would be a sun god in any other mythology and whose advice is a kind of preventive medicine. Certainly his godlike glittering appearance (made much of here), his contra-Satanic journey to earth, and the unique grace of his divinely directed mission are symbolized and enforced by the phoenix. [7]

Milton's phoenix simile emphasizes the uniqueness and wonder of the figure and aligns Adam and Eve with "the Sun's / Bright Temple" where Raphael's message and mission will be enshrined. The postlapsarian reader may go on to align *sun* with *Son*, recall Saint Paul's Corinthian metaphor for *Temple* (e.g., 2 Cor. 6:16), and interpret *Egypt* as "place of bondage," but for present purposes the basic format of epic simile itself is as significant as the simile's content.

This significance becomes even clearer when we turn to the analogous image attached to Michael's arrival. The bird image, though filtered through the classical, is here drawn from nature not from art, and is to be read differently:

nigh in her [Morn's] sight
The Bird of *Jove*, stoopt from his aery tow'r,
Two Birds of gayest plume before him drove . . .
Direct to th' Eastern Gate was bent thir flight. (11.184–90)

"The Bird of *Jove*," along with its companion image of "the Beast that reigns in Woods," has the effect of an epic simile and its characteristic homologation, but in fact the images are not similes but rather "nature's mute signs" requiring human interpretation. As readers of the epic, we are the more inclined to read this material as a compounding epic simile because we have been offered close equivalents of such animals and such hunting earlier and were there disciplined to process them appropriately, translating the "prowling Wolf, / Whom hunger drives to seek new haunt for prey" and the "Tiger, who by chance hath spi'd / In some Purlieu two gentle Fawns at play" as Satan, and the gentle fawns and flocks "In hurdl'd Cotes amid the field secure" as Adam and Eve. These occasions in Book 4 (183–87, 403–8) brought into unfallen Eden the reader's fallen experience, but by Book 11 Eden and Adam and the mode of the poetry and participation of the reader have changed. Adam has become more active as an interpreter: He assesses the natural signs as "Forerunners of [divine] purpose" (11.195), asks potentially productive questions about the meaning of "this double object in our sight" (201), and reads the attendant cosmic phenomena as "with something heav'nly fraught" (207). Michael's arrival fulfills the sign and promise written upon the natural world for this special occasion. The natural phenomena do not merely decorate the arrival but participate in the narrative action and particularly signal the internalization, the psycho-spiritualizing of epic convention. The Jove reference may seem to point in a classical direction, but the materials are processed in thoroughly Reforma-tionist Protestant ways.

By convention, epics begin *in medias res* and present the past by way of flashbacks and the future by way of prophecy. These chronological assign-ments to Raphael and Michael align with a dominant thematic conflict in *Paradise Lost*. A number of vocabularies have been set forth to convey that conflict, but the terms I shall rely on are *experience* and *faith*, that is, knowing by or the epistemology of experience or of faith. These are conven-ient terms for the distinctions John M. Steadman draws between "appear-ance and reality, secular and divine standards of judgment," and between "the universal and infallible knowledge of the Creator and the partial and often fallible knowledge of the creature."[8] In *The Reason of Church Govern-ment* Milton similarly distinguishes between "lower wisdom" and "the only high valuable wisdom," which is of God and his true worship. Lower wisdom "rests in the contemplation of naturall causes and dimensions"; it is low because its object is low. Milton proceeds to observe "that God even to a strictness requires the improvement of these his entrusted gifts" and to address the problem of knowledge: "how and in what manner [a person] shall dispose and employ those summes of knowledge and illumination, which God hath sent him into this world to trade with" (3.1.229). We shall return to the problem of knowledge, which Milton here calls "a sore burden of mind," after a closer look at the relationship of Raphael and Michael to experience and faith or, in Milton's phrasing, to "knowledge and illumination." In one sense, Raphael is primarily responsible for supplying Adam with vicarious experience and Michael for fortifying Adam's faith.

Experience is the category of fallenness in Milton's epic, of facts, things, time, and literalness, of visibilia and weight, of that which is available to the lower sensory faculties and that which is subject to the law of gravity, that is, the downward pull of earth. The psychic need to "prove" God, that is, to translate matters of faith into matters of experience, underlies several of the crises of the epic. If, for example, we answer Satan's rhetorical question about the War in Heaven—"and till then who knew / The force of those dire Arms?" (1.93–94)—by replying that the good angels knew, we are distinguishing between their epistemology of faith and Satan's reliance upon experience, his need to "put to proof his high Supremacy" (132). Again, in her decision to part from Adam on the fateful morning, Eve is governed by her need to prove, to try, to assay her virtue (9.317, 335). Satan argues from experience in tempting Eve, on the grounds that because he as a serpent ate the apple without harm and became able to speak she as a person will attain the knowledge of the gods if she will follow his precedent. She believes him, and as soon as she eats she suddenly begins to worship the tree and to worship her own experience (807). Acting on Eve's advice—"On my experience, *Adam*, freely taste" (988)—Adam also commits himself to looking only to the past and to what has already been established. After his fall Adam is described as "Submitting to what seem'd remediless"; in despair he asks, "past who can recall, or done undo?" (919, 926). He thus cuts himself off not only from God but also from the future. To idolize one's own experience includes a choice of despair over grace as of past over future. The epistemology of experience implies previously established standards and demands that the present be measured by external realities and confined by precedents. It defines reason as the faculty of such measurement and as man's highest faculty.

Raphael's challenging assignment is to supply a prelapsarian Adam with the equivalent of experience, to give him a past that will allow valid measurement of his present, but to do so in ways that will not cut Adam off from the future and future growth, from the alternative epistemology of faith. Raphael is the expounder of hierarchy and of organic unity, but he is also the advocate of synthesis and aspiration. Characteristically, even while presenting Adam with history and experience, with settled data, Raphael is simultaneously suggesting that Adam stretch his perception beyond the corporeal and toward the spiritual. Immediately after announcing that he will draw likenesses between these two realms for Adam's edification, Raphael poses the rhetorical question: "what if Earth / Be but the shadow of Heav'n, and things therein / Each to other like, more than on Earth is thought?" (5.574–76). Adam must learn to ask questions to continue his growth, but his inquiry must proceed in the right order and in the right spirit. Raphael supplies Adam with equivalents of past experience to support Adam's present complete faith and obedience and to facilitate his future judgment. Some form of moral experience is necessary, because reason is choice, and right choice requires a lesser option to reject. But Raphael also reinforces the epistemological alternative. In Adam's prelapsarian condition faith is the given, the standard that Adam both coincides with and aspires to enhance. Raphael's task is the double one of supplying experiential analogues and of providing models for and exercising Adam in recognizing the interrelationship of faith and experience. In fulfilling this task Raphael presents both a content and a method, both history and a process for mental and spiritual transcendence of history's constrictions.

Michael's complex assignment is also to reinforce Adam's faith to allow him to endure and transcend experience, but as Barbara Lewalski has pointed out, within the Protestant tradition experience is "the proving-ground of the Word."[9] In the phrasing of Heb. 11:1, faith is "the substance of things hoped for, the evidence of things not seen." Saint Paul's letters regularly distinguish between faith and experience, the unseen and the seen, the divine and the worldly, as for example 2 Cor. 7:10 and 4:17–18 or Rom. 1:17–20. For Roland M. Frye—to cite only one commentary on *Paradise Lost* that interrelates the theological and the poetic—"Faith is the existential incorporation of God's redemption, the application of it to the center of man's own being, and the individual acceptance of God's ultimate accommodation in the Son."[10] Faith is here definable, insofar as it is definable, chiefly in terms of negation and in contrast to its experiential opposite. It is a future category, looking forward to the achievement of immateriality and the transcendence of time and of the visible, sensory creation. It implies an epistemology that defies experience, history, the past, and mere reason and looks forward to the realization of what has not yet been. It argues the need that the present be kept open to and measured by future possibility and the fulfillment of God's promises, and the need for human readiness and receptivity to divine will and divine generosity. It recognizes the limitations of human reasoning even though such reasoning is essential to the responsible conduct of human life. Faith begins and moves upward from humanly defined norms. It presupposes psychic openness, freedom, aspiration, optimism, growth, and grace.

Michael's challenging assignment in *Paradise Lost* is to supply the postlapsarian Adam with a future prospect that will allow him to measure sensory fact by the light of ultimate Truth and to translate his participation in the dynamic human condition into a more fully exercised spiritual capacity. Postlapsarian growth will proceed by leaps and lapses in a world that is fragmented and for a psyche that must create its own spiritual coherence amid insistent uncertainties and with sensory and rational equipment that is known to have been faulty in the past. Michael must teach Adam how to rise above the limitations of experience and reason and how to exercise his spiritual arms in the battle for vision, faith, and salvation. Michael must therefore explicate for Adam the patterns of fragmented experience and present him with processes for interpreting and transcending the divisions in his external and internal worlds. In Adam's postlapsarian condition experience is the given, the definition and context of Adam's being and life process. Michael's task, like Raphael's, is a double one, and Michael's instruction, too, presents both a content and a method. Michael must teach Adam to transmute experience into faith and to read their dynamic interrelationship, but before he can fulfill this goal he must transmit to Adam an awakened awareness of future possibilities, a sense of hope, and a vision of ultimate goals in which he participates and to which he is responsible.

In the background of its lapsarian issues and angelic missions, *Paradise Lost* variously treats the problem of knowledge, that is, in the words of *The Reason of Church Government*, the "sore burden of mind" as to "how and in what manner [we] shall dispense and employ those summes of knowledge and illumination, which God hath sent [us] into this world to trade with" (3.1.229). Two narrative forms this problem prominently takes in the epic are the conflicts of innocence with experience and of innocence with faith. Thomas H. Blackburn helpfully sorts the issues into lapsarian alternatives by distinguishing between innocence as naive purity untouched by evil and innocence as the chronological antonym of guilt, that is, *not yet* guilty. He argues too for a dominance of conceptual knowledge in prelapsarian Eden and for the fall as supplying "experiential knowledge of an actuality rather than any intellectual enlightenment or increase in moral acuteness" and as reversing the prelapsarian balance of experiential knowledge of good and conceptual knowledge of evil.[11] Innocence and experience are not dichotomous or problematic before the fall, where we find, as Barbara K. Lewalski describes it, "a mode of life steadily increasing in complexity and challenge and difficulty but at the same time and by that very fact, in perfection," a mode of life defined by radical growth and process.[12] The problem of knowledge is, briefly, how to accumulate experience without entirely losing innocence. The human condition is vital, progressing through a time sequence that implies incremental growth. A human life begins in innocence and inevitably accrues experience. The innocent eagerly address the unfamiliar, hopeful of expanding their awareness and selves. All too often, however, in trying all things in order to embrace that which is good and true as Saint Paul recommended, the innocent encounter and are shocked and repelled by the evil and false. Reaction to such betrayals is withdrawal; thus, increasing awareness creates scars and multiplies fortifications. As these accumulate, human beings are in danger of sacrificing affirmation and hope to withdrawal and fear, of abandoning all risks in favor of self-defense and of thus turning against their own vital growth and becoming absorbed in their own wounds and enslaved by their own pasts. Egocentrism replaces love, hope, trust. Satan is the character in *Paradise Lost* who has fully achieved these negative conditions, and the epic variously sets before the reader, as Raphael variously sets before his edenic audience, the negative example of Satan's exercises in despair, spite, and self-servitude.

As teachers Raphael and Michael present their pupils with guidelines for solving the problem of knowledge. Raphael provides a format for accumulating experiences without sacrificing innocence, and Michael supplies a modus operandi for processing the experiences so that they may be properly evaluated and transcended. Before the fall Adam and Eve enjoy a secure and idyllic existence in a state of innocence. Their lives are free and full of affirmation and love of each other and the Creator. They are joyfully responsive to the external world and receptive to the lessons that emerge from it. They are vital, growing, and therefore accumulating wholesome and coherent contacts with an external world. After the fall humanity learns by experiments, testing, proofs. In the postlapsarian world things and events claim for themselves a reality and priority that exclude the options of spirit and intuition and surprise and growth. After the fall experience contrasts chiefly not with innocence but with that other way of knowing, faith. After the fall, if faith can be activated, it will serve some of the same positive ends as innocence before the fall. It will open up future possibilities and make love, affirmation, growth, and joy accessible. It will teach the believer to transcend the experiential and the self.

Two Miltonic solutions to the problem of knowledge are embedded in two of Milton's 1644 prose works, the pamphlet *Of Education* and the classical oration *Areopagitica*. In *The Second Defense of the English People* Milton explains that he prepared these two documents in order to promote domestic liberty; "nothing can be more necessary [than education] to principle the minds of men in virtue," he says there of the former, and the latter he describes as intended to promulgate "the power of determining what was true and what was false" (Hughes, pp. 830–31). The two documents underscore the lapsarian contrasts of the present study, with *Of Education* establishing the pedagogical methods and goals from and toward which Raphael works, and *Areopagitica* recognizing the conditions for learning "as therefore the state of man now is" (p. 728), learning for a fallen humanity addressing a divided and delusive world of postlapsarian experience. Milton's practical and methodically ordered educational tractate proposes a program of studies, exercise, and diet to insure the physical, intellectual, political, and spiritual well-being of his pupils. Milton's classical oration against censorship, however, is essentially an argument for freedom of learning, inquiry, and humanistic growth within the moral polarities of a fallen world.[13]

In its most famous pronouncement, *Of Education* defines the purpose and goal of learning in lapsarian terms:

> The end then of learning is to repair the ruins of our first parents by regaining to know God aright, and out of that knowledge to love him, to imitate him, to be like him, as we may the nearest by possessing our souls of true virtue, which being united to the heavenly grace of faith makes up the highest perfection. (Hughes, p. 631)

Here, as in *Paradise Lost*, Milton assumes a fundamental relationship between success or failure in reasoning and the fall of man, but in the program *Of Education* recommends for achieving perfection of learning, the educational pamphlet in fact also assumes that the teacher is dealing with young and innocent and teachable youth who differ from the unfallen Adam in years but not in moral experience. Although it speaks of postlapsarian "repair," in fact *Of Education* addresses prelapsarian prospects. The prelap-

sarian may be seen underlying the idealism of the pamphlet's other defini-
tion of its subject: "I call therefore a complete and generous education that
which fits a man to perform justly, skilfully, and magnanimously all the
offices, both private and public, of peace and war" (p. 632). Oliver M.
Ainsworth, one of the most careful students of Milton's pamphlet, distin-
guishes between its two definitions of education: On the one hand, educa-
tion studies the visible creation and infers the existence of God by a process
of reasoning, and on the other education does "not attempt to prove the
existence of God" but assumes "it as the basis of all thought and action." [14]
The first of these formulations neatly captures Raphael's role and procedures
in *Paradise Lost*, his explications of the natural visible world, and his draw-
ing out inferences of deity for Adam's edification, as the second clarifies
Michael's assumptions about faith and the limitations of the human mind in
the epic's final books.

The body of the educational pamphlet is given over to a description of the
procedures through which education may ideally be accomplished:

> Because our understanding cannot in this body found itself but on sensible
> things, nor arrive so clearly to the knowledge of God and things invisible as
> by orderly conning over the visible and inferior creature, the same method is
> necessarily to be followed in all discreet teaching. (P. 631)

The unseen is arrived at through a progressive apprenticeship to the visible;
in the elegant phrasing of Balachandra Rajan, familiarity with the compo-
nents of nature "liberates a response to entelechies which transform and
sustain the facts of the familiar." [15] Again and again Milton proved himself a
most discreet teacher, particularly in his poetry, which constantly interre-
lates the visible, inferior, and sensible creation to the invisible and transcen-
dent order and divinity inherent or incarnate in it and available to the
human understanding that will build from such a foundation.

The majority of the education pamphlet's text is devoted to setting forth a
pattern of developmental learning that moves upward from a secure grasp of
the fundamentals of experience—such subject matters as natural history,
geography, agriculture—to culminate in the reading and creation of poetry.
William R. Parker likens the sequence of learning to the Great Chain of
Being and observes, too, that when in the fourth year students were exposed
both to poetry and to field trips, "what had seemed largely theoretical
would be translated, simultaneously, into the practical *and* the aesthetic." [16]
The starting point for Milton, as for education as understood in his time,

was classical languages, but Milton differs from many of his contemporaries in his insistence that the earliest vocabulary and material should be practical and substantial and memorable and therefore both efficient in the present and foundational for later vision and growth. "Solid things" and "things useful to be known" (Hughes, p. 631) precede "the acts of ripest judgment and the final work of a head filled by long reading and observing" for which they prepare. Milton's hierarchy moves from "natural knowledge" through ethics, politics, and theology to the "organic arts" of literary composition—logic, rhetoric, and the "sublime art" of poetry (p. 636). Students are to "proceed by the steady pace of learning onward . . . until they have confirmed and solidly united the whole body of their perfected knowledge" (p. 637). They are prepared to write when through this sequence of instruction "they shall be thus fraught with an universal insight into things" (p. 637). The procedure is variously hierarchical, from rudiments to subtleties, and regularly applicable to the public and private offices of a learned and a gentle man. It moves from things to ideas to vision, from data to imitation to creativity. Students are to accumulate experience directly and borrow it vicariously from their reading and to move onward from experience to matters of faith and poetry. Proper presentation will show "what religious, what glorious and magnificent use might be made of poetry, both in divine and human things" (p. 637).

Raphael's program of instruction for prelapsarian Adam builds upon similar principles. Raphael supplies Adam with vicarious equivalents of experience that will not compromise his innocence and with the outlines of an orderly procedure for wholesome intellectual growth whose model is the Great Chain of Being, the natural universe that is Adam's textbook. Prelapsarian learning solves the problem of knowledge by moving outward in sequential circles from a secure and unified core and thus annexing and assimilating new territories that are immediately adjacent to core knowledge rather than far-fetched. It is an organic procedure, as Irene Samuel has noted, "in which every ascent keeps the circumference still linked to the center," and its governing principles are "due sequence and organic unity in learning."[17] Prelapsarian learning, which is like the natural world in being layered, hierarchical, analogous, unified, organic, and aspirational, is safe and not problematic. As such it reinforces the foundations of sequential and hierarchical learning as set forth in Milton's pedagogical pamphlet. Because human beings live in a world of sense objects and think in terms of material things, they can achieve an understanding of the invisible and the divine only as it is made available through the visible creation. In absolute terms for Milton the highest perfection and knowledge are of God and are therefore inaccessible, but what is available to the imperfect comprehension of humanity is the visible lower creation, which provides guidelines for approaching the deity. A large component of Raphael's teaching mission is to guide Adam's awareness to the patterns and continuity of the corporeal forms of creation and their spiritual analogues, to mediate "what surmounts the reach / Of human sense" (5.571–72).

Of Education was written when Milton had himself spent several years as a schoolmaster and had had a chance to apply what an anonymous early biographer describes as this "easy and delightful method for training up gentry" (Hughes, p. 1040). From the point of view of Milton when he himself was a pupil, similar sequences of developmental learning and a similar culmination in poetry are set forward in the youthful Prolusions. In these academic exercises, according to Howard Schultz, Milton "marshalled exuberant Latinity to express . . . the boundless expectations of the full Renaissance."[18] After a review of lower realms in Prolusion 3, for example, the culmination occurs in these exhortatory terms:

> But your mind should not consent to be limited and circumscribed by the earth's boundaries, but should range beyond the confines of the world. Let it reach the summit of knowledge and learn to know itself and at the same time to know those blessed minds and intelligences with whom hereafter it will enter into eternal fellowship. (Hughes, p. 607)

And exuberantly in Prolusion 7 we find:

> So at last, Gentlemen, when the cycle of universal knowledge has been completed, still the spirit will be restless in our dark imprisonment here, and it will rove about until the bounds of creation itself no longer limit the divine magnificence of its quest. (P. 625)

To the young Milton such a learned man will attain "possession of the stronghold of wisdom" and can become "a contemporary of time itself" and "the oracle of many peoples" and can enjoy "a kingdom within" (p. 625). Similarly, Prolusion 2 equates poets with "divine oracles" (p. 603); *At a Vacation Exercise* arrays the topoi to which "the deep transported mind may soar" (lines 33 ff.); *Il Penseroso* expansively celebrates the rewards of contemplating "Where more is meant than meets the ear" or eye (line 120); and *Ad Patrem*, lines 86–92, gratefully acknowledges the rich learning of heaven and earth that Milton's father's generosity provided to him. Norman B. Council summarizes Milton's primary assumption in these terms, that "Education, unfettered by vocational, rhetorical, or other limiting concerns, should ideally provide access to universal knowledge."[19] The youthfulness of these Baconian views bespeaks an idealistic, able, ambitious, and enthusiastic scholar; here we hear Milton as a young Platonist with a future of passionate study ahead of him. The Milton of such views is himself identifiably prelapsarian and a not inappropriate model for the later portrait of edenic Adam, though like the unfallen Adam this Milton too must learn to "be lowly wise."

Although Milton's pamphlet *Of Education* defines the goal of learning as repairing the ruins of our first parents, in fact the process of instruction there set forth is designed for students before and during their teenage years, students who are therefore still remarkably innocent and susceptible to learning in an orderly sequence and from the simpler to the more complex, the concrete to the abstract, the material to the spiritual. Another of Milton's prose works, indeed his most famous one, *Areopagitica*, has much to say about the process of learning "as therefore the state of man now is" (Hughes, p. 728), of learning after the fall, of learning for those whose innocence is behind them and who are seriously embarked on making coherent sense out of their own individual and disorderly accumulations of fallen experience. Reasoning is now a matter of making choices, of recognizing options as moral alternatives, and of testing the true by the false. *Areopagitica* puts these points eloquently:

> Good and evil we know in the field of this world grow up together almost inseparably; and the knowledge of good is so involved and interwoven with the knowledge of evil, and in so many cunning resemblances hardly to be discerned, that those confused seeds which were imposed on Psyche as an incessant labor to cull out and sort asunder, were not more intermixed. It was from out the rind of one apple tasted, that the knowledge of good and evil, as two twins cleaving together, leaped forth into the world. And perhaps this is that doom which Adam fell into of knowing good and evil, that is to say, of knowing good by evil. (P. 728)

> Assuredly we bring not innocence into the world, we bring impurity much rather: that which purifies us is trial, and trial is by what is contrary. (P. 728)

Many there be that complain of divine providence for suffering Adam to transgress. Foolish tongues! when God gave him reason, he gave him freedom to choose, for reason is but choosing. (P. 733)

The same lapsarian point is made in *Christian Doctrine*:

It was called the tree of knowledge of good and evil from the event; for since Adam tasted it, we not only know evil, but we know good only by means of evil. For it is by evil that virtue is chiefly exercised, and shines with greater brightness. (Hughes, p. 993; CE 15 : 115)

Even *Of Education* allows for the exercise of intelligent moral choice, Aristotle's *proairesis*, when students have attained sufficient years (Hughes, p. 635).

As we have seen, Raphael's external world is unified, hierarchical, and open-ended, inviting the intuitively able human reasoner to ascend the scale of nature toward God. In *De Doctrina* 1.10 Milton describes the law of prelapsarian nature "which is sufficient of itself to teach whatever is agreeable to right reason, that is to say, whatever is intrinsically good," a law that was "implanted and innate" in unfallen Adam made in God's image (Hughes, p. 933; CE 15 : 115). But Michael's postlapsarian world is "intrinsically bad," divided and confusing. It requires the human reasoner to weigh alternatives against each other and make choices. Moreover, Michael defines a structure of truth that is closed rather than open and that requires human beings within that framework to collect as many as possible of the fragments toward a total structure. Once fragments of truth have been collected, they must then be remembered, or re-collected, as the standard against which future options are measured and to which true additions may be made. *Areopagitica* visualizes this process through a memorable mythological image:

Truth indeed came once into the world with her divine Master, and was a perfect shape most glorious to look on. But when he ascended, and his apostles after him were laid asleep, then straight arose a wicked race of deceivers, who, as that story goes of the Egyptian Typhon with his conspirators, how they dealt with the good Osiris, took the virgin Truth, hewed her lovely form into a thousand pieces, and scattered them to the four winds. From that time ever since, the sad friends of Truth, such as durst appear, imitating the careful search that Isis made for the mangled body of Osiris, went up and down gathering up limb by limb still as they could find them.

We have not yet found them all, Lords and Commons, nor ever shall do, till
her Master's second coming. He shall bring together every joint and member,
and shall mold them into an immortal feature of loveliness and perfection.
(Hughes, pp. 741–42)

Balachandra Rajan has examined this and related images in the classical
oration and applied their model to describing the process of *Paradise Lost*,
particularly its final postlapsarian books:

> *Areopagitica* is dominated by images of labor and progress in the reconsti-
> tuting of truth—the temple built collectively from many timbers, the
> bringing together of the torn body of Osiris-Orpheus, the separation of the
> wheat from the tares, and the confused seeds which Psyche must sort
> asunder. We live in a world dominated by contending and opposite prin-
> ciples, but their shadows mix in a confusion which demands our vigilance in
> detecting the right outline. . . . We can say without being excessively
> fanciful that the movement of the poem is the bringing together of the pieces
> of the torn body. To cull out the seeds, whether in life or in art, is to come to
> understand and to respond creatively to the dialectic of contraries which
> underlies the confusions of existence. What the poem through its enact-
> ments progressively remembers and finally establishes is the homogenous
> and proportional body of truth, the unity of being which is its pattern. [20]

Elsewhere Rajan has examined the centrality of the Isis–Osiris image to the
network of Milton's thought and pointed out that, whereas the design
resembles Raphael's recommendation of progressing from the known to the
unknown, it differs from Raphael's procedure by translating the pattern
from space to history. [21]

The shift from space to time and from established unity to progressive
transcendence of divisions is precisely the difference between the prelap-
sarian and the postlapsarian. For fallen man reason is a matter of exercising
choice but also of receiving or pursuing and applying revelation. Fallen man
and especially Protestant fallen man must practice the art of gathering as
outlined in *Areopagitica* and noted also in *The Doctrine and Discipline of
Divorce*. There we find the image describing Christ's followers' relationship
to him:

> There is scarce any one saying in the Gospel, but must bee read with
> limitations and distinctions, to bee rightly understood; for Christ gives no
> full comments or continued discourses, but . . . speaks oft in Monosyllables,

like a maister, scattering the heavenly grain of his doctrine like pearl heer and
there, which requires a skilfull and laborious gatherer, who must compare
the words he findes, with other precepts, with the end of every ordinance,
and with the general *analogie* of Evangelick doctrine: otherwise many partic-
ular sayings would bee but strange repugnant riddles. (CE 3.2.490–91)

Milton held that the Bible was the principal source of Truth or of those
truths that are worth the struggle of collecting in *Areopagitica*. As a Protes-
tant he held also that much of the process of accumulating truth lay in the
individual Christian's efforts to interpret the Bible and to interrelate its
lessons and absolutes with the facts of his life and of human history. His
Christian Doctrine is eloquent testimony to the diligence and ardor of
Milton's own biblical collection and re-collection.

Reading Scripture is a special kind of exercise in gathering together the
broken and scattered pieces of Christian truth or, as it were, re-membering
Osiris. The student's difficulties with the Bible as central text are com-
pounded by the fact that the Scriptures are themselves radically divided
between the Old and New Testaments, each of which consists of the work of
varied human authors. Even the Book of Genesis is divided in content and
mode between the opening etiological myth and the subsequent historical
narrative. Milton saw human history as radically divided along the lines of
the testaments, between the Old and New Dispensations, between law and
grace. Like other contemporary and older thinkers Milton believed that the
Old Testament was to be read in the light of the New and that characters and
events from Hebrew history prefigure characters and events in Christian
history and psychology. Such typological or transtemporal interpretation
addresses materials that are still in process and open before the student, who
must actively strive to attain a unified understanding. Like the Bible itself,
typology is a system that is by definition divided and that brings to bear a
reasoning or a reading based upon choices and acts of memory. One reads by
the light of revelation, and one reasons by choices that are at once logical
and theological, factual and creative or transcendent.

Michael is Adam's instructor in typology and Scripture, as Raphael is
Adam's instructor in analogy and the book of nature. Raphael sets forth a
hierarchical structure by which our bodies may at last turn all to spirit in
contemplation of created things; Michael also presents a prospect of transla-
tion from flesh to spirit, but that translation is now to be effected not
through climbing a ladder of analogies but through leaps of faith and flashes
of revelation. In Raphael's universe and pedagogy, things expand in clearly

widening circles to open up the luminous ideas they contain. In Michael's allegorical world it is a given that things have been separated from their meaning by time and sin and that the perceivers must supply the meaning by searching their sometimes contradictory books and their memories and aligning the meanings there secured to the outward evidences. The exercise exactly fulfills the intention of *Areopagitica*. Fallen humanity sorts its data as Psyche sorts her seeds and gathers its fragments of truth as Isis gathers up the limbs of her fragmented husband. Chronologically too, postlapsarian knowing looks both backward to reattaining the original innocence and forward to the achievement of a new transcendent awareness. With the Savior's Second Coming, when Isis shall have collected all the pieces of truth, human awareness will move from seeing with Saint Paul through a glass darkly to seeing face to face.

I · *Lapsarian Structures*

Our curiosity shall have this noble satisfaction, we shall know how the Angels
know, by knowing as they know. We shall not pass from Author to Author, as in a
Grammar School, nor from Art to Art, as in an University; but . . . God
shall create us all Doctors in a minute. That great Library, those
infinite Volumes of the Books of Creatures, shall be taken away, quite away,
no more nature; . . . no more preaching, no more reading of Scriptures, and that
great School-Mistress, Experience, and Observation shall be remov'd,
no new thing to be done, and in an Instant, I shall know more,
than they all could reveal to me.

JOHN DONNE, *Sermon*

N HER comparison of *The Divine Comedy* and *Paradise
Lost*, Irene Samuel calls both poems encyclopedias of the
learning of their time and works in which angels, the epic
poet of Rome, and Beauty personified are turned into
schoolmasters and schoolmistresses. But, she goes on to
say, "in both perhaps the greatest daring was simply to
present education as the central human action, and an organic method of
teaching as the substance of poetry."[1] As we turn our attention to the
pedagogical structures of *Paradise Lost*, it is tempting to indulge in the sort
of academic conceit evident in the Donne sermon passage cited above and to
contrast, for example, Raphael's teaching practice of the lecture and
Michael's role as facilitator or discussion leader. Such a distinction does
indeed describe the lapsarian differences in the proceedings of the angelic
instructors with their edenic pupil. Thus, as the lecture calls for the stu-
dent's generally passive receptivity, the discussion requires active participa-
tion, and as the lecture seeks an immediate transfer of truth from the
knowing instructor to the eager pupil, the discussion presupposes a series of
student articulations, errors, corrections, and developing confidence and

independence. It is certainly true that the bulk of Raphael's content—the rebellion of Satan in Book 5, the War in Heaven in Book 6, and the creation in Book 7—is presented in what may be described as a lecture format.

A more telling and inclusive vocabulary for pedagogical structures, however, is available. In organizing his concise survey of educational backgrounds in the age of Milton, Kenneth Charlton makes a distinction between "The Education of the Few" and "The Education of the Many." In content the former encompasses classical languages and pagan literature; the latter has as its twofold aim "that each person should be able to read the Bible and, as part of his 'Godly calling,' to contribute to the economy through work." Whereas the former took place for the most part in formally established grammar schools and universities, the latter instruction was a normal byproduct of membership in a religious congregation and was reinforced in the home. People were here taught through Bible reading, through the sermon with its careful explication of scriptural texts, and through catechizing, that is, systematic and cumulative instruction through dialogue.[2] In terms of target audiences, the prelapsarian Adam is the ultimate of elites, and the postlapsarian widening to include the many also describes the distinction Stanley Fish so carefully draws between the tension of the reader's differences from the unfallen Adam and the reader's overlapping with the Adam of the poem's final books.[3]

Educationally, the distinction is between humanistic "improvement" and Christian "amendment." Humanistic education was focused on the trivium and quadrivium, especially the grammar, rhetoric, and logic of the former, and it relied heavily on what Donald Leman Clark calls "Textbooks for Precepts," "Authors for Imitation," and "Exercises for Praxis."[4] These categories include the range of Raphael's instruction of the prelapsarian Adam and explain the shift to Adam's greater independence toward the conclusion of Raphael's visit in Book 8. Irene Samuel locates the basic premise of this pedagogy: "Raphael can assume that if he does his part Adam will grasp his meaning, and can therefore discourse or narrate without pausing to see how much Adam has understood, affording opportunity for discussion and query afterward."[5] In examining Adam's prelapsarian "improvement," Mary Ann Radzinowicz describes how edenic education would proceed:

> Simply by the actions involved in voluntary obedience, Adam and Eve would perfect themselves, as though the steps to heaven were not fixed but moving, so that to stand would be to ascend. They were to better themselves in love so

they would ascend the scale of heavenly love, were to improve themselves in diet so that their very bodies would take on more spiritual qualities, were to better themselves so in the arts of fellowship that at will they could participate with angels and dwell either in Eden or Heaven. [6]

Such a process makes clear why Raphael devotes so much of his initial discourse to explicating the principles of hierarchy and why it is to this point that Raphael returns in his conclusion. And as several commentators have pointed out, Raphael is a professor not so much of natural science as of metaphysics, theology, and ethics.[7]

Michael's postlapsarian "amendment" is less a matter of education than of reeducation, less nourishment than cure. The central focus of this spiritual education for the many was the Scriptures, and it relied heavily on what U. Milo Kaufmann explicates under the headings "Puritan Hermeneutics," "The House of Interpreter" (House = Bible; Interpreter = Holy Spirit), "Exemplary History," "The Analogy of Faith," and "The Interior Voice in Meditation."[8] Frequently, in devotional books of the time, according to Louis L. Martz, *meditation* was loosely interchangeable with such words as "contemplation," "consideration," "prayer," "mental prayer," "good thoughts," "spiritual exercises," and "examination of conscience."[9] Adam's "amendment" at the hands of Michael proceeds through what Radzinowicz calls "demonstrations in a laboratory of historical time." Michael's themes are at once of endurance and love, patience and magnanimity, heroic virtue and charity, and the place of man in the universe and the place of reason in his soul.[10] Samuel likens Michael's instruction to Dante's purgatorial climb "in its urgency, its emphasis on the humbled spirit and the need of grace, its exchanges between questioner and expositor." In the postlapsarian format, "Michael must not only provide a series of examples in vision and narrative before proceeding to exposition, but must pause after each to discover from Adam's comments what in his teaching still needs clarification."[11]

Closer attention to the organization of the content of the angels' instruction reinforces the lapsarian contrast. In Books 5, 6, and 7, the "Divine Historian" Raphael sets forth a body of settled historical data in lecture format. After his introductory passages in Book 5 wherein Raphael lays down the principles of unity and hierarchy on which the universe is organized and articulates the methods of his own proceeding, the latter portion of Book 5 and all of Books 6 and 7 are devoted to set pieces through which Raphael lectures his pupil on the divine containment of evil and creation of good. His discourses on nature in Books 5 and 8 begin with materials familiar to Adam and proceed to relate them to their essential principles and significance. These lectures follow up on such shared experiences as meals, digestion, and vegetation and on lines of inquiry initiated by Adam. Unity is Raphael's given, and he presents it decoratively, pointing out again and again how materials from differing levels of being and thought derive from a single idea and are governed by the single intent they variously manifest. As a good lecturer should, Raphael introduces parenthetical gestures designed to heighten the immediacy of his content from time to time, and as a good lecturer should he draws his conclusions as a call for additional questions and a call for action.

In general the procedure is carefully stylized and the units are self-contained. The atmosphere is of wonderful leisure for both growth and stability. Russell E. Smith finds the central books of the epic governed by five questions which Adam asks of Raphael. For him each unit begins with thanks for the angel's visit, assurance that Adam understands his position in the hierarchy and his responsibility as a free agent, and then the questions themselves, which inaugurate Raphael's extended discourses. At the end of each unit Adam bookishly recapitulates Raphael's lesson, concluding always with a full stop in the middle of the poetic line followed by an undercutting new beginning introduced by "yet," "but," or "though." Smith sees Adam "formally, almost ritualistically," assuring Raphael of his contentment and then dramatically indicating a lack of content through increasingly ambitious questions.[12] We need not insist rigidly on this scheme to agree with its general tendency.

Precepts shift toward praxis as the visit draws to its end. In Book 8 Raphael's narratives give way to something more like an interchange between Raphael and Adam, but it is an interchange of epic set pieces rather than a dialogue. After Adam's questions about the heavens and Raphael's discourses on astronomy, Adam narrates his own history, culminating in "the sum of earthly bliss" (8.522), his love for Eve. This inspires Raphael to another brief lecture, reinforcing earlier lessons on astronomy from Book 8 and on hierarchy from Book 5 and thus unifying and rounding off the four central Raphaelean books of the epic.

As Adam's "safe Guide" and as a "Seer blest," Michael's teaching format as well as content necessarily differ from those of the "Divine Historian" of the middle books of *Paradise Lost*. Instead of setting forth a body of settled historical data, Michael provides Adam with revealed prophecy, with a future-oriented content that Michael has not from experience but from the process of enlightenment he himself is simultaneously undergoing. Fragmentation is Michael's given, and his pedagogical challenge is to draw out his pupil's capacity for regaining the unifying principle that has been lost with the fall. Michael's instruction is distinctly teleological as Raphael's is variously ontological. As Raphael left with his pupil a commodity of inspirational information, Michael is primarily concerned to prepare Adam to carry on the processes of scriptural memory and exegesis when his instructor is no longer present. As Raphael brings his pupil up to date on the past, Michael is fortifying his present and sending him all too quickly away from the ivory tower of learning and into the real world of earning his bread and of challenge that pupils normally "commence" into upon achieving "graduation."

As Raphael presents the only history then available, Michael presents the Scriptures. This he does quite literally in one sense, reviewing the data of the Old and New Testaments in chronological sequence and highlighting their progression and the differences between their premises and fulfillments. In a series of visions or pageants in Book 11 Michael shows Adam dramatic vignettes of Cain and Abel, the lazar house, the sons of God, the cities of the plain, the flood and the recession of the flood and the rainbow. As several critics have noticed, these six units of Book 11 are balanced by six units in Book 12 tracing a series of ages: Nimrod and tower, Abraham, sons of Abraham, captivity of Babylon, Incarnation of Christ, and transcendence of temporal order.[13] Although, as with the structure Russell Smith inferred from Raphael's books noticed above, we should be wary of attaching simple designs to an artist of such notable and ubiquitous complexity as Milton, it is certainly clear that these materials are marked by patterned divisions. The principal divisions between Books 11 and 12, between the evils and backward-oriented data of Book 11 and the emerging goods and forward-oriented data of Book 12, have been illuminated by a number of commentators. Joseph H. Summers, for example, has addressed the "duality of vision . . . central to the final books" and distinguished between the destruction and Adam's horror in Book 11 and the revelations, "secret consolation," and Adam's joy in Book 12. The first mode is "historical" or "moral" and the second "typological," proceeding by inward rather than physical vision.[14] For Georgia B. Christopher it is the difference between the World and the Word, as for Raymond B. Waddington it is between the first Adam and the second Adam within a design of "Christian paradoxology."[15] H. R.

MacCallum provides a containing perspective in noting that "the very arrangement of these materials creates a dialectical pattern of ascent which leads Adam from type to truth, from flesh to spirit."[16] Gradually, under Michael's guidance and presentation of Scripture, Adam undergoes Christian initiation and learns to transcend postlapsarian division, duplexity, or dialectic to achieve or reachieve unity through Christ.

Like the Puritan sermon, Michael presents both biblical texts and exegesis, and the organization within Books 11 and 12 of *Paradise Lost* follows this pattern as well. Each of the tableaux and narrations of the final books consists of a two-part structure. The first part rehearses biblical data or supplies objective data and thus provides a literal foundation; in the second part Michael provides interpretations of these data, draws out or draws in the governing principles and doctrines, and in general performs an act of literary criticism that is simultaneously Protestant exegesis. This twofold structure is in a sense a miniature of the structural contrast between Books 11 and 12 themselves. The first part of each individual unit, as H. R. MacCallum has pointed out, shows "the spiritual bankruptcy of natural man" and theology as it is available through the light of nature, and the second part of the individual unit shows "the revealed truths of Christianity."[17] The typological is thus superimposed upon the literal. The historical data of the first part are broken down and analyzed, but from the second part a new and future-oriented composition emerges. In Book 11 the second half of each unit, and therefore the whole of the duplex unit, characteristically ends with a tightly axiomatic formulation of the chief lesson. This is bare in style and abrupt in manner and thus reflects the radical lesson memorably rendered. In Ramistic and Puritan terms, as we shall consider more fully in a later chapter, it thus signals the absoluteness of the truth achieved and the consent that such truth compels from all reasoners who have been exposed to it. In the two parts of the units of Book 12, MacCallum has found a duplex structure in which a moment of triumph is followed by a review of the trials that led up to it. He labels this design "a loop in time," but it is also a loop in logic and serves to shift the focus between sources and goals, between first and final causes. It is a design, as MacCallum notes, for "placing the end before the beginning."[18]

The final two books of *Paradise Lost* are thus structured upon what Frank Kermode calls a "double purpose of presentation and interpretation" or what Boyd M. Berry distinguishes as "doctrines" and "uses."[19] The intervals between the narrations of individual units and Michael's explications allow for the objectification of data and the demonstration of the learning process. They serve also to separate and to interconnect the units of Michael's prophetic history. The narration of data—by the narrator in Book 11, by Michael in Book 12—is followed by Michael's explications relating the data to moral polarities or to patterns of faith, conduct, and Truth. Adam's responding exclamations, observations, and questions are interspersed. In keeping with the polarities of content, Adam's responses run to excesses of grief and joy in what Christopher calls "hermeneutic wobbling" and "interpretive 'drunkenness,'" which gradually resolve themselves into Reformation "soberness" and walking in the Word.[20] Michael corrects Adam's errors of interpretation and priority and gradually expands his judgment and grasp of principles. As future history and instruction progress, Adam's responses become increasingly sound, increasingly expansive and faithful, increasingly articulate. Michael's teaching provides a dynamic Adam with regular opportunities to put his learning into practice as he accumulates it.

Following the model of religious education, Michael's instructional formats supply Adam with Scriptures and introduce him to sermon structures from which he can benefit immediately and whose exegetical procedures he can himself imitate. Michael is a library resource, as it were, both primary and secondary. The interspersed comments and reactions of Adam and, more generally, the series of brief interchanges between Adam and Michael allow us to add to these structures the additional one of catechizing, that is, exercising a pupil in the defined structures of faith and through a series of questions and answers extracting from the pupil carefully graduated sequential units of understanding of the principal matters of faith and doctrine. As Stanley Fish has emphasized, what matters most is that pupils assume considerable responsibility for their own edification and effectively interiorize the meanings discovered within the scripturally based catechetical formulations.[21]

The structures through which the teachings of Raphael and Michael are organized are thus appropriately lapsarian. So are the pedagogic goals. Raphael's aim is to share with Adam what he calls "the prime Wisdom" (8.194); it consists of "That which before us lies in daily life" and is distinguished from those things that are "remote / From use, obscure and subtle" (191–93). "Prime" points in two directions: *first* as primary or principal but also *first* as earliest, first in time as well as first cause. With its ontological orientation, in effect Raphael's universe is atemporal, for the edenic world's rhythm is that of "Grateful vicissitude" (6.8), not of decay, "*Spring* and *Autumn* here / Danc'd hand in hand" (5.394–95).

Michael's "sum / Of wisdom" balances against Raphael's "prime Wisdom."
When Adam has learned the lesson of his Redeemer, Michael tells him,

> This having learnt thou hast attain'd the sum
> Of wisdom; hope no higher, though all the Stars
> Thou know'st by name, and all th' ethereal Powers,
> All secrets of the deep, all Nature's works,
> Or works of God in Heav'n, Air, Earth, or Sea,
> And all the riches of this World enjoy'dst,
> And all the rule, one Empire. (12.575–81)

Even when he commends Adam's attainment of this sum of wisdom, however, Michael insists upon a continuing future process and expands the lesson from spiritual principles and insights into the arena of "Deeds to thy knowledge answerable" (582). Michael makes disjunctive the realms of earthly and heavenly that for Raphael were continuous and unified; for Michael nature and grace are dichotomous alternatives, from which informed reasoners will opt for the absolute not the mundane, the eternal not the temporal, wisdom not knowledge, faith not reason.

On sometimes small, sometimes expansive occasions, Michael's data and themes reconstitute in postlapsarian mode materials that Raphael had called to the attention of his unfallen pupil. A brief instance will show something of the thrust of this evidence. Sherman Hawkins is one of several commentators to call attention to the distinction between Raphael's *nourishment* and Michael's *cure*.[22] Raphael's visit begins with the angel and the human couple sharing a meal and with Raphael's amplification of digestive processes and hierarchies. These matters receive postlapsarian treatment in Michael's presentation of the scene in the lazar house. In the central books of the epic God is "our Nourisher"(5.398), and the prelapsarian hierarchy of digestion has its cosmic analogues in, for example, the sun's receiving nourishment from creation in a sequence of "alimental recompense" (424). In the postlapsarian mode, through intemperance in meats and drinks (11.472–73), humanity "pervert[s] pure Nature's healthful rules / To loathsome sickness" (523–24) and brings upon itself "Diseases dire" and "all maladies" (474, 480). The postlapsarian transmutation of the earlier digestive imagery is to be recognized not merely in the adjuncts of pain and loss but also in the imposition of moral judgment and the emphasis upon consequences. The lesson is about the principle and exercise of temperance, not about an analogous and aspirational universe.

The third of Michael's tableaux in Book 11, the scene of the wedding between the female offspring of Lamech and the pious sons of Seth, recapitulates Adam's account of his own marriage and his continuing love for Eve. Both occasions take nature, marriage, and thus pleasure as their starting point, but Michael's characters are objectified and externalized as Book 8's were subjective and personalized in Adam himself. Classical and Christian categories may be invoked to highlight the lapsarian distinction. Thus, the central books of the epic assume the classical scale of *eros/philia/agape* to measure the prelapsarian, whereas the Christian *luxuria/caritas* distinction measures the postlapsarian in the final books. In both sections of the text love and knowledge are closely linked. Because in Book 8 Raphael corrects Adam's prelapsarian "errors" as Michael does in 11, the evidence anticipates what is so much more Michael's duty in Books 11 and 12.

The concluding section of Raphael's visit, by interrelating love and knowledge and by emphasizing the principle of hierarchy, brings full circle not only Book 8 but also the four books of Raphael's visit. Shortly after his arrival Raphael presented Adam with a design of contained and directed knowledge:

> the scale of Nature set
> From centre to circumference, whereon
> In contemplation of created things
> By steps [one] may ascend to God. (5.509–12)

Book 6 renders ascent, which is also the assent of faith (in contrast to the Satanic descent, which is also dissent), and Book 7 amplifies "the scale of Nature" by tracing its radical origins in God's unifying purpose and creative power. In his two lessons of Book 8 Raphael reinforces these first causes and their hierarchical and vertical foundations by correcting Adam's potential for distortion of attitude and data, of ascent and assent with regard to the cosmos and love. Astronomically, early in Book 8, Adam errs in separating order from wonder, data from faith; amatorially, late in Book 8, Adam similarly separates nature from wisdom in his attitude toward Eve. He judges Eve as his inferior "in the prime end / Of Nature" (8.540–41) and cites nature's failure in himself (534); Eve's presence and discourse "degrade" all his "higher knowledge" (551–52) and "discountenance" his wisdom (552–53). Raphael's correction advises against the accusation of nature and the desertion of wisdom, in general against the disjunction between nature and wisdom, things and spirit, that results from "attributing overmuch to things / Less excellent" (565–66). Raphael's final lesson reinforces the

Platonic hierarchical unified models with which he began in Book 5, citing now something like the *Symposium*'s hierarchical levels of love:

> Love refines
> The thoughts, and heart enlarges, hath his seat
> In Reason, and is judicious, is the scale
> By which to heav'nly Love thou may'st ascend
> Not sunk in carnal pleasure. (589–93)

When Raphael seeks to check Adam's enthusiasm for Eve by urging love's hierarchical refinement of the thoughts and enlargement of the heart, love as *philia* or *agape* is acknowledged as appropriate to humans and, as we soon learn, to angels also, but *eros* is dismissed downward to the animal creation. In explicating this final and inclusive scale Raphael is also guiding Adam to be more spiritually courageous, to fulfill his defined nature in the area of valor as well as contemplation (4.297), to accept and process the new and therefore uncontrollable possibilities that Adam's fantasy component Eve introduces to his staider reasoning component, to expand and ascend from body to spirit through accretions of love and faith, to accept and "be not diffident / Of Wisdom" (8.562–63) that for his integrated growth comes to him through—not contrary to—nature, things, and his helpmeet. He is not to overvalue ("attribute overmuch") things at the expense of spirit but is to proceed by way of things to the layered meanings they mediate. The love lesson like the astronomy lesson reinforces being lowly wise rather than arrogant and impatient, operating within a consecutive continuum of accrued information. In the prelapsarian context of the externally and exquisitely beautiful paradise, the sum of knowledge is also the sum of bliss: Increased beauty, love, and joy coincide fully with increased apprehension, knowledge, and wisdom.

Michael's lessons on love are founded upon postlapsarian categories: Now moral dichotomies, judgments, and choices within a divided cosmos and a framework of history and geography replace the ontological and hierarchically ascendant unity and continuum. Michael's "written Records" form the background of the lesson here as God's book of nature supplied Raphael's teaching. The love issue arises in the third pageant of Book 11 when the just men whose whole study is "bent / To worship God aright" descend from the hills to the plain and encounter "A Bevy of fair Women," the offspring of Cain who dwell "Unmindful of thir Maker" in "the Tents / Of wickedness" (11.556–637). The "fair female Troop" of atheists seduce the "sober Race of

Men, whose lives / Religious titl'd them the Sons of God" into their own wantonness and into unhappy marriages, which issue in the warmongering giants of the fourth pageant. Michael interprets this text to teach Adam of the postlapsarian distinction between delight ("the bent of Nature") or pleasure ("though to Nature seeming meet") and the nobler ends of holiness and purity that conform to the divine purpose, between "lustful appetence" and noble virtue, and between "Man's effeminate slackness" and "wisdom, and superior gifts."[23] The postlapsarian geography, society, motives, and psyches are radically divided and radically moral. Choices must be made and responsibility for spiritual self-determination accepted. Beauty, joy, and nature (all in their fallen forms) are in conflict with knowledge, faith, and salvation. Unlike the prelapsarian Eve whose love and loveliness inspired awe and mediated expansive spiritual possibilities through her "Greatness of mind," these women are "empty of all good wherein consists / Woman's domestic honor and chief praise" (616–17). Moral dichotomies and interpretation are addressed and imposed; gone are unity, coherence, sudden apprehension, and gradual ascendance of a spiritual scale.

Under Michael's instruction, moral polarities allow the judgment of the tents as "the Tents / Of wickedness," and the "Bevy of fair Women" translates into "Man's effeminate slackness" and thus to internal evil. The specific external is translated into the universalized internal to clarify and secure principles to guide Adam's future conduct. Raphael's scale of corporeal and spiritual love is reshaped to Michael's disposition of the sacrifice of virtue to lust. The diction of wanton playfulness in Book 11 recalls the vocabulary used to describe Adam and Eve's first fallen lovemaking, through which they confirmed and solaced their sin in Book 9. Appearance has become divorced from reality in the judgment of Book 11, and Adam is explicitly taught that rectitude has been divorced from pleasure and must now be the standard by which experience is assessed. Michael articulates the axioms that must henceforth govern Adam's conduct and be stored in his memory:

> Judge not what is best
> By pleasure, though to Nature seeming meet,
> Created, as thou art, to nobler end
> Holy and pure, conformity divine. (11.603–6)

The prelapsarian equivalent definition of human purpose reinforces the point. Then we were told that love was "not the lowest end of human life":

> For not to irksome toil, but to delight
> He made us, and delight to Reason join'd. (9.241–43)

Raphael identified for Adam the nobility of love within the natural hierarchy and posited man's place in the scale or ladder as a definition of the human condition. Michael, however, enunciates a discursive design that concludes in disposition and judgment. The comparative form of the adjective, "to *nobler* end," provides a miniature of the psychic alteration, the intrusion of contrast and rejection within the postlapsarian framework.

Adam himself attempts an axiomatic assessment when he observes to his postlapsarian teacher:

> But still I see the tenor of Man's woe
> Holds on the same, from Woman to begin. (11.632–33)

Adam is here endeavoring to build upon earlier lessons on the lazar house and "th' inabstinence of *Eve*" (476) there represented. In so doing Adam is imitating Michael's pedagogical practice of moving from concrete evidence to concise expressions of the universals implicit in it, but Adam brings forth the wrong universals, and Michael proceeds to relate the data to more accurate and responsible principles:

> From Man's effeminate slackness it begins,
> Said th' Angel, who should better hold his place
> By wisdom, and superior gifts receiv'd. (634–36)

The interpretative expansion of truth and universals is insistently continuous throughout Michael's instruction, as reasoning is vital and dynamic in the postlapsarian mode, and Adam must constantly stretch himself and exercise his reasoning as his spiritual muscles to escape the danger deplored in *Areopagitica*, that a man may be a heretic even in the truth if he does not embrace "the trial of virtue and the exercise of truth" (Hughes, pp. 739, 733). This continuing questing process contrasts with Adam's passive reception of Raphael's lessons, which each achieve a kind of closure. Having set forth one body of material, Raphael is free to pursue another quite distinct one that likewise concludes in informational satisfaction. But Michael's lessons gradually and dichotomously accumulate understanding of progressively deepened and revealed insights.

Both the dichotomy and the progress may be seen in the different handling of love in Book 11 and Book 12, and the difference manifests organizational principles noted earlier: Postlapsarian love is a matter of *luxuria* at the social level in Book 11, but after Adam's exposure to New Testament history and dogma in the second and balancing half of Michael's materials in Book 12, love becomes redefined as "Charity, the soul / Of all the rest" (12.584–85). Diane McColley eloquently distinguishes between *castitas* and *caritas* while glancing also toward *Comus* and the autobiographical section of *Apology for Smectymnuus*:

> *Castitas* is faithfulness of body, mind, and heart. *Caritas* is the outward-reaching love that cherishes the immortal well-being of every person. Charity is the highest of virtues, but chastity is its meet and necessary help. In the fallen world, on the sexual level, chastity is often regarded (or disregarded) as a merely carnal and prudential virtue, protecting legitimacy, social order, and emotional balance. In the unfallen and regenerate worlds of Milton's Paradise and the household of faith it figures forth, "the Sun-clad power of Chastity" includes far more: it is a radiant clarity and wholeness that both discloses and repels evil and empowers for good, by fitting the "living Temples" of the Spirit to be conduits of grace.[24]

In Book 12 the New Law of love that contrasts with Old Testament law is carefully articulated; under the Dispensation now inaugurated, "love / Alone fulfil[s] the Law" (12.403–4). Without love, as the blushing Raphael admits to Adam, there is no happiness (8.621), but with the fall socially love becomes an occasion of lightening "Each other's burden in our share of woe" (10.960–61), and spiritually "The Law of Faith / Working through love" (12.488–89) is written upon the hearts of believers by the Holy Spirit. The "offices of Love" are now a matter not merely of awareness but of energized belief and of virtuous deeds answerable to one's knowledge and one's service to the New Dispensation of the transforming, translating Word, Christ, in whom is substantially and visibly expressed "Love without end, and without measure Grace" (3.140–42).

In the largest structural contrast, Raphael's division between the repelling of the Satanic forces in Book 6 and the creation of the earth in Book 7 is recapitulated in the division between Michael's Books 11 and 12, "Betwixt the world destroy'd and world restor'd" (12.3). The concluding sections of Stella P. Revard's *War in Heaven* examine these analogues in thoughtful detail. She finds that both Raphael and Michael share with Adam information on the rise of sin and its spread throughout the social structure, on the rise of war, which both angels resoundingly indict, and on the rise of political tyranny, but both set forth also parallel victories and deliverances by Christ and parallel triumphal returns of the Son to the Father. According to Revard, both Books 7 and 11 close "with a great rhapsody to creation after destruction, fruitfulness after waste, new covenant after spent sin." A number of her chief points may be seen in this passage:

> That *Paradise Lost* should return at the end to the theme of deliverance fulfills not only the promise of the poem's proem, but also the great promise that the center books dramatize. The Son who came to deliver the angels, who drove his antagonist Satan from Heaven with his rebel angels, who restored the empyrean and created earth, must come to conquer Satan on earth, to redeem man, and to restore Eden. If the war in Heaven predicted the translation of evil to earth and its spread throughout human society, it must accordingly predict also its eventual downfall. Books 11 and 12 bring forth both good and evil, destruction and re-creation. Book 11 concludes with a flood that both destroys and makes possible new creation, illustrating the pattern the center books set.

For Revard, Raphael no less than Michael is a prophet.[25]

Several analogues within these large parallel structures deserve a closer look. As many commentators have noted, both Raphael and Michael present Adam with models of conduct under the "one just man" rubric. The prelapsarian model is of course Abdiel,[26] but the postlapsarian model has been variously identified as Christ and as Old Testament prefigurations of Christ, Enoch, Noah, Abraham, and Moses. Characteristically postlapsarian is this multiple distribution of the single and singular Abdiel, a division that stresses humanity and chronological continuity and progress. Abdiel is a fictive model or analogue, invented by Milton to help Raphael surmount the reach of human sense. Michael's models are not fictive but true, drawn from history and the "written Records pure" of the Bible. In the unified absolute integrity of the angel Abdiel, faithful and zealous impulses precede their renderings in discourse of reason. The human postlapsarian exemplars of rectitude achieve right action by actively and retrospectively transcending experience, reason, and history. The postlapsarian "one just man" and "one faithful man" are grounded in history and geography, the categories of experience, as the angelic Abdiel is grounded in ideality. The angel Abdiel demonstrates what the man Adam may achieve as his body works its way up to spirit. Adam moves toward or may move toward Abdiel on a vertical scale, as his movement toward the postlapsarian models is on a horizontal or chronological line. Abdiel figures forth a Platonic ideal as the patriarchs render types that look both backward to the first Adam and forward to the second Adam. Further, like the prelapsarian model Abdiel, Enoch is "the only righteous in a World perverse" and the one "beset / With Foes for daring single to be just, / And utter odious Truth" (11.701–4). As Enoch rises against his militaristic and factious context, Noah does similar battle against the analogous corruptions of peace in his era. What is a metaphoric battle in Book 6 becomes a differently metaphoric internal battle in Books 11 and 12, as Michael was himself the leading military angel in Book 6 and is now, like the Holy Spirit, striving to arm Adam "With spiritual Armor, able to resist / *Satan's* assaults, and quench his fiery darts" (12.490–92). The battle to come is not, as Adam supposes, "a Duel, or the local wounds / Of head or heel" (12.387–88), but the battle for which one dons "the whole armor of God," "the breastplate of righteousness," "the shield of faith," "the helmet of salvation," and "the sword of the Spirit, which is the word of God" (Eph. 6).

When we turn from destruction to creation, Raphael's hexaemeral history is also tellingly recapitulated in Michael's presentation of the new creation attendant upon Noah and the flood. Sea animals, land animals, birds, and vegetation all have their roles in the second as in the first of these accounts. The animal kingdom is now divinely organized and even numbered in a modified methodized version of days 5 and 6 of the original creation:

> Of every Beast, and Bird, and Insect small
> Came sevens, and pairs, and enter'd in, as taught
> Thir order. (11.734–36)

The dry lands and waters return to Chaos and are redivided. Topographical details closely echo evidence from Book 7:

> And now the tops of Hills as Rocks appear;
> With clamor thence the rapid Currents drive
> Towards the retreating Sea thir furious tide. (11.852–54)

This compares to the response to the fiat of the third day of the original creation:

> Immediately the Mountains huge appear
> Emergent, and thir broad bare backs upheave
> Into the Clouds, thir tops ascend the Sky:

So high as heav'd the tumid Hills, so low
Down sunk a hollow bottom broad and deep,
Capacious bed of Waters: thither they
Hasted with glad precipitance, uproll'd
As drops on dust conglobing from the dry. (7.285–92)

The postlapsarian account wherein we find the "world restor'd" (12.3) manifests a new covenant, a divinely imposed promise written occasionally by the deity upon the natural world to communicate a specific message, which can be discovered only with the aid of Scriptures, in this case the Scriptures mediated by Michael. The rainbow, "Betok'ning peace from God" (11.867), replaces the natural forms of light created on the fourth day of Book 7. Those served "for Signs, / For Seasons, and for Days, and circling Years" (7.341–42); their communication was by way of the natural creation, for as Raphael points out, "Heav'n / Is as the Book of God before thee set, / Wherein to read his wond'rous Works, and learn / His Seasons, Hours, or Days, or Months, or Years" (8.66–69). But the rainbow signifies the "Cov'nant new" (11.867) of grace and operates by way of human memory; it is an internal sign to govern conduct, to assure and promise future guidance and blessing. All future and occasional and conspicuous rainbows will recall this particular "triple-color'd Bow" (897) fraught with heavenly meaning whereon humanity may "look / And call to mind his Cov'nant" within the postlapsarian time frame of "Day and Night, / Seed-time and Harvest, Heat and hoary Frost . . . till fire purge all things new" (897–900). The "world restor'd" and "This second source of Men" (12.13) recapitulate the previous humanity in initial fear of the Lord, righteous and blameless conduct, worship, and peace, and in subsequent ambition, arrogance, and dispossession of concord and the law of nature. Nimrod recapitulates Satan and Satanic rebellion and plastic ingenuity; literally as well as morally, Babylon echoes Babel; and the Babylonian captivity recalls the enslavement of the Chosen People in Egypt, the ark of the covenant echoes the ark of Noah. As Michael's history proceeds, the recapitulations become linked in a series of moral polarizations. Michael's recapitulations of Raphael's material become themselves recapitulated in postlapsarian cyclical continuity and Christian teleology.

A number of commentators have found in Michael's history a variety of mathematically identifiable substructures. Thus, Boyd M. Berry finds a tripartite division of history: "The first period seems to have extended from

Creation to the giving of the decalogue; the second from Sinai to Christ; the third, of Christian liberty, from Christ to the millenium." Harry Levin outlines a similar triadic history with an initial age of the Father, the Law, and the Old Testament; a second age of the Son, the Gospel, and the New Testament; and a third age of the Holy Spirit and the Everlasting Gospel. Other critics, however, have found a four-part structure in the history of Books 11 and 12. Thus, Northrop Frye speaks of

> the four great stages of redemption covered in Michael's summary of the Bible. These we remember, are the restoring of the natural order with the giving of the law to Israel, the Incarnation and the giving of the gospel to all mankind, and the final apocalypse.

To this Edward Tayler adds the Myth of the Four Ages from Plato and the notion of the Four Monarchies from Daniel.[27]

The evidence of *Paradise Lost* may readily be marshaled in support of these structures. For purposes of lapsarian contrast, by far the most telling structure, however, is the recognition that the traditional seven ages of biblical history are the postlapsarian version of the seven days of creation. Commentators have called attention to various precedents for Milton's use of the design, though they have not agreed on either a specific source or the uses to which Milton puts such a source. For our purposes it is sufficient to note that the concept was a common rather than an esoteric one and to rely on the version readily available to Milton's contemporaries in the Geneva Bible in an appendix entitled "A Perfite Svppvtation of the Yeres and Times from Adam vnto Christ, proued by the Scriptures, after the collection of Diuers Autors." The appendix specifies the eras as: (1) from Adam to Noah's flood; (2) from Noah's flood to Abraham's departure from Chaldea; (3) from Abraham's departure to the departing of the children of Israel from Egypt; (4) from the departure from Egypt to the first building of the temple; (5) from the first building of the temple to the captivity of Babylon; (6) from the Babylonian captivity and the rebuilding of Jerusalem to the coming of Christ; and (7) from the coming of Christ to the present (i.e., 1560).[28] With some effort and ingenuity, Michael's history in *Paradise Lost* may be divided structurally into the eras of this tradition. Certainly the initial era, centering on Noah, amply demonstrates the cyclical pattern of new beginnings giving way to corruptions and to new definitions of the relationship between man and God.

However convergent or divergent Milton's treatment of the analogy of the six creational days and the six historical eras, it is generally agreed that Milton was aware of the analogy and put it to some use in the background of his epic. The analogy highlights several lapsarian distinctions. The postlapsarian Michael is necessarily concerned with chronological sequence and moral consequence rather than with the individuation and spatialization of created forms. The "days" of the hexaemeral are days "as we compute the days of Heav'n," in God's words from Book 6, line 685, that is, divine days traditionally equated each with a thousand years of earthly time. But Michael's days and years are measured according to the fallen calendar of diurnal and annual solar revolutions. There is no specified correlation in the epic between creational events—vegetation or topography, for example— and historical events. Michael's materials consist of human history, geography, and politics, of human conduct, not of the phenomena of nature and external reality. As the ontological Raphael devotes closest attention to those portions of the creation closest to Adam in space and kind, so the teleological Michael presents with greatest fullness those portions of history closest to Adam in time. His foreshortening of temporal vision accommodates Adam's perspective as does Raphael's accommodation of the lowly wisdom of Adam's mundane surroundings.

Insofar as these eras are denominated according to their principal figure, Noah and Abraham and the like, as a number of commentators have pointed out, Michael's materials are also organized along the lines of the "cloud of witnesses" in the Epistle to the Hebrews (11 and 12 : 1). Just as the Jobean dimension of *Paradise Regained* requires to be read not merely in the light of the Old Testament Book of Job but also in the light of the New Testament view of Job as a hero of remarkable patience (James 5 : 11), so in this reading Michael presents Hebrew history overlaid with Christian faith and to be interpreted in the light of the New Testament and its ultimate goals. Specifically, the catalogue of heroes in Hebrews 11 divides into two units, and the first of these contains all and only those figures that Milton also isolates for special attention:

> By faith Abel offered unto God a more excellent sacrifice than Cain, by which he obtained witness that he was righteous, God testifying of his gifts: and by it he being dead yet speaketh. By faith Enoch was translated that he should not see death; and was not found, because God had translated him: for before his translation he had this testimony, that he pleased God. But without faith it is impossible to please him: for he that cometh to God must

believe that he is, and that he is a rewarder of them that diligently seek him. By faith Noah, being warned of God of things not seen as yet, moved with fear, prepared an ark to the saving of his house; by the which he condemned the world, and became heir of the righteousness which is by faith. By faith Abraham, when he was called to go out into a place which he should after receive for an inheritance, obeyed; and he went out, not knowing whither he went. By faith he sojourned in the land of promise, as in a strange country, dwelling in tabernacles with Isaac and Jacob, the heirs with him of the same promise. (Heb. 11:4–9)

In the second catalogue Abraham again appears along with Moses and many witnesses who do not figure in Michael's summary of history. These exemplary figures dramatize the action of faith and the definition of faith with which this chapter of Hebrews begins:

Now faith is the substance of things hoped for, the evidence of things not seen. For by it the elders obtained a good report. Through faith we understand that the worlds were framed by the word of God, so that things which are seen were not made of things which do appear. (11:1–3)

The first part of the catalogue of individual elders concludes thus:

These all died in faith, not having received the promises, but having seen them afar off, and were persuaded of them, and embraced them, and confessed that they were strangers and pilgrims on the earth. (11:13)

The second half of the catalogue concludes thus:

And these all, having obtained a good report through faith, received not the promise: God having provided some better thing for us, that they without us should not be made perfect. (11:39–40)

These Old Testament figures have received the promises of salvation through Christ only by anticipation, as in the peculiar chronology of *Paradise Lost* Adam is presented with the promises in advance from as early as the protoevangelium of Book 10, line 181, and Gen. 3:15. Milton is at the same time presenting his reading audience the responsibility that is central to his conception of Protestantism and of poetry: "that they *without us* should not be made perfect" (emphasis mine). It is the Christian point of *Samson Agonistes* that future generations should make "perfect" Samson's history by inflaming their breasts to matchless valor and adventures high (*Samson Agonistes*, lines 1739–40). Michael's Old Testament heroes of faith are similar occasions for the exercise of memory and also of creative spiritual action on both Adam's and the reader's parts.

Michael sets forth the Old Testament heroes of faith as types or prefigurations of Christ or as exemplary "case histories" in Mary Ann Radzinowicz's thoughtful argument,[29] but they are also offered as immediate models of action for Adam. Like ourselves Adam is a "reader" of these narratives and is expected to apply their lessons. Georgia Christopher illuminates the Reformation reading activity in these terms:

> "Companion of the patriarchs" well describes the recommended stance of the reader of Old Testament narratives. A reader is not simply to locate "the promise" and note the paradigm of proper response, but to identify with particular figures in particular "gests" which the spirit may be directing particularly to him. Luther and Calvin set the example by identifying closely with favorite figures in the Old Testament. . . . This identification of the reader demands an attention to particulars of situation and psyche which paradoxically prevents the reduction of the story to a mere paradigm, even while insisting upon the paradigm.[30]

Michael's rendering of the history of Abraham exactly reproduces the data and emphasis of Hebrews 11 along with geographical and other specific information from the Old Testament:

> him God the most High voutsafes
> To call by Vision from his Father's house,
> His kindred and false Gods, into a Land
> Which he will show him, and from him will raise
> A mighty Nation and upon him show'r
> His benediction so, that in his Seed
> All Nations shall be blest; he straight obeys,
> Not knowing to what Land, yet firm believes:
> I see him, but thou canst not, with what Faith
> He leaves his Gods, his Friends, and native Soil
> *Ur* of *Chaldaea*, passing now the Ford
> To *Haran*, after him a cumbrous Train
> Of Herds and Flocks, and numerous servitude;
> Not wand'ring poor, but trusting all his wealth
> With God, who call'd him, in a land unknown. (12.120–34)

The story of Abraham becomes a varied lesson for Adam: It is a lesson in future history and geography, a lesson of fact, but it also presents Abraham as an immediate model for action. Adam too is in the process of being called by vision, Michael's visions, from his Father's house, the edenic garden. Adam too does not know to what land, fortune, and destiny he is being called; he knows only that he too must leave behind the safe and familiar. Abraham illustrates the action of faith: He departs, in Milton's words, "Not knowing to what Land, yet firm believes," "Not wand'ring poor, but trusting all his wealth / With God, who call'd him, in a land unknown." Adam is here clearly a "Companion of the patriarch" Abraham,[31] and this shared action is forcefully brought to mind when in the final lines of the epic Adam and Eve face the similar prospect:

> The World was all before them, where to choose
> Thir place of rest, and Providence thir guide. (12.646−47)

The processes of our memory and their memories, our and their "readings," are here enjoined, and we like them are to remember the promises of the past and address the future, both immediate and ultimate, by the light of such promise.

Structurally, the movements from days to eras and from edenic Adam to Abraham and to humanity generally serve to expand the imaginative range and application of the epic throughout time. Michael is arguing for a typological reading of the Old Testament and establishing the responsibility for Adam and for us to read and remember and thus bring to completion the divine processes and poem. In Abraham's history parallels are not drawn for Adam; he must draw them for himself. Where Raphael asks Adam to notice the unity behind his comparisons, Michael has Adam create the comparative alignments and create the imaginative unity. To see the likeness among so much and such specific difference requires a leap of faith, an application of memory, and an act of the imagination. Through such actions one can achieve the goal of education after the fall, that is, repair the ruins of the first parents.

2 · *Lapsarian Imagery*

The World is Gods book, which he set man at first to read; and every
Creature is a Letter, or syllable, or word, or Sentence, more or less,
declaring the name and will of God. There you may behold his wonderful
Almightiness, his unsearchable Wisdom, his unmeasurable Goodness,
mercy and compassions; and his singular regard of the sons of men! . . . Those
that with holy and illuminated minds come thither to behold the footsteps
of the Great and wise and bountiful Creator, may find not only
matter to *employ,* but to *profit* and *delight* their *thoughts.*

RICHARD BAXTER, *Christian Directory*

For the invisible things of him from the creation of the world are
clearly seen, being understood by the things that are made,
even his eternal power and Godhead.

ROM. 1:20

 S WE turn to a consideration of lapsarian differences
implicit in Raphael's and Michael's handling of analogous
patterns of imagery, it is appropriate to notice the con-
trasting textbooks through which the angels instruct
their unfallen and fallen pupils. DuBartas versifies the
textbook image thus: "God . . . In's Works reveales him
t'our intelligence"; "The World's a Schoole, where (in a generall Storie) /
God always reades Lectures of his Glorie"; and "The world's a Book in *Folio,*
printed all / Within God's great Workes in Letters Capitall." [1] As E. M. W.
Tillyard observes, "Milton insisted on an organic connection between God
and his universe," and "Milton's Adam attains to his belief in a creator
through the approved age-long process of seeing him through creation, *per
speculum creaturarum.*" [2] Book 1, chapter 2, of Milton's *Christian Doctrine*
defines the premises thus:

> Though there be not a few who deny the existence of God . . . yet the
> Deity has imprinted upon the human mind so many unquestionable tokens
> of himself, and so many traces of him are apparent throughout the whole of
> nature, that no one in his senses can remain ignorant of the truth. . . . There
> can be no doubt that every thing in the world, by the beauty of its order, and
> the evidence of a determinate and beneficial purpose which pervades it,
> testifies that some efficient Power must have preexisted, by which the whole
> was ordained for a specific end. (CE 14 : 25 – 27)

At its simplest in the neat phrasing of a commonplace, Raphael supplies
Adam with a reading of the book of God's works as Michael introduces him
to the book of God's word.

Paradise Lost is explicit about the texts appropriate to the two contrasting
angels. As Raphael explains, specifically "Heav'n" but more generally the
natural creation

> Is as the Book of God before thee set,
>
> Wherein to read his wond'rous Works, and learn
>
> His Seasons, Hours, or Days, or Months, or years. (8.66 – 69)

Even before Raphael's arrival, however, the untutored Adam had addressed
himself similarly to the divine as praised through the articulate creation:

> Thyself how wondrous then!
>
> Unspeakable, who sit'st above these Heavens
>
> To us invisible or dimly seen
>
> In these thy lowest works, yet these declare
>
> Thy goodness beyond thought, and Power Divine.
>
> (5.155 – 59)

As James H. Sims has noted, "The idea of the created universe as a Book of
God is based on the psalmist's view that the heavens give testimony in a
universal language to the existence and glory of God."[3] Thus, Raphael and
Adam are also expressing the opening verses of Psalm 19: "The heavens
declare the glory of God; and the firmament sheweth his handywork. Day
unto day uttereth speech, and night unto night sheweth knowledge. There
is no speech nor language, where their voice is not heard" (1 – 3). Milton's
Raphael is also following and sharing the advice that the apocryphal
Raphael gave to Tobit and Tobias in *The Book of Tobit*:

Bless God and give thanks to him. Ascribe majesty to him, and before all
the living acknowledge how he has dealt with you. It is a good thing to bless
God and exalt his name, declaring God's works and doing them honor, so do
not be slow to give him thanks. It is wise to keep a king's secret, but the
works of God should be gloriously revealed.[4]

As in *Of Education*, the prelapsarian Adam is to attend to the sensible things
of the earthly world and to arrive at his knowledge of higher matters as the
divine is made visible through the creation. Nature, then, provides Raphael
with his instructional data, especially in Books 5 and 8, and these data
figure forth in clear and coherent design the unity and creativity of the deity
and his purposes. As Abdiel points out in defining service, "God and
Nature bid the same, / When he who rules is worthiest, and excels / Them
whom he governs" (6.176–78), and the governor of the prelapsarian uni-
verse is God the creator, sustainer, nourisher. Such service contrasts with
postlapsarian "servitude" (12.89) wherein the conjunction of "true Liberty"
and "right Reason" is divorced and usurped by "upstart Passions" in both
the microcosm and politicocosm.

What Milton says of the plainness of Scripture's beauty in *The Reason of
Church Government* explicates the lapsarian loss of the validity of the book of
God's works: "All corporeal resemblances of inward holiness & beauty are
now past" (CE 3.1.246). *Christian Doctrine* 1.2 amplifies the postlapsarian
change: "No one, however, can have right thoughts of God, with nature
or reason alone as his guide, independent of the word, or message of
God" (CE 14:31). *Of Reformation* develops the contrast at length and sup-
plies the postlapsarian Protestant alternative to prelapsarian perfect sense
perception:

> The very essence of Truth is plainnesse, and brightnes; the darknes and
> crookednesse is our own. The wisdome of God created understanding, fit and
> proportionable to Truth the object, and end of it, as the eye to the thing
> visible. If our understanding have a film of ignorance over it, or be blear with
> gazing on other false glisterings, what is that to Truth? If we will but purge
> with sovrain eyesalve that intellectual ray which God hath planted in us,
> then we would beleeve the Scriptures protesting their own plainnes, and
> perspicuity, calling to them to be instructed, not only the wise, and learned,
> but the simple, the poor, the babes, foretelling an extraordinary effusion of
> Gods Spirit upon every age, and sexe, attributing to all men, and requiring
> from them the ability of searching, trying, examining all things, and by the

spirit discerning that which is good; and as the Scriptures themselvs pronounce their own plainnes, so doe the Fathers testifie of them. (CE 3.1.33)

William G. Madsen expresses the postlapsarian mode in these terms:

> Because of the Fall man is unable to see the spiritual significance of this outer book, and therefore God made a second work, Jesus Christ, "that wisdom might be seen more manifestly and be recognized more perfectly, that the eye of man might be illuminated by the second writing, since it had been darkened to the first."

More generally, Madsen summarizes Milton's position: "Scripture is the key to a proper understanding of nature, at least in its symbolic aspect. Nature is witness to its inability to reveal the will of God."[5]

The book of Michael's instruction is also a book of God, but for him Christian doctrine, story, and Truth have been

> Left only in those written Records pure,
> Though not but by the Spirit understood. (12.513–14)

These written records, "The promise of the Father," "the Law of Faith / Working though love" (487, 488–89), are not merely enrolled in the parchment of normal library resources but are also engraved by the Spirit within and upon the heart of the believer (523–24). In general, the prelapsarian visual text and instruction give way to the postlapsarian, definitively Protestant aural instruction and individual textual analysis, the public and outward to the private and inward. Milton himself in *Christian Doctrine* attaches the postlapsarian reading capacity to the operations of the Holy Spirit. As in the epic the spirit helps us to understand "those written Records pure," so here the Spirit assists in our understanding of the unwritten law of God:

> The unwritten law is no other than that law of nature given originally to Adam, and of which a certain remnant or imperfect illumination, still dwells in the hearts of all mankind; which, in the regenerate, under the influence of the Holy Spirit, is daily tending towards a renewal of its primitive brightness. (CE 16:101)

In sum, in their separate portions of the epic, Raphael and Michael explicate the divine works, Raphael addressing those of nature and Michael those of grace.

Just as the books through which Raphael and Michael instruct their pupils reflect the lapsarian distinction, so too do the languages the angels employ. Before the fall the model of language occurs in Adam's naming of the animals. In Genesis we read that "whatsoever Adam called every living creature, that was the name thereof." As Milton renders this, Adam beholds "each Bird and Beast . . . Approaching two and two," and says:

> I nam'd them, as they pass'd, and understood
> Thir Nature, with such knowledge God endu'd
> My sudden apprehension. (8.349–54)

Before the fall, language and understanding are complete and simultaneous, at once instinctive and God-given. As Harold Toliver describes it, Adam's linguistic skill reflects "his share of the Word's original creative ordinance, which from the outset gives him a kind of mental set or instinctive sense of the right ideas and words in the right order."

> Discursive reason and perception are scarcely distinguishable in him. . . . he simply finds no cross-purposes before him. All objects project a moving image of eternity in a continual enactment of harmony: they are tuneful, whether high or low in the scale, and his perceptions move along them like variations of a harmonized melody.[6]

What Adam knows and can name is quite clearly distinguished from what he does not comprehend, the deity who "Surpassest far my naming" (8.359). It is important that Adam not merely apprehend but also express his awareness; the verbalizations actualize the internal and instinctive. Thus, the deity puts Adam through a test that requires him to articulate the differences between them; God is single, perfect, and infinite, but man is numerous, incomplete, and finite. Adam then asks for a helpmeet in order to fulfill his assigned mission of being fruitful and multiplying. The request manifests his instinct, his obedience, and his faith, and also explicitly his freedom, and he is rewarded with his heart's desire.

The first gift of language from Gen. 2:19–20, which allows Adam to name the animals, carries over to verse 23 and allows Adam to rightly name Eve and understand her nature and place: "And Adam said, this is now bone of my bones, and flesh of my flesh: she shall be called Woman, because she was taken out of Man." Adam's echo of these words at Book 8, lines 494–97, reflects the precise coincidence of name and thing that constitutes prelapsarian knowledge, a knowledge both from God and from Adam's innate capacity to respond intuitively to the divine. This is the reasoning that Adam calls his "sudden apprehension" and that Raphael identifies as the soul's being (5.486–87). Milton takes up the Genesis verses and the question of Adam's prelapsarian understanding and language in *Tetrachordon*, saying that in Adam's "originall rectitude" "all that was naturall or morall was engrav'n without externall constitutions and edicts" in his breast. The discussion proceeds:

> But *Adam* who had the wisdom giv'n him to know all creatures, and to name them according to their properties, no doubt but had the gift to discern perfectly, that which concern'd him much more; and to apprehend at first sight the true fitness of that consort which God provided him. And therefore spake in reference to those words which God pronounc't before.

The *Tetrachordon* discussion concludes with an acknowledgment of the role of accommodation between human speech and divine meaning: "*Adam* spake like *Adam* the words of flesh and bones, the shell and rinde of matrimony; but God spake like God, of love and solace and meet help, the soul of *Adams* words and of matrimony" (CE 4:92–93). Here Milton posits an analogy between the human medium of flesh and God's medium of ideas or "soul." Raphael's role in *Paradise Lost* is to mediate these two spheres, and analogies are his regular practice.

Postlapsarian language is also explicitly dealt with in *Paradise Lost*. Language falls with the human fall in Book 9 of *Paradise Lost*, and language is deliberately and more widely disoriented after the destruction of the tower of Babel, which not only etiologically diversifies language but also signifies the disruption of language as a communication medium and as a union of name and meaning. *Babel* means confusion, and with this biblical event the word becomes divided from the thing it signifies, distorting the equivalence of word and understanding.[7] In *The Art of Logic* (CE 11:221), Milton distinguishes between the lapsarian languages—"both that first one which Adam spoke in Eden, and those varied ones also possibly derived from the first, which the builders of the tower of Babel suddenly received"—and asserts that both were divinely given. In Isabel MacCaffrey's neat phrasing, the first language is "univocal," the second "equivocal."[8]

In the postlapsarian analogue of the above evidence, late in Book 11 Adam puns upon *woman*—a pun is literally an *equi-voque*—and in providing a false etymology further signifies that the perfection of the original language has been lost.

> But still I see the tenor of *Man's woe*
> Holds on the same, from *Woman* to begin. (11.632–33; emphasis mine)

Michael immediately corrects Adam's language and understanding on this point and in general assists Adam's linguistic instruction. Early in Book 12 Milton collocates Nimrod from Genesis 10 with Babel from Genesis 11. Both the man and the city are handled etymologically. In Genesis Nimrod is described as "a mighty one in the earth" (8) and "a mighty hunter before the Lord" (9), which Milton—remembering the Hebrew—renders thus:

> A mighty Hunter thence he shall be styl'd
> Before the Lord, as in despite of Heav'n.
> Or from Heav'n claiming second Sovranty;
> And from Rebellion shall derive his name,
> Though of Rebellion others he accuse. (12.33–37)

God punishes the ambitious builders of Babel, the sons of Shem, by depriving them of their one language and one speech (Gen. 11:1), saying

> Go to, let us go down, and there confound their language, that they may not understand one another's speech . . . . Therefore is the name of it called Babel; because the Lord did there confound the language of all the earth; and from thence did the Lord scatter them abroad upon the face of all the earth. (11:7, 9)

Paradise Lost etymologizes thus:

> thus was the building left
> Ridiculous, and the work Confusion nam'd. (12.61–62)

That Nimrod and his followers, like the fallen angels, are ambitious to "get themselves a name, lest far disperst / In foreign Lands thir memory be lost" (12.45–46), encapsulates the contrast with the prelapsarian language in which name and thing are inseparable and name need not be sought elsewhere because it is so thoroughly and numinously present in the thing itself. Among other things, such matters are a Ramistic argument, specifically the derived argument of notation.

The Babel passage in Milton's *Logic* draws a catalogue of errors that may prevent the identification of "true notation" and that thus characterize postlapsarian vocabulary and its and human nature's fallenness:

But languages, both that first one which Adam spoke in Eden, and those varied ones also possibly derived from the first, which the builders of the tower of Babel suddenly received, are without doubt divinely given; hence it is not strange if the reason of primitive words is unknown. But as to those words that are derived or composite, either their origins are to be sought in other languages ancient and now obsolete, or by their own antiquity and the usually corrupt pronunciation of the lower classes are so changed, and by the habit of writing them falsely are so obliterated as it were that a true notation of words very seldom may be had. Therefore unless a notation chances to be very obvious, an argument from it is quite false and often ludicrous. (CE 11:221)[9]

The linguistic activity attaching to *Nimrod* and *Babel* in Book 12 is supported by the authority of the angel Michael and behind him of the Scriptures themselves, so that "false" teaching is avoided. More generally, the postlapsarian language crisis has a positive as well as a negative result. As a gift of God, postlapsarian language consists of division not precision of names but complementarily also of a means for bridging the gap between name and thing or name and meaning and a process for translating one language into another. In the prelapsarian mode, "In the beginning was the Word" (John 1:1), but in the postlapsarian mode "the word was made flesh and dwelt among us . . . full of grace and truth" (John 1:14). The Son as the unifying Word provides the possibility for translating or mediating between corporeal and spiritual, experience and faith. The *logos* signals the new order and new dispensation that Christ is and effects.

The lapsarian nature of these texts and vocabularies emerges clearly from the evidence of the epic. Raphael's initial lessons in Book 5 instruct Adam in hierarchical reality and in the relation between hierarchy and the deity and between hierarchy and himself. The overriding principle is the unity of God's universe or, as S. K. Heninger suggestively spells it, "uni-verse."[10] This Raphael outlines in one of the great set pieces of the epic:

> O, *Adam*, one Almighty is, from whom
> All things proceed, and up to him return,
> If not deprav'd from good, created all
> Such to perfection, one first matter all,
> Indu'd with various forms, various degrees
> Of substance, and in things that live, of life;
> But more refin'd, more spiritous, and pure,
> As nearer to him plac't or nearer tending

Each in thir several active Spheres assign'd,
Till body up to spirit work, in bounds
Proportion'd to each kind. So from the root
Springs lighter the green stalk, from thence the leaves
More aery, last the bright consummate flow'r
Spirits odorous breathes: flow'rs and thir fruit
Man's nourishment, by gradual scale sublim'd
To vital spirits aspire, to animal,
To intellectual, give both life and sense
Fancy and understanding, whence the Soul
Reason receives, and reason is her being,
Discursive, or intuitive: discourse
Is oftest yours, the latter most is ours,
Differing but in degree, of kind the same. (5.469–90)

The passage describes what is usually called the Great Chain of Being or the Analogy of Being, and Milton's rendition is in general conformity to the tradition as outlined popularly in E. M. W. Tillyard's *Elizabethan World Picture* and C. S. Lewis's *Discarded Image* and learnedly examined in A. O. Lovejoy's *Great Chain of Being*. At its most basic in the latter work, the creation is a carefully graduated continuum, deriving from Aristotle's *De Anima*, with "each higher order possessing all the powers of those below it in the scale, and an additional differentiating one of its own"—each, that is, contains privations and possibilities.[11] It is a spatial and atemporal model for an ontological universe in which the divine unity and perfection are distributed hierarchically through the forms of creation. The levels of creation variously, proportionately, and mutually participate in the divine energy. The mineral creation has being but no life; the vegetable creation has being and life but no motion; the animal creation has being and life and movement but no reason; the human creation has being and life and move-ment and reason or soul. The soul exercises reason of two kinds: The lower, more human discursive reasoning processes the data of the realms of matter and idea, of experience, in consecutive formats, and the other higher, more angelic reasoning is intuitive and knows innately, instinctively, simultane-ously, and totally. The deity, the cosmos, the created universe and its forms, human psychology, all are contained within this controlled design. The plan is at once contained and also and simultaneously aspirational and buoyant. Thus, Marjorie Nicolson can speak of "Nature's nest of concentric boxes" and Walter Clyde Curry of "theopantism" and of the comprehensive "hylomorphic composition."[12] Because the creation is radically unified, coherent, and continuous, Raphael looks forward to the time when, as he says to Adam, "Your bodies may at last turn all to spirit." The unfallen Adam apprehends these lessons "suddenly" and perfectly, and he summarizes them in these words:

> Well hast thou taught the way that might direct
> Our knowledge, and the scale of Nature set
> From centre to circumference, whereon
> In contemplation of created things
> By steps we may ascend to God. (5.508–12)

Adam's summary recapitulates the idealized patterns and ways of knowing outlined in Milton's pamphlet *Of Education*.

As the prelapsarian universe is unified and continuous, the postlapsarian is divided and fragmented. After Adam and Eve matriculate in experience by eating the forbidden fruit that gives them "Knowledge of Good bought dear by knowing ill" (4.222), their minds like nature itself "felt the wound" (9.782). Raphael's spatial model of the universe gives way to a temporal model; Raphael's ontology shifts toward Michael's teleology; and Raphael's emphasis on likeness is replaced by Michael's emphasis on differentiation. Divisions accumulate throughout Michael's presentation of history, and as they do so they show several repeated patterns and a sequence that reinforce Adam's grasp of the material and his awareness that it is moving toward a larger design that makes sense out of the apparent confusion and that will make more sense as time proceeds.

These postlapsarian divisions are perceived in three patterns that coincide roughly with the final three books of the epic. To Adam alone in Book 10 the world appears hopelessly fragmented, and the fragmentation in the structure of Book 10 arrays this new reality as well as Adam's fallen psyche. The varying perspectives of Book 10 provide a structural mimesis of the dislocations of the fallen mind, world, and relationship to deity. Its disjunctive scenes on earth and in Heaven and Hell, its disordering of the cosmos, and its rendering of Adam's isolation and despair give way at the conclusion of Book 10 to a reconciliation of man with woman and of humanity with God.

In the second pattern, after his arrival in Book 11 Michael teaches his pupil that the numerous divisions resolve themselves into two, that is, into moral polarities. These appear in the smallest details in his narratives as well as in the largest issues of good and evil and life and death, in the rhythm through history of freedom and bondage, peace and war, famine and plenty, the world destroyed and the world restored (12.3). The polarities operate specifically through oppositions of character: Cain against Abel, the offspring of Cain against the offspring of Seth, city dwellers against shepherds, Enoch against the factions of his time, and Noah against the lascivious corruptions of his time. As history unfolds to Adam, individual characters are identified thoroughly with one or the other of the moral poles and emerge as symbols, examples, and types: Cain, Nimrod, and Pharoah of evil; and Enoch, Noah, Abraham, and Moses of good. The same design governs the presentation of places, with evil attaching to Babel, Egypt, and Babylon and defined in terms of things and the experiential, and good containing expansive possibilities. Good is linked with Canaan, but a distinction is made clear between "earthly *Canaan*" (12.315) and the "promised land" (259–60) it signifies to those who have done their reading and whose minds and spirits are capable of transcending the literal. Such spiritual exercise calls for an ability to recognize and judge present realities and place them within the larger perspective of eternity and the ideal. Where Raphael had instructed Adam in a unified continuum of the universe, Michael sets forth parallel disjunctive categories that are moral as well as physical, interpreted as well as real. Michael's lessons are targeted on conduct rather than created nature, and his mode is not vision but revelation. Michael demands not sudden apprehension but moral judgment and choice.

This process of moral differentiation is not merely something that Michael does for Adam but something that he is in the process of teaching Adam to do for himself. Raphael's passive pupil must come to accept the responsibility to pursue truth energetically, not merely receive it by immediate and total transfer. Michael is weaning Adam away from his fugitive and cloistered virtue, exercising him to become a wayfaring and warfaring Christian, to fight the good fight and run the race where that immortal garland is to be run for, not without dust and heat, for the trial that purifies, for choice which is reason. *Areopagitica* maps out the moral territory:

> Good and evil we know in the field of this world grow up together almost inseparably: and the knowledge of good is so involved and interwoven with the knowledge of evil, and in so many cunning resemblances hardly to be discerned, that those confused seeds which were imposed on Psyche as an incessant labor to cull out and sort asunder, were not more intermixed. It was

from out the rind of one apple tasted, that the knowledge of good and evil, as two twins cleaving together, leaped forth into the world. And perhaps this is that doom which Adam fell into of knowing good and evil, that is to say, of knowing good by evil. (Hughes, p. 728)

Such a dynamic exercise of discrimination makes the pupil not a heretic in the truth but a uniter of those dissevered pieces that are yet wanting to the body of Truth (pp. 739, 742).

In Book 11 Michael replaces Adam's apprehension of the hopeless fragmentation of the fallen universe with a dichotomous design that places the divisions between good and evil, experience and faith, reality and language, God and man, time and eternity, within a containing perspective. In its final stage in Book 12, however, Michael's polarities give way to another model for reuniting the fallen division and for repairing the ruins of the fall, and that is the principle of paradox, and specifically the agency of the paradoxical Christ. In his general examination of paradoxes in *Paradise Lost*, J. C. Gray calls attention to those paradoxes that become "a mode of expressing truth" and that "initially seem contradictory but eventually prove through logical, semantical, or mystical manipulation to be resolvable at some different level of meaning." Of these he remarks, "Yet, sometimes, as the mind and the heart repeatedly batter the difficulty, cognition can suddenly occur when higher truth flashes from the dark and coiled mystery of paradox." [13]

As the culmination of Michael's history and as the inclusive design for resolving postlapsarian divisions, Christ is precisely this "different level of meaning" in the epic and this mysterious flash of illumination. Christ is by definition paradoxical in being God incarnate in man, the Word in the flesh, the strength in apparent weakness, the life in apparent death. He is paradoxical as the second Adam reversing the consequences of the first Adam's fall. Christ embodies the analogue of the relationship of earth and heaven that Raphael had presented before the fall in simpler spatial and hierarchical terms. After the fall the Son represents a kind of energy that, once revealed and received by mankind, transforms their whole mode of perception and action. He exists for fallen mankind as an exemplar and model of the divine promises, and he exists as crucial memory equipment against which all of experience, accident, and confusion must be measured. An important instrument for re-creation or for the creation of the paradise within of the New Dispensation is thus man himself. The new order celebrates the deity more gloriously the more the material and experiential are transcended. As paradox, Christ shows the way, the truth, and the life by which fallen division may be restored to the original and to the final unity and union with God, and he provides the new mode of creative vision for the now human creators. Christ is the Word, the paradox, and the means of translation between not merely two languages but also two kinds of reality and life. The temporal design that replaces Raphael's spatial chain is, then, a progression, moving from initial confusion, through a recognition of moral polarities, to a culmination in Christian paradox.

The lapsarian contrasts of books, languages, and principles will be clearer if we turn to some collections of specific evidence from *Paradise Lost*. Vegetation imagery and solar imagery not only support the lapsarian distinctions already developed but also point in expansive directions. These groups of images define the physical and spiritual contexts of the poem and illuminate the angels' contrasting theological as well as poetic proceedings. In brief, the vegetative category of flowers variously defines the prelapsarian world, and the vegetative category of seed—its biblical echoes reinforcing natural chronological realities—serves to present the postlapsarian equivalent data and instruction.

A long tradition of biblical and exegetical imagery of the cultivation of vegetation provides a provocative context for Milton's edenic setting. Thus, Diane McColley has recently and suggestively arrayed levels of interpretation:

> [Gardening] is literally the care and cultivation of nature; morally, the cultivation of virtue in response to God's laws, both natural and revealed; ethically, the nurture of marriage and children, which Milton stresses in his similitudes, and the formation of a godly community; and anagogically the regeneration of "all the faculties" and the union of Christ and the church, both celestial and terrene. Moreover, Milton so cultivates the sense of organic process, of mimesis, and of the interanimation of nature and grace emergent in the liveliest Renaissance and Reformation thought, that his fit audience might see in the handiwork of Adam and Eve the cultivation of "all kinde of seedes and grafts of life," as they integrate the contemplation of God's ways and the imitation of them and thus nurture the divine image in themselves and each other through providential and creative acts.[14]

As Boyd M. Berry has emphasized:

A Puritan would positively have loved to tend such a garden ever tending to wild. . . . Such a garden provides the perfect format for constantly imposing order on one's existence and surroundings. It is as though Milton here pastoralized Puritan theology, captured in plants and trees the stuff of Puritan summas and military sermons.[15]

As Charlotte F. Otten has so delightfully demonstrated, Milton's edenic garden is no mere metaphor for spiritual activity or "dreamlike fantasy," but it is solidly and exactly grounded in the native English gardening tradition.[16] Initially, the floral vegetation sets forth the prelapsarian as Adam and Eve inhabit and understand it before Raphael arrives to instruct them beyond what is naturally manifest in the givens of their garden universe. Flowers are the fairest or choicest part of a plant, beautiful, colorful, ornamental, sweet-smelling, delicate. Like Eden itself, they appeal to the eye, the nose, and the touch and are fixed in space. Flowers render the tone and atmosphere of Eden and supply even quite literally its furnishings. Within the edenic setting Adam and Eve work, they perform "sweet Gard'ning labor" (4.328), or in the words of Genesis they dress the garden and keep it. Work is by definition the imposition of order and thus the multiplication of the good, and work distinguishes man from animal: It "declares his Dignity, / And the regard of Heav'n on all his ways" (619–20). Thus, in their capacity for work, for reasoned order, for good, Adam and Eve share their maker's image. Before the fall, flowers serve to define that work as sensuous, exquisite, and delightful—in contrast to the sweaty Adam's painful tillage of a land cursed with thorns and thistles afterward. Prelapsarian Adam and Eve's days are scheduled around morning praise, daily garden work, evening praise, and loving restful nights, and all of these categories of work, praise, and love find expression through the flower imagery of the poem.

These are the vegetative givens upon which Raphael builds his lessons. Soon after his arrival Raphael places flowers within a hierarchical vegetative continuum to explicate the order, unity, and verticality of the divine creation:

> So from the root
> Springs lighter the green stalk, from thence the leaves
> More aery, last the bright consummate flow'r
> Spirits odorous breathes: flow'rs and thir fruit
> Man's nourishment, by gradual scale sublim'd

To vital spirits aspire, to animal,
To intellectual. (5.479–85)

As Kester Svendsen has pointed out, Milton here selects the simplest form of life to illustrate the complete Chain of Being and implies in the well-known figure that ontogeny recapitulates phylogeny. Furthermore, he notes, "the plant, a visual epitome for the whole scale, *grows* before our very eyes." [17] The flowers are *last, bright, consummate, odorous*, and in their sensuous way spiritous. "Thir fruit" is "Man's nourishment," useful rather than decorative, "sublim'd" to serve human potentialities and aspiration, transmutable into reason and faith.

Raphael uses this hierarchical example drawn from the visible world arrayed before them in the garden in order to provide Adam with an explanation of the process by which body works up to spirit, the model for Adam's life and spiritual life. In presenting the vegetative example, Raphael demonstrates the analogy between vegetative life and psychic life in order to show the unity and continuity of the whole of creation. When the explanation shifts from a vegetative hierarchy to the hierarchy of faculty psychology, an additional point emerges. Adam had himself provided a review of faculty psychology in explicating the source of Eve's dream before Raphael's arrival. Raphael is working with Adam's prior knowledge of psychology as of vegetation in order to stretch his capacities to greater spiritual awareness. He is discovering to Adam the implications of the visible data. Raphael's text is the natural world, but he is teaching Adam to read that natural world as the book of God, to see in the visible and sensible creation "the knowledge of God and things invisible" that *Of Education* recommended as available through the "orderly conning [of] the visible and inferior creature" (Hughes, p. 631).

Raphael's hexaemeral lecture in Book 7 of *Paradise Lost* builds upon this hierarchical foundation in significant ways. Raphael's copious lyric expansion of the days of creation from the first chapter of Genesis shows a quite different attitude toward this other "book of God" than Michael's. Unlike Michael's contractive biblical history with its emphasis on time, sequence, and consequence, Raphael is amplifying the thirty-one Bible verses into more than 300 lines in the poetic version. In expanding the Genesis data he provides a hymn of praise celebrating the forms and variety of the creation, thereby celebrating the Creator so amply, variously, and wonderfully manifest; the re-creation of creation is itself a significant creative act on Raphael's part. The detailed review of species in Book 7 fills out the layers of the scale of nature Raphael presented theoretically and hierarchically in Book 5. In Gen. 1:11 we read of the vegetative evidence: "And God said, let the earth bring forth grass, the herb yielding seed, and the fruit tree yielding fruit after his kind, whose seed is in itself, upon the earth: and it was so." But in Raphael's rendering we are presented with grass, herbs, flowers, vines, gourds, reeds, shrubs, bushes, and trees, especially fruit trees, each of which is described in sprightly and colorful detail.

One of the most interesting things that happens as the vegetation is being arrayed in Book 7 is that a number of the details gradually build up a portrait of a personified Mother Earth with "her Universal Face," with bushes for hair, and green clothing, and flowers to make her bosom sweet-smelling. The personification is capable of a variety of motions. Raphael is explicitly calling attention to the likeness between earth and Heaven, but he is also implicitly drawing a pattern of comparisons between one realm of creation and another, in this case between vegetation and animal life. A similar thing happens with other parts of the story. Light is spoken of as "Transplanted" (7.360) and the heavens are "sow'd with Stars . . . thick as a field" (358). Fish are spoken of as grazing in pastures of seaweed and straying through groves of coral (404–5). Land animals are described as rising out of the earth as if they were plants, most vividly in the wonderful phrases "the grassy Clods now Calv'd" and "the swift Stag from under ground / Bore up his branching head" (463, 469–70). The effect of these interrelated vegetation images is to argue the unity of the creation even as the variety is being counted off unit by unit.

In Book 7 Raphael is explicating vegetation itself and is explicating also the unified interrelationship between vegetation and the other layers of the creation. As before, Raphael is building on Adam's informational givens, but that building is intended primarily to celebrate the unity of the Creator and his creational purposes and design. Raphael is presenting the universe as unified and invites Adam to make such comparative alignments central to human perception. He is providing a model through which in contemplation of created things by steps Adam may ascend to God (5.509–12).

Seed is the form the vegetation imagery takes in the final portions of *Paradise Lost*. Within the realm of nature the implications of *seed* nicely balance against the earlier flowers to make the lapsarian point. In addition, fallen humanity is now to read vegetation data like other postlapsarian data by the light of the "written Records" more than by the light of nature, and as such *seed* points both to the Old Testament and to the New, both to Hebrew history and continuity and also to potentiality for growth in Christ. The final books of the epic repeatedly call attention to the children of Israel as Abraham's seed and to Christ as the seed of Adam and Eve or as "the woman's seed." *Seed* brings the vegetation imagery of the poem and its themes and promise emphatically into the scheme of time, including the past or Old Testament time, reviewed historically throughout Books 11 and 12, and the future or the culmination of New Testament time anticipated as the New Jerusalem, and the present or that transitional segment in which we live and Christ is operative and in which each just person may live fruitfully in outward relations and may in inward relations live spiritually in the blossoming and burgeoning of that paradise we create within ourselves.

The *seed* of the "written Records" echoes through the final books of the epic and is one of the "mysterious terms" from the Son's judgment on the serpent. As Raphael had copiously amplified the hexaemeral verses from the first chapter of Genesis, the final books of *Paradise Lost* take as their starting point a particular passage from the third chapter, the curse on the serpent in verse 15: "And I will put enmity between thee and the woman, and between thy seed and her seed; it shall bruise thy head, and thou shalt bruise his heel." The Geneva Bible glosses *head* as "the power of sinne and death" and *bruise* with this note: "Satan shal sting Christ & his members, but not overcome them." [18] The equivalent passage is rendered in Book 10 of *Paradise Lost* in precisely equivalent language:

> Between Thee and the Woman I will put
> Enmity, and between thine and her Seed;
> Her Seed shall bruise thy head, thou bruise his heel. (179–81)

The exactness of the echo from Genesis contrasts with the copious amplifications of Raphael to make a point that we see in various evidence from the final books of the epic: that Raphael and the prelapsarian generally take a poetic or inventive attitude toward their data but that the postlapsarian addresses Truth as mediated by the Bible or by the biblical agencies of Michael and Christ.

When introduced in Book 10 the passage occurs "in mysterious terms, judg'd as then best" (173). Adam recalls this mysterious promise of *seed* late in Book 10 (1031–32), and his initial effort to interpret it provides the spiritual turning point in the narrative from despair to grace. Divine motions working in Adam allow him to exercise his memory and make a dramatic interpretative leap. He undergoes the central religious experience for Puritans, which Georgia Christopher labels an "opening":

> In essence, the "opening" is a moment when the promise in a passage of scripture that has hitherto seemed dark, puzzling, or merely irrelevant, takes on clarity, certitude—and more important—a liberating application to one's immediate life situation. [19]

The half-dozen or so times in Books 11 and 12 when Michael recalls the enigma build on Adam's initial breakthrough to spiritual possibilities. Further, they may be described as Michael's efforts to gloss the poetic rendering in close analogy to the Geneva Bible's gloss for its Renaissance readers. Michael does not modify the text as Raphael's amplification does; he accepts the verbal format as data and concentrates upon the spiritual and interpretative exercises that will draw forth the mysterious and applicable meaning for the human audience. Its meaning is revealed gradually to Michael as Michael gradually reveals it to Adam: The revelation is accommodated to progressive comprehension. H. R. MacCallum analyzes the spiritual and pedagogical design in these terms:

> Michael's aim is to bring Adam to a full and spiritual understanding of the Son's prophecy concerning the war between the seed of the woman and the serpent. He leads Adam toward this goal by a series of graded steps, each one but the last inconclusive, and each consequently capable of misinterpretation. Yet as he proceeds he does sow within Adam "the seeds of a sufficient determining," so that by the close of the story every part takes its place in a total design. He does not teach oracularly, of course . . . but the events themselves, whether presented in vision or simply recounted, provide the material on which he and Adam must practice the art of gatherers. He employs ambiguity, sometimes appearing to mislead Adam deliberately in order to crystallize the false interpretations which must be rejected, and he uses the "powerful art of reclaiming" employed by Christ in which excess is administered against excess.

As MacCallum also notes, "a series of subsidiary promises mark the stages of the process and point in an increasingly specific manner to the nature of the promised seed." [20] The collection of seed passages lays before us in imitative form the need and arena for the action of re-collection that is the hallmark of the postlapsarian mode in the epic.

Harvest or the anticipation of harvest is the idea we are left with at the culmination of *Paradise Lost*, and this too activates the art of gathering. If we learn with Adam the spiritual and paradoxical lesson of the final pages, we too may triumph in the harvest of knowledge, deeds, faith, virtue, patience, temperance, and love (12.581–84):

> Henceforth I learn [says Adam], that to obey is best,
> And love with fear the only God, to walk
> As in his presence, ever to observe
> His providence, and on him sole depend,
> Merciful over all his works, with good
> Still overcoming evil, and by small
> Accomplishing great things, by things deem'd weak
> Subverting worldly strong, and worldly wise
> By simply meek; that suffering for Truth's sake
> Is fortitude to highest victory,
> And to the faithful Death the Gate of Life;
> Taught this by his example whom I now
> Acknowledge my Redeemer ever blest. (561–73)

The fruitfulness of the new Eden will more than match the abundance of the old Eden, now "The haunt of Seals, and Orcs, and Sea-mews' clang" (11.835), when place has become metaphorical and space internalized. After time has been completed, "the Earth / Shall all be Paradise, far happier place / Than this of *Eden*, and far happier days" (12.463–65). Eve had complained that the vegetation in Eden "under our labor grows, / Luxurious by restraint" and in a day or so becomes "wanton growth . . . Tending to wild" (9.208–9, 211–12). The fruit of Eden is "in such abundance"

> As leaves a greater store of Fruit untoucht,
> Still hanging incorruptible, till men
> Grow up to thir provision, and more hands
> Help to disburden Nature of her Birth. (620–24)

Adam assures Eve that there is no danger to their state in God's abundance, and when we are metaphorically released from the merely material garden we too rejoice in the fullness of the promise of fruitful opportunities and spiritual nourishment. The confined world of edenic imagery, subject to Old Testament law as to nature and reason, gives way to the open-ended dispensation of grace, imagination, and faith.

Vegetation evidence pervades *Paradise Lost* and functions variously both in the narrative itself and in the artistic rendering of the epic's themes from its opening-line reference to "the *fruit* / Of the Forbidden Tree." Vegetation provides Raphael and Michael with their different vocabularies for rendering their unified and divided worlds and for explicating their books of God's works and of God's word. When we recall that flowers send forth their incense in response to distant emanations of the divine light of the sun, we can see the difference the fall makes in the enriching transformation of the process of worship from the "floral" praise of Book 5 to the "fruitful" prayer of Books 10 and 11 (especially 11.22–30) that follows the "deflowering" of innocence. Flowers properly may send their innocent odors upward, but fruits must nourish humans, be digested and transmuted into spiritual energy. The natural dimension of Michael's *seed*—rooted, as it were, in time—fades into the background, and the biblical echoes and metaphoric significations take over. *Seed* conveys the temporal dimension of vegetation generally and Hebrew-Christian continuity and values more specifically.

Another closely related pattern of the epic's evidence, the solar imagery, makes similar and additional points about Raphael's instruction in the book of God's works, Michael's rendering of the book of God's word, and the contrasts between the two angels and their lapsarian worlds and epistemologies. In brief, the solar distinction is this: Raphael presents the *sun* to Adam's full understanding whereas Michael explicates the role of the *Son* to his fallen pupil. Within the book of nature, the sun is the source of earthly life and therefore of growth, energy, and reason. All units of creation are informed by it, participate in it, and aspire to realize themselves in it and it in themselves. The sun is the basis of unity in nature in a physical, cosmological rendering of the theological act of the begetting of the Son, undertaken in Book 3 and explicated in Book 5 of *Paradise Lost* as a means of bringing about the New Dispensation of dynamic unity in creation and ultimate union with the deity. The sun's nature and activity are precisely translatable into an account of the functioning of the Christian Son. Milton's deployment of the homonym is traditional and intentional, as varied evidence of the Nativity *Hymn* attests, but within the epic the solar imagery imposes a significant lapsarian distinction not only between the central and the concluding books of the epic but also incidentally between Raphael's immediate audience of Adam and Eve and the epic's postlapsarian reading audience. When processing Raphael's solar materials, readers put in practice the instruction that Michael exercises Adam in late in the epic. Raphael's statements about Adam's natural universe convey to a Christian reading audience quite separate Christian messages. Such readers from their fallen vantage put back together the abstract and concrete that are a single whole to Adam's consciousness with its "sudden apprehension" of the spiritual within the natural.

Milton's handling of the sun in *Paradise Lost* has received a variety of critical attention in recent years, ranging from the scientific to the imaginatively provocative. Thus, Walter Clyde Curry's *Milton's Ontology, Cosmogony, and Physics* studies the sun as "magnetic center and ruler of a magnetized world" and as an "ethereal quintessence" subject to metabolic change and as a generator of powers, especially in its interactions with earth. In "Adam on the Grass with Balsamum," Geoffrey Hartman moves outward from a detailed examination of *Paradise Lost* 8.253–56 to touch upon a wide range of solar passages and issues; and in "The Sacred Head: Milton's Solar Mysticism," Don Parry Norford examines Milton's celebration of the solar Logos and notes a tendency in the later poems for solar power to become apocalyptically destructive. For our purposes the wisest of the solar studies as well as the earliest is that of Kester Svendsen in *Milton and Science*. In addition to supplying encyclopedic backgrounds on the sun and discussing Milton's uses of the sun, Svendsen puts the solar along with the scientific more generally into perspective by observing that "cosmology was a vocabulary for [Milton], a quarry of images, not a formal statement of scientific theory," and again "The poems 'believe' in science the way they believe in classical mythology; the real truth is not in it except as it is analogue." [21]

Within the poem, it is interesting to note how frequently the sun receives initial emphasis. Literally the first fact of Adam's existence and consciousness is the physical sun, "This happy Light" (8.285). From Adam's narration of his primal moment the solar influence on human life and mind and spirit dominates. It is this—all the experience the newborn Adam can have—that teaches him the right relationship between himself and God.

> As new wak't from soundest sleep
> Soft on the flow'ry herb I found me laid
> In Balmy Sweat, which with his Beams the Sun
> Soon dri'd, and on the reeking moisture fed.
> Straight toward Heav'n my wand'ring Eyes I turn'd,
> And gaz'd a while the ample Sky, till rais'd
> By quick instinctive motion up I sprung,
> As thitherward endeavoring, and upright
> Stood on my feet. (253–61)

The sun draws Adam's birth moisture, eyes, and action toward and beyond itself, a process that has analogues throughout the natural edenic world. The relation of sun to dew and flowers is cited as an example that becomes generalized to "all things":

> Now whenas sacred Light began to dawn
> In *Eden* on the humid Flow'rs, that breath'd
> Thir morning incense, when *all things that breathe*,
> From th' Earth's great Altar send up silent praise
> To the Creator, and his Nostrils fill
> With grateful Smell. (9.192–97; emphasis mine)

Even the newly created fish in Book 7 "Show to the Sun thir wav'd coats dropt with Gold" (406). The human equivalent of the flowers' "morning incense" is their hymn of praise in Book 5. Because humans have a capacity for speech, a receptivity to the Word, the praise they send up "From th' Earth's great Altar" is not silent; their very breathing is instinct with praise as the flowers' is with aromas. Such harmony with nature and such a shared relationship to the sun define the nature and purpose of human body, mind, and spirit in Adam at his purest. The physical sun draws humanity toward itself, as fallen future humanity will be drawn toward God through the Son. The sun is a mediator of prelapsarian worship and a source of prelapsarian life; after the fall the Son is the agency of worship and life, but that life, like the paradise of Book 12, is within.

Adam's first words are an apostrophe to the sun. Adam was created with the ready capacity to name whatever he saw, and what he first saw and first named was the sun. He records his first words—his first invocation of the solar Word—in the conversation with Raphael in Book 8:

> Thou Sun, said I, fair Light,
> And thou enlight'n'd Earth, so fresh and gay,
> Ye Hills and Dales, ye Rivers, Woods, and Plains
> And ye that live and move, fair Creatures, tell,
> Tell, if ye saw, how came I thus, how here?
> Not of myself; by some great Maker then,
> In goodness and in power preeminent;
> Tell me, how may I know him, how adore,
> From whom I have that thus I move and live,
> And feel that I am happier than I know. (273–82)

Adam's relationship to the physical sun provides him with some guidelines for answers to questions of power and worship; it provides a vocabulary that facilitates its own transcendence, from nature toward grace. Poetically Adam is a reader, and his world consists of images. Adam asks the cosmos to "tell," that is, to speak to him, to facilitate revelation, by making meaning visible. The physical sun does so initially, though the Son (identified merely as "God" by the pre-Christian Adam) soon arrives to amplify the account and provide new modes of enlightenment. Adam's first articulation addresses the relationship between sun and enlightened earth and becomes a reasoned consideration of the relationship between the deity and himself, which he in his humble gratitude rightly apprehends.

A similar mood of praise shared with the silent members of the visible creation governs Adam's other major pre-Raphaelean solar observation in a stanza of the hierarchical morning hymn of Book 5. There all creations in heaven and earth are called upon to extol the creator. The sun is apprehended as an image of the greater meaning it incarnates; the prelapsarian physical sun is acknowledged as subject to vicissitudes to which the fall attaches moral categories not yet existing. The passage and surrounding stanzas are these:

> Fairest of Stars, last in the train of Night,
> If better thou belong not to the dawn,
> Sure pledge of day, that crown'st the smiling Morn
> With thy bright Circlet, praise him in thy Sphere
> While day arises, that sweet hour of Prime.
> Thou Sun of this great World both Eye and Soul,
> Acknowledge him thy Greater, sound his praise
> In thy eternal course, both when thou climb'st,
> And when high Noon hast gain'd, and when thou fall'st.
> Moon, that now meet'st the orient Sun, now fli'st
> With the fixt Stars, fixt in thir Orb that flies,
> And yee five other wand'ring Fires that move
> In mystic Dance, not without Song, resound
> His praise, who out of Darkness call'd up Light. (5.166–79)

The progress of the hymn generally is from higher to lower; specifically here the progress is also chronological, reflecting Adam and Eve's earliest morning and latest evening glimpses of light. As Eve's love song in Book 4, lines 639–56, had descriptively reviewed a diurnal array, this morning hymn in which Adam's psychological processes dominate imposes a hierarchical design upon chronology and the cosmos.

Adam and Eve praise the way things are; they affirm the divine order, wholly while their faith is whole. In so doing they are also affirming the operations of night and, for postlapsarian readers, the necessary functioning of evil within the divine dynamic diurnal scheme. Before the fall Adam and Eve's nighttime experience remains limited and indirect. That the "Fairest of Stars" in the hymn is Lucifer, the light bringer (the presunrise form of the sunset Hesperus), makes that point. [22] When one's spirit and faith are whole, evil too is a sure pledge and crown of smiling morn. The sun is constant, the world's "both Eye and Soul," but also dynamic, and its worship and worshiping show through both climbing and falling. The moon both meets and flies from the sun. God's creation and triumph harbor in the action of calling up light out of darkness, each day and in each faithful heart. The darkness is necessary to the cycling of the dynamic, but before the fall it is apprehended as participating in unity. The created world is literally a uni-verse, circling and variously articulate of affirmation. For the Christian reader—a matter of imaginative potentiality as well as historical chronology—the spiritual dimension of the solar is resonant in ways it cannot be for the Hebraic Adam. For Adam, the unnamed stellar Lucifer bears no burden of moral adversary and fall; for redeemed readers, Lucifer as morning star is a "sure pledge of Day" in both the generalized *felix culpa* design and specifically in the prehistory that Books 5 and 6 explicate: The begetting of the Son initiates the fall of Satan ("A fairer person lost not Heav'n" [2.110]; "Star of the Morning") and the luminous rise of the Sun of Righteousness. The third day of the Battle in Heaven illustrates (= makes lustrous) the Son and implies the creation (Book 7) within which and on whom that sun/Son will shine.

The action of *Paradise Lost* may be described within this shift from *sun* to *Son* as it may be described in the shift from happiness to happy fall and from flower to seed. The movement is from the simplicity of prelapsarian external reality to the complexity, elusiveness, paradox, mystery, triumph of the internal that asserts itself in defiance of the contradictoriness in the realities we postlapsarians inhabit. Milton's creation of the prelapsarian is a lively and coherent but imaginative exercise. One of the problems that Milton criticism has variously addressed itself to is anticipations of the fall built into the edenic perfection. [23] Eden is a place that we *can* as well as *must* imagine, and, to achieve this, postlapsarian readers require evidence that speaks to the principle of experience as well as of innocence within them. It must be a world of vicissitudes as ours is; in terms of solar imagery it must set forth night as well as day, shadow as well as light. Adam and Eve's lives must be touched by absences of sun as well as presences, but their innocence requires their acceptance and affirmation but also their lack of full understanding of the variations of their cosmos. Adam and Eve sleep during their nights and wake, work, and worship during their days. They even retire at noon from too full exposure to too bright sun.

A passage from Book 5 demonstrates the edenic norm:

> But first from under shady arborous roof,
> Soon as they forth were come to open sight
> Of day-spring, and the Sun, who scarce up risen
> With wheels yet hov'ring o'er the Ocean brim,
> Shot parallel to the earth his dewy ray,
> Discovering in the wide Lantskip all the East
> Of Paradise and *Eden's* happy Plains,
> Lowly they bow'd adoring, and began
> Thir Orisons, each Morning duly paid
> In various style. (137–46)

The movement is from night to day, from shade to sun, from sleep to increased consciousness. The sun draws them toward itself and "discovers" their world and happiness to them; they worship "In various style." Their rising is a reversal of their going to bed, as the sun's rising wheels reverse its decline of the night before (4.352–54). They recognize the reversals but do not yet grasp the principles of cycle and dynamism. That lesson awaits Raphael's visit and is not fully learned until the fall and its initiation into knowledge, evil, and the paradox that is Christ. At its simplest, Adam does not experience a wakeful night until after he has fallen. Prelapsarian Adam and Eve live in a world of day, of sunlight, as they know experientially only good. That there are or may be such things as night and evil is part of their theoretical awareness, but as yet safely so. Raphael several times articulates the warning that they not seek to know (to need to know) evil or good via evil. The narrator enforces the point to readers. Adam and Eve are constantly expanding the boundaries of their experience and control, and such a process inevitably bumps against unassimilable data. Morally and spiritually, the crisis comes in Book 9 with the fall. Intellectually and imagistically, the analogue is in the questions they ask and the opinions they hold about the nocturnal cosmos. Their position is one of affirmation and faith; they praise the total work and world of the Creator. They do not know what they affirm in their talk of night; lack of knowledge about night is synonymous with their innocence. Their other attitude results from their need to grow, their curiosity. Praise, innocence, and curiosity are the terms of their condition before the fall, and narratively before Raphael's arrival and discourse.

Adam and Eve are conscious of the full diurnal order, even though they have not experienced the cosmological night or the moral evil. In her love lyric Eve labels the sun *pleasant*, "When first on this delightful Land he spreads / His orient Beams, on herb, tree, fruit, and flow'r, / Glist'ring with dew" (4.642–45, and similarly at 651–53). But her affirmation is equally directed to those cosmic realities that do not yet govern her inner life: "grateful Ev'ning mild," "silent Night," "this fair Moon, / And these the Gems of Heav'n, her starry train" (647–49, and similarly at 654–56). Her innocence is apparent and only becomes endangered in the ensuing query:

> But wherefore all night long shine these, for whom
> This glorious sight, when sleep hath shut all eyes? (657–58)

That the night of the question, the immediate hours, encompasses the toad-inspired dream makes the moral and cosmic point, as does the fact that Eve has reviewed the whole diurnal sequence, but Satan's temptation in the dream echoes only the nocturnal evidence.

Adam's reply to Eve's question makes a number of important points, in sum, that the total cosmos reflects divine order and harmony and providence for human protection:

> Minist'ring light prepar'd, [the stars] set and rise;
> Lest total darkness should by Night regain
> Her old possession, and extinguish life
> In Nature and all things, which these soft fires
> Not only enlighten, but with kindly heat
> Of various influence foment and warm,
> Temper or nourish, or in part shed down
> Thir stellar virtue on all kinds that grow
> On Earth, made hereby apter to receive
> Perfection from the Sun's more potent Ray. (4.664–73)

Lines 672–73 encapsulate the *felix culpa* paradox to which Michael will give postlapsarian expression. In the lines that follow this passage Adam speaks of the "Millions of spiritual Creatures" that walk the earth; these demonstrate the earthly equivalent of heavenly stars, and in the ensuing action of Book 4 we are shown how the "stellar virtue" (671) of Gabriel and his cohort prevents the attempt of Satan to gain possession of the mind and spirit of Eve and thereby "extinguish life / In Nature and all things."

Adam's answer to Eve employs the vocabulary given to him on his creation, which allows him to name the things of nature and therefore to understand their nature. Note that it is their *nature*, not their *grace*, that he perceives. Until Raphael's visit this vocabulary is one-dimensionally scientific, not the diction of poetic resonances; it is rational rather than imaginative; it sees and states things as they are in external reality, without the influence of the Christic imaginative energy that makes them more meaningful than they appear to be, and also without the influence of the literalist Satan who seeks always to make less. That which for prelapsarian Adam has the secure clarity of physical fact has the mystery of Truth to postlapsarian Christian readers, however. Thus, when we read that the effect of the night and stars is to make growing things of earth "apter to receive / Perfection from the Sun's more potent Ray," we supply the equivalent *Son* for *sun*. Adam's world is a fully harmonized whole, whereas ours, like the one Michael addresses, is disjunctive. The energies that allow the fallen to bridge the gap between the separate units of experience are on the one hand faith and on the other imagination. We read via Christ, by remembering the promises; we read through skill in the kinds of lessons Michael will teach the postlapsarian Adam in the final books of the epic.

Raphael is the unfallen Adam's instructor, specifically for the test that Adam and Eve fail in Book 9, more generally in matters of hierarchy (Book 5), faith (Book 6), creation (Book 7), and knowledge (Book 8). Briefly in Book 5 and at length in Book 8 Raphael focuses on the operations and interrelationships of the sun to teach Adam about both his physical world and his spiritual role. Raphael expands Adam's understanding of the cosmos and the relation of earth and sun and develops Adam's capacity to read the book of nature as a source of analogues to himself and his spiritual role.

In Adam and Eve's pre-Raphaelean morning hymn of praise, lines 153–208 of Book 5, the elements in the hierarchical sequence are separate units separately and statically viewed.[24] What coherence there is derives from the stanzaic sequence; variations on the word *praise* as noun and verb and images invoking the idea of circularity occur within nearly every unit. Adam and Eve's stasis coincides with their prelapsarian state. Raphael's several hierarchical accounts in Book 5, however, view the universe dynamically; it is their function to call attention to the interrelationships within the created world, to the downward and upward movements of matter and grace, to the process and possibility of growth.

It is especially significant that the hierarchy of Adam's pre-Raphaelean morning hymn moves from high to low. That pattern governs Adam's other pre-Raphaelean hierarchy of the psychological faculties also, the descending line of reason, fancy, the senses. The principle of hierarchic descent from Heaven to earth is characteristic of Adam's untutored thought; it is inseparable from his consciousness of himself as humble and grateful dust. Raphael's hierarchies, however, move in the precisely opposite direction, from down to up, from root to flower/fruit, from vegetable spirits to angelic intuitive reason, from animal to angelic and even cosmic digestion, in general from earth to Heaven, not from Heaven to earth. The accumulation of Raphael's hierarchies argues an intention to reverse the direction of Adam's hierarchical awareness. In its larger shape this intention includes instructing Adam not only in the divine dynamic but also in his own participation in the divine dynamic.

That Raphael's theory deals with a dynamic and that the edenic world that Adam knows, the prelapsarian, is necessarily static create a serious problem. It may be said that this is what Raphael's pedagogical challenge is chiefly about. Adam's consciousness of the good that descends to him is full and grateful, but from Adam's first speech in the poem we have also his sense of the limitations of his own participation. He and Eve

> at [God's] hand
> Have nothing merited, nor can perform
> Aught whereof hee hath need. (4.417–19)

Adam is correct that God does not need, but God's purpose is to multiply the good through his creatures, to share his creative nature with mankind by making them also multipliers of the good. Adam must learn to act and how to act. Before Raphael's arrival Adam judges the good only in solar terms; the nature of good in earthly terms—earth both as Eden and as the dust of his own being—must be defined as a guide to his understanding and conduct and as a completion of the cycle of the divine dynamic.

In reshaping Adam's thinking Raphael takes as his starting point the immediate evidence of Adam's world as they are in the process of sharing it. Because that world is defined by vegetation, Raphael reviews the sequence of root, stem, and the like; because they are in the process of sharing a meal,

Raphael discusses hierarchical aspiration and the cosmic vista surrounding them in the language of digestion. Raphael's interpretation of the interrelationships of the cosmos builds upon the data of the morning hymn, as Raphael's psychological account amplifies and redirects Adam's faculty psychology. Moreover, Raphael's goal is to instruct Adam in the unity of the creation. Thus, his vegetation analogy may also illuminate a psychological process and his digestion a cosmic process that is also spiritual. Raphael builds from Adam's basic principle that "one Almighty is, from whom / All things proceed," but his examples emphasize the completion of the dynamic cycle and Adam's participation and moral responsibility: "and up to him return, / If not deprav'd from good" (5.469–71). Raphael's lesson that for humans body can work up to and can at last turn all to spirit (478, 497) presents in immediate terms what he will explicate late in Book 5 in narrative and historical terms, the divine intention toward unity and ultimate participation in divinity. As God describes it and Abdiel understands it, Christ's role as newly begotten Son will effect this unity.

Raphael's speech is characterized by analogies. Taking as their starting point Adam's immediate data, these analogies move in widening circles of understanding around that central core; they provide the model for prelapsarian learning that is both memorable and free from threat or risk. Analogies enforce unity and span the gulf between things and ideas, images and themes, microcosm and macrocosm, man/earth and God/Heaven. Analogies are Raphael's mode of accommodation.

These generalizations will be examined more particularly in a later chapter, but for the present they are amply supported by the evidence of Book 5. Taking occasion from the meal before them, Raphael uses the digestive process to explicate the transmutation of corporeal to incorporeal: "whatever was created, needs / To be sustain'd and fed . . . / The Grosser feeds the purer." Macrocosmically this pattern moves through earth, sea, air, fires ethereal, the moon, and higher orbs. For our purposes the most important lines are these:

> The Sun that light imparts to all, receives
> From all his alimental recompense
> In humid exhalations; and at Even
> Sups with the Ocean. (423–26)

The cosmic relationship of sun to elements below it is a two-way process; the sun gives and receives—gives of its own nature, receives those portions or emanations of lower natures that are most like itself. In plants these are the odorous spirits that bright consummate flowers breathe (481–82); in humans these are such gestures of praise as the morning hymn in Book 5. Raphael is describing what will become the role of the Son, the creative and redemptive light of human history mediating between the otherwise inaccessible divine idea and "Grosser" human creation.

The explication of the relationship of Adam/man/earth to God/Heaven/sun is expanded in Raphael's discourse on the heavenly bodies in Book 8. Adam's troubled and troubling questions about this opacous and apparently sedentary earth (23, 32) take shape from his need for fuller understanding of himself and his participation in the dynamic and from pursuing the implications of Raphael's previous lesson in the creation. Given Adam's basis for evaluation of the world around him and given the reader's initiation into the light values of the poem in Book 3, one of the most astonishing statements in the poem is Raphael's assertion "that Great / Or Bright infers not Excellence" (90–91). The full context deserves close attention, keeping in mind what Raphael indicates in lines 98–99, that in speaking of earth he speaks simultaneously and metaphorically of "Earth's habitant." Adam and his future offspring are said to err in supposing

> That bodies bright and greater should not serve
> The less not bright, nor Heav'n such journeys run,
> Earth sitting still, when she alone receives
> The benefit: Consider first, that Great
> Or Bright infers not Excellence: the Earth
> Though, in comparison of Heav'n, so small,
> Nor glist'ring, may of solid good contain
> More plenty than the Sun that barren shines,
> Whose virtue on itself works no effect,
> But in the fruitful Earth; there first receiv'd
> His beams, unactive else, thir vigor find. (87–97)

That this proposition is not more startling to Adam derives from its restructuring of ideas familiar to him. He knows of earth's fruitfulness both in theory (from Book 7) and in his constant practice, as he knows his own life to be a participation in promoting that fertility. He is himself to "Be fruitful and multiply" and also to tend the garden. The idea of plenty (8.94) is linked with "Be fruitful and multiply" and more importantly with Adam's early acknowledgment of the difference between himself and God. God is perfect and already infinite (415, 420):

> But Man by number is to manifest
> His single imperfection, and beget
> Like of his like, his Image multipli'd,
> In unity defective. (422–25)

What Adam has not fully understood, Raphael's present lesson, is that good may be *solid* as well as or even rather than glistering. In that distinction is contained one of the poem's largest and most varied mysteries. That is the "new Law" that Satan revolts against when Christ is begotten in Book 5; it is the motive impelling all material form and the creation of earth. It is a way of describing the New Dispensation that is Christ, though in doing so we must keep in mind Christ's paradoxical nature, for it is also true that the Christian dispensation operating on earth promulgates freedom, imagination, growth, eternity, by setting aside the bondage of Old Testament law, fact, experience, history, time. Spirit and form, matter and light—all move toward the transformation, dissolution, re-creation when "the Earth / Shall all be Paradise" (12.463–64), when "The World shall burn, and from her ashes spring / New Heav'n and Earth . . . [and] God shall be All in All" (3.334–35, 341), when man's deficiencies of unity will be supplied and transcended through Christ's mediation.

At present we need not belabor such mysteries, but we must not leave the present passage without glancing at the idea of the sun's barrenness. The small, fruitful, potentially good earth images Adam and humanity. The sun manifests deity and images specifically the Son. Receiving his beams invigorates good; without such a target for his influence as human spirit, that Son too is barren and unactive. That the New Dispensation is dynamic— "mazes intricate, / Eccentric, intervolv'd, yet regular / Then most, when most irregular they seem" (5.622–24)—and that it requires man's active participation are again the point.

In his initial speech in Book 4, Adam expressed the view that humanity cannot perform "Aught whereof [God] hath need" (418–19). In the sonnet on his blindness Milton says similarly: "God doth not need / Either man's work or his own gifts" (Hughes, p. 168, lines 9–10), and *De Doctrina* expresses the same principle. In pointing to the sun's barrenness, its absence of effects and activity, Raphael is developing, even reversing this tenet. If

God does not "need" humanity's effects in an absolute sense, Milton's deity is at least susceptible to human influence in revising and fulfilling his design. In describing to Eve the effects of human prayer after the fall, Adam shows that his initial assumption has been suspended:

> Eve, easily may Faith admit, that all
> The good which we enjoy, from Heav'n descends;
> But that from us aught should ascend to Heav'n
> So prevalent as to concern the mind
> Of God high-blest, or to incline his will,
> Hard to belief may seem; yet this will Prayer,
> Or one short sigh of human breath, up-borne
> Ev'n to the Seat of God. (11.141−48)

If the Old Dispensation balances benefits received with obedience, downward donation with passive receptivity, the New Dispensation depends upon the mediation of the Word—their prayers are "up-borne" by Christ—and realizes ascent, completion of and participation in the divine dynamic. Raphael's goal in the lessons on hierarchy in Book 5 and on the cosmos in Book 8 is to instruct Adam in these patterns and prospects, to teach Adam as much as he can about Christ / the Son, even though that Word has not yet gone forth, and his medium for such lessons is the book of God's works, specifically the analogous sun.

Raphael's discourse also instructs Adam and humanity to admire rather than merely scan the book of God. The movements of the cosmos bespeak divine magnificence (8.101), Omnipotence (108), and mystery ["uses to [man's] Lord best known" (106)]. The proper human or creaturely attitudes are wonder, praise, and faith. Raphael admonishes Adam to avoid attempts to impose his limited judgments upon the operations of the illimitable God. Raphael himself carefully avoids the angelic equivalent of such hasty assumption. Even when "Admitting Motion in the Heav'ns" (115), Raphael cautions:

> Not that I so affirm, though so it seem
> To thee who hast thy dwelling here on Earth. (117−18)

Raphael eludes the danger, too, in carefully couching most of the remainder of his account in the optative mode, with his questions, "what if's," and "whether's."

The central lecture on astronomy, though lengthy, deserves full attention here, the more so because it is generally neglected by commentators on the poem. That the passage is extremely scientific in matter and diction must be admitted; it will help to keep in mind that Adam's immediate reaction to these materials is the admission that through them he is "clear'd of doubt" (8.179), "fully . . . satisfi'd" (180), "And freed from intricacies" (182):

> What if the Sun
> Be Centre to the World, and other Stars
> By his attractive virtue and their own
> Incited, dance about him various rounds?
> Thir wandring course now high, now low, then hid,
> Progressive, retrograde, or standing still,
> In six thou seest, and what if sev'nth to these
> The Planet Earth, so steadfast though she seem,
> Insensibly three different Motions move?
> Which else to several Spheres thou must ascribe,
> Mov'd contrary with thwart obliquities,
> Or save the Sun his labor, and that swift
> Nocturnal and Diurnal rhomb suppos'd,
> Invisible else above all Stars, the Wheel
> Of Day and Night; which needs not thy belief,
> If Earth industrious of herself fetch Day
> Travelling East, and with her part averse
> From the Sun's beam meet Night, her other part
> Still luminous by his ray. What if that light
> Sent from her through the wide transpicuous air,
> To the terrestrial Moon be as a Star
> Enlight'ning her by Day, as she by Night
> This Earth? reciprocal, if Land be there,
> Fields and Inhabitants: Her spots thou seest
> As Clouds, and Clouds may rain, and Rain produce
> Fruits in her soft'n'd Soil, for some to eat
> Allotted there; and other Suns perhaps
> With thir attendant Moons thou wilt descry
> Communicating Male and Female Light,
> Which two great Sexes animate the World,
> Stor'd in each Orb perhaps with some that live.
> For such vast room in Nature unpossest

By living Soul, desert and desolate,
Only to shine, yet scarce to contribute
Each Orb a glimpse of Light, convey'd so far
Down to this habitable, which returns
Light back to them, is obvious to dispute.
But whether thus these things, or whether not,
Whether the Sun predominant in Heav'n
Rise on the Earth, or Earth rise on the Sun,
Hee from the East his flaming road begin,
Or Shee from West her silent course advance
With inoffensive pace that spinning sleeps
On her soft Axle, while she paces Ev'n,
And bears thee soft with the smooth Air along,
Solicit not thy thoughts with matters hid,
Leave them to God above, him serve and fear. (122–68)

This speech is intended to be dazzling, not explanatory. Even confusions of the syntax evidence the point that God moves in various and mysterious ways. The speech is thus a kind of equivalent of the voice of the whirlwind to Job, humbling Job by its questions and suggestions of his relative insignificance even while ratifying Job's highest vision of the glory of God's power and creativity. Even careful reviewers and interpreters of the action of *Paradise Lost* pass quickly over this section, apparently considering it—to borrow C. S. Lewis's familiar phrase about Books 11 and 12—an "untransmuted lump," but of science not futurity, theology, history. The speech concludes with aphoristic advice, "be lowly wise" and "Dream not of other Worlds," which readers generally take to be the core of the message. In so doing they neglect Raphael's final summation—"thus far hath been reveal'd / Not of Earth only but of highest Heav'n" (8.177–78).

The discourse generally explicates the relationship and interrelationship between sun and earth and therefore between God and man. For chronological and dispensationary reasons Raphael's information on the Son remains indirect and accommodated; Adam's characteristic "sudden apprehension," his instinctive intuitive quickness, makes discursive, fully rational presentation and precision unnecessary. "Reveal'd" describes Raphael's mode here as it later attaches to Michael's, and revelation necessarily coincides with the highest of mysteries. Several propositions emerge with some clarity: The first is the centrality of the sun, whose "attractive virtue" activates the other cosmic participants; and as sun to earth, so Christ to man. The other participants are subject to vicissitudes and varying proximities and intensities within this centrifugal design. Earth's "three different Motions" build on an etiological fact with Trinitarian suggestions. "Thwart obliquities" imply the functions of postlapsarian divisiveness within an as yet unified design, as do the balances of nocturnal and diurnal and the earth part luminous, part averse from the sun. Against Adam's assumption that the earth is the center of the universe, Raphael posits the sun in that role. To put the matter otherwise, Raphael substitutes the sun's "attractive virtue" for Adam's experiential force of gravity. Further, Raphael is supplying an analogue, distanced from him so that Adam can "read" it, and an analogue that is dynamic rather than static. Raphael's procedures as well as goals are poetic to enforce the point of reciprocality or dynamism from his earlier speeches. In addition, the cosmic disputation of Book 8 provides Adam with a human psychological analogue of the presentation of angelic faith through the narrative of the Battle in Heaven. Raphael corrects Adam's erroneous inclination toward saving appearances when divine realities are the transcendent issue.

Raphael's extended discourse on astronomy accomplishes a wide range of lessons. The speech provides the principal example of what Virginia R. Mollenkott calls "Milton's Technique of Multiple Choice."[25] With line 140 Raphael's characteristic introduction of possibilities and options teams with his characteristic expression of analogies to posit both other worlds and an imaginative domestic application of the theory and pattern. The complexly reciprocal interrelations of sun, moon, and earth may be seen to mirror the *felix culpa* theme, the indirect route to good via evil, to light via dark. Topography, weather, fruitfulness, and digestion are posited for the moon, and the relationship of suns to moons is made an analogy for masculine and feminine to guide Adam in his own relationship to Eve and his own participation in the macrocosm and microcosm. Adam as sun forecasts the second Adam. The cryptic syntax of lines 153–58 dismisses as pointless any theorizing about astral populations and about mutual contributions of light between earth and stars/other suns/planets.

Lines 159–66, and even the summary advice of lines 167–68, return to Raphael's optative mode to present the crucial mystery of the New Dispensation. Given the intricate interdependence of the cosmos, it does not matter whether the sun circles the earth or the earth circles the sun, as spiritually it does not matter whether grace is more preveniently given or earned, more received or initiated, because it is so much simultaneously both. Raphael's discourse is thus a revelation, but it is a limited and modified revelation: "thus far hath been reveal'd / Not of Earth only but of highest Heav'n." It is limited even as it is facilitated by Raphael's cosmic imagery and characteristic modes of expression, and limited too by the prelapsarian circumstances of its immediate audience. On the one hand, the complexities of the divided or balanced universe are unavailable to a creature who knows only good and only unity; on the other hand, such a creature can know (as we fallen readers cannot) by "sudden apprehension," by intuitive reason, and the discourse is more, and more easily, available to Adam than to us. The discourse also establishes guidelines for Adam's future growth, ways in which his body may at last turn all to spirit; should he not fall and not require the mediation of Christ, he can still attain something like the ordained union with deity, thus mediated by Raphael and the sun of the natural universe.

The postlapsarian *Son* is necessarily handled quite differently than its prelapsarian solar analogue. The principal medium for the altered expression is the typological, which will be examined in detail along with Raphael's analogies in a later chapter. Some instructive smaller things, however, happen to the physical sun in the final books of *Paradise Lost*. The relationship of sun/earth, like the relationship of God/man and Christ/ man, changes with the moral, spiritual, epistemological, and historical crisis. With the human fall in Book 9 "Earth felt the wound" (9.782); Book 10 provides the complementary:

> At that tasted Fruit
> The Sun, as from *Thyestean* Banquet, turn'd
> His course intended. (687–89)

The Thyestean simile conveys reversal, revulsion, betrayal. The fall signifies the shift from unity to division and from direction to indirection. Numerically the uni-verse, as we have seen, is replaced not only by duality, multiplicity, or contradiction but also by that complex, potentially unifiable design of paradox.

The sun in the final three books of *Paradise Lost* continues to equate with Son, but as with the Raphaelean analogue, the evidence includes a distinction between the understanding Adam is capable of before Michael's visit and that which he attains under the angel's tutelage. Before Michael's arrival, attention focuses on the natural sun, and Book 10 records the alterations in the relationship of sun and earth along with the division between God and man. In its annual career the fallen sun's relationship to earth assumes a variety of motions and interacts with an array of lower astral influences. Within the context of Book 10, the narrator presents the facts available to an Adam who is lost, confused, and despairing, the soliloquizing Adam whom John S. Hill calls "Adam Agonistes."[26] Such an isolated Adam perceives the alterations in the relationship of earth and heavens but not their spiritual import and promise. He has lost the direct availability of sun and meaning and sees only a world of apparent confusion and disorder.

The apparently contradictory changes attaching to the turning athwart of the sun in Book 10 illustrate the new division between sun and earth, God and man.

> Some say he bid his Angels turn askance
> The Poles of Earth twice ten degrees and more
> From the Sun's Axle; they with labour push'd
> Oblique the Centric Globe: Some say the Sun
> Was bid turn Reins from th' Equinoctial Road
> Like distant breadth to *Taurus* with the Sev'n
> *Atlantic* Sisters. (668–74)

The qualification of "Some say . . . Some say" casts the changes in a tentative mode. Such *doubts* are transitional between the earlier and later *faiths*. The "three different Motions" of the sun that Raphael hinted at in Book 8 are here realized. The hints of the Trinity are less available to Adam than the confusion of such astral "mazes intricate." The passage continues into a zodiacal catalogue, a confusion of names, each pulling in its own significatory direction. Lacking as yet a grasp of the pattern, the redemptive order and Word, the imaginative energy—uninitiated, that is, into Christ—Adam perceives only his own loss and isolation amid such change and multiplicity.

In the process of restructuring the cosmos it is the sun, as so often earlier in the poem, that receives first attention:

> The Sun
> Had first his precept so to move, so shine,
> As might affect the Earth with cold and heat
> Scarce tolerable, and from the North to call
> Decrepit Winter, from the South to bring
> Solstitial summer's heat. (10.651–56)

"Pinching cold" and "scorching heat" (691), winter and summer, signal the extremities of the now divided cosmos. These polarities do not—or do not yet—coincide with moral polarities, but like good and evil they come together "from out the rind of one apple tasted" (Hughes, p. 728), to be discerned and sorted asunder by human response. Human judgment must seek some fulcrum for balancing alternatives and extremities before it can proceed to fulfill the human responsibility of moral choice. The evidence, even at this stage, is extraordinarily complicated, for the moon and planets with their "noxious efficacy" (10.660), "Synod unbenign" (661), and "influence malignant" (662) may operate in congruence with or discordance from the sun.

The context stresses the sun's effects as a matter of temperature rather than light. Satan's quarter is of course the North, the area of predominant cold as well as darkness. Within the context of Book 10, a solution to the human difficulty that arises with changes in temperature and weather has already been provided as part of the divine plan, but that providence must be activated through the memories of the human beneficiaries. Immediately after sentencing the first couple and the serpent, the Son has provided a solution to the new problematic circumstances: "As Father of his Family he clad / Thir nakedness" (10.216–17). The scene provides also the model that governs his role and the verbal action through the remainder of the poem; Christ, the Word, translates outward data to their spiritual analogues:

> Nor hee thir outward only with the Skins
> Of Beasts, but inward nakedness, much more
> Opprobrious, with his Robe of righteousness,
> Arraying cover'd from his Father's sight. (220–23)

Through Christ, outward experiential facts are translated into the vocabulary of faith, imagination, the inward Jerusalem, the paradise within. As with the vegetative evidence, outward reality gives way to biblically based metaphor. Christ provides humanity with comfort both outward and inward, but initially humanity is more aware of the merely outward.

The sun comes in for another kind of attention later in Book 10, and this completes the spiritual design, taking as its starting point the human aspiring energy that complements and completes the dynamic cycle of divine donation to man. The focus is again on solar temperature rather than light. The passage occurs as, reunited with Eve, Adam remembers the divine visit and sentence from the opening of Book 10, a recollection that leads to the prayer with which Book 10 closes. Specifically, Adam remembers the "mild / And gracious temper" (1046–47) of their judge and provider:

> lest Cold
> Or Heat should injure us, his timely care
> Hath unbesought provided, and his hands
> Cloth'd us unworthy, pitying while he judg'd. (1056–59)

And this glance backward via memory is followed immediately by a turning forward through faith to the merciful promises implicit in what is remembered:

> How much more, if we pray him, will his ear
> Be open, and his heart to pity incline,
> And teach us further by what means to shun
> Th' inclement Seasons. (1060–63)

These seven lines exactly capture the new pattern of proper fallen intercommunication between human and divine: Memory, *timely care*, implicit promise, human prayer, inclinable divine ear and heart, and "teach us further," progressive revelation. Adam performs a creative act; he puts together disparate levels of his experience as a foundation for a leap of faith.

This definitive action of memory is further represented in the scene with which Book 10 concludes. Adam responds to Eve's recommendations of barrenness and suicide with an exercise of judgment and memory that establishes the new pattern again precisely:

> But *Adam* with such counsel nothing sway'd,
> To better hopes his more attentive mind
> Laboring had rais'd. (1010–12)

"Nothing sway'd" replaces the "slack hand" and "joints relax'd" of Adam's falling from Book 9; mental exertion, though laborious, leads to elevation and aspiration as "better hopes" transcend the despair enacted in Adam's soliloquy in Book 10. Adam's exercise of judgment upon Eve's evidence leads him from the tyranny of the present to an act of memory and its divine promise for the future:

> Then let us seek
> Some safer resolution, which methinks
> I have in view, calling to mind with heed
> Part of our Sentence, that thy Seed shall bruise
> The Serpent's head. (1028–32)

The sentence is remembered in the "mysterious terms" (173) in which it was delivered; it is remembered in biblical words that Adam does not yet understand, but the affirmation of divine promise and even of divine mystery is a definitive act of faith that leads to the prayer that concludes Book 10 and to further enlightenment, specifically to Michael's revelations in Books 11 and 12 of the Word and the Christian vocabulary and mode of translation. Again *seeking* and "calling to mind with heed" interact with "timely care" and "teach us further" to define the structures and epistemology of memory and faith.

As with the good angels in the battle in Book 6, right human conduct requires independence, acceptance of responsibility, action, and invention insofar as these fulfill rather than intrude upon the divine intention. Arguing again from analogy, Adam explains to Eve that perceived change in their immediate weather and nature

> bids us seek
> Some better shroud, some better warmth to cherish
> Our Limbs benumb'd, ere this diurnal Star
> Leave cold the Night, how we his gather'd beams
> Reflected, may with matter sere foment,
> Or by collision of two bodies grind
> The Air attrite to Fire, as late the Clouds
> Justling or pusht with Winds rude in thir shock
> Tine the slant Lightning, whose thwart flame driv'n down
> Kindles the gummy bark of Fir or Pine,
> And sends a comfortable heat from far,
> Which might supply the Sun: such Fire to use,
> And what may else be remedy or cure
> To evils which our own misdeeds have wrought,
> Hee will instruct us praying, and of Grace
> Beseeching him, so as we need not fear
> To pass commodiously this life, sustain'd
> By him with many comforts, till we end
> In dust, our final rest and native home. (10.1067–85)

Even the periphrasis of "this diurnal Star" (cf. "Day-star") reflects the altered human relationship in the cosmos within a context of "remedy or cure," not Raphael's simpler "nourishment." As prelapsarians received and responded directly to the sun governing the unified cosmos, postlapsarians must in part "supply the Sun." In "gather'd beams / Reflected," reflection suggests both mirroring and intellection. The combination of "gather'd beams" and "matter sere" nicely models the new relationship of sun and earth, God and man. That in thus "supplying the Sun" for their survival the humans follow a process modeled in the cosmos itself—where lightning kindles the earth's woods—illustrates the revised revelatory relationship between humans and their instructional surroundings, surroundings implicit with divine messages as were those Raphael explicated, but the messages themselves are now of process rather than of static design and are available to active discursive pursuit rather than to passive "sudden apprehension." The fire is *useful*, but external kindling is also the kindling of hearts and spirits, and this remembered lesson shifts quickly too in the direction of future promise of further enlightenment: "Hee will instruct us praying" (1081). When nature "bids us seek / Some better shroud," nature becomes an argument for its own transcendence, for spiritual action and grace. The fall has split the inhabited world into what is beginning to be seen as moral polarities, into evils and their remedy and cure. Adam and Eve have learned to ask for grace and to be assured that they need not fear. On their own they have not yet learned to translate the key terms of *life* and *death*, but Michael's instruction will reveal that mystery and supply them with the divine books that will teach and fortify the first couple to read and revise their reading of the book of nature by that revealed light.

As the prelapsarian couple joined voices with the components of the natural world in praising God in the morning hymn of Book 5 and as the newborn Adam could enjoin nature to tell him of his origins and receive some kinds of answers, so the fallen Adam derives messages from the natural world. That world contains messages that have been deliberately and occasionally implanted rather than instinct, and the messages must be achieved by an active dianoetic process rather than by "sudden apprehension." Such messaging precedes and attends Michael's arrival. Adam acknowledges the syntactical structures—the vehicles—of the messages but not yet their tenors when he sees an eagle driving "Two Birds of gayest plume" and a lion pursuing a hart and hind toward the eastern gate of paradise (11.184–90). The "Air [is] suddenly eclips'd / After short blush of Morn" (183–84). Adam judges these as divinely devised "mute signs in Nature" and as "Forerunners of [God's] purpose" (194–95). The coming of Michael represents in solar imagery the pattern with which we are now familiar and in its final phrase makes the communicational strategy explicit:

> why in the East
> Darkness ere Day's mid-course, and Morning light
> More orient in yon Western Cloud that draws
> O'er the blue Firmament a radiant white,
> And slow descends, with something heav'nly fraught. (203–7)

That heavenly freight is Michael and his revelation, but to the fallen Adam's dimmed eye, such enlightenment must come in the mixed mortal mode: darkness at noon, cloud against blue sky, eastern light reflected in western cloud. These data, like fire, Adam assesses as implicit with promise to be divinely fulfilled. Adam's acknowledgment of meaningful signs shows him ready for the instruction Michael brings. That instruction might be described as fortifying Adam's memory with the promises that will prepare him to read nature by way of divine books and with the spectacles of faith. Like Uriel and Raphael to an unfallen Eden, Michael arrives in a solar mode, but that is now accommodated to the human audience rather than directly coincident with sunbeams.

After Michael's arrival, *Son*, not *sun*, becomes the primary issue, and rather than immediately perceivable nature it is abstract aural theology that dictates the format of fallen instruction through the media of biblical text, typological process, and acknowledgment of Christ as Logos. The apparent division that the fall imposes upon nature is susceptible to the "safer resolution" of Protestant faith thus exercised. The old unity violated, a new unifying principle facilitates unity even when the evidence is at its most contradictory, even when experience and faith seem most irreconcilable. Christ is the Word, and paradoxically the Word made flesh. Christ is the focus of paradox in the poem—most dramatically and definitively in Book 12 when he is "nail'd to the Cross . . . But to the Cross he nails [Adam's] Enemies" (413, 415). The example of the Redeemer, which Adam acknowledges in his final summarizing speech of the poem, defines the divine presence and providence through paradox:

> with good
> Still overcoming evil, and by small
> Accomplishing great things, by things deem'd weak
> Subverting worldly strong, and worldly wise
> By simply meek; that suffering for Truth's sake
> Is fortitude to highest victory,
> And to the faithful Death the Gate of Life. (565–71)

Christ is the essential promise to be remembered and the mediator of radical new unity. He achieves this within the contradictions of his own double nature and his double role as creator and redeemer, and he is the inspirational mediator and model for humans to participate in and follow.

As the central paradox in the poem, as in Christianity, the Son facilitates a new transcendent union between God and man as between the two halves of his incarnate nature and as between poetic vehicle and tenor. The fall divides man's outward and inner selves, body from spirit, experience from faith, and Christ is the model by which humanity too can achieve a new transcendental unity out of that contradiction and paradox. With the fall the Son assumes a new relationship to God and man, becoming not merely the voice of God to man but also the word by which human prayers are conveyed from man to God. In this Christ fulfills the dynamic model Raphael tried to communicate to the prelapsarian Adam. The greater distance between God and man that comes with the fall is balanced by a greater closeness now possible. In this dynamic, fall implies potential rise, as it did not need to before the fall. The new possibility and potentiality must be stressed as options rather than necessities or absolutes. Raphael could speak of absolute principles and designs, but after the fall human choice and judgment become fully operative. The one standard of obedience has multiplied into myriad tests, and choice itself has become a dynamic continuing process.

As word, promise, unified paradox, and agent of the New Dispensation of divine openness, human participation, and ultimate union, the Son— "Divine Similitude" (3.384)—provides humanity with new energies and new creative options. Translated into faculty psychology, Christ aligns with imagination as well as with memory. Christ provides the poet—and the everyman hero and reader of *Paradise Lost* is a poet—with the essential word and with the format for deploying that word variously. Christ makes reading and literary criticism poetic or creative acts also. Reading like writing has recourse to memory storage and from thence a creative address to present realities and future options. As the "Divine Similitude" Christ makes the absolute available—"Whom else no Creature can behold"— and mediates transcendent vision. Christ's role is to "bid the Deep / Within appointed bounds be Heav'n and Earth," whereas for the paternal deity "Boundless the Deep, because I am who fill / Infinitude" (7.166– 69). The Son as creator and the Son as redeemer merge in the redemptive act of poetry. It is not surprising that a Milton who saw the poet's role as "beside the office of a pulpit" and who set out to make his life "a true poem" (Hughes, pp. 669, 694) should understand the deity as an epic poet also, responsive to the generic claims of flashback and prophecy and expressing himself through typology. It is also not surprising that Milton anticipated readers very much like himself—"fit audience though few" (7.31)—and deployed his theology as a mode of participatory self-transcending discourse, not merely as an artistic fabric and construct.

3 · *Lapsarian Logic*

When you are criticizing the philosophy of an epoch, do not chiefly direct your
attention to those intellectual positions which its exponents feel
it necessary explicitly to defend. There will be some fundamental assumptions
which adherents of all the variant systems within the epoch unconsciously
presuppose. Such assumptions appear so obvious that people do not
know what they are assuming because no other way of putting things has ever
occurred to them. Within these assumptions a certain limited number
of types of philosophic systems are possible, and this group of
systems constitutes the philosophy of the epoch.

ALFRED NORTH WHITEHEAD, *Science and the Modern World*

NE VOCABULARY that significantly articulates the lap-
sarian contrast is Ramistic logic. In its largest designs as
well as in its minutiae, Ramistic logic is radically dichoto-
mized in ways that can broaden and deepen our under-
standing of Raphael's and Michael's modes of instruction,
expression, and epistemology. Because modern pedagogy
has eschewed the format as well as the structures of thought of what was for
Milton and his age a matter of elementary instruction, it is difficult for us to
retrieve—and even to take seriously—the miasma of abstractions, catego-
ries, and distinctions that are the hallmark of logical systems such as
Ramus's. But because Milton himself treated them with high seriousness, as
witnessed by his preparing a revised and expanded edition of Ramus's *Artis
Logicae*—Milton's title is *Plenior Institutio, ad Petri Rami Methodum concinnata
[A Fuller Course in the Art of Logic Conformed to the Method of Peter Ramus]*—
we must concern ourselves with this tool to achieve a full understanding of
his presentation of solutions to the problems of knowledge in his epic.[1]
Because Milton was himself instructed in these materials and formats from

his earliest studies, they necessarily inform the assumptions behind his thinking, even his instincts, in ways that we must try to recover.

Ramism is the system of schoolboy logic that flourished in sixteenth- and seventeenth-century Europe, especially in Protestant countries and crucially among Puritans in Old and New England. It reformed traditional, chiefly Aristotelian logic in a number of ways and embodied some identifiable new attitudes toward reality, epistemology, and expression. It derives from Peter Ramus, or Pierre de la Ramée (1515–72), a Paris academic, the author of textbooks in numerous fields, who much prided himself as an academic innovator and reformer of Aristotle but who has come down to the twentieth century chiefly as a notorious oversimplifier and inveterate dichotomizer, the propagator of methodical bifurcating chains running from generals to specials that his twentieth-century biographer and analyst Father Walter J. Ong, S.J., has likened to a sideways pinetree pattern.[2] He prided himself too on the usefulness of his systemizings and considered his logic to be a guide to the study of all subject matters, he purported to follow natural models to insure the soundness, even the divine validation of his proceeding, and he emerges as what we might call a pedagogical efficiency expert, bent on supplying memorable schematizations, recourse to which was expected to illuminate all experience and thought and thereby eliminate all difficulties and uncertainties. Because Ramus himself reconstitutes the data and arguments of the traditional logic he inherited and because his own logic undergoes a number of changes and editions and because his followers and imitators were so numerous and often vanished behind his and their own texts, I have used the term *Ramism* to cover a wide territory whose boundaries have some clarity but whose topographical features are elusive.

As Walter Ong comments: "Ramus was known to his contemporaries as the *usuarius*, the usufructuary, the man living off the increment of intellectual capital belonging to others." Ramistic logic is a fusion of pedagogy and philosophy, didactic and dialectic, arts and charts. It tends to "regard knowledge as a set of objects and to identify those objects with curriculum subjects" and to make these subjects the genera of a system in which "all intellectual movement takes place with reference to the genus-species apparatus." It is a system in which definition and division take primacy and in which general principles and universals are presumed to be more available, conspicuous, and better known than particulars and individuals, and thus it can stress the use of specials or individual examples to prove generals or universal propositions. It emphasizes disjunction and sees judgment as an act of comparison or matching by juxtaposition and thus suggests that reason is virtually automatic. It essentially equates spatial arrangements of thought with judgment and judgment therefore with memory. The principal features of Ramistic logic derive from his redistribution of the five areas of traditional Ciceronian rhetoric: invention, arrangement, style, delivery, and memory. Ramus appropriated invention and arrangement (which he called judgment) to logic, absorbed the category of memory under judgment, and assigned style and delivery as the province of rhetoric. Specifically, the rhetorical art of memory is replaced by Ramistic Method, the diagrammatic schemes of inclusive and included categories arrayed according to nature and degree of generality so as to make all relationships and priorities immediately clear. Ramus substituted a series of what he called "arguments" for the Aristotelian categories or topoi. Ramism generally emphasized the discovery and statement of axiomatic and self-evident truths, founded on nature and the Scriptures, over the use of logic as an instrument for inquiry or for the creation of new truths. Epistemology and communication coincide in the Ramistic view of reality. Because truth exists in things and because the human mind naturally answers to the natural world and its patterns, truth does not need to be produced or proved but need only be apprehended and asserted. To the Ramist, as Perry Miller points out, reason "is not an instrument but a doctrine; logic is the instrument by which the doctrine is made evident." [3]

Ramus was a notorious oversimplifier. In *The Massacre at Paris*, Christopher Marlowe complains of Ramus's superficiality and calls him "a flat decotamest" (= dichotomist), and more recently Hardin Craig labels him "the greatest master of the short-cut the world has ever known." More philosophically, in Ramism has been found

> a connecting link between Puritanism and scholasticism, establishing in the Puritan mind its obsession for logic, and distaste for symbolism, shaping its views of nature, determining its literary preferences and style, and in great part accounting for its attitudes, if any, toward epistemology. Seen as an outgrowth of a kind of simplified logic which imposed itself by implication on the external world to make this simple too, Ramism here is correlated also with the Puritan preference for the plain style and hence with a good many Puritan virtues and vices associated with a *simpliste* view of things. Ramism is a kind of downrightness. [4]

What would draw a thinker of such sophistication and subtlety as Milton to the work of the simplistic Ramus? Answers cannot certainly be found. Perhaps the immeasurable ramifications of exposure in childhood, a boyish admiration for Ramus's conversion to Protestantism or his martyrdom, even an instinctive responsiveness to his iconoclasm or to his frequent use of examples involving blindness, perhaps the inevitable convenience of taking up the data of one's own learning experience and schoolbooks when one sets himself to teach, perhaps a capitulation to the underground spirit of Ramus's place in history and the history of ideas.

Whatever the motives, the basic principles of Ramism have much appeal to Milton, and a number of his works are organized according to its characteristic formats. His *Christian Doctrine*, for example, is radically Ramistic in conception and execution; at the outset Milton describes his "method," his intention of "assisting the memory" by conveniently reducing into a coherent whole the dispersed parts of Scripture, "digested under certain heads," and his bifurcations of Christian doctrine under the heads of "Faith, or the knowledge of God,—and Love, or the worship of God." In this "methodical tractate of Christian doctrine," as he himself describes it, Milton outlines his plan of "winnowing and sifting every doctrine," his "habit of classing under certain heads whatever passages of Scripture occurred for extraction," and his filling his pages "even to redundance with quotations from Scripture that so as little space as possible might be left for my own words, even when they arise from the context of revelation itself." His goals are to establish his faith, assist his memory, and to "remove from my mind all grounds for hesitation, as often as it behoved me to render an account of the principles of my belief." Proceeding "with all possible fidelity," he satisfies himself "that I had discovered, with regard to religion, what was matter of belief, and what only matter of opinion." Following the lines of independent inquiry outlined in *Areopagitica*, Milton recommends that others follow his example and not his resulting treatise: "that every one should suspend his opinion on whatever points he may not feel himself fully satisfied, till the evidence of Scripture prevail, and persuade his reason into assent and faith." [5]

Milton's affinity for Ramism may also rest largely upon their shared commitment to the principle of order governing external and internal structures and perceptions; God is order, and man approaches the deity by ordering energies within himself, by developing the Apollonian principle. Milton's poetic imagery powerfully exploits the implications of general principles within experiential particulars or individuals. Though Milton retains subtlety for his poetic ends, like Ramus he often manifests a keen resistance to ambiguity. Milton's thought seems to fall automatically into dichotomous designs, a fact that may attest to his early absorption of this aspect of Ramism or testify to his natural affinity for such procedures and their inseparability from the whole of his mind and work. Critics who fault Ramus do so with special emphasis upon the bifurcating tendency of his schemes, but although Ramism may have been responsible for over-emphasizing and rigidifying the process of dichotomization in the interests of pedagogical tidiness, the binary plan itself is basic to all thinking. Less charitably, it must be added that Ramistic logic is a logic for dogmatists. One need not know Milton well to realize that this too has a claim to register with regard to his character and his sense of the role and mission of his life and art.

Milton may have been drawn to Ramism through a shared commitment to what is useful in general and what is useful in teaching in particular. In large and in small matters *Paradise Lost* abundantly demonstrates that Milton like Ramus delights to find models of mind and action in nature—at least in unfallen nature—rather than in artifice and the manufactured complexities of "the habit of learned vaporing" that obscure the truth and the right. For both men logic is the medium through which art and nature can be reconciled and through which the logical and the theological can be at once aligned and distinguished from each other. Milton like Ramus is a vigorous proponent of clarity, simplicity, and the unity of truth. As Milton's title (*A Fuller Course . . .*) indicates, his *Logic* will expand upon what he finds to be excessive brevity in Ramus's logic, and as his early pages show, Milton proposes to remedy "the suspicion of novelty" that attaches to Ramistic documents by drawing upon precepts and commentaries of the ancient authors. Here, as in so many of his prose works, Milton inveighs against Aristotelian accumulations of rules, labeled as "uncertain or futile" additions to the heap (Milton's word), which "impede the learner and burden rather than aid him, and if they have any usefulness or show any wit, it is of such a sort as any one might more easily understand by his native ability than learn by means of so many memorized canons." Milton insists that art, specifically the art of logic, should be "used for the purpose of aiding nature, not of hindering it," and he objects that traditional logics have often labored "too anxiously and too subtly" and sometimes unnecessarily with the result of blunting rather than sharpening the student's capacities. On the one hand

Milton does not wish to intrude upon the acute natural abilities of his pupils by being tedious and superfluous, and on the other hand the ruins of our first parents must be repaired through a proper education so that we may regain to reason and to know God aright. In the preface to his *Logic*, Milton several times distinguishes between two logics, "that merely natural logic with which we are born" and "that artificial logic which we learn later," within a context that recognizes that God is the efficient cause of all arts as of all nature and is "the author of all wisdom." Through practice and instruction, art (specifically the art of reasoning well) can become in Milton's phrase "second nature" (C5–13; Y211–14).

As these passages indicate, Milton's Ramistic logic in particular, like Ramistic logic in general, is explicit about the lapsarian nature of the human exercise of reason. Perry Miller expresses the general Ramistic and Puritan attitudes toward the prelapsarian and postlapsarian Adam's reasoning in these terms:

> Adam had been created in the image of God, possessed of perfect holiness and an intuitive grasp of the principles of right reason, but after the fall he was no longer able to tell what should follow upon what, or to perceive the interconnectedness of things.

And again Miller explains:

> Before Adam lost the image of God, Ramus said, almost all of his judgments had been simply axiomatical; in his integrity he had been able to see and to pronounce sentence immediately, as when he named the animals; he had uttered what was true and perceived what was false, and had discoursed by infallible progression from one proposition to its inevitable successor.

As Miller quips, "innate depravity might most accurately be defined as a congenital incapacity for discursive reasoning" and "the loss of an ability to use the syllogism."[6] With a God who is truth and who participates largely in all exercises of right reason, logic becomes, like grace, a gift of God bestowed upon fallen humanity to provide light and access to himself and to protect humanity from suffering the full consequences of the errors it brought upon itself. Ramism stresses both the original human and natural capacity in the prelapsarian condition and the postlapsarian return to something like that original rational perfection through exercises of reason that restore our capacities to regain to know God aright.[7]

In several direct ways lapsarianness is taken into account in Milton's *Logic*.

A number of operations in the first or Invention half of the *Logic*, for example, distinguish between "perfect" and "imperfect" kinds. A distinction is early drawn between "the perfection of the art" and "the imperfection of the natural faculty." There is "perfect" consent between cause and effect but only "imperfect" consent between subject and adjunct. The latter, however, is capable of "perfect" adjustment if the reasoner establishes the "proper adjunct" of a subject, that with which it exactly coincides and reciprocates. The "imperfect" analogue of definition is description. The former is based on causes; the latter may be erroneous when "many things are brought together, of which some perhaps extend more widely than that which is described" (C19, 27, 71, 79, 97, 265, 267, 271; Y217, 221, 239, 242, 249, 311, 313, 315). In the fallen context, descriptions may be made reciprocal through Disposition, which methodically establishes causes and the relationship of units of experience to causes.

Raphael's and Adam's conversations in Books 5–8 are conducted in terms of the perfection of these categories, or in what I shall call "true speech." In true speech, perfect descriptions and definitions are the norm. As himself an inartificial argument mediating the deity and divine mission and records, Raphael cannot express himself otherwise. As an unfallen man living and reasoning perfectly, Adam cannot perform otherwise, though his edenic state is one of educable or expandable perfection. True speech consists of a knowledge of causes that includes a full grasp of effects so that when one or the other is voiced the whole interplay and meaning are present to the consciousness of the speaker and auditor. The paradigm of such understanding and such expression is established when Adam describes his ability to name the animals, his divine endowment with useful knowledge:

> I nam'd them, as they pass'd, and understood
> Thir Nature, with such knowledge God endu'd
> My sudden apprehension. (8.352–54)

In true speech such reciprocity is the norm.[8] In Raphael's books of the poem, the arrayed data of Adam's created or invented cosmos present material as luminous, indeed numinous, truth and invite perfect as well as sudden apprehension and affirmation of it. In particular, as we shall see, the data of Book 7 precisely illustrate the ideal of Ramistic reality, the equation or reciprocation of words and things, mediated through Raphael's true speech.

The second half of Ramistic logic texts, Disposition, Michael's province in *Paradise Lost*, also regularly acknowledges lapsarian categories. Ideally,

Ramistic schematizations are arrayed from generals to specials in keeping with Ramus's view of the order of nature and of the human mind. As Walter Ong points out, variations from this order "can be tolerated only where a particular audience makes special demands, by its recalcitrance, ignorance, or other ineptitude."[9] In *Paradise Lost* the fall creates such special demands in its lapsed audience, who must be educated by Michael to a return to the ideal norm set forth and practiced by Raphael. Except where axioms are necessary and self-evident, Disposition is a procedure for dealing with a fallen world and a lapsed reality and for repairing the ruins of reason. Thus, the second half of the *Logic* regularly warns against erroneous data and supplies tools for correcting the errors. There are three kinds of error, together called crypsis or concealment, which the reasoner must begin by identifying; these are defect, redundance, and inversion of parts. As the *Logic* explains, "If on account of these crypses there is uncertainty, what lacks must be supplied, what is superfluous must be cut off, and any part must be restored to its place" (C299; Y324). Although the *Logic* calls upon all three kinds of crypsis under the headings of axiom, syllogism, and Method, there is an important sense in which one form of crypsis accompanies one of these kinds of Disposition in the final books of *Paradise Lost* and in general. Eliminating excesses or paring down the data to central propositions aligns with axioms; supplying what is lacking, especially bringing to bear the third argument, aligns with syllogisms; and putting the materials in proper order is precisely the goal of Method. Milton warns against crypsis in his opening chapter, again in his second chapter, and at considerable length in an appendix to chapter 16 of Book 2. As Adam's postlapsarian instructor in faith and truth Michel refines Adam's thinking through these exercises. Crypsis requires that the reasoner sort out and fill in the terms precisely, and such sorting requires judgment that in general is assumed rather than developed in the reasoner. Because Ramism is a system for putting oneself in touch with self-evident truths, those truths need only to be apprehended to be affirmed by the reasonable mind. Checking the crypsis in a statement provides the clarity in the things themselves that makes judgment automatic. It is Michael's assignment to equip Adam with the self-evident or the axiomatic and with syllogistic access to the absolute and necessary truth, to fill in omissions, to lop off the distractions of the superfluous, and to restore arguments and the syntax of arguments to their secure and clear places. Crypsis must be eliminated because it creates uncertainty; it is a barrier to truth and to confidence in truth and therefore to sound judgment. Crypsis is synonymous with concealment, and Michael brings forward what has been hidden beneath the surface.

Technically, Raphael and Michael are themselves among other things inartificial arguments. Artificial arguments are self-evident, what we see with our own eyes as aided by the *art* of logic; inartificial arguments are what we see through the eyes of another witness, either human or divine. In this case the character of the witness becomes their efficient cause. This distinction allowed Ramists a place for revealed theology. In *The Art of Logic* Milton is careful to distinguish testimony from proof in a passage that is often excerpted as foundational to much of his thinking:

> Yet I commonly attribute to testimony very little power for proof in investigations of the deepest truth and nature of things; this would seem to apply to divine as well as human testimony, and I do not see why it should offend any one, for testimony whether human or divine equally gets all its force from the author, and has none in itself. And divine testimony affirms or denies that a thing is so and brings about that I believe; it does not prove, it does not teach, it does not cause me to know or understand why things are so, unless it also brings forward reasons. (C283; Y319)

That Milton was himself willing to take up the radically Protestant challenge of proving his own faith from the evidence of the Scriptures is testified to by the process governing the making of *Christian Doctrine*. The sorting out of artificial from inartificial truth is a logical as well as a theological challenge. *Paradise Lost* is Milton's epic investigation of "the deepest truth and nature of things," and its avowed goal is to "justify the ways of God to men." It affirms and denies transcendent and mundane realities, and the poem may serve to bring about belief in its readers, but its procedures intend rather to prove, teach, and cause the readers to know and understand the reasons and the why of the materials it sets forth. It "asserts Eternal Providence" in terms that make Milton's "great argument" self-evident and inescapably true to the reader's rational as well as suprarational faculty.

Raphael and Michael are by definition inartificial arguments and the source of inartificial arguments in *Paradise Lost* both as characters and speakers, especially when they are presenting Adam with materials whose source and corroboration are in the Bible itself. As angels Raphael and Michael witness direct and immediate divine testimony, and as characters they are intermediary agents of the divine testimony. As inartificial arguments, they mediate human access to the body of self-evident arguments and axioms that constitutes truth; they give access to the finest and truest knowledge, and they bring forward reasons to eliminate the gap between divine and human, between truth and belief. Specifically, Raphael affirms the Creator and creation while articulating Genesis 1, and Michael denies the validity of the merely experiential while providing a précis of the Old and New Testaments. In order to teach as well as witness, they in their differing ways bring forward reasons, artificial arguments, to complement their given inartificiality of argument. Both provide Adam with a balance of faith (bringing about that he believes) and of knowledge and understanding (bringing forward reasons). Raphael presents Adam with insight into and validation of the deepest truth and nature of things by guiding him to a recognition of efficient and material causes, especially as these normally elude human perception. Michael guides Adam to insight into and validation of another kind of truth, deep, elusive, transcendent of things and of human perception unaided by revelation. Michael guides Adam's awareness to final causes and provides Adam with formulations of commonly received wisdom, but he is also himself a divine testimony and variously presents the Bible, those "written Records pure," which combine divine intention and human (or something like human) agency divinely inspired.

One particular Ramistic dichotomy governs the epic's prelapsarian and postlapsarian teachers, and that is that Ramistic logics invariably begin by dividing themselves into two halves and two books, Invention and Disposition. As Milton explains early in Book 1 of his *Art of Logic*, "All reasoning is made up of reasons either considered alone and for themselves or related to each other" (C21; Y219); or, in Perry Miller's phrasing, "God has created the world by creating individual entities, and then by establishing them in sequences, relations, and patterns; they exist first by themselves and then in connections."[10] The Ramistic thinker performs the two answering exercises of Invention and Disposition. Invention (= *to come upon* or *find*) is the discovery of truth in the things themselves, especially as they are distributed in designs of cause/effect and subject/adjunct; Disposition is the consideration of the relationships of arguments or reasons with each other, and it variously includes time processes, priorities, and sequences of truth and judgment. Both Raphael and Michael guide Adam toward awareness of preexistent divine truth, but Raphael's emphasis is upon the discovery of what Adam had not fully realized before; Michael's is upon recovery. Raphael's hierarchical universe Platonically and inductively guides the learner as on a ladder toward the fullest perception of divine idea. The movement is an ordered, guided sequence of revealing the transcendence contained within the unit, leading to expanded awareness of the unity and coherence of the total creation. Michael is concerned with temporal and other patterns within the mind, the products of Disposition, Method, and memory. As Raphaelean reasoning centers on induction, "the process of judging immediately from the evidence of the senses,"[11] so for Michael reasoning centers on the organization of information within frameworks of priorities and sequential bifurcations that facilitate the recall of prior knowledge from memory storage.

When we turn to a detailed consideration of Raphael's domain of arguments, distribution, and Invention, we find that the major blocks of Raphael's evidence in Books 5 through 8 divide conveniently along the lines of the chief categories of *The Art of Logic*; it falls, that is, into consenting arguments, dissenting arguments, and comparatives. Consenting arguments are for proving and confirming, dissenting arguments are for refuting and contradicting, and comparatives serve chiefly to make things plain and to produce confidence. As a deployer of arguments, Raphael's purposes are put concisely in the phrases confirming the deity, refuting the adversary, making plain the universe as a reflection of its creator, and thus producing confidence in his audience. Throughout his books but especially in Book 5, Raphael's procedural mode is solidly founded upon comparatives of various sorts. Book 7 arrays Ramistic consenting arguments, and the format of those arrays is the governing format of Invention, that is, distribution. The Satanic materials of Raphael's Books 5 and 6 set forward dissenting arguments. The governing purpose of Raphael's proceeding is definition, that is, technically the identification of an argument's causes; and, as we shall see, the principal cause for the ontological Raphael is, of course, the efficient or first cause. The following materials are arranged according to these categories. In discussing Raphael's Invention, I shall begin, as the *Logic*s do, with consenting arguments, for in the words of Milton's *Logic*, "from affirmation and consent all art and teaching, like all knowledge, are deduced" (C99; Y250).

When we turn to a detailed consideration of Michael's domain, the second half of Ramistic logic, Disposition, again we find that much of the angel's evidence from Books 11 and 12 divides conveniently along the lines of *The Art of Logic*, that is, into axioms, syllogisms, and Method. Roughly, Book 11 sets forward the axiomatic and Book 12 the syllogistic. Both books are governed by the governing format of Disposition, that is, Method.

Disposition is a decidedly postlapsarian matter. Throughout and complexly it is based upon divisions, distinctions, and alternatives, and its procedures and results are divisions and distinctions. Such doubleness occurs even when Disposition is noetic, as with axioms, for even direct and self-evident cognition requires realignment of the errant reasoner and absolute reality. The governing cause for the teleological Michael is final cause, and final cause is itself double, a matter of both duration (end-of-which) and perfection (end-for-which). In the epic those two ends are to be simultaneously realized with the achievement of the New Jerusalem.

The first, finest, truest knowledge, indeed "the fount of all knowledge," according to *The Art of Logic*, is a knowledge of causes. Cause is "that by the force of which a thing exists" or "that which gives being to a thing," and "in fact if the cause of something can be comprehended it is believed to be known" (C29–31; Y221). There are four causes—efficient cause, material cause, formal cause, and end cause—and these four establish *by which, from which, through which*, and *on account of which* a thing exists. These four causes divide into two groupings: on the one hand, prior (efficient and matter) and posterior (form and end); and on the other hand, external (efficient and end) and internal (matter and form).

Milton's epic, which aspires "to the highth of this great Argument" of justifying God's ways to man, takes questions of cause as both its starting point and its goal. Its action is inaugurated with the epic question:

> say first what cause
> Mov'd our Grand Parents in that happy State
> Favor'd of Heav'n so highly, to fall off
> From thir Creator? (1.28–31)

One answer to this question leads back to the deity as the all-creator, but another answer leads forward to the divine intention in the creation and in the patterning of time and trial toward its ultimate goal, that culpa that is, or is to be, felix. To generalize, God in *Paradise Lost* is the beginning and end of creation, the idea from which it springs and the perfection toward which it tends.

In the *Logic* as in *Christian Doctrine* (especially 1.5) and the epic itself, God is explicitly identified as the absolute first or efficient cause: "The efficient is the cause by which the thing is or is brought about," "procreating that which not yet is that it may come into being, and conserving what now is that it may continue to be." [12] The remote first cause of God works through proximate secondary causes that are impulsive or instrumental, working from either within or without, working either of themselves or through accidents, that is, either by nature and according to plan or by some external power. Milton's discussion of this point in the *Logic* directly addresses a number of issues in the epic:

> Absolutely, God alone freely does all things, that is whatever he wishes, and is able to act or not to act. The Bible frequently asserts this. Those causes merely which work according to reason and thought, as angels and men, act freely *ex hypothesi*—on the hypothesis of the divine will, which in the beginning gave them the power of acting freely. For liberty is the power of doing or not doing this or that, except, to be sure, God wished otherwise, or force from some other quarter assailed them. (C43; Y227)

Similarly, there is one true end, though subordinate ends may be perceived as conducing to that end. Technically, final cause, or the cause *for the sake of which* a thing is, is what the efficient cause has led up to and in which the efficient cause acquiesces and finds its completion. End cause, or a thing's aptitude for use, is a matter of both chronology (*end of which*) and its good or perfection (*end for which*). The final cause is the initial intention of the efficient cause though last in realization; or, in the words of Milton's *Logic*, "the end is first in the mind of the efficient, last in act and effect." As the *Logic* also makes clear, in its ignorance of divine purpose or lack of foresight, humanity has fabricated the categories of "fortune" or "chance" or "necessity," errant misnomers for what deserves to be called divine providence (C63–65, 49–51; Y236, 229).

Causes are difficult to discover, and indeed untutored humanity (like Raphael's Adam) or fallen humanity (like Michael's Adam) regularly has to make do with grasping less than absolute causes. The two angels function in the epic, however, to direct their pupil toward the controlling design of God's creation and providence. In broad terms, Raphael's answer to questions of cause, and specifically to the question of "what cause / Mov'd the Creator . . . to build / In *Chaos*" (7.90–93), is the deity as first or efficient cause, and Michael's answer is the deity as end or final cause. The ontological Raphael conduces to wonder and mystery and in general the prior, and the teleological Michael conduces to will and hope and in general the posterior. For Raphael, whose world view is simply unified, the first and final causes coincide, as when he cites the deity as that "from whom / All things proceed, and up to him return" (5.469–70). Raphael qualifies this with the phrase, "if not deprav'd from good" (471), but it is a qualification he does not need to deal with except as a warning to Adam. Michael addresses a situation that includes such depravity, and with sin come time and sequence and consequence and thus also division and paradox and hard-won judgments of priorities. Michael looks forward to the end of time when God shall be all in all, but such unity must be laboriously achieved through a process that is temporal and through a complex vision that includes the paradoxical.

Milton's logical theory, and especially the causal foundations of it, sheds light not just on the procedures and goals of Raphael and Michael but also on some of the governing ideas of the epic as a whole: on the relationship between God and the angels (good and bad), God and man (or God and the divine within man), grace (impulsive from within or from without), free will and predestination and providence, and the effects of the fall on action, language, and knowing. "Whatever is the cause of a cause is the cause of what is caused" (C39; Y225) voids the issue of whether man falls deceived or "not deceiv'd, / But fondly overcome with Female charm" in Book 9. Eve as the cause of Adam's downfall and the serpent and Satan in the serpent as the cause of Eve's downfall, and therefore of Adam's, initiate a chain of inquiry that leads the active reasoner back to the deity as the remote first cause and forward to the divine intention of multiplying the good and achieving a loftier ultimate unity within the creation as the remote final cause.

One way of perceiving Adam and the creation is as effects, that is, the things caused; another way is to examine these as internal causes. They are material relative to the prior genre of efficient cause and formal relative to the posterior genre of final cause. Raphael deals with Adam as a material cause, that is, as a made thing, a part of the common creation. Matter is that which is acted upon, and in the words of the *Logic*, "the efficient cause prepares the matter that it may be fit for receiving the form" (C51; Y230). Similarly, Michael stresses "the strength of the form," the uniqueness, by defining what constitutes "the peculiar essence" of individual human nature—"one just man," "one faithful man"—from all others. Michael takes into account Adam's "rational soul," his nature and uniqueness, his internal form. In noting that forms differ in number and essence but not in matter, the logician Milton exclaims, "Here let the Theologican awake" (C59; Y233), and proceeds to cite the example of the rational soul as the form of man. The distinction between man's material (*from which*) and formal (*through which*) natures does not mean that Raphael or Michael deals with Adam's physical or spiritual nature exclusively. In the *Logic* "Matter is common to all entities and non-entities, not peculiar to sensible and corporal things" (C53; Y230). Raphael's emphasis upon man as material cause, man's common essence, does, however, help explain why the prelapsarian Adam is necessarily less "formed" as a character and therefore a less than fully engaging personality within the audience's fictional norms and expectations. Raphael is dealing with common denominators. Michael, however, is dealing with a particularized individual personality, recognizable as is Odysseus by his scars.

Turning briefly to the second category of consenting arguments and the significance of subject/adjunct relationships to the larger issues of *Paradise Lost*, we see that Adam is regularly the subject of his adjunct Eve and the temporal/spatial setting of Eden is regularly in an adjunctive relationship to the human characters who occupy it. As proper adjunct, Eve, "though by nature posterior to [her] subject, and besides less important, yet is temporally simultaneous and to us generally better known." The logical theory is precisely translatable into glosses on the human evidence of the epic:

> When a proper adjunct is given, a subject is given, and the opposite; for the subject is in a way properly essential to the adjunct, and the adjunct arises from the form of the subject; it depends therefore on the form of the subject, not on its own nature, because the subject causes it to be and takes it away.

Adam provides Eve's form, both physically through his rib and psychically by being the prop of reason in the floral garden. The adjunctive Eve is an extrinsic addition to her subject Adam, who "is already perfect and constituted by its causes" (C91–93, 79; Y247, 242). Adam and Eve relate to each other mutually as well as simultaneously, but they consent after a fashion rather than absolutely. They do not give or receive being to or from each other after receiving the breath of life. The adjunctive Eve is extrinsic to her subject Adam and posterior in reason, consciousness, and nature as well as in time. As initially described, Eve's form "impli'd / Subjection" (4.307–8), and she is worthy of Adam's love, "Not thy subjection," in Raphael's admonition (8.569–70). The subject (Adam) receives the adjunct (Eve) to or into itself; the adjunct (Eve) is sustained by or contained by or collocated with its subject (Adam); the subject (Adam) is not essentially changed by the accession or removal of the adjunct but then merely exists in another mode, as Adam might have done had he not accepted the fruit and as Adam does in the private scientific part of the interview with Raphael in Book 8;

and finally the adjunct (Eve) is more copious and plentiful than the subject, because there can be several adjuncts of one and the same subject. Eve is Adam's receiving adjunct; Eden is Adam's occupying adjunct. The subject sustains or maintains its receiving adjuncts, which are called ingrafted or inherent; it contains its occupying adjunct or "is that in which the located thing is contained" (C81–87; Y243–46). The theoretical bases of common adjuncts also illuminate their relationship: The first couple are separable or inseparable; their relationship is definable in terms of quantity, quality, passion, and motion. That *Paradise Lost* sometimes treats them as parts of a single entity and sometimes as separate units is explicated in the logical theory of consenting arguments:

> In whatever number of modes several things are said to consent among themselves, in so many modes they are called one and the same, absolutely or in some way or other; they are absolutely one or the same by cause and effect, and are in some way one and the same in subject and adjunct, in cause or efficient or matter or form or end. (C97; Y249)

Adam's relationship to God is founded upon cause/effect, but his relationship with Eve—after the causal occasion of the rib—is grounded in subject/adjunct.

The business of the first half of Ramistic logic is the Invention of arguments, and arguments equate with nouns, with what Walter J. Ong calls "the corpuscular units" of reality or with what Perry Miller calls "any counter employed in thinking."[13] A Ramistic argument, however, is simultaneously the thing, the name of the thing, and the mental conception of the thing. In Downham's version of Ramus (the specific text from which Milton prepared his own version), an argument is "an affectation in a thing to make its meaning clear, the reason in a thing by which it becomes intelligible"; and in Milton's own *Logic*, "an argument is that which has a fitness for arguing something," "a tendency for arguing not merely in itself, but also of itself" (C23, 27; Y220, 221). Milton's *Art of Logic* formulates the role of simple arguments thus:

> But the proper and primary potency of a simple argument is to explain and prove how one thing follows or does not follow from another; that is, it is judged that when one thing has been laid down as true something else is or is not also laid down originally. (C25; Y220)

Invention is both the act of such discovery and the intellectual faculty by which the discovery is made.

Invention begins with the unit or argument and discovers its nature; it proceeds from apprehension to an exploration of its natural components and the relationships that are simultaneous with, contained in, and inseparable from the thing itself. The emphasis is always on the unit as self-referential. "In the process of inventing arguments," according to Perry Miller, "the mind follows its natural bent through the acts of sense, observation, induction, and experiment, and thus extracts from the objects of experience the arguments with which it forms true ideas about the nature of things."[14] Like other logics Ramus's provides a sequence of kinds of relationships that may inhere in individual arguments and thus a structure by which students may articulate their recognition of an argument's implications, but such serial recognition is a matter of the reasoner's temporary emphasis rather than of the nature of the thing itself. The implicit relationships can generate a spatial pattern, as with comparisons and classifications of genera and species, but the patterns matter in their success in illuminating the thing itself. A whole is divided into its components in order to provide a clearer understanding of the central wholeness. Invention is thus aimed at breaking through the barriers of ignorance or unawareness to an apprehension of inherent and inevitable truth that thence compels the reasoner's allegiance. Invention is an enhancing of awareness through heightened consciousness of the implications of the unit of reality.

Raphael's hierarchies in Book 5 and his "discovery" of the individual units of creation in Book 7 follow these lines precisely. Raphael and the prelapsarian pupil Adam address the created universe in *Paradise Lost* as an array of artificial arguments. Raphael "proves" the world to Adam by guiding him to look with care and intuition at the units of the creation and "invent" or realize their full implicit meaning or allow them to present their full meaning to him. In Book 7 Raphael proceeds as through a dictionary to present Adam with a vocabulary of the corpuscular units of the world of created nature. Raphael's goals, like the theoretical goals of Invention in logic, are to produce knowledge and confidence as well as to make the nature of the units manifest.

All knowledge, according to the *Logic*, derives from affirmation and consent; through the category of consenting arguments, "anything agreeing with another can be called either the same or one with it; and all the modes of unity and, so to speak, of identity here are to be assigned as to their first and simple sources" (C97; Y249). The consenting arguments are cause/effect and subject/adjunct. Cause and effect consent and reciprocate absolutely; subject and adjunct consent only after a fashion, except that a subject consents absolutely with its *proper* adjunct. The goal of the characteristically "affirmative" Raphael in Book 7 is to establish the first and simple sources of the creation and its arguments and by emphasizing likenesses and agreement, that is, consent, within those units to prove overall unity and individual identity. Book 7 is a lyric hymn of praise, a creation that celebrates creation, an invention of Invention itself, and its final cause is celebration, to magnify the divine through increased understanding of his works, to grow closer to him through an increase in knowledge, especially the fount of all knowledge, the knowledge of causes. *Christian Doctrine* defines the creation as "that act whereby God the Father produced every thing that exists by his Word and Spirit, that is, by his will, for the manifestation of the glory of his power and goodness" (CE 15:5), and Prolusion 7 expresses the assumptions behind Milton's hexaemeral proceeding with characteristic enthusiasm:

> The builder of this great work has made it for his own glory. The more deeply we search into its marvelous plan, into this vast structure with its magnificent variety—something which only Learning permits us to do— the more we honor its Creator with our admiration and follow him with our praise. (Hughes, p. 623)

The governing reciprocation of Book 7 of *Paradise Lost* is of the creation from Genesis 1 as "Answering [the] great Idea" (7.557) of the Creator, and the "great Idea" of Book 7 is the deity as efficient cause. *Christian Doctrine* illuminates the process here operating:

> Though there be not a few who deny the existence of God . . . yet the Deity has imprinted upon the human mind so many unquestionable tokens of himself, and so many traces of him are apparent throughout the whole of nature, that no one in his senses can remain ignorant of the truth. . . . There can be no doubt that every thing in the world, by the beauty of its order, and the evidence of a determinate and beneficial purpose which pervades it, testifies that some supreme Power must have pre-existed, by which the whole was ordained for a specific end. (CE 14:25−27)

The perceptive process here outlined is qualified a page later in these terms: "No one, however, can have right thoughts of God, with nature or reason alone as his guide, independent of the word, or message of God" (14:31).

Raphael carries such a message directly to the prescriptural, prelapsarian Adam to illuminate the human understanding and develop human capacities for Invention.

Even before Raphael's arrival the units of the creation are predisposed to articulate both their own natures and their praise of the Creator, that is, predisposed to present themselves as Ramistic arguments. In the morning hymn of Book 5 Adam and Eve address the wondrous and unspeakable deity who is invisible to humans or "dimly seen / In these thy lowest works." The works of creation are said to "declare / Thy goodness beyond thought, and Power Divine" (155–59), and the hymn proceeds through a series of stanzas that invoke the realms of creation to articulate their praises of the divine. "Speak yee" is the basic verb of the imperatives, but it is varied into "extol / Him," "praise / Him," "acknowledge him," "sound his praise," "resound / His praise," "Vary to our great Maker still new praise," "In honor to the World's great Author rise . . . Rising or falling still advance his praise." The winds are enjoined to breathe his praise, the plants to wave "in sign of Worship," the waters to warble his praise, the animals to "join voices," the birds to "Bear on your wings and in your notes his praise," and the whole creation to witness Adam's vocal song that reflects his way of sharing the praise of the deity with all its other units. It is useful to remember the function the *Logic* assigns as the principal role of effects: "From this place of the effect come praises and dispraises" (C73; Y240). Before Raphael's arrival to explicate causes, Adam's universe is variously articulate, its units discovering their own arguments, especially the argument of effects within a context of praises, and the universe in "various style" teaches and shares its messages of the creator.

Only after Raphael's arrival, however, does the causal foundation of this material become clear. The logical propositions in Raphael's key speech in Book 5 govern the procedure:

> O *Adam*, one Almighty is, from whom
> All things proceed, and up to him return,
> If not deprav'd from good, created all
> Such to perfection, one first matter all
> Indu'd with various forms, various degrees
> Of substance, and in things that live, of life;
> But more refin'd, more spiritous, and pure,

> As nearer to him plac't or nearer tending
> Each in thir several active Spheres assign'd,
> Till body up to spirit work, in bounds
> Proportion'd to each kind. (469–79)

The passage sets forth the four causes in tidy array: In terms of the external causes, the efficient cause is that "from whom / All things proceed," and the final cause is that to which all return as their end or "perfection"; in terms of the internal causes, we have here the "one first matter all" and the "various forms" or "various degrees" or "several active Spheres assign'd." The passage anticipates the two actions of Invention that will be realized in Book 7, identification or definition of units and distribution of units. Walter J. Ong has called attention to Ramus's insistence "on the absolute monarchy of definition and division (distribution) in all cognition."[15] The mode of identity is definition: "it defines the essence of a thing, and circumscribes it as though by its boundaries"; it presents "a universal symbol of the causes constituting the essence and nature of a thing." Such causes "are comprehended in genus and form." Definition cites the nearest genus (which implies the more remote); form is also sometimes called *difference*, which is described as "the fruit of form." A definition reciprocates with the thing defined (C261–65; Y310–11). The units of Book 7 establish the reality to which the mind responds, purely and truthfully in a prelapsarian mode. Its units develop the vocabulary Adam had demonstrated when he named the animals and provide the vocabulary and grammar, as well as the implicit prelapsarian epistemology, of Raphael's "true speech."

Raphael's copious version of the days of creation from Genesis 1 occurs in response to Adam's "desire to know"

> . . . how this World
> Of Heav'n and Earth conspicuous first began,
> When, and whereof created, for what cause,
> What within *Eden* or without was done
> Before his memory. (7.61–66)

Adam's is a question of causes—inquiring as to the categories *by which, from which, through which,* and *on account of which* a thing is—and Raphael's answer takes shape in comparable logical terms: The "Filial Godhead," the divine Word, "gave *effect*" to the Almighty's creative intention (7.175;

emphasis mine). Again, through a second question of causes early in Book 7 Adam initiates the retelling of the creation story, asking Raphael to explain:

> what cause
> Mov'd the Creator in his holy Rest
> Through all Eternity so late to build
> In *Chaos*, and the work begun, how soon
> Absolv'd, if unforbid thou mayst unfold
> What wee, not to explore the secrets ask
> Of his Eternal Empire, but the more
> To magnify his works, the more we know. (90–97)

The cause that "Mov'd the Creator" is the final cause, the desire specified at lines 190–91 to "diffuse / His good to Worlds and Ages infinite." Adam has asked also "How first began this Heav'n which we behold / Distant so high" (86–87), a question of efficient cause. The deity as both efficient and final causes is captured in the epithet of line 591, "Author and end of all things," as to Adam the "sovran will" of the deity is "the end / Of what we are" (79–80). The "Omnific Word" is seen "circumscrib[ing] / This Universe, and all created things" (217, 226–27). To "Matter unform'd and void" he gives form and being and in it infuses "vital virtue" (233, 236).

As we have seen, Raphael's principal cause, and it includes his conception of the deity, is efficient cause, and efficient cause is that *by which* a thing is or is brought about. Similarly, matter is the cause *from which* a thing is, but these two causes are closely bonded. To read Milton's commentary on material cause when the epic deity has been equated with efficient cause is to set up a foundational gloss on Book 7 of *Paradise Lost*:

> In the order of nature matter follows the efficient cause, and is a sort of effect of the efficient cause; for the efficient cause prepares the matter that it may be fit for receiving the form. As the efficient cause is that which first moves, so the matter is that which is first moved; hence the efficient cause is called the principal cause of acting, matter the principal cause of being acted on. (C51; Y230)

Material cause is difficult to separate from formal cause because it is simultaneous with the existence of a thing. An example from the epic will make Milton's view of the interrelationship of matter and form clearer. On the first day of creation the creating word takes the golden compasses in his hand:

> to circumscribe
> This Universe, and all created things:
> One foot he centred, and the other turn'd
> Round through the vast profundity obscure,
> And said, Thus far extend, thus far thy bounds,
> This be thy just Circumference, O World.
> Thus God the Heav'n created, thus the Earth,
> Matter unform'd and void: Darkness profound
> Cover'd th' Abyss: but on the wat'ry calm
> His brooding wings the Spirit of God outspread,
> And vital virtue infus'd, and vital warmth
> Throughout the fluid Mass, but downward purg'd
> The black tartareous cold Infernal dregs
> Adverse to life; then founded, then conglob'd
> Like things to like, the rest to several place
> Disparted, and between spun out the Air,
> And Earth self-balanc't on her Centre hung. (7.225–42)

The extension of "vital virtue" out of the procreating deity and its imposition upon the previously *unformed matter* renders dramatically the relationship of efficient and material causes, and the "conglobing" of like things to like and the dismissal of the unlike dramatize the consent and affirmation that are foundational to consenting arguments. The lines also actualize the "one first matter" of Raphael's theoretical account from Book 5; as the account continues, that "one first matter" becomes "Indu'd with various forms."

Once the common matter has been established, Book 7 is chiefly devoted to arraying the distinct identities, effects, and forms of creation. Logically, form is the cause *through which* a thing is what it is; it emphasizes something's uniqueness, its difference in number and essence from all other things. Matter argues that a thing exists, but form argues its identity. As the *Logic* tells us, "the efficient produces the form not yet existing and induces it into the matter" (C59; Y232). The complex interrelationship of matter and form may be seen in the differences between light as created on the first day of Book 7 as material cause and lights as created on the fourth day as formal cause. The first-day light is light

> Ethereal, first of things, quintessence pure
> Sprung from the Deep [which] from her Native East

> To journey through the airy gloom began,
> Spher'd in a radiant Cloud, for yet the Sun
> Was not; shee in a cloudy Tabernacle
> Sojourn'd the while. (244–49)

The lights of the fourth day appear as formed and also as notably useful and as participating in the dichotomous distributions so favored by Ramists:

> Let there be Lights
> High in th'expanse of Heav'n to divide
> The Day from Night; and let them be for Signs,
> For Seasons, and for Days, and circling Years,
> And let them be for Lights as I ordain
> Thir Office in the Firmament of Heav'n
> To give Light on the Earth; and it was so.
> And God made two great Lights, great for thir use
> To Man, the greater to have rule by Day,
> The less by Night altern. (339–48)

The separation of light as matter and light as form is a difficult feat for the poet to present and for the audience to receive, grounded as the audience necessarily is upon its human nature and mortal perception with its radical dependence upon formal cause itself. Within the hexaemeral sequence, perception becomes notably more accessible when the fourth-day light forms are fiated.

In general the data of *Paradise Lost*, Book 7, array and identify the unique forms of creation, the "active Spheres," into which the "one first matter" of the created world has been assigned, distinguishing each from all others. In thus establishing individual identities, Raphael is providing definitions (in the technical sense) for Adam's vocabulary by calling attention to the causes that constitute their essences. Within the arrays of Book 7, however, the category of material cause shades into the category of formal cause and both, deriving from their common efficient cause, shade into the category of effect. Simultaneity and reciprocity of being and argument are foundational to the process. The Ramistic vocabulary may be variously invoked to describe the separate units of creation: They are effects of the efficient cause; they are themselves material and formal causes; they are adjuncts of subjects and subjects of adjuncts. They are sometimes genus, subaltern genus, and species. Their individual presentations are sometimes definitions and sometimes descriptions. That the Ramistic vocabulary may be thus variously invoked is part of the proof, both as that proof is by, from, through, and for the sake of divine unity and as it sets forth the prelapsarian perfection of language and reality. When viewed as matter, the data argue the unity of creation; when viewed as forms, they argue uniqueness and variety; when viewed as effects, they argue all the causes in a context of praises. Effects are less clear and less weighty in argument than causes, but effects are regularly better known to human reasoners and therefore "more plainly argue the causes than they are argued by the causes" (C73; Y239). We need not look far in Book 7 to find occasions when all these categories are applicable, as for example,

> The Swan with Arched neck
> Between her white wings mantling proudly, [which] Rows
> Her state with Oary feet. (438–40)

Or again,

> The crested Cock whose clarion sounds
> The silent hours, and th' other whose gay Train
> Adorns him, color'd with the Florid hue
> Of Rainbows and Starry Eyes. (443–46)

Or again,

> The parsimonious Emmet, provident
> Of future, in small room large heart enclos'd,
> Pattern of just equality perhaps
> Hereafter, join'd in her popular Tribes
> Of Commonalty. (485–89)

Or finally,

> The Female Bee that feeds her Husband Drone
> Deliciously, and builds her waxen Cells
> With Honey stor'd. (490–92)

Each of these units of creation is absolutely itself and no other, though sharing in the "one first matter" of creation and divine love. Each unique item is reciprocal with a unique explanation, which, if achieved, gives access to true knowledge, the knowledge of causes. In the lyric celebration, praise effects wonder. Raphael thus expands Adam's knowledge by linking the items to the remote first cause; Raphael's instruction carries Adam's awareness beyond the bounds of nature and reason alone and supplies "right thoughts of God" as recommended in *Christian Doctrine*.

Additionally, the hexaemeral units of Book 7 of *Paradise Lost* are presented through arrays of, for example, vegetation or fauna. The technical name for such arrays is distribution, that is, identification of arguments that consent within a whole (genus) but dissent among themselves (species). The genus vegetation on the third day is distributed into the species of grass, herbs, flowers, vines, gourds, reeds, shrubs and bushes, stately trees and fruit trees; fauna on the fifth day of creation are arrayed into eagles, storks, cranes, nightingales, swans, cocks and peacocks, along with unspecified birds remarkable for such adjuncts as loci, colors, and songs. Distribution is itself a kind of Ramistic argument, derived, composite, and realistic, but it is more importantly a process or format that establishes the relationships between collections of simple arguments within the reciprocating categories of whole/parts or genus/species and thus represents the movement from universals to particulars. Distribution is the division of a whole into its parts; technically it is said to reciprocate with induction, which is a gathering of the parts to make up the whole (C227; Y297). According to the *Logic*, "Genus and species are signs of causes and effects"; *genus* signifies common causes or common essences (cf. material cause), and *species* signifies effects or distinct forms. Distribution is based upon arguments that consent in the whole but dissent among themselves, and it is more perfect and accurate the greater and clearer the consent and dissent. Imperfect distributions occur as examples and enumerations.

Distributional formats are central to Raphael's and Genesis's presentation of hexaemeral materials, both in the sequence of days and in the data of individual days. In Distribution, items are arranged in sequences that proceed usually in bifurcations from the most general to the most specific. It is worth noting that Genesis itself proceeds by distribution and bifurcation.[16] That Distribution is a governing organizational format for Milton's Book 7 needs only to be stated to be agreed upon, but we may examine some detailed evidence to clarify the procedure and also to note some variations on the basic model. On the third day the genus earth is distributed into the subaltern species/genera of dry land and waters. The common essence is established in the opening lines:

> The Earth was form'd, but in the Womb as yet
> Of Waters, Embryon immature involv'd,
> Appear'd not: over all the face of Earth

> Main Ocean flow'd, not idle, but with warm
> Prolific humor soft'ning all her Globe. (276–80)

The Distribution is launched with God's fiat:

> Be gather'd now ye Waters under Heav'n
> Into one place, and let dry Land appear. (283–84)

Dry land is distributed into high land and low land, the high into degrees of height as mountains and lesser hills. Waters are distributed according to their height, speed, and receptacles:

> Immediately the Mountains huge appear
> Emergent, and thir broad bare backs upheave
> Into the Clouds, thir tops ascend the Sky:
> So high as heav'd the tumid Hills, so low
> Down sunk a hollow bottom broad and deep,
> Capacious bed of Waters: thither they
> Hasted with glad precipitance, uproll'd
> As drops on dust conglobing from the dry;
> Part rise in crystal Wall, or ridge direct,
> For haste; such flight the great command impress'd
> On the swift floods. . . . so the wat'ry throng,
> Wave rolling after Wave, where way they found,
> If steep with torrent rapture, if through Plain,
> Soft-ebbing; nor withstood them Rock or Hill,
> But they, or under ground, or circuit wide
> With Serpent error wand'ring, found thir way,
> And on the washy Ooze deep Channels wore. (285–303)

The individually arrayed arguments consent with the wholes of waters and dry lands, and they dissent among themselves, especially in the balanced bifurcations so favored by Ramists. The common or shared matter is distributed into individuated species. Between the extremes of the most inclusive genus and the most indivisible species, genus and species are in a chain, each serving as genus of one kind and species of another. The distribution here, as later in Book 7, begins as perfect, but as the prospect widens the examples multiply toward infinitude and the process halts with subordinate genera/species. The exhaustiveness and inclusiveness of the categories and halting the chain before it reaches to indivisibles have the effect, however, of all-inclusiveness. An exhaustive distribution of nature would require an infinitude of parts to balance the infinitude of the creative cause.

Later on the third day of creation, *Paradise Lost*, Book 7, presents a distribution of vegetation based upon subject/adjunct rather than cause/effect. The subject, "the bare Earth" or the Mother Earth, consents "after a fashion" with the adjunctive vegetation that emerges from it:

> He scarce had said, when the bare Earth, till then
> Desert and bare, unsightly, unadorn'd,
> Brought forth the tender Grass, whose verdure clad
> Her Universal Face with pleasant green,
> Then Herbs of every leaf, that sudden flow'r'd
> Op'ning thir various colors, and made gay
> Her bosom smelling sweet: and these scarce blown,
> Forth flourish'd thick the clust'ring Vine, forth crept
> The smelling Gourd, up stood the corny Reed
> Embattl'd in her field: and th' humble Shrub,
> And Bush with frizzl'd hair implicit: last
> Rose as in Dance the stately Trees, and spread
> Thir branches hung with copious Fruit: or gemm'd
> Thir Blossoms. (313–26)

Causes identify being or essence, but the subject/adjunct relationship is based upon additions to essences or agreement of extrinsics. Adjuncts are less weighty arguments than subjects, but in the *Logic* they are "more copious and commonly used." The adjunct of color, here in the green and variously colored flowers, is the readiest evidence of adjunctive addition to essence. Subjects are prior to adjuncts but do not give being to them, although at one point in the *Logic* Milton describes subjects as "a sort of cause" of adjuncts (C87; Y245). In this unique instance the subjective Mother Earth does in fact give being to the vegetation; "the bare Earth" is a proximate efficient cause of its vegetation as well as the receiving subject of its occupying vegetational adjuncts. In the Chain of Being, vegetation is defined as having being and life but no motion. Being is manifest here in the sense categories of color, odor, texture, size, and height. Life is manifest throughout, but especially in the capacity, even urgency, for growth. By way of metaphor even movement is attached to the vegetative units. In this artful and creative context, the categories of logic as of nature are deliberately and effectively overstepped.

In a very direct appropriation of the categories of the *Logic*, the various modes of the relationship of subject to adjunct and of adjunct to subject may be seen in the evidence of the fourth day of creation where light is literally as well as logically distributed. The metaphors that present that distribution—of sowing seeds, of drawing liquid from a fountain—testify again to infinitude, to the impossibility of enumerating the individuals exhaustively. The four modes of the relationship of subject to adjunct are: the subject receiving ingrafted or inherent adjuncts; the subject containing the adjuncts in itself; the subject receiving adjuncts to or about itself; and the subject occupying and employing the adjunct. Similarly, in their four modes adjuncts are: inherent or placed within, either separably or inseparably; contained or located in the subject; received near the subject; and, finally, the mode of the adjunct occupied (C81–85, 91–97; Y242–44, 246–49). Following the fourth-day fiat, we read:

> For of Celestial Bodies first the Sun
> A mighty Sphere he fram'd, unlightsome first,
> Though of Ethereal Mould: then form'd the Moon
> Globose, and every magnitude of Stars,
> And sow'd with Stars the Heav'n thick as a field:
> Of Light by far the greater part he took,
> Transplanted from her cloudy Shrine, and plac'd
> In the Sun's Orb, made porous to receive
> And drink the liquid Light, firm to retain
> Her gather'd beams, great Palace now of Light.
> Hither as to thir Fountain other Stars
> Repairing, in thir gold'n Urns draw Light,
> And hence the Morning Planet gilds her horns;
> By tincture or reflection they augment
> Thir small peculiar. . . .
> First in his East the glorious Lamp was seen,
> Regent of Day, and all th' Horizon round
> Invested with bright Rays, jocund to run
> His Longitude through Heav'n's high road: the gray
> Dawn, and the *Pleiades* before him danc'd
> Shedding sweet influence: less bright the Moon,
> But opposite in levell'd West was set
> His Mirror, with full face borrowing her Light
> From him, for other light she needed none

> In that aspect, and still that distance keeps
> Till night, then in the East her turn she shines,
> Revolv'd on Heav'n's great Axle, and her Reign
> With thousand lesser Lights dividual holds,
> With thousand thousand Stars, that then appear'd
> Spangling the Hemisphere. (7.354–84)

This example of celestial bodies includes a series of varying modes of distribution in terms of subject (celestial bodies) and adjuncts of light, and also the subject of light and the adjuncts of celestial bodies, depending on whether light is judged the formal or the efficient cause, the essence or addition to essence, intrinsic or extrinsic. At first the sun, moon, and stars are given forms; in the second series light is distributed into those forms and the forms contain and retain the distributed light (C81, 91; Y243, 247). In the next series the distribution is according to place, east and west, and according to quality of light dispensed rather than received. The series includes a distribution according to the time categories of day and night also. Inherent adjuncts, those of the first mode above, may be either common or proper. The common (of quality, quantity, passion, and motion) are either separable or inseparable; the proper divide into those proper to one but not all, to all but not one, to all and to each but not always, and to all and each always. In the present passage, light is the proper adjunct of the genus of celestial bodies; but, in the patterns of distribution into various celestial bodies, light is the inseparable inherent common adjunct, varying in place, time, motion, intensity, and dignity. In evidence already cited, on the third day the subject earth receives its topographical features as adjuncts, and the adjuncts of the subject earth themselves become subjects of adjuncts. We need not draw fine lines between the receiving and occupying or between *to itself* and *into itself* or between what is thereafter separable and inseparable—though it is possible to attempt that exercise—to note that we are here provided with the modes of common adjuncts, arrayed in terms of quality, quantity, passion, and motion, and these in the order in which they are listed in *The Art of Logic* (C93; Y247). In this example the various modes of distribution through the subject/adjunct relationship may be thus distinguished with some readiness. Two of the logical principles governing adjuncts are demonstrated: (1) that they are copious, and (2) that they tend to provoke conjecture and thus playfulness of mind rather than more confirmed secure knowledge. In theory, "Subjects and adjuncts for the most part bring forth conjecture" (C89; Y246), but they can be powerful arguments, making truth and confidence available, when the adjunct is truly proper and reciprocal with its subject. This is the realm of prelapsarian language, of Raphael's "true speech," of belief that coincides precisely with the Ramistic argument, knowledge with the thing itself.

Success in Ramistic distributions is measured by inclusiveness and reciprocity. The logical theory takes into account the limitations of human capacity—and, because infinitude is the issue, of human patience. The sequence of the days also to some extent participates in the distribution process. The distribution by effects into land and water of the second and third days becomes the foundation for later distributions as the fish are adjoined to the waters on day 5 and as the mammals of day 6 are adjoined to land. The fowl of day 5 are defined by their airy element and special feathered and winged forms, but some are adjoined to waters and others to land. As we proceed along the chain, we necessarily move farther away from direct consciousness of causes, except for formal cause. In *The Art of Logic* imperfect distributions from effects are said to occur when the units are effects of the parts, not of the whole, and this distribution is said to be as frequent as it is imperfect and is very serviceable. When distributions are imperfect, the *Logic* allows for or calls for the use of examples and enumerations. Enumeration—that is, several causes of the same effect, several effects of the same cause, several subjects of the same adjunct, several adjuncts of the same subject—occurs where the elements are distinguished as modes but not as sufficiently differentiated species and where the arrays of units do not exhaust and therefore reciprocate with the genus. With examples, whether one or several together, the genus is treated through the species, and what is true of one is also true of the other. Although imperfect in distribution, examples, according to the *Logic*, are valid in argument, supplemental, and much used by poets.

Enumerations and examples are the most prominent feature of the catalogues of fish, fowl, insects, and mammals on days 5 and 6 of *Paradise Lost*, Book 7. Normally these enumerations proceed through arrays of species and culminate in named examples that mark the extent of the distribution into species and that by their added length provide finality and suggestions of further possible specific enumeration and exemplification into infinity. The fish of day 5 establish the pattern:

> Forthwith the Sounds and Seas, each Creek and Bay
> With Fry innumerable swarm, and Shoals

Of Fish that with thir Fins and shining Scales
Glide under the green Wave, in Sculls that oft
Bank the mid Sea: part single or with mate
Graze the Seaweed thir pasture, and through Groves
Of Coral stray, or sporting with quick glance
Show to the Sun thir wav'd coats dropt with Gold,
Or in thir Pearly shells at ease, attend
Moist nutriment, or under Rocks thir food
In jointed Armor watch: on smooth the Seal,
And bended Dolphins play: part huge of bulk
Wallowing unwieldy, enormous in thir Gait
Tempest the Ocean: there Leviathan
Hugest of living Creatures, on the Deep
Stretcht like a Promontory sleeps or swims,
And seems a moving Land, and at his Gills
Draws in, and at his Trunk spouts out a Sea. (399–416)

The fish are distributed according to sites, community or individuality, physical attributes, motion, procreation, nutrition, the inherent adjunct of "passion," and size. Only the dolphins and Leviathan are named, and the former is plural, whereas the latter by varied implication is notably singular. The catalogue of fowl of lines 417–38 shows a similar patterning. Here the distribution is by generation and growth, distinctive physical characteristics, subject site (air) and adjunct site (land or sea), domicile, community, time (seasons and hours), number, song, and color. The passage continues into accounts of named species: from crane and nightingale to swan and cock. The peacock, though unnamed, is absolutely individuated as an example. The insects are similarly arrayed as genera and conclude with the examples of the ant and the bee that are handled as a kind of equivalent of the epic simile elsewhere in the poem. This catalogue ends with a forward look toward inexhaustibility of species: "The rest are numberless, / And thou thir Natures know'st, and gav'st them Names, / Needless to thee repeated" (492–94). This conclusion rescues Raphael's proceeding from the accusation of imperfection that normally attends enumerations and establishes that he has been citing examples in order to prove or clarify the genera. Specific names dominate the account of the land animals and remove the examples from the genera to be inferred. The content of the lists draws closer to Adam's immediate experience and to Adam's own nature. The accumulations of examples in each category of the animal creation give validity to the inductions produced about the genus/genera. Within the governing context of enumeration, the examples accumulate as either similar and arguing similar points about the Creator or special and arguing their own forms and genus. With such a content as Raphael's, examples are "obviously indispensable" (C251; Y306), and their function is illustration—but illustration in two senses: first, to give examples, and, secondly, to shed light upon or draw forth the light (the divine creative energy) that shines within. Raphael's re-creation of creation and his progressing systematically through the consenting arguments as he invents Invention to Adam is itself a large-scale argument of the wondrous efficient cause, the power, wisdom, and love of God the Creator.

Although I began with the consenting arguments—they are foundational and explicated first in Ramistic logics—it must be noted that Raphael's early narratives focus not on consent but on the dissenting Satan at the end of Book 5 and throughout Book 6. The *Logic* makes this strategy clear. Affirmation and consent have priority over negation and dissent, a priority based not only on nature but also, it is said, on use and dignity (C99; Y250). To enforce and clarify the warning to Adam that is his mission, Raphael cites the radical paradigm of dissent, war, and the radical distinction between the obedient "Angelic Host that stand / In sight of God enthron'd" (5.535–36) and the disobedient host that have fallen to deepest Hell (541–43). In answering to himself the rhetorical question, so often cited as the modus operandi of his narrative procedure, "how shall I relate / To human sense th'invisible exploits / Of warring Spirits" (564–66), Raphael is making a choice of strategies. He posits what is foundational to dissenting arguments, that the dissenting units are "both equally known and equally firm among themselves" and "equally argued by the other." But dissenting arguments make differences *more evident* (C99–101; Y250); through such alignment, dissenting arguments lay the groundwork for reason, because "Reason is choice." The role of Satan as dissenting argument is captured neatly in several lines from *Paradise Regained*: "Error," we are told there, is "by his own arms best evinc't" (4.235), and at greater length Satan explains:

> The trial hath indamag'd thee no way,
> Rather more honor left and more esteem;
> Mee naught advantag'd, missing what I aim'd. (206–8)

Indeed, the dramatic juxtaposition of the Son and the Adversary through-out the brief epic sets forth these operations at large. As Milton's late *Of True Religion* states:

> In logic they teach that contraries laid together more evidently appear; it follows then that, all controversies being permitted, falsehood will appear more false, and truth more true; which must conduce much . . . to the general confirmation of implicit truth. (CE 6:178)

Consenting arguments "are valuable chiefly for arguing, proving, and con-firming, but dissenting arguments are useful in contradicting, overthrow-ing, and refuting" (C101–3; Y251). The supporting proposition illumi-nates the function of the strategy relative to fallen audiences, and although Adam is unfallen his innocence makes it adaptable to his condition also: "so that he who does not wish to be taught by a consentany argument is led back to it by the absurd result of a dissentany argument, so that even an unwill-ing man is unable not to assent to the truth." Adam is not, of course, recalcitrant, but the *reductio ad absurdam* is in line with the tone of mockery that arises at times in Books 5 and 6. An argument contains its message within itself, which requires only recognition, not explication. From the dissenting arguments represented through Satan, Adam may come to know, deny, and avoid their threat, just as through the model of right action, Abdiel—whose perfect adjunct is zeal—Adam may bring himself into consent with the divine plan, may affirm and imitate.

Dissenting arguments are susceptible to two formats, one based on the relationship of one to many (diverses, a category that Ramus introduced) and the other based on the relationship of one to one. The general rule is that opposites dispose of each other and that when one opposite is affirmed the other is thereby denied—with emphasis on the *thereby*. The emphasis of opposites is thus upon exclusion rather than merely on identifying differ-ence. As the degree of dissent increases, that is, when we reach the catego-ries of dichotomous contraries, the Aristotelian proposition that "Con-traries are to be assigned to the first differences of being" (C135; Y263) comes to govern the logical materials and the evidence. In *Paradise Lost* "first difference of being" is quite literally that. Given the nature of the deity as creator of being, life, form, and order, denying contraries are available in the presentation of the original distinction from Chaos. As the creating Word addressed himself to his task, he "far remov'd" the "loud misrule" of Chaos, "lest fierce extremes / Contiguous might distemper the whole frame" (7.271–73). Contradiction is further illustrated in the conception of the cosmos, at the point where the deity

> . . . downward purg'd
> The black tartareous cold Infernal dregs
> Adverse to life; then founded, then conglob'd
> Like things to like, the rest to several place
> Disparted. (237–41)

Contrary dissenting arguments divide into those that affirm (relatives and adverses) and those that deny (contradictories and privatives). Raphael's Satanic evidence in Books 5 and 6 illustrates all four categories, making evil plain to Adam and rendering what Satan stands for absurd, so that even if Adam were an unwilling student he would be unable not to assent to the divine truth thus made evident. One of the modes in which *Paradise Lost* presents Satan is as a relative of God; in other words, one of the ways in which evil is to be understood is as a simultaneous mutual affect of good (C121; Y258). This is a stage of understanding that readers like Adam soon pass beyond as they come to employ more fully the finest and truest knowledge, the knowledge of causes, but it is foundational to and in the background of deeper inquiry into the existence of evil and the nature of the Satanic. Satan's very name, the Apostate, the Adversary, marks him as radically in dissent, and he is literally, even etymologically, the embodiment of the adverse argument. In the *Logic*, "Adverses are affirming contraries, which are absolutely diagonally adverse to each other"; here the dissent of members is absolute, "in every way, perfectly," and occurs in qualities, substances, quantities, and indeed in all things (C131; Y262). Satan is the great contradiction of the divine, the adversary of unity, glory, new laws, truth, and incarnation. He is the "Antagonist of Heav'n's Almighty King" (10.387) and "th'Arch-Enemy" (1.82). [17]

The other dissenting arguments, the denying contraries of privatives and contradictories, are also well manifest in the characterization of Satan. Here the members negate each other, either universally or finitely. Privatives involve a denial of something that is expected to be present, "the negation of essence," the "extinction of some habit which by nature ought to be or is able to be within a subject" (C145; Y267). Raphael's and Milton's Satan is essentially deprived of God and is therefore lacking in those attributes of the deity, such as reason, self-knowledge, joy, glory, faith, hope, charity, light, and on and on. These, as a creation of the deity, Satan was born to have and they are habits appropriate to his original angelic nature. Satan also manifests the contradictory that denies universally, especially within the format of *is/is not* because it is difficult to find words to express the fullness of such negation. This is the mode of pure denial (C137; Y264). Like Goethe's Mephistopheles, Milton's Satan is the spirit that denies, but in a special logical sense as well as in general.

In the *Logic* Milton examines the backgrounds for measuring degrees of contrariety and states his position:

> Aristotle assigns the greatest contrariety sometimes to adverses, sometimes to contradictories. But there seems to be the greatest dissent among the privatives, the next greatest among the adverses, less still among the contradictories, the least among the relatives, for the relatives on account of that mutual affect are partly consentany.

He finds adverses indeed directly opposed but still able to be mingled, whereas "privatives admit of no mixture" (C149; Y268). The specific category for Satanic negation need not be defined absolutely, for it suits Milton's various epic purposes that at many points in the poem the options remain open. Here, as elsewhere in the central books of the epic, the reader's assessment hovers with varying uneasiness over the question of Satan's acting from his own essence or as an instrumental agent of divine purpose, mirroring the largest question the poem seeks to justify in describing God's ways with man, that is, whether evil is or is not under control in a universe supposedly targeted always on the attainment of the absolute good.

As arguments and Invention establish the nature of things, so Disposition and Method focus on the relationships among things or, in view of Ramus's inexorable bifurcating, between things. In Invention one draws out meaning; in Disposition one imposes order or judgment. The *Logic* describes Invention as the matter of dialectic and Disposition as its form. Invention identifies or discovers corpuscular units and interchangeable parts. It looks at things and discovers the simultaneous and reciprocal meanings implicit within them. The implicit may be made explicit but is returnable to its container. In Disposition the reasoner collocates arguments into axioms and places them in priorities in order to achieve access not to knowledge (as in Invention) but to truth, access not so much to nature as to the abstract. Disposition is neither simultaneous nor reciprocal. As a process of establishing relative sizes of units and placing them in order of precedence, whether that is measured by time or by value, Disposition necessarily involves sequence and therefore precedence and consequence. It is postlapsarian in its acknowledgment of time sequence and of the possibilities of error in human perception of and processing of data. Disposition works with and within contexts. As Invention concerns itself with substantives and semantics, Disposition emphasizes verbs, conjunctions, and correlatives. In the metaphor used by the *Logic* itself, Disposition is a matter of syntax, of purposeful arrangement. Syntax is subject to parsing but not to essential redistributions of the subject, verb, and period. It sorts out the true from the false, the valid from the invalid, antecedent from consequent, the necessary from the contingent, truth from opinion in a process of judgment, deduction, chronology, and implicit persuasion. To Milton Disposition teaches one to think well, and thinking in his words includes the varied functions of understanding, judging, debating, and remembering (C294; Y324).

Like Invention, Disposition is both a transcript of reality and an intellectual process of aligning the reasoner's mind with reality. Rightly managed, it allows one to give a true verbal form to the relationships that truly obtain between and among things as they are. Whereas in Invention reality is the data of the world of nature, in Disposition reality resides in ideas and universals. To align one's mind with the transcendent calls for special exercises of the order-making and order-perceiving faculties. The goal of Disposition is truth, and for Ramists truth was one, simple, inviolable, and available. As Perry Miller formulates the Ramist position:

> Truth does not need proof, but only assertion. Hence true doctrine is a
> series of axioms, and correct propositions are so self-evident that in almost all
> cases doubt can be resolved by the mere statement of alternatives in the
> disjunctive syllogism. [18]

Disposition remains then a chiefly organizational matter, but its organizations were believed to answer to reality, and therefore its organizational procedure coincided with reality. Hence, some Ramistic logics called their second halves Arrangement or Disposition while others, including Ramus's, called them Judgment. Milton chooses to call his second half Disposition, because for Milton judgment is implicit in both noetic and dianoetic reasoning, implicit in both Invention and Disposition. Disposition for Milton includes simultaneously arrangements and judgments of data and is thus the more accurate term (C295–97; Y323–24).

Disposition consists of axioms, syllogisms, and Method; the latter two being arrangements of axioms. The following discussion and evidence are organized into these three categories. Michael's role in Books 11 and 12 of *Paradise Lost* is to supply Adam with formulations of self-evident truth or axioms and with access to the syllogistic process for resolving doubtful cases by examining their relationship to axiomatic truth and thereby eliminating logical as well as theological doubt. Michael supplies Adam with the universals, the biblical givens, and teaches Adam how to evaluate the particulars of experience by that light, to dispose experience within a methodical scheme of spiritual priorities. Axioms compose arguments in the relationship of subject/predicate or antecedent/consequent in order to determine what may and may not be said about a matter, to determine truth or falsity. Like arguments, axioms are noetically available and address self-evident absolute truth. Syllogisms are available to deal with doubtful cases in arrangements that allow questions to be developed into necessary conclusions. Ramus demoted the Aristotelian syllogism to a position equivalent to axioms and Method, and he promoted to prominence a kind of syllogism that traditional logics did not allow, the disjunctive syllogism, a syllogism that disposes simplified alternatives to facilitate choice. Ramistic Method is the format of Ramism's characteristic sideways pinetrees representing sequential relationships of genera and species; Method is also the process of seeking, weighing, and putting a series of axioms in order of their conspicuousness or priority. The human order of Method, in Ramus's view, transcribes and answers to the divine order of reality, making the natural world theological as well as logical. Disposition is a process of building upon what one already knows; it is basically a postlapsarian mode, which seeks to put the reasoner back in touch with the truth that has been dimmed or lost through time and faltering human capacity. Disposition is a gathering of the fragments of homogeneal truth, as in *Areopagitica*, and a placing of those fragments in orderly and memorable patterns. It is, in *Of Education*'s words, a repairing of the ruins, a regaining to know God aright.

The axiomatic is both a kind of proposition and a procedure. Its formal components divide into antecedent and consequent; it either puts together or separates its arguments; its band either affirms or denies a relationship between them. Its expression may be lengthy or as brief as two words, subject plus verb. It is a matter of both arrangement (establishing what is and what is not, what may or may not be said about something else) and judgment (distinguishing between the true and the false, and between necessary and contingent truths, and therefore between truth and opinion).

The soundness of an axiom is determined by checking it against its own contradiction. Necessary true axioms, like arguments founded upon secure causes, produce "the truest and first knowledge":

> It is first because it is knowledge of principles, which, though indemonstrable through themselves, are completely manifest by their own light, and do not need the light of the syllogism or any plainer argument for producing knowledge; it therefore is of necessity completely true as well. (C323; Y333)

Such axioms provide a dimension of Disposition that overlaps with Raphael's "true speech" by identifying the structures that are returned to when the ruins of the first parents are repaired. That overlap explains why it is possible for the prelapsarian Adam to describe axiomatic structures and processes in his psychological account to Eve in Book 5. After outlining hierarchically the roles of reason, fancy, and the senses, Adam calls attention to the data or arguments from

> Which Reason joining or disjoining, frames
> All what we affirm or what deny, and call
> Our knowledge or opinion. (106–8)

Finally, the axiom simultaneously formulates an idea in the mind and an enunciation for an audience.

The finest and truest axiomatic knowledge resides in the judgment of axioms that obey the Ramistic laws of truth, justice, and wisdom. These laws are foundational to Ramistic Method. As Ong points out, although these laws were carefully nuanced in Aristotle, "In Ramus, they serve only for mystification."[19] Put simply, these laws require that the axiom be "always true about every antecedent or subject, and the whole of it," that the parts of the axiom be homogeneous and essential to each other, and that the antecedent and consequent be reciprocal (that is, proximate and immediate, proper and equal). The law of truth establishes the necessary verity of the axiom through the consenting affect of its parts; the law of justice requires the essential relation of the parts; and the law of wisdom "prohibits the vices contrary to wisdom, inequality or lack of agreement of the antecedent with the consequent, and tautology." The latter is also called "the law of brevity" and is recommended as "mindful of intelligence and memory" (C317–23; Y331–33). The third law includes the former two, but their distinction is said to aid perspicuity. These Ramistic laws expand upon the goals noted earlier, that "What is affirmed is firm, certain, very brief."

The laws orient us toward the truth that resides in things, the knowledge of indemonstrable principles "completely manifest by their own light." The very names of the laws point directly to Michael's teaching goals.

The theoretical principles of Disposition may be seen clearly from the outset of Michael's fulfillment of his mission to the fallen Adam; indeed, the axiomatic foundations of his procedure are laid in the first of Book 11's tableaux. The story of Cain and Abel from Genesis divides into two parts, the first narrative, the second dramatic.[20] The narrative unit presents arguments: the characters, the setting, and the plot. Adam is identified as the cause of his sons (effects), and Adam's crime as the cause of corrupt effects among his heirs (11.423–28, especially "effects," line 424). Identification of logical arguments moves to Disposition of those arguments. In the first of the alternating speeches of the dramatic unit, Michael explicates the relationships between the arguments and articulates arrangements and the foundations for judgment.

> These two are Brethren, *Adam*, and to come
> Out of thy loins; th' unjust the just hath slain,
> For envy that his Brother's Offering found
> From Heav'n acceptance; but the bloody Fact
> Will be aveng'd, and th' other's Faith approv'd
> Lose no reward, though here thou see him die,
> Rolling in dust and gore. (454–60)

Cain and Abel are identified (though not by name) as to proximate efficient cause, as diverses, relatives, and opposites, as to their proper adjuncts, as comparatives, and the like. The explication points toward future lessons and revelations, thus logically toward final causes. The specific scene is explored, disposed, and judged in relation to the generals of mortality, justice, and faith. *In relation to* is the key phrase and focuses on the core of Disposition. Cain and Abel are dichotomized by profession, temperament, spiritual as well as physical attitudes. Even the field of the scene is dichotomized into "Part arable and tilth" and "the other part sheep-walks and folds." "First Fruits" are balanced against "the Firstlings of his Flock." One sacrificer is "sweaty," the other "more meek." One gift is "Uncull'd, as came to hand"; the other's sacrifice is performed with "all due Rites." One's is sincere and gratefully received, the other's not. The account is structured on dichotomies at virtually every point. The arguments imply values (sweaty, uncull'd, due, sincere) that a teacher or reasoner may easily draw forth, but the values, the judgment, are secured within the evidence itself, which requires only to be seen correctly. One begins with arguments, and the arguments are then disposed into axioms, that is, into syntactical arrangements in which the verbs and conjunctions emerge as more important than the nouns. The axioms are sorted out chronologically into antecedents and consequents, Disposition's analogue of causes and effects. The data reach toward universals, especially of justice and mortality, and toward guidelines for the conduct of human life. Adam's response to Michael's explication, for example, laments both the deed and the occasion of death, the effect and the cause. Michael proceeds to deepen the inquiry here begun and, for example, to open up the term *death* for Adam by examining its matter and form, as well as its efficient and end.

Michael's presentation of the Cain and Abel scene is itself a twofold process, the presentation of data and the identification and interpretation of those data. The double presentation builds into the educational process several definitive Ramistic principles. To dispose properly is simultaneously to judge. If the scene is clearly viewed—and it is so by Michael and is so deployed that Adam may absorb the design—it implies a value system that is inseparable from its own data. Proper vision or Disposition, however, requires that the crypsis of the matter be eliminated, that excess, deficiency, and disorder be sorted out. In Michael's hands the axioms are made homogeneous; antecedents and consequents become a moral as well as a chronological matter; and patterns of precedence and therefore of value are recognized and set forth. Universals take precedence over the experiential, and thus the account relates the arguments to justice versus injustice, faith versus envy, and related dichotomous patterns and judgments, within a context that looks forward to divine approval, reward, vengeance, and further revelation. If Abel receives less immediate attention than Cain, he is not less the bearer of promises to be opened up more fully in the other shepherds to follow in history.

On the one hand, axioms are enunciations. Because Michael is describing factual historical truth to his pupil, there is a sense in which everything he says is axiomatic; that is, he disposes arguments to show that something is or is not. Although what he describes to Adam attaches to a future occurrence that is to the reader a past event, Michael's pronouncements have a present and absolute validity founded upon universal principles. Especially in Book 11 Michael tends to conclude each unit by enunciating its lesson in concise and memorable form: "Man's woe" begins "From Man's effeminate slackness," he avers at line 634, and at lines 836–38 "God attributes to place / No sanctity, if none be thither brought / By Men who there frequent, or therein dwell." The exemption of Enoch from death demonstrates "what reward / Awaits the good, the rest what punishment" (709–10); death is "to sense / More terrible at th' entrance than within" (469–70); "since they / God's Image did not reverence in themselves" the diseased persons of the lazar house disfigure "not God's likeness, but thir own" (524–25, 521); "th' Earth shall bear / More than anough, that temperance may be tri'd" (804–5); and the rainbow betokens "peace from God, and Cov'nant new" (867). In these axioms the emphasis on antecedent and consequent is made clear and telling. In such pronouncements as these, Michael is articulating what thereafter become self-evident and inescapable truths for Adam. Within her context of Reformation theology, Georgia Christopher makes the same point: "[Adam] is acquiring the verbal structures for patience, and in the process of internalization [of God], Michael's narrative undergoes an abstraction into sentences of great integrative and mnemonic value."[21] In such speech Michael is setting forth "the truest and first knowledge," and his axioms follow the laws of truth, justice, wisdom, and supplementarily brevity.

Besides being enunciations, axioms are also a procedure, a clarified arrangement of arguments with each other, and the *Logic* moves from an analysis of axioms according to their content and judgment to a consideration of axioms according to their form and disposition. As some of the examples show, an axiom need not be a simple, even two-word deployment of argument with argument where the band is a verb but may be syntactically complex where the band is a conjunction. Some of the simple axioms in Michael's commentary on the first scene may be listed as follows: Cain is unjust; Cain envies; Cain kills his brother; the murder will be avenged; heaven will reward the just brother and therefore the just generally. The common consequent justice is generally attributed to both brothers but affirmed for one and denied for the other. The common consequent reward is attributed particularly to some brothers. The proper consequent, Michael's "bloody Fact" (457), is attributed to its peculiar antecedent Abel. The true may be separated from the false axiom by measuring an axiom against its contradiction. If we consider, for example, "Cain is just" or "the just brother is not pious," the readiest reference to external reality demonstrates the thorough falseness of the proposition and thereby the truth of the original axiom. Reversing the band of general axioms cannot, however, sort out true from false. External reality cannot attest absolutely that Heaven does not reward the pious or that both brothers do not receive justice, because two standards of measurement apply separately to the two brothers.

Compound axioms are either congregative (expressing consenting arguments) or segregative (expressing dissenting arguments). Congregative are either copulative (with *and*) or connex (with *if* or *unless*). Michael's second scene provides examples. If we eliminate the crypsis of the scene and relate it to the preceding scene, we come up with these compound axioms: Violence and intemperance cause death; if a man lives, he will die; if one does not die prematurely, he dies maturely. In these examples, death is a consequent of life, and mature death a consequent of not premature death and *for that reason*. Segregative axioms are either discrete (with *not this . . . but that*) or disjunct (with *either . . . or*). The discrete set forth diverses, the disjunct opposites, only one of which is true. Necessary disjunctions produce knowledge, contingent disjunctions produce opinion. These matters may be illustrated from Michael's formulation at the conclusion of the second tableau:

> Nor love thy Life, nor hate; but what thou liv'st
> Live well, how long or short permit to Heav'n. (11.553–54)

Michael begins and ends with disjunctive formulations here and disposes them into a distinction between quantity and quality of life, a *not this . . . but that* formulation. Michael corrects Adam's "opinionated" disjunction at lines 502–7:

> Why is life giv'n
> To be thus wrested from us? rather why
> Obtruded on us thus? who if we knew
> What we receive, would either not accept
> Life offer'd, or soon beg to lay it down,
> Glad to be so dismist in peace.

The correction is brought about through the appropriate axiomatic contradiction, by showing that neither of the alternatives is true. Love *and* hate as well as love *or* hate can provide the basis for the contradiction. Michael offers discrete and disjunct axioms in considering whose image is disfigured through intemperance: the human image, the maker's image, or the brutish image of ungoverned appetite. The diseased did not reverence God's image or their own; they disfigured "not God's likeness, but thir own" (521). Diverses and opposites are disposed to make distinctions and to enunciate the opposition of temperance and intemperance and thus to affirm "the rule of not too much" (531), but that too is left behind in favor of submission to the divine will and its allotment of life span, the larger necessary axiomatic truth. Michael is here as in general disposing arguments with each other to show things to be or not to be and to state what may and may not be said about the relationship of one argument and another.

The alternative to necessary true axioms are axioms whose truth is contingent, with the judgmental alternative of opinion. Axiomatic structures allow for distinguishing true from false and truth from opinion through the soundness of the apprehension of the things themselves and the degree of certainty inhering in the things. Necessary truth attaches to the divine, but contingent truth is the general domain of human, especially postlapsarian, judgment. Contingent things, the area of the experiential and the fallen, are matters of opinion unless the reasoner proceeds to a full awareness of causes. Although necessary truths are fully certain, if the human reasoner is ignorant of causes, he or she can have only opinion in this area also. If, however, one has difficulty determining whether a truth is contingent or necessary, he or she exercises not opinion but doubt (C309–11; Y328–29). Michael's mission to Adam is to eliminate the area of doubt by sorting out the contingent from the necessary, by distinguishing experience from faith, and by "gathering up limb by limb still as they could find them . . . those dissevered pieces which are yet wanting to the body of Truth" (Hughes, p. 742). The reasoner pursues appropriate causes, especially final causes. If successful, Michael will replace doubt with faith, opinion with full certainty. When we move from the noetic axioms to the dianoetic syllogism, we are moving also fully into the realm of contingencies and uncertainties where the goal is necessary conclusions rather than necessary apprehension and assent. In terms of the evidence of *Paradise Lost*, we are also moving for the most part to the evidence of Book 12 rather than Book 11.

Father Walter Ong establishes the relationship of the syllogism to the process of Invention in these suggestive terms:

> Syllogistic reasoning is less a way of or a substitute for discovery than a sequel of and complement to it. To some extent in Aristotle himself, and to a greater extent in the commentaries, discovery of first principles tends to be assimilated to the *via inventionis* and thus to the topical tradition and to dialogue as represented in dialectic whereas demonstration is the *via iudicii*, in the sense of a check-up operation verifying the results of invention, or

testing by means of syllogism (a notion which Ramus would exploit wildly). Demonstrative ratiocination follows as a further step after the inventive process and is thus an ordering of items discovered in such a way as to produce intelligibility, to illuminate discovery and explain it.[22]

The syllogism is a reckoning together, or, in Ramus's metaphor, it involves a "gathering." It deduces one axiom from another. It is discursive, that is, literally "passing from one subject to another," as discourse is literally "to run to and fro." Milton makes the dianoetic explicitly postlapsarian in commenting:

> Such gathering up or deduction has arisen from the weakness of the human intellect, which because it is not able by the first intuition to see the truth and falsity of things in the axiom, turns to the syllogism in order to judge of their consequence and lack of consequence by its means. (C367; Y350)

This is the discourse of reason that Raphael distinguished for Adam in Book 5 as the human norm in contrast to the angelic intuitive mode or "the first intuition." It is Michael's pedagogical province. *Gathering* is also a natural, indeed inevitable, metaphor for the operation of memory; collection is inseparable from recollection. Both imply a sequence and a chronology.

As axioms aim at sorting out necessary truth, so the Ramistic syllogism is a dispositional structure for dealing with doubtful axioms, or with contingent truths, or with what are called "questions." Its professed goal is to sort out consequence from inconsequence and to move the reasoner from contingencies and doubts to necessary conclusions and therefore necessary truths. Its emphasis on form allows it to determine what does and what does not follow from what is given. Doubt is the postlapsarian state, and phenomenological contingency the postlapsarian reality; both result from the loss of a direct and clear relationship to the deity without and within. Reason itself is fallen, but its new role is to aid in the return to the original state and truth, and it mediates between the reality and the absolute, between experience and the divine plan. Ramus cites the syllogism as reflecting "the image of some sort of divinity" in man and as what distinguishes men from animals; he allows induction "to be a common possession among all forms of life, whereas the syllogism is the property only of the highest form of life and the expression only of the highest intelligence." Perry Miller puts the case wittily in saying:

> Considered therefore in the light of logic, the fall of man had amounted in effect to a lapse from dialectic; the loss of God's image, reduced to the

most concrete terms, was simply the loss of an ability to use the syllogism, and innate depravity might most accurately be defined as a congenital incapacity for discursive reasoning.[23]

Ramus rejects Aristotle's distinction between necessary and contingent syllogistic conclusions; for him every syllogism concludes necessarily because that necessity results not from the content but from the arrangement of the syllogism itself. The Ramistic syllogism is thus an instrument for the verification of preexisting truth, not for original inquiry; it leads backward in time. This is especially apparent in the reasoner's quest for the key element in the syllogistic arrangement, the third argument or the middle term of the syllogism. The third argument functions like the band of the axiom to determine the consent or dissent between the antecedent and consequent. To find the third argument, the reasoner searches through the places of Invention for an argument that agrees with both sides of a question to be affirmed or one that agrees with one side and dissents from the other in a question that is to be denied (C389; Y359). The third argument participates in both the proposition and the assumption but does not enter the conclusion. Two laws assist the reasoner in finding the third argument, one from the place of equals ("Things which agree in some third thing agree among themselves") and the other from the place of genus ("What is generally attributed to a genus is also attributed to all the species contained under the genus" [C387; Y358]). When the antecedent has been laid down and the question legitimately disposed with the third argument, it is necessarily concluded. Because the necessity is of form not matter, the syllogism produces necessary rather than contingent results. One example recurs frequently throughout the *Logic* and will serve for clarification: If the question is whether Socrates is an animal, the third argument is man, a species of the genus animal, and the genus of the species Socrates. The conclusion is and ought to be the same as the question posed, Is Socrates an animal? . . . Socrates is an animal. The conclusion is the same as the question, with the difference that the species has now been deduced from the genus. The third argument (man) mediates the consent or dissent between the antecedent (Socrates) and the consequent of the question (animal).

As with warnings against crypsis in the axiom, the *Logic* also gives large and early space to clarifying the errors to be avoided in the disposition of syllogisms. The faults are similar to axiom's excess, deficiency, and disorder. Excesses in the syllogism occur chiefly through homonymy or equivocation of terms and ambiguity of syntax; the terms must be precisely three, and each must be used in its single consistent meaning. Deficiency of terms in the syllogism occurs chiefly as the lack of the third argument and specifically as using a third argument that is equal to one of the terms and does not mediate between the terms as genus, subgenus/supraspecies, and species. The third fault of the syllogism resides in the matter or in a combination of matter and form rather than in the form alone; it occurs when a non-cause is taken as cause, when an adjunct is taken for a subject or a subject for an adjunct, "when the laws of opposition are not observed for the same number, according to the same thing, in relation to the same thing, and at the same time," and "when it is argued that contraries are the consequents of contraries" (C383–85; Y356–57). Similarly, a concluding appendix supplies the crypses of the disposition of the syllogism under the headings of enthymeme, prosyllogism, dilemma, and sorites. In the examples from Michael's materials of Books 11 and 12 of *Paradise Lost*, it is clear that Michael applies these forms of testing as a way of establishing the truths he communicates and as a structure that Adam may absorb and later apply in his own solitary processing of the truth. The reasoner who seeks to proceed from doubtful questions to necessary truths must check and recheck data and procedures at every turn. Both senses of *checking*, that is, *testing* and *restraining*, describe Michael's procedures in instructing a postlapsarian Adam.

This alien vocabulary may be translated into the theological with ease, and it is worth noting that in Ramus's first version of his logic, he divided Judgment into the three phases of (1) syllogism, (2) collocation (which involved Method), and (3) "the conjunction of all the arts and relation of them to God," which he called First, Second, and Third Judgment. According to the analysis of Father Walter Ong, such Third Judgment (which "Ramus had piously described as the *only* true dialectic") is "that by which all men are freed from the shadows of the cave (Plato's cave, clearly) and all things referred to the divine light, that is, to God." Ong evaluates such an "ascent of the mind to God through dialectic" as "largely an elaborate exercise in mystification."[24] In the Ramism that Milton inherited, the discovery of the third argument and the capacity to achieve such a discovery indicate the presence of the divine in the mental equipment of the reasoner. It is this that "by its presence permits the conclusion of the question" (C371; Y351). The question presents the matter of experience, the doubtful contingencies of daily living; the experiential matter is examined and interacted with what is attained by reason and faith; the issue is reason and faith. One begins with faith and returns more secured in faith. In the postlapsarian world of contingencies or questions or "doubtful axioms," as Michael presents it, the units of experience are always in question, and the conclusion derives from a measurement of such uncertainties against first or settled principles, against faith—in other words, from a carefully formulated disposition of the data that brings to bear (remembers) the intuitive. Its goal is "to produce confidence."

Syllogisms bifurcate into the simple and the compound and into the contracted and the explicated. The *Logic* reviews the various modes of the syllogism in expansive detail; indeed, here as with comparatives Milton fulfills his intention stated at the outset to expand upon Ramus's brevity by supplying illustrative examples from classical authors. Because the discussion of simple explicated syllogisms generally rehearses Aristotelian categories and because it would be tedious in the extreme to consider in detail here, for example, the six modes of each of its species, I shall attend chiefly to what in the *Logic* and the evidence is of lapsarian interest. It is, however, worth noting that the *Logic* particularly recommends the simple contracted syllogism through examples because of its clarity and simplicity. Here the example assumes the duties of the third argument, mediating between the antecedent and the consequent of the question (C395–97; Y361–62). In presenting his instruction, Michael relies upon the examples of the one just and one faithful man within the context of general history and thus makes the particular into a genus or subaltern genus. In the process he avoids specifically named individuals and cites, for example, Cain as "th' unjust," Abel as "the just," and Abraham as "one faithful man."

When we move into instances of the syllogism from Michael's conversation with Adam, the evidence and the deployment of it are illuminated by the theoretical formulations. Adam's response to the vision of Cain and Abel includes two literal questions that may be formulated as the logical questions of syllogisms:

> But have I now seen Death? Is this the way
> I must return to native dust? (11.462–63)

The first question must be answered by determining what death is, that is, by establishing the third argument. From the information given, Adam determines that death is a "bloody Fact," a "Rolling in dust and gore." Because he has seen a "bloody Fact," a "Rolling in dust and gore," he concludes with a reshaping of the question, that, therefore, he has seen death. This looks valid as a syllogism and concludes in a truth. As is soon discovered, however, the term *death* has been inadequately defined. Adam assumes he has seen *all* death, but as Michael shows he has seen only *some* death. The conclusion shows only what Adam has seen, not what is more largely to be learned about the concept of death itself. Michael corrects the errors of the matter by discovering here a lack of a proper third argument; Adam has begged the question by taking something identical in meaning or something equally obscure for a viable argument (C379; Y355). Adam's second question and Michael's response to it are similarly fallacious and move quickly to expand both the meaning of the term *death* and the range of Adam's vicarious experience. In asking if this is the way he himself must die, Adam attempts to make death the third argument. But, as Michael soon demonstrates, death cannot serve in such a capacity because it is genus to a bloody fact, not species to a bloody fact. Again Adam implies *death* is *all death* rather than *some death*, and Michael proceeds to add "many shapes / Of Death" to Adam's witness of death's "first shape on man." In these examples of simple syllogisms, the text's and Michael's emphasis has been upon correction of errors of procedures and of axiomatic data.

If we turn to some of Adam's first questions in Book 12, the logical as the moral and historical atmosphere has altered, and the emphasis now falls upon perfecting a more complex use of the syllogism. Adam's questions follow Michael's accounts of Abraham and Moses:

> This yet I apprehend not, why to those
> Among whom God will deign to dwell on Earth
> So many and so various Laws are giv'n;
> So many Laws argue so many sins
> Among them; how can God with such reside? (280–84)

Adam attempts here to work his way through a series of formally sound premises but finishes with his question, not with a syllogistic conclusion. His reasoning is not unsound, but his opening premise is. God resides with all men, and all men since Adam and because of Adam are subject to sinfulness, as Michael proceeds to point out. In what follows Michael does what he does throughout Book 12; he uses the opportunity to expand the material beyond its Old Testament or rationalistic base into the more expansive categories of New Testament grace.

In addition to the simple syllogisms favored by traditional logic, we may see in this evidence also examples of those compound syllogistic formats Ramus added to and preferred to the Aristotelian models, the connex syllogism and the disjunctive syllogism. As a connex syllogism we find: If there are laws, there are sins; but there are laws; therefore, there are sins. In another of the formats of the connex syllogism, this may be formulated thus: If men were sinless, there would be no need for laws; but there is a need for laws; therefore, men are not sinless. As disjunctive syllogisms, the matter may be disposed thus: God resides with the sinless or the sinful; but God does not reside with the sinful; therefore, God resides with the sinless. Alternately, it may be disposed disjunctively thus: Man is either sinful and given laws or sinless and free from laws; but man is sinful and given laws; therefore, man is not sinless and free from laws. Thus, the connex syllogism, formatted as *if . . . then* or, in time matters, *when . . . then*, assumes an antecedent and concludes a consequent or takes away the consequent that it may take away the antecedent, and the disjunctive syllogism, formatted as *either . . . or*, takes away one and concludes the other or assumes one and takes away the rest.

Both kinds of compound syllogism are foundational to Michael's postlapsarian proceeding and address. In them the third argument resides in the syntactical structure itself; it is this that by its presence allows the conclusion but does not enter it, and it is this syntax that the reasoner brings to bear in mediating the matter at hand. The connex (or *if . . . then*) syllogism with its acknowledged frequency and dominance is basically the model for disposing contingencies from experience against abstract absolutes from faith in order to resolve truth and repair the ruins of humanity and the world. Because the proposition of the connex syllogism sets forth an antecedent that is less than the consequent, the format of the connex syllogism requires an act of judgment in comparing those parts. The relationship of antecedent/consequent will follow the pattern of effect/cause, adjunct/subject, or species/genus. The disjunctive syllogism's characteristic syntax of *either . . . or* marks it as singularly central to Michael's duplex presentations and to the foundations of moral choice implicit in the very nature of a morally polarized world. The third argument of the disjunctive syllogism, that is, the syntactical structure, comprehends opposites, and normatively Michael's opposites are moral polarities.

One extended series of syllogisms from Book 12 of *Paradise Lost* will serve to illustrate variations and implications of compound syllogisms. As with the earlier examples, the same units may be disposed in various syllogistic

formats, but the *Logic* avers that all syllogisms are reducible to the model of
the connex syllogism (C447; Y379). The textual unit I have chosen occurs
in Michael's interpretation of the occasion of Nimrod and Babel:

> . . . yet know withal,
> Since thy original lapse, true Liberty
> Is lost, which always with right Reason dwells
> Twinn'd, and from her hath no dividual being:
> Reason in man obscur'd, or not obey'd,
> Immediately inordinate desires
> And upstart Passions catch the Government
> From Reason, and to servitude reduce
> Man till then free. Therefore since hee permits
> Within himself unworthy Powers to reign
> Over free Reason, God in Judgment just
> Subjects him from without to violent Lords;
> Who oft as undeservedly enthral
> His outward freedom: Tyranny must be,
> Though to the Tyrant thereby no excuse.
> Yet sometimes Nations will decline so low
> From virtue, which is reason, that no wrong,
> But Justice, and some fatal curse annext
> Deprives them of thir outward liberty,
> Thir inward lost. (12.82–101)

Among this wealth of instances, the opening of this passage disposes the
following syllogisms: If right reason is lost, true liberty is lost; but right
reason is lost; therefore, true liberty is lost. And similarly: If man has right
reason, he has true liberty; but man does not have right reason; therefore,
man does not have true liberty. These examples of the connex syllogism
assume an antecedent (right reason) that is less than the consequent it
concludes (true liberty). The second format of the connex syllogism, which
takes away the consequent in order to take away the antecedent, may also be
disposed from the quotation: If upstart passions govern man, then man's
right reason has been obscured or not obeyed; but man's right reason has
been obscured or not obeyed; therefore, upstart passions govern man. Or,
again: If right reason is clear and obeyed, upstart passions will not govern
man; but upstart passions do govern man; therefore, right reason is ob-
scured or not obeyed. In the first of this pair, *man's right reason* is the

consequent, greater than the antecedent *upstart passions*. In the second, however, *upstart passions* and the whole concept of disorder there implied are the consequent of and are greater than man's instrument for attaining order, that is, the antecedent *right reason*. This transposition makes clear the act of judgment that is simultaneous with the disposition, the determination of what is greater than/less than what else. Connex syllogisms may also dispose relationships of time (*when . . . then*) and relationships that assume a greater rather than an equal. These may be seen in the cited passage in Michael's concern for temporal consequences and his shift from microcosmic internal government to macrocosmic external government.

Michael's discourse on rational liberty may also be disposed into disjunctive syllogisms, as, for example, in this: Man is governed by either right reason or upstart passions; but man is not governed by right reason; therefore, man is governed by upstart passions. And, similarly: Man is governed by either right reason or upstart passions; but man is governed by upstart passions; therefore, man is not governed by right reason. Additionally, the opening materials suggest these disjunctive syllogisms: Man is either free or reduced to servitude; but man is not free; therefore, man is reduced to servitude. And, similarly: Man is either free or reduced to servitude; but man is reduced to servitude; therefore, man is not free. In the first species of disjunctive syllogism, the reasoner takes away one in order to conclude the other, and in the second, where the parts are all affirmed, the reasoner assumes one and takes away the other or the rest. The parts of the proposition are opposites, and the third argument or syntax disposes oppositional equals.

The redeployments of the same units of evidence in the preceding examples are an important part of the point. Ideally, inward and outward liberty, for example, are in God-given balance. Man's lapse has abrogated the ideal and effected a reversal of this balance. Man gives up inward and therefore outward liberty, or man gives up inward liberty and therefore God (or Justice) takes away outward liberty. The repetitious formats allow subtle implications and distinctions to emerge and be explored. The apparent repetitiousness here is like the apparent repetitiousness of the examples in the *Logic*; it may be seen as only apparent, for in its own way it allows for subtlety and precision of reasoning and affirmation of faith. The question and its argument have to do with inward and outward liberty in relation to reason. The context disposes these matters in relation to the ideal and the postlapsarian. Such givens dictate the conclusions and dispose and judge the relationships, but in order for Adam or for us to regain to know God aright, the givens require to be seen clearly and within their wide-ranging context. The goal of syllogisms, we may recall, is to produce confidence.

Clearly, these preferred Ramistic syllogisms are radically different from their counterpart in traditional logic. They are instruments for dichotomists and dogmatists, not for inquiry. The forms are altered as well as the content and intent. Both connex and disjunctive syllogisms clarify why for Ramists there was so little to choose between the headings of Disposition and Judgment. If the units of the argument are plugged into the required format, all difference is reduced, and preexistent truth is served. Logicians align themselves and their materials with the essential "natural models" and thus attain theological as well as logical ends.

Method is the final category of Ramistic Disposition, and it supplies the models so characteristic of Ramistic documents, the schemes running in linked and generally bifurcated chains from the most general and universal on the left to the progressively most individuated on the right. The *Logic* defines Method as "a dianoetic disposition of various homogeneous axioms arranged one before another according to the clarity of their nature, whence the agreement of all with relation to each other is judged and retained by the memory" (C471; Y390). Ramism assumes and addresses an orderly world, and Method is the Ramistic category for that world, that address, and for reasoning generally. The *Logic* equates Method with the concept of order, but Method is Ramistic order of a special and limited sort with particular bases and goals. It is a matter of both Disposition and Judgment. Because the homogeneous axioms pertain to the same thing and are referred to the same end, they can be mutually subordinated and therefore ordered in a temporal or spatial or other sort of continuum. The *Logic*'s rule clarifies the goal and nature of Method as well as its relationship to the other forms of Disposition:

> So as truth or falsity is seen in the axiom, in the syllogism consequence and inconsequence, so in method care is taken that what is clearer in itself should precede, what is more obscure should follow; and in every way order and confusion are judged. Thus the first in absolute idea of the homogeneous axioms is disposed in the first place, the second in the second, the third in the third, and so on. (C371–73; Y391)

Like other modes of Disposition, Method is a process of sequential accumulation and judgment, requiring the reasoner to sort out antecedent from consequent, true from false, greater from lesser. It is also a chronological process, looking toward a goal, a final cause, a perfection, a completion. The most important, Ramistically most complex and characteristic terms in this account attach to Ramistic "clarity" and "absoluteness" of idea, but we may attend first to some simpler points.

Some contrasts with Invention analogues, especially with Invention's distribution format, will clarify the issues. Distribution is also a sequential progressive array of bifurcation from more to less inclusive, but in Method the data shift from arguments to axioms, and the basis of inclusiveness shifts from what is to what is perceived. As the cornerstone of Invention, distribution consists of the division of the whole into its parts and is balanced by induction, which is the collection of the parts to make up the whole. Within Invention induction is the reasoning process that allows men to know universals. Invention is nonjudgmental and atemporal and based upon reciprocation; it is simultaneous rather than sequential. As Invention implies perception, discovery, heightened awareness, and grasp of knowledge and causes, so Disposition implies a communicative usefulness in the reasoner's relationship to others and a usefulness within the reasoner's own psychology, as memory storage for later retrieval replaces perception. Time categories, past and future, take the place of Invention's immediacy and simultaneity. The *Logic* itself draws the contrast through a distinction between the Platonic and the Aristotelian:

> For the method of inventing which by Plato is called *synthetic* proceeds from single things which are before in time and first offer themselves to the senses; by induction from these general notions are collected. . . . A contrary way, as Aristotle (*Metaphysics* I.1 and 2) teaches, proceeds from universals, which by nature are before and better known; not since they are known first or more easily, but because after they are known they have precedence by the nature and clarity of the notion in proportion as they are more remote from the senses. (C475; Y391–92)

Method is the grounds for deduction, and deduction is central to Michael's instruction and the postlapsarian world view, expression, and epistemology. Method gives precedence to the most general and moves from it to the subaltern and lastly to the most special, as the synthetic mode moves from the simple to the composite. As Invention reaches principally *toward* causes, "So method continually progresses *from* universals, as those which contain causes, to particulars," from known antecedents to unknown consequents (C475; Y391; emphasis mine).

Besides being such a format, Method is also the process of putting the pieces of chains back together in their proper order of priority. It assumes a reasoner who is in the process of accumulating truths and who will commit himself or herself to measuring by the highest truths yet attained. The second half of the *Logic* may be described as outlining processes for collecting universal precepts, but when judgment is superimposed upon arrangement induction is no longer reciprocal with distribution. Judgment compels an acknowledgment of precedence and establishes a truth from which there is no turning back or away. Method serves to establish and reinforce the universals in the reasoner's mind so that the mind can suffer no lack of confidence in measuring particulars and special cases against their standard. Under Invention the first and truest knowledge is a knowledge of causes, but under Method a new definition emerges when the terms are reconstituted in such rules as this: "The most general will be first in place and order, since it is first in light and knowledge" (C471; Y392). In Invention, the reasoner performs the complementary acts of moving from wholes to parts and from parts to wholes within a context that is fundamentally synthetic and where the corpuscular units contain and imply the relationships the reasoner discovers within them. But in Disposition and Method, the reasoner, having striven to reconstruct the original synthesis, then works from the universals and absolutes that she or he has achieved and that constitute a compelling higher reality. In Method remoteness from the senses itself dictates truth and confidence. Such an epistemology overlaps with faith, faith that grows out of and away from the experiential. Both Method and faith are ways of knowing difficult to attain, and once won they compel the assignment of predetermined value to every lesser thing.

Michael's presentation is variously "methodical" in the special Ramistic meaning of that term. In *Paradise Lost* and the transition of the final books from the prelapsarian to the postlapsarian, Michael functions to establish the universals and the new route of progress and precedence securely for the human race. The universals are the deity, and the route is that of faith. His materials are securely rooted in the chronological and the teleological. He sets forth the sequence of history in progressive temporal order but also establishes clarity and agreement of data within abstract orders of priority and facilitates an understanding of universals and their retention by the memory. The Isis image from *Areopagitica* and the expressed end of education in *Of Education* exactly apply to Michael's procedures and goals in instructing the postlapsarian Adam.

The key to Method must necessarily be the foundations from which one establishes priority, sequence, and precedence. The *Logic* specifies five modes for determining clarity and absoluteness of idea: (1) that of time (old before young); (2) that of nature (cause before effect, genus before species); (3) that of consecutiveness of existing, including precedence in production (parts before wholes, means before end) and precedence in intention (whole before parts, end before means); (4) that of place, including what is nearer the beginning and what excels in dignity; and (5) that of cognition, including (*a*) what is in itself easier to grasp and (*b*) what the perceiver finds easier to grasp (C473–75; Y391). The possibilities as the *Logic* describes them become increasingly complex and compounded as the series proceeds. The final three modes in particular build upon the foundations of the simpler first two. Priority based on cognition is of two sorts. The first is labeled "perfect cognition" and bespeaks ideal reasoners; it assumes as does prelapsarian Invention that things manifest their essential natures and can be immediately so received as well as that generals or universals are more conspicuous than individuals or particulars. The second category of cognition is postlapsarian and takes into account the limitations of fallen perception and the need to repair one's reasoning process. It is later in time and more sensorily based. The former or Natural Method and its attendant perfect cognition are to be preferred and are appropriate for communication with a learned audience. The second or Prudential Method modifies the so-called natural order to accommodate content to the limitations of a more general (fallen) audience.[25]

Priorities based on the formatting modes of time, nature, consecutiveness, and place are inseparable from Michael's presentation of human history and the multiplication of the race. As a whole and within the parts, Michael's tableaux of Book 11 are laid out in a chronological, dichotomized sequence of serialized and overlapping units. At its simplest, the sequence is of the genealogical multiplication of humanity: Adam takes precedence over his sons in time and in nature; he is father/cause to those sons/effects. Michael's methodized racial history builds also upon the Ramistic preference for dichotomies. Adam multiplies into Cain and Abel, though the sons go unnamed in the text. At a further stage "him who slew / His Brother" (11.678–79 and 608–9) multiplies into the race inhabiting "the Tents / Of wickedness" (607–8). Those sons of Cain are dichotomized against the offspring of Adam's other son Seth, those "Just men" who come down from the hills and whose study is "bent / To worship God aright" (575–78). These align with the epithet for Abel, "a Shepherd next / More meek"

(436–37), as their enemies with the epithet for Cain, "A sweaty Reaper" (434). Adam's immediate future will involve tillage and exertion—"In the sweat of thy Face shalt thou eat Bread" (10.205)—and his long-range future will involve Christ as the Good Shepherd as well as the mediary "Shepherd, who first taught the chosen Seed" (1.8). In the dichotomization into Cain and Abel and the later alignments of the offspring of Cain against the offspring of Seth and of the inhabitants of the "Cities of Men" against the Shepherds (11.640, 650), the sequences and priorities of time and nature are moral as well as generational. Similarly, in the categories of Book 12 and the "world restor'd" (3), these generational and moral polarities multiply into the "vicious Race" of Ham, "th'irreverent Son / Of him who built the Ark" (101–4) and the "one peculiar Nation" springing from the faithful Abraham (111–13), in whose seed "all Nations of the Earth / Shall . . . be blessed" (147–48). Within the genus, the species are normally dichotomized into moral oppositions. Michael's emphasis upon moral polarity is designed to make a habit of dichotomy and thus translate Ramistic exercises into piety and righteousness. The pattern is both an internal and an external arrangement and judgment. The perceiver's truth answers to external truth if the reason/the reasoner is sound, and when the Method is soundly, faithfully, applied.

As additional arrays of evidence show, Michael's presentation of humanity proceeds regularly through such patterning and chronological/moral identification. Michael cites Enoch's enemies as "the product / Of those ill-mated Marriages" witnessed earlier "where good with bad were matcht, who of themselves / Abhor to join" and which produced "prodigious Births of body or mind" (11.683–87). Michael cites Noah's contemporaries as

> . . . Those whom last thou saw'st
> In triumph and luxurious wealth. . .
> First seen in acts of prowess eminent
> And great exploits, but of true virtue void. (787–90)

Adam too picks up the practice, relating the military contemporaries of Enoch to "Death's Ministers, not Men, who thus . . . multiply / Ten thousandfold the sin of him who slew / His Brother" (676–79). The chronological and familial identification is sometimes simply offered: Enoch is "hee the sev'nth from thee" (700); Noah is "the Patriarch . . . who scap'd the Flood" (12.117); we and Adam are told of "A Son [of Abraham], and of his Son a Grandchild" (153) and of "the Grandchild with twelve Sons increase" (155) and of "a younger Son" (160) with "his Race / Growing into a Nation" (163–64) and then of "the twelve Tribes" (226) of Israel. Israel is identified as "the third / From *Abraham*, Son of *Isaac*, and from him / His whole descent" (267–69). Sequential patriarchs and sequential shepherds establish patterns of continuity and implication. Kings, judges, and the various implications of *seed* trace the same design. In the further reaches of history, enumeration is set aside on the grounds that "the rest / Were long to tell" (260–61). Eras as well as generations are methodized in the progress from "the world destroy'd" to the "world restor'd" and in "Thus will this latter, as the former World, / Still tend from bad to worse" (105–6), and in the reference to "the World's great period" (467). A geographical expansion progresses from Cain and Abel in a field, to the site of the lazar house, to "a spacious Plain" (11.556) on which the sons of Lamech pursue their activities, to the "wide territory" (638) of Enoch's contemporaries, and to "the face of things" (712) on which Noah gazes. Time precedence gives way to precedence in status or dignity with the Patriarchs and heroes of righteousness and faith. "The Sons of *Abraham's* Loins" expand to "the Sons / Of *Abraham's* Faith wherever through the world" (12.447–49). Such methodized arrays are very much conditioned by Ramistic dogmatics; they facilitate memory storage and thereafter invite the reasoner to give back what he or she has been given.

In their treatment of death, the tableaux of Book 11 follow the guidelines of Ramistic Method more expansively, variously deploying and interweaving all the patterns of priority and precedence set forth in the logic textbook, and especially making available to view priorities based on cognition, both that perfect cognition of what "is easier to grasp . . . in itself because it is before by nature" and that less perfect cognition of what is easier to grasp "because it is later and presented to the senses" (C373–75; Y391). Similarly, the third mode of consecutiveness allows for some of the complexities that underlie Michael's proceedings and especially for the transition between an emphasis on efficient cause and an emphasis on final cause. This mode distinguishes between consecutiveness in production and consecutiveness in intention; in the former the parts precede the whole, the simple the composite, the means the end, but in the latter the whole precedes the parts, the compound the simple, the end the means. As the former evidence showed a progressive array of data from genus to species, so this evidence shows the use of Method to restore the pieces of truth to their proper sequential order. Method fills in the blanks of the model by determining the homogeneousness of the bifurcated species and disposing these toward the left, that is, toward the inclusive generals and universals, and toward the right, that is, toward careful distinctions and refinements of thinking. The process is cumulative and, at least within Book 11, inconclusive, for the serial accumulation regularly calls for revision (or reseeing) of what has preceded as well as reorientation as new distinctions and new truths and priorities are taken into account.

Verbally, *death* provides one of the richest entries into the texture as well as themes and structure of the epic.[26] Death is the penalty posed and imposed for disobedience and is central to the paradoxes illuminated by Michael. From the divine perspective established in the scene in Heaven and offered educationally through Michael's rendering of the new dispensation of Book 12, death is itself dichotomized with life, as body with spirit, nature with grace, and experience with faith within a methodized design whose higher genera can be defined only in terms of the paradoxical Christ and the mysterious divine intention. Within Michael's visions of Book 11, physical life and physical death are our and Adam's chief concern and cognitive starting point. Nature will be transcended by grace increasingly in Michael's prophecy/history, but within Book 11 explication of grace is deliberately postponed. Such postponement reflects the mode of Method that distinguishes between imperfect cognition based on sensory immediacy and limited human capacity and perfect cognition based on absolute priority.

Before Michael's arrival, the epic secures these two extreme views of what death is, one the divine or absolute idea of death and the other Adam's limited and insecure or conjectural opinion about death. On his own in Book 10 Adam speaks often and eloquently of death, but also conjecturally and uncertainly. His questions and guesses set forth an array of views of death, all fallen and despairing and based on nature:

> Why do I overlive,
> Why am I mockt with death, and length'n'd out
> To deathless pain? How gladly would I meet
> Mortality my sentence, and be Earth
> Insensible, how glad would lay me down
> As in my Mother's lap! (773−78)

He fears that he cannot die, that he must "die a living Death" (788), that God will draw out finite to infinite to punish man (801–3) and "extend / His Sentence beyond dust and Nature's Law" (801–5):

> That Death be not one stroke, as I suppos'd,
> Bereaving sense, but endless misery
> From this day onward, which I feel begun
> Both in me, and without me, and so last
> To perpetuity. (809–13)

Because he has not yet been initiated into Christ, the idea that God could "make deathless Death" is to him a strange and impossible contradiction, an "Argument / Of weakness, not of Power" (798–801). He longs for "one thrice acceptable stroke" of Death to end him (854–56). In conversation with Eve, Adam defines death as "a slow-pac't evil, / A long day's dying to augment our pain" (963–64). The uncertainty and repetitiousness of this evidence manifest Adam's state of mind and what is available from the experiential natural world, untouched by and unaided by revelation. Not all of Adam and Eve's prerevelation views are errant: Prayer assures Adam "that the bitterness of death / Is past, and we shall live" (11.157–58) and provides Eve with the awed recognition "That I who first brought Death on all, am grac't / The source of life" (168–69). But even with such capacity the truth and confidence in the truth must be secured for the reasoner. Adam can have only doubt or opinion about death at this point because he lacks a knowledge of its causes. Michael arrives to review and dispose its form, matter, efficient, and especially its end and thus to replace Adam's uncertainty with secured truth.

The ultimate and inclusive meaning of *death* is clarified in conversations between the Son and the Father before Michael's arrival. In Book 10 Death is a kind of ghastly vacuum cleaner to keep pollution in check:

> I call'd and drew them thither
> My Hell-hounds, to lick up the draff and filth
> Which man's polluting Sin with taint hath shed
> On what was pure, till cramm'd and gorg'd, nigh burst
> With suckt and glutted offal, at one sling
> Of thy victorious Arm, well-pleasing Son,
> Both *Sin*, and *Death*, and yawning *Grave* at last
> Through *Chaos* hurl'd, obstruct the mough of Hell
> For ever, and seal up his ravenous Jaws. (629–37)

In Book 11, when the human prayers arrive, the Son mediates reconciliation between man and God and a continuation of human life on earth "till Death . . . To better life shall yield him" (40–42), and the Father emphasizes the remedial and providential nature of death:

> So Death becomes
> His final remedy, and after Life
> Tri'd in sharp tribulation, and refin'd
> By Faith and faithful works, to second Life,
> Wak't in the renovation of the just. (61–65)

In large measure, Michael's mission may be described as aimed at bringing Adam to the understanding of this concept and its implications. It is not, however, sufficient for Michael merely to explain the matter, for as Milton makes clear in the *Logic*, testimony or witness, even when divine, requires translation into the modes of reason:

> And divine testimony affirms or denies that a thing is so and brings about that I believe; it does not prove, it does not teach, it does not cause me to know or understand why things are so, unless it also brings forward reasons. (C283; Y319)

In the final books of *Paradise Lost*, Michael is the mediator of such reason and more largely of reasoning that is also revelation, and Method is the necessary disposition for this information. Michael must take as his instructional starting point Adam's present psychic and informational state, his imperfect cognition, insecure and based on sensory data rather than universal and transcendent principles. Michael's first, unprefaced statement upon his arrival acknowledges that death, though due as their punishment, has been postponed to allow them time to repent and perform compensatory good deeds and proposes that such acts will appease the deity and "Redeem [them] quite from Death's rapacious claim" (11.258). The announcement serves doubly to stabilize Adam's previous conjectures and to provide a foundation for Michael's further revelations through vision and prophecy. Those revelations will culminate in Book 12 in the perfect cognition of Christ's role and the Christian paradoxical translations of language, the Word generally and *life/death* specifically. Perfect cognition will bring Adam to the point of grasping and repeating the divine view of death as "second Life" (11.64).

A quick review of the early evidence, some of it glanced at previously, will establish the materials to be methodized. In the first historical instance of death, Cain's murder of Abel, the text neatly avoids the word *death* itself: Cain smote Abel "with a stone / That beat out life; he fell, and deadly pale / Groan'd out his Soul with gushing blood effus'd" (11.445–47). This is for Adam "some great mischief" (450) and for Michael "the bloody Fact" (457). In response to Adam's troubled queries ("But have I now seen Death?" and "Is this the way / I must return to native dust?" [462–63]), Michael replies by opening up an array of species whose genera will later be supplied:

> Death thou hast seen
> In his first shape on man; but many shapes
> Of Death, and many are the ways that lead
> To his grim Cave, all dismal; yet to sense
> More terrible at th' entrance than within. (466–70)

The suspense of the periphrasis and Michael's introduction of·death's many shapes lead us forward in the array of visions, humanity, history, and their lessons. Michael merely glances without illustration at deaths "By Fire, Flood, Famine," those other horses of the Apocalypse, but he lingers over deaths by intemperance in the lazar house, "wherein were laid / Numbers of all diseas'd, all maladies" (479–80). Within this scene the emphasis shifts away from physical manifestations and toward human attitudes:

> Dire was the tossing, deep the groans, despair
> Tended the sick busiest from Couch to Couch;
> And over them triumphant Death his Dart
> Shook, but delay'd to strike, though oft invok't
> With vows, as thir chief good, and final hope. (489–93)

By contrast with despair, the death of the spirit, physical death becomes potentially affirmative, a deliverance from burdensome mortality. An addendum to this second tableau presents slow-paced death from old age, distinguishing between those "harshly pluckt" (like the diseased, like the young Abel) and those who are ripe and who may "drop / Into thy Mother's lap, or be with ease / Gather'd" (535–37, and cf. 10.778). To the idea of delayed death as to the early murder of Abel, Adam responds by extremes; he is now "bent rather how I may be quit / Fairest and easiest of this cumbrous charge" (11.548–49). Not wanting to live balances Adam's earlier not wanting to die. As the first vision invited a lesson in divine

justice, this one turns toward patience. Michael's formulation looks forward
to further clarification of living and of faith:

> Nor love thy Life, nor hate; but what thou liv'st
> Live well, how long or short permit to Heav'n. (553–54)

The lesson in faith is suspended to invite a later synthesis that will resolve
the dialectic of merely physical life/death, too early/too late. The scene
allows for a crystallization of Adam's errors that they may be left behind,
logically fully known and denied.

This evidence from the opening tableaux invites a recognition of the
Method model on which it is based. In the priority of time, humanity
multiplies; in the priority of nature, the genus death is distributed into its
species. The first shape of death expands to the "many shapes / of Death,"
and in Michael's emphasis the genus physical death becomes dichotomized
into mature death and premature death and into natural and unnatural
death. Unnatural death bifurcates into death by violence and death by
intemperance. The former applies the priorities of time and nature, the
latter of cause and effect, matter and form. The species intemperance is
traced to a proximate cause in "th'inabstinence of *Eve*" (11.476) and to a
more conspicuous efficient cause in the debasement of the divine image and
similitude in man. Adam's redefinition of death as *dissolution* (552) looks
forward chronologically and logically from formal to final causes. Death as
the termination of life widens to include preterminal mortality and spiri-
tual death as well as physical. The despair of the lazar house inhabitants
evokes distinctions between externals and internals and between death to be
avoided and death to be desired. Such death, which is "to sense / More
terrible at th'entrance than within," introduces a larger and more inclusive
distinction of points of view between human and divine. Most prominent of
the characteristic principles of Method in this evidence is the tendency
toward bifurcation; even when the evidence is of "many shapes," the treat-
ment pursues a bipartite pattern. Further, the disposition of Method regu-
larly calls for a pursuit of universals and consequently a frequent revision of
the design and redeployment of the evidence to fit the newly recognized
priorities, bifurcations, and emerging genera. Errors are corrected as one
progresses and achieves new recognition that smaller genera have been ill
disposed or inadequate as the larger, more universal principles emerge.

Such methodical dispositions continue and expand in the remaining
visions Michael presents in Book 11. The discussion of the first scenes

concludes with the advice, "what thou liv'st / Live well," and Adam must next be brought to some securer judgment of *life* to complement his expanding awareness of *death*. The third scene distinguishes between physical life and spiritual life in a more wholesome atmosphere than the lazar house, between the arts that polish life and the practices that can lead to true life. In the third vision, the "fair Atheists" (625), those daughters of Jubal and Tubal-Cain, seduce into marriage the sons of Seth, "the Sons of God" (622), "Just men" whose study was "bent / To worship God aright" (577–78) and who "yield up all thir virtue" (623). Adam at first errs in thinking that "Here Nature seems fulfill'd in all her ends" (602), until Michael teaches him that pleasure and nature no longer have priority as the standard of judgment. Though the evidence has progressed beyond the obvious, Adam must be taught to apprehend the "Tents of various hue" (557) as "the Tents / Of wickedness" (607–8) and taught that the race is Cain's (tracing its causes); that the unacknowledged gifts of artifice and artifact are to be measured and condemned "By wisdom, and superior gifts" of spirit (636); that no matter how rare the arts that polish civilization, if the inventors are Mammon-hearted and "Unmindful of thir Maker" (611) and refuse to acknowledge the gifts and teaching of the divine creative spirit, they promulgate "a world of tears" (627); and that even the most just and sober race of men are vulnerable to degradation, surprise, and, like Adam himself, seduction by "some fair appearing good" (9.354) and betrayal of the image of God in themselves. Adam attempts to attach man's woe to the blamable proximate cause of woman and thus link the data to his edenic past, but Michael is severe in defining the cause as internal, not external, and in drawing the lessons of fortitude and patience. In contrast to the earlier visions, *living* has become a matter of quality, not quantity, and *well* is measured by faith, or mindfulness of the maker, not pleasure, nature, dust. Death in this scene is of the spirit, not the body; the enemy of grace is no longer despair but now emotional and spiritual slackness and hardness of heart. It is easy and "natural" to prefer the comforts and delights of civilization and the bevy of fair women to the horrors of the lazar house and dismay over one's own decay, but that very ease is treacherous, and nature—as the youthful Milton argued in a Prolusion—is subject to decay. The scene is disposed from the same foundations of Method and axioms as the earlier ones. Humanity has multiplied in number and is bifurcated socially, geographically, and morally. General principles are pursued, applied, and left behind in favor of principles with greater clarity and universality and thus greater Ramistic priority. The moral principles like the human generations are aligned with their homogeneous and reciprocal analogues in earlier visions and in Adam's earlier experience. The abruptness of the scene shift after Michael's axiomatic pronouncement on "Man's effeminate slackness" (634) underscores its absoluteness as truth and the unqualified assent such truth must compel immediately from all hearers. The forcefulness of the expression gives it a resonance far beyond its few words and recalls the Ramistic preference for brevity as serviceable to memory.

The fourth and fifth visions of Book 11 expand upon the earlier distinctions. In the lazar house the results of intemperance were reflected in the catalogue of individual struggles with diseased mortality, but in the fifth scene Noah's contemporary society as a whole suffers from the moral and social corruption of intemperance. Similarly, the violent death of Abel and the violent sin of Cain concerned only the individual, but the multiplied violence in the time of Enoch affects a whole society. War and "factious opposition" (664) dominate, in contrast to and as a bifurcation and consequence of the peaceful artful civilization of the third vision. Giants and military prowess pillage the shepherds; carcasses replace cattle in the fields. The warriors are, in Adam's words,

> Death's Ministers, not Men, who thus deal Death
> Inhumanly to men, and multiply
> Ten thousandfold the sin of him who slew
> His Brother. (676–79)

Michael's epithet is comparable and reinforcing, "Destroyers . . . and Plagues of men" (697). Adam draws the generational design and tightens the sequential structure in a methodical way. Physical violence, now vastly multiplied, is again the mode of death as the population grows beyond Adam's immediate family. The agency of death is now clearly embodied within humanity itself and its institutions and is no longer an external abstract character or principle. In exploring the methodized pattern, Michael supplies the comfort of a miraculous alternative to death in Enoch, whom "a Cloud descending snatch'd . . . thence" (670). Michael's explanation illuminates the bifurcation:

> Him the most High
> Rapt in a balmy Cloud with winged Steeds
> Did, as thou saw'st, receive, to walk with God

> High in Salvation and the Climes of bliss,
>
> Exempt from Death; to show thee what reward
>
> Awaits the good, the rest what punishment. (705 – 10)

The final phrases here show Michael following up on an expansion of a lesson left hanging in the Abel tableau. This unique exception to *death* and mortal norms calls for a revision of the previous methodizing of death and placement of experience. A distinction is here drawn that looks to a more inclusive general principle: Physical death is now dichotomized with exemption from physical death; spiritual life is distinguished more securely from physical life, and a transcendent alternative and divine power are affirmed. Earlier the universal principle was "all die," but now that is distributed into "some die" and "some like Enoch are exempt from death."

The fifth scene culminates in a further explication of the design of death/life/exemption. Now we find that "some who are exempt from death are made the source of new life, world, and generation." In the peacetime setting of the fifth vision as in the homogeneous wartime setting of the fourth vision, the opposition continues between general humanity and the exceptional man, the Enoch and the Noah. The warring urban men and the self-indulgent or intemperate peaceful men descend in a chain from the murderous Cain through the inhabitants of the tents of wickedness, as Abel's and Seth's kind, the righteous, multiply through the Sons of God in scene 3 to the victimized shepherds and the wise and just Enoch of scene 4 and the reverend sire Noah and his sons in scene 5. The moral polarities reduce to the same pattern in peace and war, in families as in politics and society. That pattern is both a Ramistic dichotomy and a lesson in the limits of experiential process and history. As the repetitions of the pattern accumulate, they testify to the universals of the pattern but also highlight the exceptions. As with Enoch there is again unique divine intervention, but Noah's exemption from death shows God's effort to maintain rightly directed life on earth. Instead of eliminating the righteous Enoch from mortal context, the flood eliminates the corrupt context and establishes a fresh basis for earthly and moral life. The virtuous Noah in his ark "swum / Uplifted" (11.745 – 46), elevated above the mortal "Depopulation" (756). The doubleness of the results of the flood, destruction and restoration, is also represented in the doubling of visions and conversational commentaries in the fifth scene. This duplex structure marks the transition from negative to positive that will emerge more largely in the transition between Books 11

and 12, and this doubleness sets in motion a yet larger and more in-
conclusive dichotomization or methodizing of biblical history and of
Michael's instruction. The first visual unit of the Noah scene looks as usual
backward to the genealogical relationship to Adam and thus the past gener-
ally; the second visual unit looks forward and is implicit with promise,
including those promises written in the cosmos and henceforward available
to human memory, the promise of a new covenant, matters that Michael
will explicate more fully in Book 12 and the basis of his lessons in revelation
that transcends reason.

In terms of the *Logic*, the transition between Books 11 and 12 may be
described as a transition within final cause itself, a shift from end-of-which
to end-for-which (C69; Y237–38), the movement toward recognition of
the perfection rather than the conclusion of the thing. This distinction
roughly encapsulates the attitudes taken toward death in the two final books
of *Paradise Lost*. Michael's Book 12 instruction in the meanings of *life* and
death shifts from visual to abstract, from temporal to eternal, from nature to
grace. Death becomes triumph not defeat, beginning not end, and indeed
not even death but "second Life." An examination of Michael's presentation
of death in Book 12 provides some additional insights into structural,
artistic, and thematic designs. It is true that the rendering of Christian
paradox and mystery transcends the merely logical and in important ways
leaves Ramus behind, but it is also true that the Ramistic foundations and
philosophy make such transcendence not only possible but preferred.

Death is barely mentioned in Book 12 until Michael's explication of
Christ's defeat of the serpent, but in the hundred lines of this conversation it
is amply arrayed to arrive at a solid conclusion and guidelines for Adam's and
humanity's futures. In the discourse following the account of Christ's birth,
death is opened up to a nonliteral review and to the paradox of Christ's
transformation of the bases of human life: "nail'd to the Cross . . . But to
the Cross he nails thy Enemies" (413, 415). Experientially viewed, Christ
will undergo "a reproachful life and cursed death" (406), "to death con-
demn'd / A shameful and accurst" (412–13). He is "slain for bringing Life"
(414), for the attempt to bring life. With the exercise of faith (specified in
line 409), such death becomes a proclamation of "Life to all who shall
believe / In his redemption" (407–8):

> . . . so he dies,
> But soon revives, Death over him no power

Shall long usurp; ere the third dawning light
Return, the Stars of Morn shall see him rise
Out of his grave, fresh as the dawning light,
Thy ransom paid, which Man from death redeems,
His death for Man, as many as offer'd Life
Neglect not, and the benefit embrace
By Faith not void of works: this God-like act
Annuls thy doom, the death thou should'st have di'd,
In sin for ever lost from life; this act
Shall bruise the head of *Satan*, crush his strength
Defeating Sin and Death, his two main arms,
And fix far deeper in his head thir stings
Than temporal death shall bruise the Victor's heel,
Or theirs whom he redeems, a death like sleep,
A gentle wafting to immortal Life. (419–35)

Faith is again specified as the key (427). Repeatedly *death* and related terms
are gracefully balanced against *life* and related terms. The balance expands
and reverses the meaning of both. "The Victor's heel, / Or theirs whom he
redeems" leads toward the generalizing of the Christic energy to all men,
and similarly baptism washes men "from guilt of sin to Life" and prepares
them, "if so befall, / For death, like that which the redeemer di'd"
(443–45). "Third dawning light"—a fact—balances with "fresh . . .
dawning light"—a simile that focuses the sun/light imagery from the
preceding range of the poem. The balance of *death/life* diction culminates in
the distinction between "temporal death" and death as a transition from one
mode of lesser being to another mode of higher being. This transition recalls
Adam's initiation into life, "As new wak't from soundest sleep" (8.253), the
"gentle sleep" (287) that admitted Adam's first interview with deity and
Adam's translation from lower earth to Eden where, as Adam says, "I wak'd,
and found / Before mine Eyes all real, as the dream / Had lively shadow'd"
(309–11), and the sleep whose issue was Eve (457 ff.). All such sleeps for
Adam have been gentle waftings, and always he wakes to increased delights.
The culminating reference to death in *Paradise Lost* describes it as "the Gate
of Life" to the faithful (12.571). Christ's ahistorical defeat of Sin and Death
is thenceforth a compelling priority of individual histories until the bliss of
the New Jerusalem, which is the final cause of death, the end-of-which and
the end-for-which.

In sum, the range of evidence on *death* throughout Michael's Books 11 and 12 brings Adam to the ultimate comprehension of death shared by the Father and Son but unavailable to humanity before Michael's methodical and paradoxical initiation of Adam's reason and faith. The methodized design builds from simple data, through an extended series of bifurcations, toward increasing conspicuousness of principles and toward the reasoner's increasing security in the truth. As vertical hierarchies govern Raphael's reasoning and content, so such horizontal Method governs Michael's.

One final point must be made, and it leads directly into the subject matter of the following chapter: that is, that Ramistic logic texts, and Milton's is no exception, conclude with sections of praxis. Three matters were essential in the traditional study of logic: natural ability, knowledge of theory, and practice. And practice, as Donald Leman Clark describes the normal contemporary school curriculum, took two forms: analysis and genesis. Analysis is the exploration of written works, and genesis is imitation or the production of new disputations. In the tradition the former generally accompanied Invention and the latter Disposition. Ramistic interpretational praxis, as Ong presents it, advises thus:

> When you have cut out from the parts of the continuous discourse the many syllogisms therein [after having found them, for they are often concealed], take away all the amplifications, and, after making brief headings to note the arguments used, form into one syllogism the sum total of the discourse, this sum total being ordinarily self-evident, although it may be swelled to undue proportions by accumulations of ornaments.[27]

Ramus's metaphor for analysis is "unweaving." This passage summarizes many points raised in the preceding discussion; it also looks forward to several principles of postlapsarian stylistics. In Milton's epic, to some extent both Raphael and Michael lead their pupils toward imitation of themselves as masters and to some extent toward more creative and analytical activities, but analysis of texts is the special province of Michael's instruction, and in particular he is concerned to present both biblical texts and a procedure for reading such texts along the lines defined by Renaissance humanism and by Reformation theology.

4 · *Lapsarian Poetics*

> What Milton means by revelation is a consolidated, coherent,
> encyclopaedic view of human life which defines, among other things, the
> function of poetry. Every act of the free intelligence, including
> the poetic intelligence, is an attempt to return to Eden, a world in
> the human form of a garden, where we may wander as we please
> but cannot lose our way.
>
> NORTHROP FRYE, *Return of Eden*

> The study of Scripture was for Milton the staff of life, not an idle occupation of
> children gathering pebbles by the seashore (cf. *PR* 4.330). Everything
> important here and hereafter, he thought, depended upon certain
> "motions" of consciousness in response to Holy Writ, and upon the permanent
> acquisition of a "literary" cast of mind. As in New Criticism, the
> relation between text and reader was held to be inviolable; one was to puzzle
> and search out meaning without the intervention of any "arbiters," save the Spirit
> (*CD*, p. 124). Adam, with his absolutely "virgin mind," stands as the
> prototype of the evangelical Christian who studies Scriptures
> in all "newness of life."
>
> GEORGIA B. CHRISTOPHER, *Milton and the Science of the Saints*

HE POETICS of Raphael and Michael, by which I mean the ways in which they characteristically address themselves to their content and to their pupil and the ways in which they normally express themselves in fulfilling their missions, may be distinguished in lapsarian terms. Raphael's expressional norm of analogy and Michael's of typology rest upon theoretical foundations in contrasting kinds of allegory and accommodation. Several theoretical principles warrant preliminary review. Raphael supplies Adam with what we may call a creative poetic as Michael offers a critical poetic. The prelapsarian angel is himself something

of a poet, as the postlapsarian angel is something of a literary critic. These roles and intentions coincide with the kinds of lapsarian characteristics we have noted earlier, especially Raphael's Hellenism and Michael's Christianity, even his quite specific Reformationist Protestantism or Puritanism with its characteristic emphasis on the individual's interpretative processing of the Word. Raphael regularly practices a metaphorical mode of expression as Michael practices a Calvin-based metonymy.[1] The Platonic Raphael aligns also with the open hand of rhetoric, and the Aristotelian Michael with the closed fist of logic. For Michael rhetoric is the art of persuasion, not, as it is for Raphael, the art of adornment of speech. Insofar as Michael practices secular oratory, as opposed to the art of preaching, it is deliberative oratory, not Raphael's epideictic oratory, the art of praise.

At the outset of *Protestant Poetics and the Seventeenth-Century Lyric*, Barbara K. Lewalski distinguishes two Renaissance poetics that align with and expand our categories. The first

> presents the poet as maker of fictions which allegorically conceal and reveal profoundest philosophical truths; or as the inspired shaper of myths and symbols which shadow forth cosmic truth and divine revelation; or, in Sidney's terms, as the creator of a golden world which embodies and mediates a truer vision of the real than can nature's brazen world.

The second or biblical poetics "proposes instead a direct recourse to the Bible as repository of truth." It is marked indeed by what Lewalski judges "an overwhelming [Reformationist] emphasis on the written word as embodiment of divine truth." In this second tradition "the speaker calls upon biblical models and biblical poetic resources . . . and associates himself straightforwardly with the Psalmist in heartfelt and uncontrived (plain) utterance." The second poetics may underlie either private, devotional, generally lyric expressions or public prophetic ones.[2]

A series of key words will clarify some lapsarian stylistic differences. In Milton's prelapsarian garden God is called "Presence Divine" (8.314), but in the postlapsarian garden we find only "track Divine" (11.354). From Raphael Adam learns that "In contemplation of created *things* / By steps [he] may ascend to God" (5.511–12; emphasis mine); Prolusion 7 speaks too of "the contemplative way which leads to all that is supremely desirable" (Hughes, p. 623). Things here are the medium through which the body works up to spirit (5.478). Comparably, Michael teaches Adam to progress from "Flesh to Spirit" not through the medium of things but through the discipline of "shadowy Types" (12.302–3), through following the "track Divine."

Contrasting uses of the word *shadow* by the two angels provide a miniature of the larger lapsarian contrast in poetics. Soon after his arrival, Raphael posits the proposition that earth may be "but the shadow of Heav'n" and that "things therein [may be] / Each to other like, more than on Earth is thought" (5.574–76). This is a recasting of Adam's phrasing in the morning hymn of praise, that the deity is "To us invisible or dimly seen / In these [his] lowest works" (157–58). As Balachandra Rajan says,

> There is a strain in our imagination which takes the transcendent to lie inviolably beyond the reach of human sense, known by its unlikeness rather than its likeness to the ordinary world of our perceiving. The shadow is not an intimation but a deformity. . . . We know the invisible only as it chooses to manifest itself.

Michael too uses the term *shadow* in a definitive way, when he speaks of the "types / And shadows, of that destin'd Seed" (12.232–33) and of the discipline that moves

> From shadowy Types to Truth, from Flesh to Spirit,
> From imposition of strict Laws, to free
> Acceptance of large Grace, from servile fear
> To filial, works of Law to works of Faith. (302–6)

Noting the echo of Raphael's phrases in the first line cited here, Rajan again comments that for the postlapsarian Michael and the promises he mediates, "the shadow is a means of finding the light, not a betrayal of the light's nature. We move forward step by step in the continuities of self-renewal as we might have done in a better world where perfecting rather than renewing could be seen as the objective."[3] Michael's *shadow*, that is, foreshadowing, signifies the validity not of hierarchy but of history and the dynamic drama of salvation. William G. Madsen has discussed the two angels' uses of the term *shadow* against the background of conflicting traditions:

> In Platonic and Neoplatonic thought man's nature is defined by the rational categories of Being and Becoming, the intelligible and the sensible; his immersion in the meaningless cycle of time is a misfortune, and the duty of man is to become a philosopher and thereby escape from the world. In Christian thought man is defined primarily by moral categories, and the

Platonic distinction between the intelligible and the sensible is replaced by
the Christian distinction between the Creator and His Creation; man's im-
mersion in time is the condition of his salvation, and the duty of man is to
become a saint and thereby redeem the world.[4]

As in a religious context *shadow* normally signifies *type*, so in a Renais-
sance literary context *shadow* often points to allegory or symbol. Don
Cameron Allen has described *Paradise Lost* as in part "an allegory about
allegory."

> In general [says Allen] Milton probably defined allegory as a downward
> descent of knowledge, a revealing of suprarational information that enabled
> the humble learner to ascend. . . . For [Milton], allegory is the only means
> of communication between a superior mind aware of grand principles, such
> as the enduring war between Good and Evil, and a lesser mind incapable of
> higher mathematics. It is essentially a form of revelation, or, as Vaughan
> would put it, "a candle tin'd at the Sun."[5]

Specifically, two traditions of allegory in the Renaissance underlie the
lapsarian contrasting poetics in *Paradise Lost*. The two develop Lewalski's
two Renaissance poetics as well as Dante's distinction in the *Convivio* be-
tween the allegory of poets and the allegory of theologians, between inter-
preting and applying an acknowledged fiction ("thematic analysis" in our
terms) and divinely inspired history whose full import is only gradually
revealed.[6] On the one hand, allegory descends from the rhetorical tradition
and draws its theory from classical and Neoplatonic sources and goals.
Michael Murrin has traced this strain in *The Veil of Allegory*, finding Renais-
sance rhetorical allegory "an oral art in which the poet expresses a truth he
has received in contemplation . . . through the medium of tropological
figures." The poet unifies fact and moral value through myth in order to
induce a conversion and a new kind of sensibility in his auditors. Because
man's nature unites the visible and the invisible, its proper expression is in
allegory, a term that becomes equated with poetry itself.[7] This view of
allegory nicely articulates Raphael's role and relationship to his prelapsarian
pupil. *Veil* in this tradition is what one passes beyond in order to be initiated
into divine mysteries.

In its second mode, allegory derives also from the Patristic tradition
rooted in the Pauline epistles. This early Christian allegory had as its
medieval issue the notorious four levels: the literal, the allegorical (*cre-*

denda), the tropological (*agenda*), and the anagogical (*speranda*), drawing out analogous interpretations in relation to the society, the individual, and the afterlife, or in relation to the past, the present, and the future. In this tradition as in the former *veil* is a ruling metaphor, but here *veil* explicitly echoes 2 Cor. 3:13–16 with its distinction between the Old Dispensation where "the vail is upon their heart" (15) and the New Dispensation under which, as Paul says, "we all, with open face beholding as in a glass the glory of the Lord, are changed into the same image from glory to glory even as by the spirit of the Lord" (18). In Exod. 34:33 Moses vailed himself to deliver God's word from Mount Sinai, but now the "Vail is done away in Christ" (2 Cor. 3:14). *Veil* in this tradition is both a matter of initiation as in Heb. 6:19–20 and the beholder's subjective obstacle rather than an objective signifier of upward passage.

Madsen has distinguished between two modes of accommodation that illuminate our lapsarian contrast. In one, accommodation is a mode of expression, and in the other it is a mode of interpreting the Bible for homiletic purposes. In the former tradition, "in the humanist and Neo-platonist theory," "divine poets like Moses and Orpheus veil arcane truths in poetic allegories because they cannot be communicated in any other way or because they would otherwise be profaned by the vulgar," but in the other, the Protestant tradition, the "veils and shadows of the Old Testament" are contrasted with "the full light of the New."

> Before the advent of Christ God did indeed veil His saving truths in shadowy types and ceremonies, but for Christians, who live in the full light of the Gospel, the purpose of types is not to veil but to illuminate and make "lively" the truths that are already known.[8]

In their instruction of Adam, both Raphael and Michael practice theological accommodation. Put briefly, theological accommodation, which has been called "one of the great commonplaces of the Renaissance,"[9] is the mediated vocabulary through which human beings, because of their "imperfect comprehension," can be said to "know" the transcendent God. Milton expands upon this basic definition of his in *Christian Doctrine* 1.2:

> Our safest way is to form in our minds such a conception of God, as shall correspond with his own delineation and representation of himself in the sacred writings. For granting that both in the literal and figurative descriptions of God, he is exhibited not as he really is, but in such a manner as may

be within the scope of our comprehension, yet we ought to entertain such a conception of him, as he, in condescending to accommodate himself to our capacities, has shewn that he desires we should conceive. For it is on this very account that he has lowered himself to our level, lest in our flights above the reach of human understanding, and beyond the written word of Scripture, we should be tempted to indulge in vague cogitations and subtleties. (CE 14 : 31 – 33) [10]

Within the basic definition of accommodation must be distinguished two complementary thrusts, the one bringing truth down to earth, the other gradually raising the earthly mind to Heaven. The first of these Geoffrey Hartman calls "authoritarian and condescending," the second "initiatory." [11] H. R. MacCallum develops a similar distinction between what he calls "social accommodation" and "epistemological accommodation." Social accommodation stresses condescension to an audience's limitations and has the effect, MacCallum suggests, of inducing a student to read between the lines, "to penetrate behind the veils of imagery to the hidden meaning." Epistemological accommodation, on the other hand, defines the limits of human comprehension; it calls for a resting in the words and images of Scripture, not seeking to penetrate behind them. [12] Accommodation is at once a closing and an opening, a builder of confidence and a provocation of inquiry. It is a process of teaching employed by the Scriptures and is of course every parent's and teacher's strategy for communicating with those whose information and capacities are less than or lower than her or his own.

Raphael's teaching is aimed precisely at inducing Adam to read between the lines and to penetrate behind the veils of, for example, vegetation or solar phenomena to apprehend their full divine meaning. Michael, on the other hand, labors to provide Adam with the full light of the Gospel, to induce him to find enlightenment and fulfillment in the terms of the Scriptures themselves. This is a lively exercise, however, rather than a reductionist literalism. Because the written records are "not but by the Spirit understood"(12.513–14), the Protestant reader's life-giving spirit transcends the letter that killeth (2 Cor. 3 : 6). Further, in Milton's view such a reader has access to the superior scripture that is internal, the superior and peculiar possession of each believer written on the heart, as in 2 Cor. 3 : 3 where "the epistle of Christ ministered by us [is] written not with ink, but with the Spirit of the living God; not in tables of stone, but in fleshy tables of the heart."

The nature of the problem that accommodation solves may be seen in the introductory lines of Book 3 of *Paradise Lost*: on the one hand the invocation to elusively fluid heavenly light, and on the other acknowledgment of the poet / narrator's blindness. Book 3 plays variously with the relationship between essence and form and between the divine and the human. In the opening lines of "the great encomium of light" may be found, as Don Cameron Allen outlines it, a "Threefold distinction between essential light, material light, and the Divine Light by which inwardly the poet sees." Light is "a graduated divine impulsion." [13] God's "unapproached Light" here hymned contrasts with the poet's blindness. According to Anne Davidson Ferry's study of "the blind bard," the speaker in these early lines of Book 3 is both a "limited human creature whose vision was dimmed by the Fall" and an "inspired seer whose divine illumination transcends the limits of mortal vision." [14] It is important to recognize also that the narrator's physical blindness includes and generalizes the reader's varying and definitively human limitations in receiving light unless divinely aided. "Dark with excessive bright" describes human perception as well as the divine mind and formlessness, and the poet's "ever during dark" becomes the reader's participation in the poem if she or he remains reluctant or rebellious in the presence of the emotionless clarity of God's theologizing. In sum, the opening section of Book 3 presents divine and human extremes that require the mediation that accommodation can provide.

When the mode of Book 3 shifts from hymn or invocation or biographical digression to narrative, light characterizes the uncharacterizable God and his filial image. Here the role of the Son is fundamentally designed to enact accommodation and to make the inaccessible paternal deity accessible to the limited comprehension of humanity. Recalling the logical categories discussed earlier, God in *Paradise Lost* is the beginning and end of creation, the idea from which it springs and the perfection toward which it tends. As the efficient cause of the universe, the deity manifests himself through form and matter; his final cause will be attained when the realms of form and matter are transcendently redefined as "New Heav'n and Earth" (3.335) where "God shall be All in All" (341). The divine purpose is twofold: First, it is creative purpose, to "diffuse / His good to Worlds and Ages infinite" (7.190–91); and second, it is redemptive purpose, to establish "his great Vice-gerent" Son under whose reign the multitudinous created universe will "abide / United as one individual Soul / For ever happy" (5.609–11). As Abdiel describes this second purpose, God's New Law or New Dispensation is designed "to exalt / Our happy state under one Head more near / United" (829–31). Sequentially, the infinite and formless unified deity will proceed into form and matter, into number and diversity, and from thence progress to a new unity that is transcendent rather than increate. Further, the double-natured Son is by merit and by birthright the Son of God; he is the agency both through which God enters into form and matter and through which these are transcended in the reunion with God. By birthright he fulfills God's creative purpose mediating downward from God to angels or men; by merit he will fulfill God's redemptive or transcendent purpose mediating upward from men or angels to God.[15] These roles coincide with the double thrust of accommodation.

These theological mysteries are variously enacted throughout the epic, with God's creative purpose dominant before the fall and God's redemptive purpose dominant after the fall. The governing proposition of both purposes is this: The accessible Son gives form to the inaccessible Father; Christ makes the invisible visible; the Word makes the inexpressible articulate. Boyd Berry's consideration of the Puritan context of *Paradise Lost* puts the point in terms of grammar: The Son's characteristic use of *me* rather than *I* "places him as syntactic object within a larger, circumscribing framework—paternal control." Berry's chapter title makes a similar point: "The Son: The Hero as Expressive Definition."[16] The angelic hymn in Book 3 establishes the relationship of Father and Son and celebrates the Son's claims of birthright and assumption of merit:

> Thee Father first they sung Omnipotent,
> Immutable, Immortal, Infinite,
> Eternal King; thee Author of all being,
> Fountain of Light, thyself invisible
> Amidst the glorious brightness where thou sit'st
> Thron'd inaccessible, but when thou shad'st
> The full blaze of thy beams, and through a cloud
> Drawn round about thee like a radiant Shrine,
> Dark with excessive bright thy skirts appear,
> Yet dazzle Heav'n, that brightest Seraphim
> Approach not, but with both wings veil thir eyes.
> Thee next they sang of all Creation first,
> Begotten Son, Divine Similitude,
> In whose conspicuous count'nance, without cloud
> Made visible, th'Almighty Father shines,

Whom else no Creature can behold; on thee
Impresst th'effulgence of his Glory abides,
Transfus'd on thee his ample Spirit rests. (372–89)

Milton's God has what might be called a problem of accessibility, or ap-
proachability, which the Son solves. Logically, as God is cause, the Son is
and brings about the effects of that cause. "God is Light," but that light is
eternal and "unapproached" (3–6). When this "Fountain of Light" exerts
himself to become available, even "brightest Seraphim" are prevented from
approaching through the excess of dazzling, blazing brightness. In biblical
terms the Son is "the light *of the World*" (John 8:12; emphasis mine); in epic
terms, he is the "Divine Similitude" who makes the Father conspicuous and
available. Biblically, "no man cometh unto the Father, but by me" (John
14:6); epically, the Son mediates the Father "Whom else no Creature can
behold." The accommodating Son both gives form to God and provides self-
transcendent access to God.

Milton's account of the creation of light on day 1 and of the creation of the
sun on day 4 in the hexaemeral Book 7 presents an analogue of the relation-
ship of Father and Son in Book 3. Both the Son and the sun are divine
similitudes; the sun from the physical creation is analogous to the Son in the
logical and theological framework of the epic. Among other points of
likeness, the sun is the natural fact and light source which most com-
pellingly represents divine light to human eyes, and the sun's light is both
sufficiently accessible and sufficiently inaccessible to mediate the divine
principles. Within Book 7 the sun is "of celestial Bodies first," "A mighty
Sphere . . . of Ethereal Mould," and "Regent of Day" (354, 355–56, 371).
The sun and other heavenly bodies created on the fourth day give temporal
and spatial form to the illimitable and eternal light, the "quintessence
pure" (244), of God's fiat on the first day. In these bodies the essential light
becomes formed for human perceivability and benefit. Within the confines
of Genesis 1 and of a realized cosmos, we find here enacted the theological
and poetic structure that readers of *Paradise Lost* meet with in Book 3: that
pattern by which the invisible Godhead, that inaccessible "bright essence
increate" (3.6), is "made visible" in the "Divine Similitude" of the "Begot-
ten Son." With the other heavenly bodies, the sun's "Office in the Firmament
of Heav'n" (7.344) is twofold: "To give Light on the Earth" but also to give
pattern to time, to serve "for Signs, / For Seasons, and for Days, and circling
Years" (345, 341–42).[17] In their first office, as it is the sun's function to give
light to earth, it is Christ's function to give light and enlightenment to

earth's inhabitants, and the Christic enlightenment, like the solar and like the double movement of accommodation, is both a downward donation and an upward inspiration and guide. In their second office also, like the sun, Christ functions to give pattern to time. With the Incarnation so eloquently celebrated in Milton's *Nativity* ode, time becomes structured and purposeful; with Christ's assumption of his redemptive role, history begins its progress toward the transcendence of the New Jerusalem when "God shall be All in All."

In fulfilling his divine assignment, to bring on such discourse as will advise Adam of his happy state (5.233–34), Raphael undertakes a "process of speech" that allows him to tell of divine matters in such a way "as earthly notion can receive" (7.178–79) and be thereby fortified by full understanding. His job is to "measur[e] things in Heav'n by things on Earth" (6.893) and thus "lift / Human imagination to [the] highth / Of Godlike Power" (299–301). This we have seen Raphael achieving through the large figures examined in the evidence of previous chapters. By early establishing the fact and pattern of a hierarchical universe, Raphael positions himself to explicate the interlocking levels of an allegorical continuum, à Platonic ladder founded upon the corporeal, conspicuous, and material and reaching upward to the incorporeal, visionary, and spiritual. He aligns earth with its inhabitants, the heavens with the divine, and earth and Heaven with each other. Parallel kinds explicate each other; thus, digestion, vegetation, faculty psychology, and cosmology all modulate into one another and resonate the same aspiration that combines knowledge and wonder. Thus, the hexaemeral creation of earth is underscored by a personification and realization of the image of the Great Mother Earth, stars are sown like seeds across the sky, animals arise from the ground like branching plants, fish rove through pastoral groves, plants execute animal motions, all to manifest the wondrous unity of the divine creation, and thus Raphael can speak simultaneously of sexual distinction and the relative lights of the sun and moon. In such large figures and, as we shall see in a moment, in certain patterns of smaller, less noticeable examples, Raphael employs an artfulness to which we can attach a variety of names: It is a matter of comparisons, of metaphors, of analogies, of Platonic graduated resonating emanations. Such terms as *analogy, similitude, emblem, hieroglyph, figure, image, metaphor,* and *shadow* were used interchangeably in the seventeenth century to characterize the relationship between the physical and spiritual worlds and to reflect Milton's contemporaries' "emblematic habit of mind."[18] Even as a merely grammatical matter, comparatives mediate between the basic term and the superlative, as between Raphael's earth and Heaven.

Within *Paradise Lost* itself, at several points Raphael articulates the prelapsarian poetic, a theory of comparison that governs much of his process of speech. His challenge is to find a way to relate the invisible and immaterial angelic activities and the secrets of another world to human sense without compromising the integrity of that spiritual realm and without betraying Adam into excesses of complacency and either pride or humility. The solution—in lines frequently cited as Milton's own modus operandi—is to draw comparisons, true or feigned, between the spiritual and the earthly, to make truth plain, to produce confidence, and to equalize the knowledge of speaker and listener. These descriptive phrases are, as we shall see in a moment, drawn from the definition and rules of comparisons in Milton's *Art of Logic*. Within the epic poem, however, Raphael's theory of analogy reads thus:

> High matter thou injoin'st me, O prime of men,
> Sad task and hard, for how shall I relate
> To human sense th'invisible exploits
> Of warring Spirits; how without remorse
> The ruin of so many glorious once
> And perfet while they stood; how last unfold
> The secrets of another World, perhaps
> Not lawful to reveal? yet for thy good
> This is dispens't, and what surmounts the reach
> Of human sense, I shall delineate so,
> By lik'ning spiritual to corporal forms,
> As may express them best, though what if Earth
> Be but the shadow of Heav'n, and things therein
> Each to other like, more than on Earth is thought? (5.563–76)[19]

In supplementary formulations Raphael says:

> to recount Almighty works
> What words or tongue of Seraph can suffice,
> Or heart of man suffice to comprehend? (7.112–14)

And again:

> Immediate are the Acts of God, more swift
> Than time or motion, but to human ears

Cannot without process of speech be told,
So told as earthly notion can receive. (176–79)

Such accommodated communication is based on the assumptions of basic
and available likeness and of heavenly things Platonically shadowed on earth
in ways that humans can apprehend but not exhaust. Raphael's accommoda-
tion through such analogies is a matter of setting forth great things by small
(6.310–11), of "measuring things in Heav'n by things on Earth" (893), of
likening the heavenly "unspeakable" (297) and "unimaginable" (7.54) to
things "on Earth conspicuous" (6.299).

In the prospect of translating spirit to things, heaven to earth, Raphael
here outlines his metaphoric mode of speech, but in an ensuing question—
"what if Earth / Be but the shadow of Heav'n?"—he also opens the possibil-
ity of expanding the human capacity to receive and while receiving tran-
scend the limits of the information imparted. Raphael thus proffers the
double pattern of accommodation that is necessarily a matter of the pupil's
aspiration beyond epistemological limits and the teacher's condescension.
Indeed, the word Adam uses to describe Raphael's conversation is "conde-
scension" (8.649), and again Adam expresses gratitude for Raphael's
"friendly condescension" in relating "Things else by me unsearchable, now
heard / With wonder, but delight, and, as is due, / With glory attributed to
the high / Creator" (9–13). Likeness is never identity, and in the com-
monplace warning, "Every likeness hobbles," but the goals and processes of
relating, likening, lifting, measuring, and thus revealing are poetic, open-
ing, imaginatively exercising. Before proceeding to the indirectness of
narrative instruction, Raphael makes his metaphoric procedure quite clear
and directs Adam to participate in imaginative reading and meditation on
what is to follow so that Adam may in contemplation of created things
ascend to God.

Raphael's smaller analogues accumulate into patterns within the larger
outlines of the major narratives to serve his largest goal of establishing
clearly the relationship between God and man. Raphael draws a number of
incidental parallels between the heavenly and the knowns of Adam's world
and accumulating experience by breaking his narrative with parenthetical
alignments as in these examples:

when on a day
(For Time, though in Eternity, appli'd

> To motion, measures all things durable
> By present, past, and future) on such day
> As Heav'n's great Year brings forth. (5.579–83)

Or, again, in

> Ev'ning now approach'd
> (For wee have also our Ev'ning and our Morn,
> Wee ours for change delectable, not need). (627–29)

Or, again, in

> Grateful Twilight (for Night comes not there
> In darker veil). (645–46)

The evidence is sometimes spatial rather than temporal as in

> Wide over all the Plain, and wider far
> Than all this globose Earth in Plain outspread,
> (Such are the courts of God). (648–50)

Or, again, in

> Regions to which
> All thy Dominion, *Adam*, is no more
> Than what this Garden is to all the Earth,
> And all the Sea, from one entire globose
> Stretcht into Longitude. (750–54)

The alignments are sometimes vegetative, as in line 635, and sometimes cosmic, as in comparing angels' "Mystical dance" with Adam's view of "yonder starry Sphere / Of Planets and of fixt in all her Wheels" (620–21). Within the story of creation, Raphael several times explicitly focuses the materials of his lectures on Adam's experience: in likening the marshaling of earthly terrain with the marshaling of armies Adam has heard of in Book 6 (7.295–97), in the new perspective on Adam's creation out of dust and divine image (524 ff.), in recalling the seventh day's heavenly harmony Adam heard (561), and in likening the road "To God's Eternal house" to Adam's Milky Way (576–81). In Book 6, too, Raphael regularly draws particular analogues between Adam's experience of earth and the heavenly phenomena that surmount the reach of human sense. These analogues serve as an equivalent of epic similes in the larger epic. In describing the commotion of battle, specifically the duel between Satan and Michael, Raphael says the process is

> such as, to set forth
> Great things by small, if Nature's concord broke,
> Among the Constellations war were sprung,
> Two Planets rushing from aspect malign
> Of fiercest opposition in mid Sky,
> Should combat, and thir jarring Spheres confound.
> (310–15)

On the first day of battle the divine army is likened to the "orderly array" of birds summoned to receive their names from Adam (73–76), and Satan's recoil is likened to an earthquake (195–98). On the second day Raphael notes a likeness between the entrails of earth and Heaven (516–17) and between heavenly and earthly hills and dales (640–41). On the third day Raphael reaches the limit of comparison, however, for there is no edenic analogue for the dawning of "the Chariot of Paternal Deity" (750) when Christ rises "from the right hand of Glory" (746–47). To the prelapsarian Adam this event is indescribable—"instinct with Spirit" (752), "wondrous" (754), "radiant" and "divinely wrought" (761). Raphael is apologetically parenthetical about the number of attendants (769) when he must descend again from the mystical into experiential fact. Finally, the creation that Raphael will explicate in Book 7 is anticipated in the description of Christ's charioted arrival:

> At his command the uprooted Hills retir'd
> Each to his place, they heard his voice and went
> Obsequious, Heav'n his wonted face renew'd,
> And with fresh Flow'rets Hill and Valley smil'd.
> (6.781–84)

The lines return Adam to the Eden he inhabits, but the passage reaches beyond its context into Books 7 and 4 and 5 to remind readers variously of the fall and unfallenness.

The analogues teach lessons in transcendence, in wonder, and in the limits of human rationality. Such gestures take away even as they give; they accommodate the instruction to Adam's givens and enhance his faith. They serve also such orational goals as change of pace, immediacy of application, and the like, appropriate to Raphael's lecturing mode. Such smaller occasions call attention to a dimension of *Paradise Lost* that commentators on the epic seldom acknowledge in discussions of its central books, that is, that Raphael is addressing himself to the specific audience of Adam or of Adam and Eve. For many readers of these books Raphael fades from his narrative role in Eden to become Milton's voice speaking without narrative mediation to the poem's readers. By concentrating on the communication between Raphael and Adam we can redress the balance and see more clearly how the effects of these communications and on these audiences differ and position ourselves to correctly assess the Battle in Heaven.

Thus, from beginning to end Raphael's mission and communication are governed by the need to reinforce and expand Adam's unified consciousness and unified cosmos by presenting comparative alignments between Heaven and earth. Raphael's very presence argues the point, as his sociability mirrors the possibility of human access to the divine. But Raphael must enforce both the likeness and the difference between angelic "pure / Intelligential substances" (5.407–8) and human "Rational" beings (408), between man who is "in part / Spiritual" and thus receives divine gifts that are "in part / Spiritual" (405–6) and angels who are "spiritual Natures" (402) able to "transubstantiate" (438) what is less than purely spiritual. Raphael also acknowledges likeness in kind but difference in quality:

> though in Heav'n the Trees
> Of life ambrosial fruitage bear, and vines
> Yield Nectar, though from off the boughs each Morn
> We brush mellifluous Dews, and find the ground
> Cover'd with pearly grain: yet God hath here
> Varied his bounty so with new delights,
> As may compare with Heaven. (426–32)

Adam takes up the concluding hint with the question: "yet what compare?" (467), which prompts Raphael's ensuing discourse on the large-scale analogue of the Satanic disobedience. Adam's humility and his eagerness to respond to Raphael's analogical goals and sociability are emphasized in the narrative link:

> sudden mind arose
> In *Adam*, not to let th' occasion pass
> Given him by this great Conference to know
> Of things above his World, and of thir being

> Who dwell in Heav'n, whose excellence he saw
> Transcend his own so far, whose radiant forms
> Divine effulgence, whose high Power so far
> Exceeded human, and his wary speech
> Thus to th'Empyreal Minister he fram'd. (452–60)

In much of Book 5 and in Books 6 and 7 Raphael speaks not in hierarchical arrays and generalizations but in narratives of specific character and action. Again the underlying goal stresses likeness.

> Myself and all th' Angelic Host that stand
> In sight of God enthron'd, our happy state
> Hold, as you yours, while our obedience holds;
> On other surety none. (5.535–38)

"Happy state" mediates neatly between the angelic here and Adam's "happy state" of line 504. Raphael is throughout at pains to clarify both the distinction and the likeness and potentially greater likeness between Heaven and earth. Raphael points also to differences, most notably in Book 8 where Eden and Heaven are separated by "distance inexpressible / By Numbers that have name" (113–14), and more largely:

> Heav'n is for thee too high
> To know what passes there; be lowly wise:
> Think only what concerns thee and thy being;
> Dream not of other Worlds, what Creatures there
> Live, in what state, condition or degree,
> Contented that thus far hath been reveal'd
> Not of Earth only but of highest Heav'n. (172–78)

The general progress in logic as in nature is from comparison to contrast. The processes and spiritualizing intent are present in their final exchange as in their first one, but now differences receive more emphasis, especially contrasts between love of fellow beings and carnal pleasure and between experiential and faithful ascendant expansive "true love" (588–94):

> Whatever pure thou in the body enjoy'st
> (And pure thou wert created) we enjoy
> In eminence, and obstacle find none
> Of membrane, joint, or limb, exclusive bars. (622–25)[20]

In small and large ways throughout the four central books of *Paradise Lost*, Raphael employs analogies. In such a proceeding Raphael is very much the Ramistic pedagogue, and according to Milton's *Art of Logic*, all knowledge and all teaching are based on consent, on established and establishing likeness. Indeed, *The Doctrine and Discipline of Divorce* claims that "God's doing ever is to bring the due likenesses and harmonies of his workes together" (CE 3.2.418). *The Art of Logic* provides a more specific theoretical vocabulary to describe and illuminate Raphael's poetic. Comparatives are one of the categories of primary arguments. As consenting arguments serve mainly for proving and dissenting arguments for refuting, comparatives function primarily "to make plain" (CE 11.153). A comparative is duplex in form and reciprocal in arguing, a compound of simple arguments in which the quantity (equals/unequals) or quality (likes/unlikes) of one subject is measured against the quantity or quality of another, or in which one subject and its adjunct are aligned with another subject and its adjunct. Equals have the same either mathematical or logical quantity; unequals are either greater or less in magnitude, measure, number, authority, potency, distinction, probability, difficulty, and the like. The recognition of greaters implies the acknowledgment of lessers; unlikes align diverses and argue dissimilitude. Under likes the *Logic* discusses the literary categories of similitude, analogy, metaphor, the apologues of Aesop, and the parables of Socrates. Nowhere is Milton more antithetical to the Ramistic principle of brevity than in the discussion of comparisons; he illustrates variations of comparison amply and subtly from classical poets. His assignment of abnormal space shows perhaps a personal enthusiasm for this form of argument and a poet's recognition of its frequency and usefulness.[21]

"Laying together" is the verb phrase used at several points to describe the mental action of comparison. The general rules are that "there is nothing which when compared with another in quality is not either like it or unlike it" but that likes "are not to be urged beyond that quality which the man making the comparison intended to show as the same in both." In the words of Boethius, "Similitude is unity of quality," that is, proportion or analogy, but Milton warns in familiar commonplaces that "nothing similar is identical" and "every likeness hobbles" (C193, 195). [22] As with consenting and dissenting arguments—the point must be stressed—comparatives manifest reality, the way things are in their own natures, not patterns of priority in the mind; their format is that of being not of judgment; their energy is centrifugal or centripetal, not externally imposed.

As we have seen, Raphael shows a very marked preference for making comparisons in his conversations in Eden, and he uses them with their primary function in view, that is, to make things plain to his pupil. In small and large matters Raphael points out that Heaven and its data are unequal in quantity and unlike in quality to earth and its data within the foundational assumption that the two are essentially similar though differing in forms. We need not rehearse the evidence here, but several theoretical principles in the *Logic*'s presentation of comparatives deserve special notice.

The first of these has to do with knowledgeability and therefore with the usefulness of comparatives in argument. The logical theory is this: "Though by the very nature of comparison comparatives are equally known, yet one must be better known and more evident to some one than another is" (153). Milton expands on this as follows:

> Before comparison is begun that which the comparatives argue by their nature should be better known and clearer to him with whom we discuss a comparative than is the thing argued, for something equally obscure would make nothing plain. Hence the extraordinary usefulness of comparatives stands out, for by this it comes about that an unequal knowledge of things by force of comparison is made equal. (C153)

Comparatives compare things equally known by the user but not equally known by the hearer. The process thus serves for the transfer of knowledge. The theory obviously describes Raphael's practice in the epic. He possesses familiarity with the realms of both Heaven and earth and transfers his data to Adam, whose knowledge of the unfamiliar and incorporeal realm of Heaven is thus elevated and made equal.

A second theoretical point clarifies the intent. The goal of comparatives is to produce confidence, and this is precisely Raphael's goal. Raphael is arguing from the familiar earth and arguing for the unfamiliar Heaven in order to secure the foundations of Adam's experience, knowledge, reason, and faith and in order to produce confidence in his pupil, who so well knows himself to be made of dust but must advance into a more active, dynamic spiritual mode.

A final theoretical proposition in the *Logic* lays to rest the question of Raphael's truthfulness in choosing to recount divine history to Adam by likening spiritual to corporeal forms. In the *Logic* "feigned greaters"— those using *if*—"are of the same value either in refuting or in proving their consequences" as true ones. Milton says of feigned comparisons and fictitious similitudes that

> they evidently argue that the thing is true, and in this are more excellent
> than other arguments, which, if feigned, argue that the matter in question is
> merely feigned . . . . But even feigned comparisons argue not by their
> nature but by force of comparison that things are true and produce confidence. (C155)

Another poetic Ramist of the English Renaissance, Sir Philip Sidney, says similarly in *The Defence of Poesy*, "A fained example hath as much force to teach, as a true example," while acknowledging also that feigned examples are powerfully moving, indeed, "may be tuned to the highest key of passion."[23] This theoretical principle legitimizes Raphael's proceedings with Adam, proceedings that Balachandra Rajan, for example, has complained against under the headings of both "prevarications" and "fumblings."[24] Because it is the force of the comparison, not the validity of the data contained in the comparison, that matters, Raphael's artifice is exonerated. From another perspective, that the information imparted may have a fictive base or may lack scientific accuracy does not signify, for as Roland M. Frye says of the accounts of the creation and fall in Genesis: "The central conception here is of an existential truth, a truth relevant to man's present condition and his ultimate redemption. The truth of Genesis accounts is a figurative truth; that is, it is both figurative and true."[25] Milton's *Art of Logic* describes the validity of fictional comparisons in different terms, but from either vantage the point is the same: The truth is not compromised by this process either logically or theologically.

That poets lie is the oft-cited reason for their exclusion from Plato's *Republic*, specifically that they tell lies about and thereby demean the gods on whose conduct humans are supposedly to model their own. The problem is, of course, that Plato is himself so poetic. Thus, Milton calls him "the supreme fabler" (Hughes, p. 58; and see *Paradise Regained* 4.295), and similarly for Sidney, Plato is "the most *Poeticall*" of philosophers who in exiling poets is not so much "defil[ing] the fountaine out of which his flowing streames have proceeded" as "banishing the abuse." Sidney avers, as he says "*Paradoxically*, but truly," that "of all writers under the Sunne, the *Poet* is the least lyer": Because "he nothing affirmeth," he "therefore never lieth"; he does not labor "to tel you what is, or is not, but what should, or should not be." [26] When Socrates proposes a censorship of writers in *Republic* 2 "when anyone images badly . . . the true nature of gods and heroes," his point is that "the true quality of God we must always surely attribute to him," and that is as the author of good, as himself truly good and unchanging, and as "altogether simple and true in deed and word." *Republic* 10 qualifies what is usually taken as a total interdiction of poets with a proposition of which Milton could thoroughly approve: "We can admit no poetry into our city save only hymns to the gods and the praises of good men." The Socratic distinction is between narrative poetry and lyric poetry, but in his Raphaelean materials Milton has combined the two modes and purposes.

In view of Book 6 of *Paradise Lost* it is important to notice that in complaining against fictional narratives Socrates especially reprehends the presentations in which "gods war with gods and plot against one another and contend." Ideally, young people should rather be taught "that no citizen ever quarrelled with his fellow-citizen and that the very idea of it is an impiety."

> For the young are not able to distinguish what is and what is not allegory, but whatever opinions are taken into the mind at that age are wont to prove indelible and unalterable. For which reason, maybe, we should do our utmost that the first stories that they hear should be so composed as to bring the fairest lessons of virtue to their ears. [27]

The most basic way that Plato's Attic commonwealth differs from Eden generates varied lesser differences. Plato's Republic is in our terms postlapsarian; it is designed to repair the ruins inherited from the past and presupposes flawed citizens. Raphael's audience, though fresh in point of years and experience and susceptible to indelible impressions on their minds, inhabit a world without precedent of quarreling. To Adam such a thing as war in Heaven is "unimaginable" (7.54). Furthermore, there is a striking contrast between the Greek gods as represented in the poetry available to Plato and Plato's own alignment of the divine with the highest good. No such contrast presents itself to Milton, and his celebration of the deity through Raphael and through *Paradise Lost* generally answers to Plato's requirements. Both Milton's poets and Raphael's audience make poets proper, even ideal, rather than excluded citizens in Milton's imaginative creation of a perfect society. It is lies not feigned comparisons and greaters that are to be excluded. Earth may be for Milton "the shadow of Heav'n," but the prelapsarian earth at least does not answer that other and complementary Platonic given: It is not the dungeon of the soul so much as an arena of opportunity.

As Irene Samuel has made clear, Milton wholeheartedly endorses Plato's other view of poetry, that "poets are the inspired oracles of the gods." He embraces too the personal discipline and sacrifice necessary to align the poet's character and destiny and thus to make himself "a true poem, that is, a composition and pattern of the best and honorablest things—not presuming to sing high praises of heroic men or famous cities, unless he have in himself the experience and the practice of all that which is praiseworthy" (Hughes, p. 694). In the introduction to the second book of *The Reason of Church Government*, Milton captures a range of poetic subject matter and purpose which applies to Raphael's practice as well as his own:

> These abilities, wheresoever they be found, are the inspired gift of God rarely bestowed, but yet to some (though most abuse) in every nation; and are of power beside the office of a pulpit, to inbreed and cherish in a great people the seeds of virtue and public civility, to allay the perturbations of the mind and set the affections in right tune, to celebrate in glorious and lofty hymns the throne and equipage of God's almightiness, and what he works and what he suffers to be wrought with high providence in his church, to sing the victorious agonies of martyrs and saints, the deeds and triumphs of just and pious nations doing valiantly through faith against the enemies of Christ, to deplore the general relapses of kingdoms and states from justice and God's true worship. Lastly, whatsoever in religion is holy and sublime, in virtue amiable or grave, whatsoever hath passion or admiration in all the changes of that which is called fortune from without, or the wily subtleties and refluxes of man's thoughts from within, all these things with a solid and treatable smoothness to paint out and describe. Teaching over the whole book of sanctity and virtue through all the instances of example, with such delight to those especially of soft and delicious temper who will not so much as look upon Truth herself, unless they see her elegantly dressed. (Hughes, pp. 669–70; and see *Elegy* 6.55–78)

The passage builds on such biblical passages as Col. 3:16 ("Let the word of Christ dwell in you richly in all wisdom; teaching and admonishing one another in psalms and hymns and spiritual songs, singing with grace in your hearts to the Lord") and Eph. 5:19 ("Speaking to yourselves in psalms and hymns and spiritual songs, singing and making melody in your heart to the

Lord"). More importantly at present, here, as Samuel observes, "Milton pretty well condenses his whole theory of poetry," and she places this prelapsarian poetic platform within a context of Plato's *Laws* as she also views *Areopagitica* as a Miltonic counter to the postlapsarian threat for which Plato banished poets in his *Republic* and espoused censorship in his *Laws*,[28] Milton characteristically and ardently requiring all citizens to accept full moral and intellectual responsibility for trying all things and in Pauline fashion cleaving to the good.

The Raphaelean fiction that has most troubled critics of *Paradise Lost* is the narrative of Book 6, the Battle in Heaven. In assessing it, we may recall both Socrates' particular reprehension of wars in Heaven and Milton's expectation that poetry's task is to celebrate the throne and equipage of God's almightiness and to deplore moral (which is simultaneously political) relapses. Adam gratefully speaks of the battle narrative as "what might else have been our loss, / Unknown, which human knowledge could not reach" (7.74–75). The large figure of the Battle in Heaven has a proleptic thrust for Adam as for readers of the poem, and in interpreting its lesson we should assume that it is a particular lesson in fulfillment of Raphael's overall mission and that it too is material to be processed comparatively as analogous to Adam's future temptation. We must consider, that is, the way these materials are feigned and the way they are comparative.

The artistry of Book 6, like the artistry of Books 11 and 12, has often been singled out for critical complaint. C. A. Patrides calls it "possibly Milton's greatest artistic failure." For Louis Martz, it is "diminished," "futile," "stiff," "clumsy," and poetically "dangerous"; for William Riggs, it is "lame" and "grotesque." At the extreme, for William Empson, the War in Heaven is "unusually stupid Science Fiction," as for Samuel Johnson it was "the favourite of children, and gradually neglected as knowledge is increased." A selection of both negative and positive criticism has recently been sorted out in Stella P. Revard's full-length thoughtful and expansive study of Book 6 of *Paradise Lost*.[29] Also very helpfully, Priscilla P. St. George places this difficult material within a nested sequence of artistic categories: "The War in Heaven is, almost simultaneously, epic entertainment (therefore fictional), sacred history (therefore true), and allegory (therefore symbolic)."[30]

Examined within the context of Raphael's prevailing uses of analogy, the narrative of the Battle in Heaven is seen to be designed to communicate to Adam one overriding lesson in faith as well as several lesser recommendations for the conduct of his experiential life. As history, the Battle in Heaven fills in a gap in Adam's experience and thus fortifies him to exercise his reason (which is choice) in the crisis in his future. Adam was created for valor and contemplation (4.297), and the basis of his reasoning is comparative. Thus, he was created on nonedenic earth so that when transported to Eden he would be equipped to evaluate it appropriately. In Book 6 Adam can witness Satan's destructiveness and self-destructiveness, his pain and increasing loss of freedom and spiritual being and perception, and opt for the alternatives that devolve from obedience. Late in Book 6 Adam can distinguish and choose between Christ as terror, the fallen perception, and Christ as wonder, the unfallen view, and Adam can affirm his allegiance and faith through the positive choice.

The lessons in faith that Raphael teaches through the Battle in Heaven are necessarily less obvious than the experiential instruction. Faith is crisply defined in the phrase "trusting in th'Almighty's aid" (6.119). If the literalizing Satan were to attempt to communicate the biblical maxim that faith can move mountains, he would do so merely by means of quite experiential mountains. He would reduce the matter to the kind of continuing wordplay applied to the cannon on the second day of battle. Because Milton and Raphael, like their source, seek to teach a different lesson from and to a different mindset, their methods also differ. Their lesson is more like this: that faith can accomplish apparently impossible tasks or unimaginable ends. Because the deity has shaped the universe for his ultimate purposes far beyond the human capacity to perceive or control, it is the task and challenge of lesser beings to so far attune themselves to his will that they may serve as instruments to realize his idea. It is neither necessary nor possible for created beings to grasp these ends, but it is their responsibility to follow the guidance he has given them and validate their worthiness for fuller awareness of and participation in those ends. Because, like Adam, everything the good angels have encountered assures them that God's goals are for their own well-being and growth as well as his own ends, they should approach the present and the future with the expectation of continuance of revelation and fulfillment. To do so demonstrates faith. In Abdiel's words to Satan,

> By experience taught we know how good,
> And of our good, and of our dignity
> How provident he is, how far from thought

To make us less, bent rather to exalt
Our happy state under one Head more near
United. (5.826–31)

Abdiel is the role model for action based on faith and zeal, the heavenly
counterparts of Adam's contemplation and valor. Abdiel's habit of obedience
to superiors led him to make the trip northward with the Satanic host, but
when the crisis of self-definition came, he rose to the occasion for the kinds
of reasons just outlined and in spite of the huge social and political pressures
that sought to compromise his integrity.[31]

Like the other good angels Abdiel acts as if the whole universe would bear
the consequences of his deeds, as is in fact in important ways the case for
both fallen and unfallen angels and for humans. Abdiel's whole care is "To
stand approv'd in sight of God" (6.35–36). Similarly, of the good angels en
route to the first day's battle we read that "each on himself reli'd, / As only
in his arm the moment lay / Of victory" (238–40). When Abdiel returns
from the fallen host to deliver his message of uprising with the most
absolute urgency, he finds the message already known, but the evidence of
his urgency wins him the highest accolade:

> Servant of God, well done, well hast thou fought
> The better fight, who single hast maintain'd
> Against revolted multitudes the Cause
> Of Truth, in word mightier than they in Arms;
> And for the testimony of Truth hast borne
> Universal reproach, far worse to bear
> Than violence: for this was all thy care
> To stand approv'd in sight of God, though Worlds
> Judg'd thee perverse. (6.29–37)

At the onset of the second day's battle Zophiel (the "spy of God") carries his
message with similar absolute urgency and self-validation and a similarly
unsurprised reception: "So warn'd he them aware themselves" (547). As
Milton explains in *Christian Doctrine*, in performing such heroic acts "the
good angels are upheld by their own strength no less than man himself was
before his fall" rather than acting specifically from God's grace (Hughes,
p. 990). Such self-checking, even on God's part, is central to Puritan views
of heroism.[32]

In these as in other ways the terms in which the Battle of Heaven is fought
are irrational: The number of good angels is artificially limited; the strength

of individual good warriors is confined; neither side can suffer permanent diminution except for the fallen adjunct of pain. That irrationality or suprarationality is precisely the point Raphael labors to impress most strongly upon Adam. The good angels and Adam are to do what is right not only *although* they do not understand but even *because* they do not understand and indeed do not feel the glimmer of a need to understand. They are exercising their faith thereby, acting on the evidence of things not seen, the substance of things hoped for. This famous definition of faith from Hebrews 11 is amplified in Saint Paul's letter to the Romans:

> For therein is the righteousness of God revealed from faith to faith: as it is written, the just shall live by faith. For the wrath of God is revealed from heaven against all ungodliness and unrighteousness of men who hold the truth in unrighteousness. Because that which may be known of God is manifest in them; for God hath shewed it unto them. For the invisible things of him from the creation of the world are clearly seen, being understood by the things that are made, even his eternal power and Godhead; so that they are without excuse. (1:17–20)

The lesson is presented in miniature within the action of the second day's battle: that clinging to one's armor, one's apparent experiential materialized protection, contributes to one's harm.[33] Satan seeks "more valid Arms, / Weapons more violent" (6.438–39). At one stage the bad angels cling to and are crushed by their arms; the good angels throw away their armor in a gesture of faith and proceed quite literally to move mountains (cf. 1 Cor. 13:2: "And though I have all faith, so that I could remove mountains, and have not charity, I am nothing").

In the Battle in Heaven Adam is being equipped with exemplary analogues of faith so that he may face his own crisis and apply them to his edenic situation. The Tree of Knowledge is his test of obedience and faith. He does not need to know experientially what knowledge or evil is or what death threatens; he does need the consciousness that the deity has negatived these terms and presented them as contrary to his own well-being and future happiness. The Battle in Heaven in Book 6 shows the working-out of the alternatives of obedience and disobedience in heavenly analogues, as the final portion of Book 5 presents Abdiel and Satan in the acts of choosing rightly and wrongly.

Satan's refusal of obedience to the Son and the New Order is the heavenly analogue of what for Adam is a garden matter: "The high Injunction not to taste that Fruit" (10.13) neatly equates with the divine decree: "him who disobeys / Mee disobeys" (5.611–12). On an occasion that Georgia B. Christopher describes with the phrases "Primal Scene," "Primal Text," "Prime Decree," and "Primal Word,"[34] the test of Satan's obedience and faith hinges on the "new Laws" of the begetting of the Son, the heavenly abstract analogue of concrete edenic fruit.

> New Laws thou see'st impos'd;
> New Laws from him who reigns, new minds may raise
> In us who serve, new Counsels, to debate
> What doubtful may ensue.
> (5.679–82; note also "new commands" [691] and "Laws" [693])

His scornful response to Beelzebub demonstrates his refusal of grace, glory, union, and joy, a refusal of the New Dispensation of Christ.

Like sun/Son and faith moving mountains, "New Laws" triggers complex responses in the poem's reading audience who exist in postlapsarian and post-Christian time and bring to bear upon the epic the remembered texts of the Old and New Testaments that are being reshaped within the poem's procedures. A remarkable instance of Raphael's biblically based communication with the reader occurs in his greeting to Eve:

> Hail Mother of Mankind, whose fruitful Womb
> Shall fill the World more numerous with thy Sons
> Than with these various fruits the Trees of God
> Have heap'd this Table. (5.388–91)

This early example of Raphaelean analogy and expansion of vegetative imagery is accompanied by the narrator's guidance of the reader's assessment:

> On whom the Angel *Hail*
> Bestow'd, the holy salutation us'd
> Long after to blest *Mary*, second *Eve*. (385–87)

The allusion is to Luke 1:28 (and see the narrator's similar gesture in "*Jesus* son of *Mary* second *Eve*" [10.183] along with "Our second *Adam*" [11.383], as well as 1 Cor. 15:45–47 and Rom. 5:14–21). Adam reads the book of nature and apprehends through his untainted, unified, and sudden apprehension, but fallen readers respond with greater complexity because they have recourse to additional texts and live within a different vocabulary, perception, and dispensation. Their skills are both superior to Adam's because of the Logos and inferior to Adam's because of the fall of reason and the undermining of language at Babel.

For readers the communication is typological or anagogical; for Adam, insofar as allegory applies it is merely tropological allegory. For readers, it is a matter of past and present, time and eternity, as for Adam the atmosphere is one of immediacy. In the hexaemeral account of Book 7 God is "Author and end of all things" (591) as similarly "Author of all being" (3.374) or "the World's great Author" (5.188), and for prelapsarian Adam *author* means the maker of things, but for the fallen reader *author* refers quite specifically to the writer of books. Insofar as Christ and New Testament material are available to Adam before the final books of *Paradise Lost*, they are imported through the reader's memory. Meaning is pursued and achieved through creative effort in weighing biblically based memories and divine promises. Thus the fallen reader, at least the fit one, is presumed capable of the wisdom and reading skills Michael communicates to the postlapsarian Adam. The prelapsarian Adam is supplied with the capacity to respond to resonances of meaning on a vertical scale, and the reader of the poem responds to resonances of meaning on a horizontal or chronological scale as well as on the Platonic one. Such responsiveness is the mark of spiritual energy and redemptive prospects, of hearts from which the stony is absent or removed, and of poetic or imaginative capacity.

Before leaving the evidence of Book 6 we should attend to a particular verbal form this principle is given: Satanic punning is the defining parody that illuminates the spiritually mysterious alternative of responsiveness to the vitalizing word, a matter both of Christian doctrine and of poetics. The second day of the battle offers three collections of puns, the first two from Satan, the third from Belial in imitation of his master:

> Vanguard, to Right and Left the Front unfold;
> That all may see who hate us, how we seek
> Peace and composure, and with open breast
> Stand ready to receive them, if they like
> Our overture, and turn not back perverse;
> But that I doubt; however witness Heaven,
> Heav'n witness thou anon, while we discharge
> Freely our part: yee who appointed stand
> Do as you have in charge, and briefly touch
> What we propound, and loud that all may hear. (558–67)

> O Friends, why come not on these Victors proud?
> Erewhile they fierce were coming, and when wee,

To entertain them fair with open Front
And Breast, (what could we more?) propounded terms
Of composition, straight they chang'd thir minds,
Flew off, and into strange vagaries fell,
As they would dance, yet for a dance they seem'd
Somewhat extravagant and wild, perhaps
For joy of offer'd peace: but I suppose
If our proposals once again were heard
We should compel them to a quick result. (609–19)

Leader, the terms we sent were terms of weight,
Of hard contents, and full of force urg'd home,
Such as we might perceive amus'd them all,
And stumbl'd many; who receives them right,
Had need from head to foot well understand;
Not understood, this gift they have besides,
They show us when our foes walk not upright. (621–27)

It is a matter of considerable interest that the two dimensions of the puns in these series systematically align the artifacts and processes of cannon with the arenas of logic, rhetoric, and oratory. At first glance such alignment might appear a poetic or metaphoric process, for the wordplay links two disparate realms within a single verbal form, but the intention of the verbal structure differs radically from what Anne Davidson Ferry calls "sacred metaphor." It is to call attention to the self and its isolated cleverness at the expense of the encompassing harmony. Its goal is to show off rather than guide and elevate. The wordplay closes off rather than opens creative energies. It posits an external reality subject to the exploitable accidents of conjunction. Such "Ambiguous words" (5.703), characteristic of Satan, are the verbal antithesis of the unificatory and transcending Logos and of the deliberately unambiguous, indeed "plain," style of the deity and the final books of *Paradise Lost*. Walter Savage Landor famously complained "It appears then on record that the first overt crime of the refractory fallen angels was *punning*: they fell rapidly after that."[35] What Landor intended to instance his own wittiness in fact turns out to capture a profound truth!

Satanic punning establishes a clearly definable antipoetic. The vocabularies for accessing a definable poetic are more elusive and more varied and thus more rich and suggestive. One fairly simple category encapsulates much of the mode of Raphael's "process of speech," that is, that Raphael's poetic proceeding is muse-governed or muse-dictated, as Michael's emphatically is not. When the Muse of Astronomy Urania (= "heavenly"), who governs *Paradise Lost*, is invoked specifically at the opening of Raphael's Book 7, it is in a context that recognizes her inseparability from her sister Wisdom. All the Muses are the daughters of Memory and literally *call to* the *mind* and thus supply their wide-ranging knowledge to and inspire their favorite agents with the materials of their creation. In Hesiod's *Theogony* after the Muses have been introduced, the author defines and implores their aid in lines that look forward to Book 7 of *Paradise Lost*:

> Daughters of Zeus, I greet you. . . . Tell how in the beginning the gods and the earth came into being, as well as the rivers, the limitless sea with its raging surges, the shining stars, and the broad sky above. [36]

The most famous human poetic agent of the Muses, and the son of one of them, was Orpheus, whose skill allowed him to harmonize and move not merely men and gods but even animals, plants, and rocks. In the enthusiastic phrasing of Prolusion 7: "The very trees, and shrubs, and the entire forest tore away from their roots to run after the elegant music of Orpheus" (Hughes, p. 629). Orpheus has often been seen as a Miltonic self-defining myth. Adam's own pre-Raphaelean morning hymn shows that he too is a poet in tune with and responsive to Orphean resonances. Indeed, Adam's own poetic is well defined in the dawn orisons with their "various style," "holy rapture," "fit" and "unmeditated" strains, and "prompt eloquence" (5.145–49). Because the hymn itself evolves out of Psalm 148, Adam can simultaneously be seen as a Hebraic, Davidic poet, overlaying pagan pastoral with "*Sion's* songs, to all true tastes excelling" (*Paradise Regained* 4.347).[37]

Balachandra Rajan has balanced this one of Milton's two poetic modes, which he calls "the Urania principle of vision," against "the Osiris principle of the search." Such poetic vision and its call to the Muse he describes by analogy with Milton's invocation of Light at the opening of Book 3 of *Paradise Lost*:

> Light . . . is first the offspring of heaven and then the first-born of the offspring. It is coeternal beam of the eternal, an unapproachable radiance which God has inhabited from eternity, an effluence of essence, an ethereal stream springing from an unknowable fountain. The tentative delineations,

superseded before they are fully evolved, keep the mind in movement round a still center. It is as if the mind can only know this center by the way in which the center moves the mind. Raphael's difficulties in likening spiritual to corporal things are lived out by the reachings of the verse. But the inadequacies of metaphor are not felt as defeat. The successive discardings are fitted into the flowing movement, suggesting the harmony rather than the strife of elusive possibilities.

It is "a world arranged as metaphor reflected in metaphor [in which] poetry as a metaphor-seeking act becomes an education in the nature of reality," "a world in which reality can only be compromised by whatever metaphors are chosen to manifest it." [38]

Such a poetic has in its background a Coleridgean principle of organic poetry, and it is not surprising that in setting forward his theory of imagination Coleridge should draw his illustration from precisely those portions of Milton's epic that are presently before us. In chapter 13 of *Biographia Literaria*, which is headed by lines 469–88 of *Paradise Lost* Book 5, Coleridge famously distinguishes between primary and secondary imagination: "The primary IMAGINATION [is] the living Power and prime Agent of all human Perception, and [is] a repetition in the finite mind of the eternal act of creation in the infinite I AM." Such an imagination is prelapsarian, as Coleridge's secondary imagination aligns with the postlapsarian as it "dissolves, diffuses, dissipates, in order to re-create." [39]

Coleridge's views of organic poetry and of primary imagination may be seen to lie acknowledged or unacknowledged behind a number of commentaries on *Paradise Lost*. In her discussion of *Paradise Lost* as myth, for example, Isabel G. MacCaffrey provides a concise foundation for inquiry into the epic's interlocking circular analogues:

> Milton's worlds all fit exactly inside each other; in noting their points of similarity, he is not so much joining different objects as observing the same thing on a smaller or larger scale. Because the same forces operate in all parts of a self-consistent, mutually dependent universe, the images may be used interchangeably for what we should now separate into "subjective" and "objective" situations.

The unity of fact, symbol, and import, as MacCaffrey remarks, "makes us feel, in reading *Paradise Lost*, that we are observing familiar forces operating in different physical areas, rather than comparing similar areas in different hierarchies or 'worlds.'" She summarizes thus: "Milton's distinction is not that he characterized the elements of his myth in a new way, but that he succeeded in revealing so clearly the outlines of the universal themes behind them."[40]

Although her focus is on the role of the narrator rather than the foundations in myth, Ferry outlines a vision and artistry similar to the Orphean and the Coleridgean.

> We are made to feel that this world, and everything with which God filled it in the six days of creation, has the reality and meaning of divine truth in itself as well as metaphorical value for the abstract or inward meaning of the epic argument.

For Ferry the language of metaphor in the poem, thus hexaemerally based, is "a world of archetypes, of things apprehended in their essences, and the only language to describe this world is a language of comparable clarity and generality," "a world now strange, awesome, distant but perfectly distinct . . . a world in which words perfectly identify things, as the names which Adam gave to the animals corresponded to their natures . . . a world of uninterrupted patterns of motion and unclouded light." Ferry's term for the language and data of such wholeness, harmony, and radiance is "sacred metaphor." In sacred metaphors fact and meaning are inseparable, and "each expresses the other in the unity of divine truth so that the two references to a single word become the two terms of a metaphor by which their meanings are identified." Metaphor is thus the "only kind of figure appropriate to divinity." It is the polar alternative of Satanic punning.

The fall Ferry sees as dividing concrete fact and abstract meaning, as shattering the once unified vision, and as resulting in debased language and "disunified experience." She is careful to distinguish Raphael's similes accommodated to Adam's limited experience from the narrator's similes, which make "the invisible world known to us by its analogies with our mortal experience," that is, the fallen world of nature, history, and art with all its variety and abundance, his compounding series of similes with their names, times, seasons, and particularity. For Ferry his similes reflect the narrator's double nature and double participation in experience and transcendence and emphasize difference or contrast, whereas sacred metaphors insist "upon unity rather than separation, identity rather than contrast," especially the identity of the abstract and concrete, physical and spiritual reality, both "the particular historical references of the story and its universal and inward meanings."[41]

Marjorie Nicolson draws a comparable distinction between the Renaissance vision as metaphoric and the modern vision as founded upon the artificial parallels of self-conscious similes. For our Elizabethan ancestors "the world was not simply *like* an animal; it *was* animate." What once were identical are now viewed self-consciously as similar. We know we are drawing analogies, but as Nicolson adds, "Our ancestors believed that what we call 'analogy' was *truth*, inscribed by God in the nature of things."[42]

If we turn to two comparable passages from the archangels Raphael and Michael, these distinctions may be seen clearly and some additional observations on the contrasting poetics drawn. In Raphael's account of the third day of the hexaemeral creation, we read:

> The Earth was form'd, but in the Womb as yet
> Of Waters, Embryon immature involv'd,
> Appear'd not: over all the face of Earth
> Main Ocean flow'd, not idle, but with warm
> Prolific humor soft'ning all her Globe,
> Fermented the great Mother to conceive,
> Satiate with genial moisture, when God said,
> Be gather'd now ye Waters under Heav'n
> Into one place, and let dry Land appear.
> Immediately the Mountains huge appear
> Emergent, and thir broad bare backs upheave
> Into the Clouds, thir tops ascend the Sky:
> So high as heav'd the tumid Hills, so low
> Down sunk a hollow bottom broad and deep,
> Capacious bed of Waters: thither they
> Hasted with glad precipitance, uproll'd
> As drops of dust conglobing from the dry;
> Part rise in crystal Wall, or ridge direct,
> For haste; such flight the great command impress'd
> On the swift floods: as Armies at the call
> Of Trumpet (for of Armies thou hast heard)
> Troop to thir Standard, so the wat'ry throng,
> Wave rolling after Wave, where way they found,

> If steep, with torrent rapture, if through Plain,
> Soft-ebbing; nor withstood them Rock or Hill,
> But they, or under ground, or circuit wide
> With Serpent error wand'ring, found thir way,
> And on the washy Ooze deep Channels wore;
> Easy, ere God had bid the ground be dry,
> All but within those banks, where Rivers now
> Stream, and perpetual draw thir humid train.
> The dry Land, Earth, and the great receptacle
> Of congregated Waters he call'd Seas:
> And saw that it was good. (7.276–309)

Raphael is versifying Genesis:

> And God said, Let the waters under the heaven be gathered together unto
> one place, and let dry land appear: and it was so. And God called the dry land
> Earth; and the gathering together of the waters called he Seas: and God saw
> that it was good. (1:9–10)

Here Raphael is amplifying, not merely paraphrasing and ornamenting, the biblical givens. Order, creation, and joy are the process as well as the content of Raphael's account, and Raphael's own order, creation, and joy answer to the deity's he affirms through the amplification.

In a comparable passage, this time of re-creation rather than creation, Michael's explication of Noah's flood for Adam contains some remarkable poetic gestures that are quite different in kind from the procedures normal to Raphael:

> He look'd, and saw the Ark hull on the flood,
> Which now abated, for the Clouds were fled,
> Driv'n by a keen North-wind, that blowing dry
> Wrinkl'd the face of Deluge, as decay'd;
> And the clear Sun on his wide wat'ry Glass
> Gaz'd hot, and of the fresh Wave largely drew,
> As after thirst, which made their flowing shrink
> From standing lake to tripping ebb, that stole
> With soft foot towards the deep, who now had stopt
> His Sluices, as the Heav'n his windows shut.
> The Ark no more now floats, but seems on ground
> Fast on the top of some high mountain fixt.

And now the tops of Hills as Rocks appear;
With clamor thence the rapid Currents drive
Towards the retreating Sea thir furious tide. (11.840–54)

The passage renders part of the eighth chapter of Genesis:

And God made a wind to pass over the earth, and the waters asswaged;
The fountains also of the deep and the windows of heaven were stopped, and
the rain from heaven was restrained; And the waters returned from off the
earth continually: and after the end of the hundred and fifty days the waters
were abated. (8:1–3)

We are here within the domain of what some critics consider the fallen
style of the final books of *Paradise Lost*. Jonathan H. Collett finds a "stiffen-
ing" in the language "paralleled by a quite sudden harshness in imagery."
From its earliest criticism, in, for example, Addison who found Milton
overly attentive to divinity and neglectful of poetry, Books 11 and 12 have
been faulted in content and style as careless, fragmented, prosaic. Northrop
Frye is typical in judging these books "a hurried and perfunctory summary
of the Bible." C. S. Lewis supports his now famous assessment of Books 11
and 12 as "an untransmuted lump of futurity" by suggesting an inartistic
design on Milton's part, a temporary failure of talent, and "a natural,
though disastrous, impatience to get the work finished." "The actual writ-
ing," Lewis avers, "is curiously bad." Louis Martz feels a "painful" "deterio-
ration in the quality of the writing," "with long stretches of barren para-
phrase," and John Peter finds passages "clotted with semi-personifications"
and generally an "integument of half-formed and jumbled images."[43]

There have also been a number of defenses of the style of the final books,
especially in recent decades when the artistry of *Paradise Regained* has been
more fully understood, and several of these are of immediate interest.
Northrop Frye also suggests, for example, that to give the New Testament
materials "their full poetic resonance" would make the epic top-heavy, and
thus they must be "assumed to have their importance already understood by
the reader," and F. T. Prince claims that "the imaginative intensity is to be
found rather in the vibration of the story in Adam's reacting consciousness"
and that these books compress a number of Miltonic artistic effects, espe-
cially "a prevailing sweep and force." The eighteenth-century editor
Thomas Newton, though finding the final books more history than poetry,
still recognizes a positive dimension:

> We may still discover the same great genius, and there are intermix'd as
> many ornaments and graces of poetry, as the nature of the subject, and the
> author's fidelity and strict attachment to the truth of Scripture history, and
> the reduction of so many and such various events into so narrow a compass
> would admit. It is the same ocean, but not at its highest tide; it is now
> ebbing and retreating. It is the same sun, but not in its full blaze of meridian
> glory; it now shines with a gentler ray as it is setting. [44]

In general and against a background of such suggestions, I wish to counter
complaints against the style and procedure of the conclusion of *Paradise Lost*
by suggesting some of the altered foundations on which the content and
poetry are built and the standards by which that poetry is to be measured, as
these alterations are inseparable from the action of the epic's theme, the fall
itself. I would argue that in style, form, and content Books 11 and 12 fill out
the epic's essential prelapsarian/postlapsarian pattern of contrasts, that they
balance and recapitulate earlier data within the governing framework of the
lapsarian parallel of Raphael's visit.

Some of Newton's "ornaments and graces" may be quickly identified. The
passage is remarkable for its uses of similes: "as decay'd"; "As after thirst";
and "as the Heav'n his windows shut." The first of these recalls the effects of
the fall, the second reinvokes the dynamic cosmic interrelationship of sun
and earth, and the third points to the disruption of direct intercourse
between humans and divine agents. The passage is remarkable also for the
pictorial energy of much of its expression: "Wrinkl'd the face of Deluge";
"his wide wat'ry Glass"; "stole / With soft foot"; "stopt / His Sluices"; and
more generally the verb actions of fleeing, driving, blowing, gazing, and
drawing. The concentration of personification and the microcosmic in pas-
sages such as these counters claims that the style of the final books is fallen,
if by "fallen" is meant deficient in poetic skill and merit. This pictorial energy
reflects mundane or secular metaphor with its division and artifice, not
Ferry's sacred metaphor with its transcendent unity. It may even be labeled
as metaphysical with an eye to Samuel Johnson's definition of that category:

> a kind of *discordia concors*; a combination of dissimilar images, or discovery
> of occult resemblances in things apparently unlike. . . . The most heteroge-
> neous ideas are yoked by violence together; nature and art are ransacked for
> illustrations, comparisons, and allusions; their learning instructs, and their
> subtilty surprises; but the reader commonly thinks his improvement dearly
> bought, and, though he sometimes admires, is seldom pleased. [45]

The contrasts are perhaps most striking between the prelapsarian domi-
nant organic image and the wrinkles and decay of Michael's numerous
incidental ornamental images. Michael too gestures toward personification
in his "Wrinkl'd the face of Deluge," but Raphael's personification of "the
face of Earth" is just one step toward realizing a full figure of "the great
Mother" Earth with all her organic unity and fecundity. Raphael's similes
differ from Michael's formally in that Michael offers *as* plus substantive, but
Raphael offers *as* plus substantive plus predication: "As drops . . . conglob-
ing from the dry" presents a comparison that is also the fact of the matter.
The more expansive "as Armies at the call / Of Trumpet (for of Armies thou
hast heard) / Troop to thir Standard" recalls to readers epic simile norms,
but for Adam the comparison has the effect of unifying the several levels of
his experience, including what we would call Books 6 and 7; it puts
together congenial not disparate matters. Raphael's "humid train" is
Michael-like and Michael's "Hills as Rocks" is Raphael-like, but the differ-
ences are sufficient to secure the argument. Both Michael and Raphael
present the relation between earth and the flow of waters and the emergence
of earth's highest points, but Raphael does so to celebrate life and earthly
life, the interrelationship of God, cosmos, and man, ascent and descent, the
essential sympathy and analogy of the whole of creation. Michael's *decay* and
fury bespeak the altered relationship of man and God, Heaven and earth,
and the aberration and even apparent antipathy that intrude between them
and that can be bridged, psychologically, spiritually, and verbally, only by
the special mediation of God's mysterious covenants of memory and prom-
ise, here in the form of the rainbow, later in the form of Christ. The
ontological Logos is Raphael's theme, and the language of the passage is
radically that which Adam received with the names of the animals. *Concep-
tion* is simultaneously birth and idea. The metaphoric mode is sacred, not
secular or metaphysical.

Within the postlapsarian scheme of things, the sun is still operative,
mightily operative, and its operations take effect with or against the results
of the unparalleled storm. The flooding of this storm reflects God's will and
cleansing vengeance against the almost universally sinful mankind. The
reminder that Satan has been identified with weather variations as with sin
throughout the epic is hardly necessary, but it is useful to recall that a
rainbow from the human perspective occurs with the interaction of sun,
rain, and clouds. Unlike Raphael's characteristic analogies, the present
passage's similes and secular metaphors draw upon two disparate earthly

categories rather than upon prelapsarian likenesses between earth and Heaven, upon horizontal rather than vertical likeness. This description is realistic rather than transcendent; the world addressed is fractionated rather than unified. The sense of abatement, stoppage, restraint, along with the lingering on an extended temporal process, all reflect the postlapsarian cosmos and theme. The small separate poetic events occur as fragments around the central core of the historical sequence with its supporting categories of decay, pride, and mechanics. The poetic units function as ornaments or brief occasional decorative gestures; they savor of metaphysical conceits.

In content as in intent the poetic units here demonstrate the postlapsarian. The poetic gestures are self-conscious, and their manipulative deliberativeness is a postlapsarian consequence of Adam's infected wit and infected will, which require instruction that is sugarcoated. Sidney's *Apology* lies behind the instruction, but so does Milton's *Reason of Church Government* with its recognition of "those especially of soft and delicious temper who will not so much as look upon Truth herself, unless they see her elegantly dressed" (Hughes, p. 670). In *Of Reformation* Milton says:

> The very essence of Truth is plainnesse, and brightnes; the darknes and crookednesse is our own. The *wisdome* of *God* created *understanding*, fit and proportionable to Truth the object, and end of it, as the eye to the thing visible. If our *understanding* have a film of *ignorance* over it, or be blear with gazing on other false glisterings, what is that to Truth? If we will but purge with sovrain eyesalve that intellectual ray which *God* hath planted in us, then we would beleeve the Scriptures protesting their own plainnes, and perspicuity. (CE 3.1.33)

As Michael proceeds through biblical history and Book 12 of *Paradise Lost*, he brings his "soft" but docile pupil to a verbal and historical confrontation with "Truth herself" and to a rigorously unadorned articulation of fallen spiritual processes that apprehend and affirm the paradoxical Christ who is both Word and Truth. But even in the present passage divinely mediated instruction, despite the decorative gestures, is only a step away from a radically plain style.

The basis of the poetry has shifted away from imagery, or Ferry's sacred metaphors, or Platonic allegory, in which a lower experiential level precisely coincides with or contains or dissolves into the higher level of meaning, and it has shifted toward occasional or secular metaphor or a typological procedure where difference, not union, dominates and where readers and Adam are obliged to exercise their creative and interpretative skills in putting back together the fragmented pieces. The prelapsarian equation of, for example, sun and deity gives way to a disjunction between data and meaning. The phenomenal world makes sense only as mediated by the Scriptures or only as viewed from a higher perspective. Experience must be processed to be understood, and that process is discursive: collecting and registering data and reconciling them to preestablished, revealed patterns of meaning. Revelation as inherited prophecy looks to the future from the past, and it requires humanity to look from the present to the past in order to glimpse the future and thus to put itself in tune with the unifying eternal vision and goal. The human memory becomes operative with the fall into history. Time and space continua, process, a horizontal line replace the prelapsarian unity, stasis, and vertical line.

As suggested above, one of the literary categories to describe this artistic shift is "plain style," which Walter J. Ong has attached to Ramus's Puritan followers and described as "a basically chirographic, nonoratorical, non-ornamental style . . . in effect rejecting or at least minimizing rhetoric . . . [as] indeed nothing but superficial ornament." [46] Adam's final lesson is expressed in a language quite free from adornment: "Henceforth I learn, that to obey is best, / And love with fear the only God, to walk / As in his presence, ever to observe / His providence" (12.561–64). As Peter Berek has argued, Milton links plain style with perfection, Truth, and revelation and ornate and contrived verbal skill with corruption, depravity, and ma-nipulation. Finding that the essence of the style in the final two books is "a lack of overt adornment," Robert L. Entzminger joins William Haller in observing that

> an important convention of Puritan hagiographical writings . . . was that they should seem to possess no art but the art of the holy spirit, which was simply to report the facts. The medium does not call attention to itself because it sought to be perfectly transparent, absorbed as fully as possible into the content.

Such style dominates *Paradise Regained* as well, and its poetic insists, in the words of Barbara Lewalski, that the reader identifies with the story and New Dispensation hero, not totally and automatically "but only partially and by deliberate choice." "Thy Word is all, if we could spell," says George Herbert in "The Flower." For Milton's Puritan contemporaries *word* included at least the seven senses that Georgia B. Christopher has collected:

> the complete biblical narrative from Creation to Judgment Day, the verbal promise given in a single sentence from Scripture, a doctrinal abstract of the Bible, a retelling of a biblical story with elaboration and commentary, an inventory of Creation, a review of the history of the world, and finally, the mere name of Christ, which covered and implied the rest. [47]

Michael leads Adam to make such an ultimate choice and to execute such orthography. The plain style or "puritanism" of style on which *Paradise Lost* ends is a matter of Protestant theology and Christian doctrine and Puritan poetics. History, literary history, and religious history are made to coalesce in the finale of Milton's epic.

Balachandra Rajan labels his second mode of Miltonic poetic the Osiris principle; it matches our postlapsarian as Rajan's Urania principle describes our prelapsarian. As with the Osiris image in *Areopagitica*, in this poetic mode fragments of the body of truth are identified and gradually accumulated in a process coextensive with time and to be completed at the Second Coming. A poem in this mode for Rajan is

> a controlled experiment of the imagination in which turbulence is allowed to rage against the endeavors of order so that order can be made more significant by what it subdues . . . [and] in which the structure of order is brought into being by the evolving consciousness rather than displayed to us, or tested and maintained under assault. When finding-making involves the recovery of a previous order catastrophically lost, knowledge both in the poem and in the larger undertakings of which it is a model will appear as both discovery and remembrance. . . . The weight of implication of the image is that the unknown is not the unknowable. What we find is a trustworthy testimony to the nature of what we have yet to find.

As in the Urania mode language is betrayal, in the Osiris mode language is discovery. [48] It is a nice point that Osiris's fate parallels Orpheus's.

Rajan errs, I think, in labeling this principle according to its fragmented subject Osiris rather than according to its unifying agent Isis, according to its "turbulence" rather than its "discovery and remembrance." Such "recollection" as Isis practices is no longer a matter of the Muse as a daughter of Memory but is theogonic in a different sense, a matter now of "the Oracle of

God" (1.12), of the interaction of the third person of the Trinity, that mighty-winged creative Spirit of the Invocation of Book 1 of *Paradise Lost* (17, 20), and "th' upright heart and pure" (18).

Like the Isis procedure, typology is an art of gathering, of accumulating fragments within a design progressing toward fulfillment of a presumed encompassing unity and perfection. In the discussion of Ramistic foundations for Michael's procedures, we noted what (following Rajan and *Areopagitica*) we might call the Psyche principle, the procedure of sorting out according to positive and negative moral categories. The Isis and typological principle of gathering is also a sorting-out process, but one based upon a chronological array, not on moral polarity. Typology is a process of God's prefigurative writing and humanity's retrospective reading, specifically the writing and reading of Old Testament characters, settings, and events as imperfect prefigurations of the perfect New Testament equivalents that fulfill their intent. In the famous phrasing of Irenaeus, typology is a tradition of "recapitulation in Christ" (and see Eph. 1:10). Typology is a matter of recapitulation of, for example, psychic history and the history of individuals in the careers of nations, of the first Adam in the second Adam Christ, of Adam's relation to Eve in Christ's relation to the Church, of both Adams in each believer, and of mankind in Christ. Types are both exemplary to us and recapitulated in us. The most prominent traditional types are those explicitly but not exclusively interpreted within the New Testament. In typology as Jean Danielou defines it, "all the outstanding persons and leading events of Scripture are both stages and rough outlines to prepare and prefigure the mystery which is one day to be fulfilled in Christ"; prefigured data are both expected at the last day and realized here and now in Christ and in the individual's Christic analogue; typology reveals unifying analogies through history and guarantees the authenticity of Scripture as God's writings; and the antitype denotes ultimate reality.[49] Natural objects may be types only as they are biblically endowed with special occasional significance.

An author may write from typological intentions, as Milton is often said to be doing, for example, with the title character of *Samson Agonistes* or with Job in *Paradise Regained*, but primarily typology is a mode of reading rather than writing. The interest is less with the catastrophic distribution of Osiris's members than with the unity available for achievement or reachievement when experiential data are left behind; progressively, the text is transcended in favor of the act of textual interpretation. One of the most striking ways in which chronological typology differs from Raphael's spatial analogy is that the type does not dissolve into the antitype but remains literally secured and distinct in what Erich Auerbach calls "figural realism."[50] This reading of history presupposes God as a poet whose foreshadowings are carefully modulated in anticipation of an anagogical climax. It casts humanity, especially Christians, especially Protestants, in the role of readers, exegetes, or literary critics who, apprised of the outcome, can interpret the textual evidence as miniatures of and contributions to the overall literary design in a process that is at once aesthetic and spiritual. From the reader's point of view, typological interpretation is retrospective. Only subsequent manifestation of the antitype invests the type with symbolic meaning. Knowledge is gradually achieved through a process of reevaluating old information retained in the memory by the light of new informational increments. Typology is temporal not hierarchical, horizontal not vertical, multiple not single, teleological not ontological.

Thus, typology is analogy of a special kind. It "lays together" equivalents from a temporal line rather than a vertical line; its thrust is chronologically forward rather than transcendently upward. If earth is the Platonic shadow of Heaven in the prelapsarian mode, the postlapsarian is measured by foreshadowings, umbrous anticipations of future and ultimate fulfillment of signified promise. As generating comparisons is Raphael's wont, processing already formulated comparisons is Michael's. It is the difference between the poet and the literary critic, and as Roland M. Frye has stressed, "the application of the literary skills of Renaissance intellectuals to the Biblical literature—their humanistic concern for textual accuracy and full literary exegesis—makes the Reformation at large a scholar's movement." We can say of Milton what Christopher says of Luther, that his exegesis "makes a radical shift from physical to *verbal*, not simply from physical to mental reference":

> For Luther, and even more so for Protestants after him, the Holy Spirit provided the experiential authentication for a reading of Scripture. The Holy Spirit's work, formally considered, was that of rhetorical expertise. In a very important sense, faith became a "poetic" activity—a passionate reading of a divine text (in which the figures were identified and read aright) followed by a reading of experience through this text. With the Reformation, Religious experience, to an overwhelming degree, became "literary experience."

Specifically of *Paradise Lost* Christopher says: "Books XI and XII are a *mimesis* of the protracted 'literary' experience that comprises 'explicit faith,' a faith confirmed 'by attentive study of the Scriptures & full perswasion of heart' (CE VI.177)." Michael initiates Adam not merely into Christianity but specifically into the sort of Christianity that was Milton's own combination or "reformation" of Puritanism and humanism. In the process of a full examination, Lewalski identifies Protestant expectations of figurative scriptural language and therefore expectations of rhetorical and poetic analysis and "the Protestant habit of referring to biblical figures and tropes to interpret and authenticate the signs and emblems presented by nature and our individual lives." [51] This neatly captures the principles underlying Michael's procedures with the Adam of the final books of *Paradise Lost*.

Typology is founded upon a series of passages from Saint Paul's writings and developed in Patristic tradition. That tradition of arraying allegorical levels is recorded with characteristic carefulness and thoroughness, for example, in Thomas Aquinas's *Summa Theologica* 1.1.10, "Whether in Holy Scripture a Word May Have Several Senses?":

> The author of Holy Writ is God, in whose power it is to signify His meaning, not by words only (as man also can do), but also by things themselves. So, whereas in every other science things are signified by words, this science has the property, that the things signified by the words have themselves also a signification. Therefore that first signification whereby words signify things belongs to the first sense, the historical literal. That signification whereby things signified by words have themselves also a signification is called the spiritual sense, which is based on the literal, and presupposes it. Now this spiritual sense has a threefold division. For as the Apostle says (Heb. x. 1) the Old Law is a figure of the New Law, and Dionysius says (*Cael. Hier.* i) *the New Law itself is a figure of future glory*. Again, in the New Law, whatever our Head has done is a type of what we ought to do. Therefore, so far as the things of the Old Law signify the things of the New Law, there is the allegorical sense; so far as the things done in Christ, or so far as the things which signify Christ, are types of what we ought to do, there is the moral sense. But so far as they signify what relates to eternal glory, there is the anagogical sense. Since the literal sense is that which the author intends, and since the author of Holy Writ is God, Who by one act comprehends all things by His intellect, it is not unfitting, as Augustine says (*Confess.* xii), if, even

according to the literal sense, one word in Holy Writ should have several senses.[52]

Gregory the Great speaks similarly:

> First we lay the foundations in history; then by following a symbolical sense, we erect an intellectual edifice to be a stronghold of faith; and lastly, by the grace of moral instruction, we as it were paint the fabric in fair colors. . . . For the word of God both exercises the understanding of the wise by its deeper mysteries, and also by its superficial lessons nurses the simpleminded. It presents openly that therewith the little ones may be fed; it keeps in secret that whereby men of loftier range may be rapt in admiration.

Such multiplicity, in Dante's word such polysemousness, produces not equivocation but secured richness of meaning.[53]

Patristic typology tended toward a rigidity of application of the multiplied schematic levels of literal, allegorical, tropological, and anagogical. Jerusalem supplies a concise traditional instance of such schematizing. Literally, it is the historical, geographical, experiential city of the Jews; allegorically, the Holy Church; tropologically, "the faithful soul of whosoever aspires to the vision of eternal peace"; and anagogically, "the life of the dwellers in Heaven who see God revealed in Zion."[54] More expansively and of special frequency and definitiveness is the interpretation of Exodus, as recorded, for example, in Dante's "Letter to Can Grande":

> Now if we look at the letter alone, what is signified to us is the departure of the sons of Israel from Egypt during the time of Moses; if at the allegory, what is signified to us is our redemption through Christ; if at the moral sense, what is signified to us is the conversion of the soul from the sorrow and misery of sin to the state of grace; if at the anagogical, what is signified to us is the departure of the sanctified soul from bondage to the corruption of this world into the freedom of eternal glory.

The passage from Egypt to Canaan is a model for Christian psychic rebirth. The Exodus example is definitive because it was allegorically interpreted nót only in the Pauline epistles but also in the prophetic books of the Old Testament and in the Gospels, Acts, and Apocalypse of the New Testament.[55]

By the seventeenth century typology had an extensive history, some of which Milton rejected as he rejected other Patristic excesses and rigidities but some of which he also inherited with satisfaction and reshaped according to his own lights. Milton was in general antagonistic to the mechanical scholastic applications of this allegorical tradition—he does not draw out four levels, for example—but his own expressed view of typology in *Christian Doctrine* builds on such a foundation:

> No passage of Scripture is to be interpreted in more than one sense; in the Old Testament, however, this sense is sometimes a compound of the historical and typical, as in Hosea XI. 1. compared with Matt. II. 15. "out of Egypt have I called my son," which may be explained in a double sense, as referring partly to the people of Israel, and partly to Christ in his infancy. (CE 16:263)

The opening words of *Christian Doctrine* announce a typological foundation and its goals:

> The Christian Doctrine is that DIVINE REVELATION disclosed in the various ages by CHRIST (though he was not known under that name in the beginning) concerning the nature and worship of the Deity, for the promotion of the glory of God, and the salvation of mankind. (14:17)

Immediately ensuing paragraphs develop the point: "Under the name of CHRIST are also comprehended Moses and the Prophets, who were his forerunners, and the Apostles whom he sent" (p. 19). From a wide range of proof texts, "what is dispersed throughout the different parts of the Holy Scriptures" will be collected into a unified body of doctrine by Milton working "from the Holy Scriptures alone, under the guidance of the Holy Spirit" (pp. 21, 19). The preparation of the treatise itself is thus an analogue of the typological procedure, bringing unity ("one compact body" "for the sake of assisting the memory" [p. 21]) out of diversity by reading past data through New Dispensatory illumination. As implicitly in his three late poetic masterpieces, at a number of explicit later points in the treatise Milton acknowledges his typological proceedings. Thus, Moses is a type of Christ (15.287), and he refers to "David, that is, Christ" (14:201); "the destruction of Jerusalem [is] the type of Christ's advent" (16.341); "Noah's ark was the type of baptism" (16:191); and "Under the law, the Lord's Supper was typified by the manna, and the water flowing from the rock" (16:197, and see 1 Cor. 10:3–4). Milton's word in this evidence is *typus*. In *Christian Doctrine* 2.7 Milton amplifies Col. 2:16–17, specifically to articulate the anagogy of the Sabbath and generally to set forward the theory of typology. The Colossians letter reads thus:

> Let no man therefore judge you in meat or in drink, or in respect of an holyday, or of the new moon, or of the sabbath *days*: Which are a shadow of things to come; but the body is of Christ.

Milton's gloss reads thus:

> Of what things to come the sabbaths are a shadow, we are taught Heb. iv. 9, 10. namely, of that sabbatical rest or eternal peace in heaven, of which all believers are commanded to strive to be partakers through faith and obedience, following the example of Christ. (CE 17:175)

Such proceeding is clarified also by a parenthetical observation tucked into one of Milton's earlier interpretations: "(if we may reason by analogy respecting spiritual things, from types of this kind, as was done before in the case of Esau)" (14.167).

Within *Paradise Lost* as Michael breaks down his prophetic history into its component parts, he articulates a series of stages but these reduce essentially to two stages, aligning with the Old Testament and its basis in law and with the New Testament and its basis in grace. That division—though it may recall the appeal of Ramistic bifurcations and moral polarities—has its more important foundation in the Pauline dialectic of letter and spirit and Pauline typological practice. Pauline allegory is most expansively and explicitly demonstrated in Gal. 4:22–5:1, in the story of Abraham's two sons, one by the bondmaid and the other by the free woman, the one "after the flesh" and the other "by promise," representing "the two covenants," one the "Jerusalem which now is" and the other the "Jerusalem which is above" and is "the mother of us all" (and see Rom. 9:7–8).

Because of Pauline theory and practice, Milton could not avoid altogether the methods of allegorical interpretation, but, in William Madsen's phrasing, typology for Milton was "a mode of discourse," not "a dictionary of ready-made symbols," as for Boyd Berry Puritan typology generally equates with "figurative literalism."[56] Like the Reformers generally, Milton professed loyalty to the *one*, that is, the literal, sense of Scripture, but he also practiced "the doctrine of the compound sense" as argued by his contemporary John Weemes, and H. R. MacCallum, who is concerned with Milton's theological theory rather than poetic practice, outlines Milton's relation to the tradition of Christian allegory in a series of stages:

> He upholds the Protestant rejection of multiple meanings, rejects allegory as an instrument of exegesis, permits a compound sense but prefers types clearly established by the New Testament, denies all authority to types in matters of doctrine and discipline, and stresses the spirituality of the antitype.[57]

D. C. Allen describes Milton's fine typological discriminations and his practice of "dynamic typology" or "typological evolution."[58] Indeed, John C. Ulreich extends Milton's theological typology to its poetic analogue: "Typological fulfillment, then, is not merely a process of analysis and redefinition; it is also a rebirth of the spirit *in* the letter, a reembodiment of abstracted meaning," and further, "The activity of the verse is an image of the imaginative process; in fact, the lines *are* 'substantially expressed' (III 140), the action they imitate, the reincarnation of meaning."[59]

Typologically, Milton rejects multiple meanings in one way but not in another; Old Testament data are "sometimes a compound of the historical and the typical," but New Testament antitypes are emphatically to be interpreted in only one sense, and that stresses their spirituality, especially by contrast with the experientiality of types. We have seen something of both the doubleness and the increasing spirituality in evidence already glimpsed, such as in the sequential revelations of the imagery of *seed*, in the biblically based solar occasions, in the structural design of historical eras reconstituting the hexaemeral creation, and in the catalogue of Old Testament faithful from Hebrews 11. Old Testament data giving way to New Dispensationary spiritualized and poetic meanings may be seen further in such incidentals as the distinction between Canaan and "earthly *Canaan*" (12.309–15), between "the Sons of *Abraham's* Loins" and "the Sons / Of *Abraham's* Faith" (12.447, 448–49), and between "The blood of Bulls and Goats" and "Some blood more precious" (12.292, 293). Milton was guided to such New Testament typological overlays by, for example, the Abraham of Galatians 3 and "blood" in Hebrews 9 and 10; and on Canaan see Heb. 11:15–16.

In more scattered evidence, the forward and spiritualizing thrust of typological allegory may be seen in the sequence of Michael's shepherds: The meek Abel, sacrificing "the Firstlings of his Flock," "On the cleft Wood," is himself sacrificed but finds "From Heav'n acceptance" and will have his

"Faith approv'd" (11.436–37, 440, 457–58); later in Book 11, the shepherds attacked by city dwellers (650, 640) provide the background out of whose wars Enoch is translated to Heaven; again, right-minded, right-worshiping shepherds people the interval between Noah's restoration of the world and the rising of Nimrod (12.19–24); the faithful Abraham is a shepherd (131–32); the Moses we encounter in Book 12 has been "That Shepherd, who first taught the chosen Seed" (1.8–9) from the epic's opening lines; and finally "simple Shepherds" (12.365) are rewarded with the solemn angel's carol of Christ's birth. These pastoral anticipations find their fulfillment in "the good shepherd" of John 10:11 ff., who lays down his life for his sheep (see also Heb. 13:20 and 1 Pet. 2:25, 5:4). In characteristically bifurcated data, shepherds define the positive pole, and the full and widening scope of their import emerges only gradually and with reference to the textually applied New Testament. Old Testament agents worked with literal sheep, but the antitype evolves through a series of poetic resonances. The Cain and Abel scene is, in MacCallum's words, "a kind of dumb show which reveals through mime, and in cryptic fashion, the essentials of the drama to come," [60] and the progressively revealed drama activates poetic as theological energies as it proceeds.

The very few references to the sun and solar variations in Michael's biblical materials are distinctly typological; they identify explicitly biblical divine messages to be stored in Adam's remembrance and recollected as promises of future guidance and glory. Examples include the ninth plague of Egypt, that of darkness; the pillar of cloud by day and of fire by night; the thunder and lightning that accompany Moses' receiving of the Ten Commandments. Noah's rainbow, "Betok'ning peace from God, and Cov'nant new" (11.86), is the most dramatic of these events, the most colorful, and the most memorable. Adam identifies the occasion as fraught with a heavenly meaning, which Michael explicates as the grace available to one just man—Noah, Adam himself, everyman—and as covenant, a promise to be remembered.

> But when he brings
> Over the Earth a Cloud, will therein set
> His triple-colored Bow, whereon to look
> And call to mind his Cov'nant: Day and Night,
> Seed-time and Harvest, Heat and hoary Frost

Shall hold thir course, till fire purge all things new,
Both Heav'n and Earth, wherein the just shall dwell. (11.895–901)

Mary Ann Radzinowicz has pointed out interestingly that the word *covenant* does not occur until Book 11. That word in Book 12, like *bruise* and *death* discussed earlier, progressively is made "amplier known." [61] The promise remains experientially elusive and mysterious but faithfully powerful as assurance of divine power, order, and fulfillment. The human roles of judgment and memory are captured in the two verb phrases *to look upon* and *to call to mind*. Book 11 ends with this acknowledgment of the New Covenant, the newly defined and promising relationship between God and man. Until Michael's revelations of the Son and the New Testament truth to Adam in Book 12, the covenant of the rainbow remains a "shadowy type." In Book 12 Michael teaches Adam about both the antitype and the process of typology.

As Raphael is explicit about the theory governing his analogies that surmount the reach of human sense, so Michael makes explicit the theoretical bases of his typological procedure, but in Michael's case the theory like their content is gradually revealed and demonstrated rather than immediately announced. When given his mission, Michael was told to "intermix [God's] Cov'nant" (11.115) in his enlightenment of mankind, and the proportions of the intermixture shift gradually. It is an anticipatory process, as introduced in Michael's explication of Abraham's significance and of the "mysterious terms" of the curse on the serpent:

> This ponder, that all nations of the Earth
> Shall in his Seed be blessed; by that Seed
> Is meant thy great deliverer, who shall bruise
> The Serpent's head; whereof to thee anon
> Plainlier shall be reveal'd. (12.147–51)

"To ponder" is the human "reading" assignment, and such contemplation will be divinely rewarded with progressive revelation of full meaning and with salvation or deliverance. It is revelation in time rather than Raphael's revelation in space. Indeed, when Michael completes this designed enlightenment his revelation reaches beyond time to explicate the ultimate return of the Messiah:

> Him so lately promis'd to thy aid
> The Woman's seed, obscurely then foretold,

> Now amplier known thy Savior and thy Lord,
> Last in the Clouds from Heav'n to be reveal'd
> In glory of the Father, to dissolve
> *Satan* with his perverted World, then raise
> From the conflagrant mass, purg'd and refin'd,
> New Heav'ns, new Earth, Ages of endless date
> Founded in righteousness and peace and love,
> To bring forth fruits Joy and eternal Bliss. (542–51)

Within time, obscurely foretold promises become "amplier known," but even that secured knowledge self-consumes in anticipatory dissolving visions of the realization of eternity. Verbally, as we have seen, this is reflected in such transformations of language as are imposed on *bruise* and *death*. *Bruise* leaves behind the literalism of its Satanic equation with a black-and-blue mark—"A World who would not purchase with a bruise, / Or much more grievous pain?" (10.500–501)—and becomes "this God-like act" of the Son's ransom of and redemption of mankind (12.427, 424). *Death* ceases to signify "temporal" dissolution or more generalized mortality, "a slow-pac't evil, / A long day's dying to augment our pain" (10.963–64), and becomes through Christ "A gentle wafting to immortal Life" (12.435).

Like Raphael's poetic, Michael straightforwardly lays the foundations of his procedures within the epic. Typologically Michael's theory is made most explicit and is most directly illustrated through the presentation of Moses, the New Testament's favorite Old Testament "example." Moses receives the laws from God on Mount Sinai:

> part such as appertain
> To civil Justice, part religious Rites
> Of sacrifice, informing them, by types
> And shadows, of that destin'd Seed to bruise
> The Serpent, by what means he shall achieve
> Mankind's deliverance. But the voice of God
> To mortal ear is dreadful; they beseech
> That *Moses* might report to them his will,
> And terror cease; he grants what they besought,
> Instructed that to God is no access
> Without Mediator, whose high Office now
> *Moses* in figure bears, to introduce
> One greater, of whose day he shall foretell,

And all the Prophets in thir Age the times
Of great *Messiah* shall sing. (12.230–44)

Earlier we noted the paradigm of Abraham's "call by Vision from his Father's house" (121) as the model for Adam's departure from Eden; here the most prominent impression is the equation of Michael's mediation to Adam with Moses' mediation on behalf of his people, both mirroring Christ's mediation for humanity.

When we look at the career of Moses that Michael presents outside of these procedural passages, Moses as a type emerges clearly. Moses guides the Chosen People in their journey (12.204), he commands the division of the Red Sea so that they may gain the shore (199), he leads them safely toward the Promised Land (215), though not by the readiest way (216), and he founds their new government in the wilderness (224–25). Egypt, bondage, the parting of the Red Sea, Canaan, the Promised Land, Mount Sinai, all are resonant with allegorical, tropological, and anagogical meanings. Even Milton uses *Egypt* when arguing for Scripture's one but compound sense uniting the historical and the typical. The style like the content, and of course like the Exodus into promise, is not by the readiest way; as in *Hamlet*, typology is a finding of directions by indirections.

God speaks through history, and if man will ponder its meaning, salvation and divine purpose will become gradually more amply known through both progressive data and progressive revelation. Douglas Bush has summarized one of Milton's most fundamental and recurrent ideas in these terms:

> In a word, the Mosaic law was not only positive and truly religious and moral but also restrictive, arbitrary, and ceremonial; it was a precise external code imposed upon man. When Christ came, the Mosaic law was abrogated for the law of the gospel. With his soul illuminated by a new revelation, man was released from his involuntary subjection to the Mosaic law and became, through divine grace and his own insight and effort, a free agent, a self-directing son of God. Regenerate man is in fact freed from dependence upon and allegiance to all external authorities and institutions.[62]

The law of Moses' dispensation gives way to the "better Cov'nant" of grace through human participation. Law evinces natural depravity (12.287–88) through such "shadowy expiations" as "the blood of bulls and Goats," but such discovery serves chiefly to persuade humans to draw transcendent

conclusions, to exercise their imaginations and memories as Adam did in
the crisis of Book 10:

> So law appears imperfect, and but giv'n
> With purpose to resign them in full time
> Up to a better Cov'nant, disciplin'd
> From shadowy Types to Truth, from Flesh to Spirit,
> From imposition of strict Laws, to free
> Acceptance of large Grace, from servile fear
> To filial, works of Law to works of Faith. (12.300–306)

Experiential data are a springboard for leaps of imagination and faith.

God's chosen mode of communication is through types, shadows, and
figures, and Moses is one link in a figurative chain of chronologically
progressive mediators:

> And therefore shall not *Moses*, though of God
> Highly belov'd, being but the Minister
> Of Law, his people into *Canaan* lead;
> But *Joshua* whom the Gentiles *Jesus* call,
> His Name and office bearing, who shall quell
> The adversary Serpent, and bring back
> Through the world's wilderness long wander'd man
> Safe to eternal Paradise of rest. (12.307–14)

This passage provides Milton's and Michael's most explicit guidelines for the
typological reading of Old Testament history. Later, in Book 12, lines
263–67, humanity's/Joshua's voice commands the sun/Son to alter its nor-
mal rhythm of shining to make a point about divine responsiveness to the
sure faith of one just man or the Chosen People. The moral lesson of faith
and man's relationship with God, as with the covenantal rainbow, is writ
large on the cosmos as in the individual heart. As with the cloud/pillar of
light, the biblical sun here provides Milton with an inherited image to
convey an array of meaning. Against the background of dispositions of the
solar throughout the preceding epic, Joshua's sun enforces the link between
sun and Son while bringing that equation into human history and familiar
fallen experience. The physical sun now fallen, veiled, and athwart, God's
light to man is altered in meaning as well as form. Access to it depends
newly upon human energy and responsibility and upon the mediator,
whether we name him Moses, Joshua, or Jesus. The act of memory makes

them all the same name, for all imply the same promise of ultimate future fulfillment and glory.

The account of the modulation of Moses into Joshua, the most explicit of Michael's theoretical formulations, coincides with remarkable exactitude with a comparable phrasing in *Christian Doctrine*, where we read:

> Thus the imperfection of the law was manifested in the person of Moses himself; for Moses, who was a type of the law, could not bring the children of Israel into the land of Canaan, that is, unto eternal rest; but an entrance was given to them under Joshua, or Jesus. Hence Peter testifies that eternal salvation was through Christ alone under the law, equally as under the gospel, although he was not then revealed. . . . But what neither the law itself nor the observers of the law could attain, faith in God through Christ has attained, and that even to eternal life. (CE 16:111)

The office of mediator, as studies of *Paradise Regained* have often acknowledged, divides into the three functions of prophet, priest, and king (15.287), and such name and office are ascribed to Moses and Joshua as types of Christ as well as to Christ himself. In Jason Rosenblatt's nice phrasing, Moses is a figure "of fortunate beginnings and incomplete endings."[63] The complementary Joshua provides happy completeness to the figure, especially when, as in both *Christian Doctrine* and *Paradise Lost*, the names Joshua/Jesus are linked etymologically. As Jean Danielou has pointed out, the typology of Joshua is a late addition to the testamentary tradition with almost no New Testament support and is indeed a piece of Christian propaganda relative to a failed Moses. In a number of ways, however, it is an overlay of the typology of Moses: Joshua replacing Moses to succeed in leadership into the Promised Land, the baptism of the Jordan displacing the baptismal dimensions of the Red Sea, the destruction of Jericho replacing that of Egypt.[64] This overlay is more optimistic than the Mosaic one and less trammeled by tradition. The progressively transcendent typological line of Moses/Joshua/Jesus thus leaves behind even the New Testament interpretational grids.

Typological procedures in *Paradise Lost* are both direct and indirect, and the indirectness is a matter of both poetics and theological theory and practice. In instructing a psychically divided Adam on how to survive and transcend a radically divided world, Michael must perform exercises that are also duplex. Ramistically, truth must be separated from falsehood, and the former affirmed, the latter denied. A natural Adam whose religion is natural theology and whose reasoning is by the light of nature must be transformed into man regenerate and redeemed who acts and reasons by the lights of grace and revelation. The Old Man must be logically as spiritually denied and the New Man affirmed (see Eph. 4:22–24 and Col. 3:9–10). Michael's instruction is sequential, gradual, and graduated. H. R. MacCallum describes that instruction as "a series of graded steps, each one but the last inconclusive, and each consequently capable of misinterpretation." The instruction is by way of indirection and dialectic. Such pedagogic method is practiced by Michael on Adam and by Milton on his readers, and it is a method of teaching that Milton identified as Christ's own. *The Doctrine and Discipline of Divorce*, for example, defines "Christs manner of teaching" in these terms:

> Thus at length we see both by this and by other places, that there is scarce any one saying in the Gospel but must bee read with limitations and distinctions, to bee rightly understood; for Christ gives no full comments or continued discourses, but . . . speaks oft in Monosyllables, like a maister, scattering the heavenly grain of his doctrine like pearl heer and there, which requires a skilfull and laborious gatherer, who must compare the words he findes, with other precepts, with the end of every ordinance, and with the generall *analogie* of Evangelick doctrine: otherwise many particular sayings would bee but strange repugnant riddles. (CE 3:2.490–91)

Tetrachordon develops a complementary agricultural image:

> Yet did [Christ] not omitt to sow within them the seeds of a sufficient determining, agen the time that his promis'd spirit should bring all things to their memory. (4.188)

MacCallum applies this Christic pedagogy to Michael's relationship with Adam and finds "the 'powerful art of reclaiming' employed by Christ in which excess is administered against excess, bending the crooked wand the contrary way, 'not that it should stand so bent, but that the overbending might reduce it to a straightness by its own reluctance.'"[65]

A number of Milton commentators have described Michael's direct instruction of Adam as a pulpit technique. By definition preaching is "the fitting and suitable communication of the Word of God," "an exposition of Holy Writ by division and subdivision." More expansively:

> Preaching by word of voice—our present subject—is open and public instruction in faith and morals, devoted to the informing of men, and

proceeding along the path of reasoning and from the source of authori-
ties. . . . Two aspects of theology whereof use is to be made in preaching are
involved: the rational, which strives after knowledge in things divine, and
the moral, which offers information in ethics. For preaching is instruction
now in divine matters, now in moral conduct. This is imaged forth by the
angels descending and ascending on the ladder which Jacob saw. Mystically,
the angels are those learned men who ascend when they preach heavenly
things. They descend when they conform to things mortal. [66]

Specifically, for J. B. Broadbent Michael is

preaching a 17th-century sermon of the plain Puritan kind recommended in
William Perkins's *Art of Prophesying*. He takes a text, explains it, derives
"close and natural" doctrine from it, and applies the doctrine "to the life and
manners of men in a simple and plaine speech." [67]

As the role of the clergy after Christ's death in *Paradise Lost* is to "win / Great
numbers of each Nation to receive / With joy the tidings brought from
Heav'n" (12.502–4), so *Christian Doctrine* also defines the role of Christian
teachers. Though not compromising the primacy of individual readings of
Scripture, Milton's guidelines for the public interpretation of Scripture
coincide with what we have seen of Michael's procedure:

They consist in knowledge of languages; inspection of the originals; exam-
inations of the context; care in distinguishing between literal and figurative
expressions; consideration of cause and circumstances, of antecedents and
consequents; mutual comparison of texts; and regard to the analogy of faith.
Attention must also be paid to the frequent anomalies of syntax. . . . Lastly,
no inferences from the text are to be admitted, but such as follow necessarily
and plainly from the words themselves; lest we should be constrained to
receive what is not written for what is written, the shadow for the substance;
the fallacies of human reasoning for the doctrines of God: for it is by the
declarations of Scripture, and not by the conclusions of the schools, that our
consciences are bound. (CE 16:265)

Such proceeding provides one format for defining the role and poetics of
Michael in *Paradise Lost*. Michael is such a textual mediator, and his instruc-
tion is of both theory and practice. As *Christian Doctrine* divides between
Faith and Love, under Michael's tutelage Adam attains the sum of earthly
wisdom in the arena of faith and doctrine and is then enjoined to "Add deeds
to thy knowledge answerable."

A supplementary format addresses additional possibilities. Late in Book 12 of the epic the burden of interpretation shifts from Michael as "public interpreter" to Adam as reader or literary critic, and the applicable genre shifts to Protestant meditation, which Barbara K. Lewalski has outlined with such recent care. Profoundly concerned with interior life and specifically with the conversion experience, Protestant meditation began from the Word, the self, or the creatures. As Lewalski describes it:

> Essentially, the Protestant concern in both categories of meditation, occasional and deliberate (as in the sermon), is to trace the interrelationship between the biblical text and the Christian's own experience, so that the one is seen to be the reflection or manifestation of the other. In occasional meditation the starting point is some occasion or event or observation in the meditator's personal experience, and his purpose is to interpret that in terms of God's providential plan and Word; in deliberate meditation the starting point is usually a biblical text or event or theological doctrine, and here the emphasis is upon "application to the self." The Christian's experience is to comment upon the biblical text, and the text upon his experience.

Typically, Protestants applied the subject to the self rather than seeking to participate in or lose themselves to the subject.[68] Such procedure should again be read against the theory of *Christian Doctrine*:

> Every believer has a right to interpret the Scriptures for himself, inasmuch as he has the Spirit for his guide, and the mind of Christ is in him. Nay, the expositions of the public interpreter can be of no use to him, except so far as they are confirmed by his own conscience. (CE 16:265)

Christian Doctrine develops the reader's proper role further by distinguishing a "twofold Scripture":

> Under the gospel we possess, as it were, a twofold Scripture; one external, which is the written word, and the other internal, which is the Holy Spirit, written in the hearts of believers, according to the promise of God, and with the intent that it should by no means be neglected. . . . Hence, although the external ground which we possess for our belief at the present day in the written word is highly important, and, in most instances at least, prior in point of reception, that which is internal, and the peculiar possession of each believer, is far superior to all, namely, the Spirit itself. (Pp. 273−75)

Similarly, "the light of the gospel . . . is not to be sought in written records alone, but in the heart," which "enlighten[s] us inwardly through the medium of faith and love" (p. 271); it is "the inward persuasion of the Spirit working in the hearts of individual believers" (p. 279). *Christian Doctrine* carries the latter, internal Scripture to its extreme, indeed elevating it beyond even the Scriptures:

> It is difficult to conjecture the purpose of Providence in committing the writings of the New Testament to such uncertain and variable guardianship, unless it were to teach us by this very circumstance that the Spirit which is given to us is a more certain guide than Scripture, whom therefore it is our duty to follow. (Pp. 277–79)

Michael encapsulates the same lesson in poetic form in his reference to "those written Records pure, / Though *not but by the Spirit understood*" (12.513–14; emphasis mine).

The kind and spirit of active and creative participation in the reading of biblical texts here recommended is central to Protestant and Puritan traditions as defined by Lewalski and Christopher and is what Milton himself practiced and regularly requires of the readers of his poem; he assigns it to Adam as to humanity in their pursuit of understanding and growth. It includes the possibility and even the necessity of error along the route and thence the crystallization and abandonment of error, but it also includes the transcendence of texts. It moves from "surprise by sin" to provoke the requisite judgment and denial central to Ramistic proceedings, but it includes also those settled principles of *Paradise Regained*, Book 4, that a man must bring to his reading, "A spirit and judgment equal or superior" to the texts, "And what he brings," Milton insists, "what needs he elsewhere seek?" (321–30). Basil Willey quips that Milton thus "frees himself from that last infirmity of noble Protestants—subservience to holy writ." [69] In such exercises Milton defines also the coinciding boundaries of Christian humanism and Protestant exegesis.

5 · *Widening Perspectives*

The change from pre- to postlapsarian life is neither radical, dramatic,
nor conclusive. Important ties still bind us to that blessed state. Milton challenges
the reader to figure out which elements of his millenial pastoralism apply to
this world in which we live and which apply only to the future.
Insofar as paradise really was lost, finally and for all, *Paradise Lost* is
utopian or escapist fantasy; it does not talk about this world but about
a world radically different from it. But insofar as the Puritan ordering suggests
that paradise was never entirely lost, the poem implies that talk about
Eden is really talk about our condition; to that extent the poem is utopian in the
way it blunts the distinction between fictive and external reality while
suggesting that the former should determine and shape the latter.
The questions I have posed about events before the fall do not have a simple
answer. Adam and Eve resemble us and are different from us; a change did
occur yet certain things remain constant. It is the double quality of our answers to
these questions, the tension between change and lack of change, which creates
the distinctive veiling of utopian impulses in *Paradise Lost*.

BOYD M. BERRY, *Process of Speech*

E MAY CONCLUDE by placing the contrasts developed
in preceding chapters between Raphael and Michael and
between the prelapsarian and postlapsarian into some
broad, suggestive, and interlocking perspectives. Com-
prehensively, the arena of faculty psychology variously
illuminates the poetics and pedagogies we have been
examining. In its simplest terms, the prelapsarian mode attaches to the
fantasy and the postlapsarian to the memory. This frame of reference will
serve both to review the categories of the previous discussion and to set forth
some suggestive widening perspectives.

Theological contrasts, as I have been arguing variously, have their basis in logical issues and are underscored by certain historical changes of which they are perhaps cause, perhaps effect. At the conclusion of his essay on Ramus and *Paradise Lost*, Walter J. Ong locates Milton between coordinates of openness and closure, aligning openness with epic and closedness with Ramistic logic.[1] Although Ong does not distribute the categories between Raphael and Michael, the distinction is suggestive for our purposes. Harold Fisch distinguishes between "classical amplitude" and "Hebraic intensity" and between

> the hexaemeral tradition represented by Du Bartas, Pererius, and a host of Christian authorities early and late [which] had emphasized the meta-historical region of theogony and eschatology, [and] the Hebraic tradition [which] had emphasized the quotidian, the concrete, and the historically visualizable aspects of the story. [2]

We can see behind the contrasting practice of Raphael and Michael a shift from classical oratory with its presumption of a broad audience to pulpit technique with its presumption of a more personal communication geared to its audience's memory storage and retrieval. The shift is also from Raphael's Platonic synthesizing to Michael's systematically chosen analytical examples, and from prelapsarian poetic resonances to postlapsarian techniques of literary criticism with their foundations in Renaissance humanism and Reformation Protestantism. It is also a shift from spatial models recognized in the natural and cosmic data of the created universe to memorably abstract and explicitly verbal models, which are products of a mind predisposed to dichotomies and disjunctions that can be arrayed in continuous sequences dependent upon a system of logical and simultaneously theological priorities, and thus a shift from language as indicative to language as commemorative.[3]

Combinations of logic, rhetoric, and poetics modulate toward categories of faculty psychology. As Murray W. Bundy has pointed out, by the sixteenth century in England, through a marriage of rhetoric and faculty psychology, logical Invention became linked with imagination:

> Invention is nothing else but the natural good of an imagination, conceiving the ideas and forms of everything that can be imagined, heavenly as well as earthly, animate or inanimate, in order afterwards to represent, describe, and imitate them.

Rosemond Tuve has similarly observed, "Puttenham's defense of the Imagination clearly regards it as the faculty responsible for logic's first division,

Invention." [4] Indeed, Puttenham begins his *Arte of English Poesie* by calling attention to God himself as poet or literally "maker," "who without any trauell to his diuine imagination, made all the world of nought." Puttenham laments that in his age poetry is so despised that men equate a poet with "a light headed or phantasticall man," whereas in fact the imagination is rather like a glass or mirror wherein "are represented vnto the soule all maner of bewtifull visions, whereby the inuentiue parte of the mynde is so much holpen, as without it no man could deuise any new or rare thing." There are many sorts of glasses, such as we would call telescopes and rosy-colored glasses, but Puttenham continues: "Euen so is the phantasticall part of man (if it be not disordered) a representer of the best, most comely and bewtifull images or apparances of thinges to the soule and according to their very truth." [5] Imagination thus linked with Invention is freed from the dangerous implications of the fantastic, and it can become in Raphael's hands an avenue of access to the divine. In this tradition, as classically, Memory is the mother of the Muses.

Speaking of the memory, Puttenham says:

> There is nothing in man of all the potential parts of his mind (reason and will except) more noble or more necessary to the active life then memory: because it maketh most to a sound iudgement and perfect worldly wisedome, examining and comparing the times past with the present, and by them both considering the time to come, concludeth with a stedfast resolution, what is the best course to be taken in all his actions and aduices in this world: it came vpon this reason, experience to be so highly commended in all consultations of importance, and preferred before any learning or science, and yet experience is no more than a masse of memories assembled, that is, such trials as man hath made in time before. (P. 39)

Although the term *memory* occurs rarely in Milton's *Logic*, as Frances Yates, Walter Ong, and others make clear, Ramistic Method was primarily a strategy for memorizing. In its basic definition in the *Logic*, "Method is a dianoetic disposition of various homogeneous axioms . . . whence the agreement of all with relation to each other is judged and retained by the memory," and memory itself is "an internal sense conserving the images of things that have been recognized." In the preface to the *Logic* Milton places memory in the context of the sequential process of reasoning:

> Reason or logic—first the natural reason just spoken of, then trained reason—attaches to itself . . . four helpers: sense, observation, induction,

and experience. For since the precepts of the arts are general, these cannot be gathered except from specific instances, and specific instances can be observed only by the senses; without observation, which commits individual examples to memory, the senses avail nothing; without induction, which by working on individuals rather than on large numbers sets up some general rule, observation is useless; without experience, which judges the conformity with one another and as it were agreement of all individuals, induction is useless.

Milton, like Ramism generally, honors brevity, "and brevity is mindful of ["is in the interests of" (Y)] intelligence and memory." [6] Memory is by definition a temporal process, and although within the mode of Invention memory may follow observation and precede induction, for prelapsarians even memory is primarily immediate and simultaneous with apprehension. For postlapsarians memory, like everything else worth achieving, is difficult to come by and requires discipline and training, and these Michael contributes.

The act and art of memory are fundamental to the dispositional processing of Michael's prophecy/history and to Adam's and the reader's processing of Michael's materials in relation to Raphael's. Memory is to Michael and Disposition as Imagination is to Raphael and Invention. The postlapsarian emphasizes the priority of words as the prelapsarian relies upon natural images. The sensory reception of images, the sense impressions, the phantasmata are at the foundation of the body of information communicated to Adam by Raphael; they are the arguments, the units of an external reality. The universals, the abstracting of universals from particulars and arranging of them in their natural and theological order, however, are the domain of Michael. Further, the postlapsarian must at every turn take into account the dimension of time as well as of human fallenness. The art of memory, that is, the mnemotechnic art, works with places and images and emphasizes their serial order to allow moving backward and forward, from generals to particulars, from faith to experience and experience to faith. Michael literalizes the memory component of topoi by pointing to actual places and their loads of meaning, which Adam can subsequently re-collect. Michael facilitates Adam's memory similarly by establishing meanings for individual historical personages disposed morally and only later attaching to these convenient handles their names, names that may later serve to trigger Adam's mind to re-collect their full and universal import.

"To think is to speculate with images," says Frances A. Yates quoting
Bruno, and this is precisely what in their quite different ways Raphael and
Michael guide Adam to do. In the tradition so ably traced in Yates's *Art of
Memory*, the Middle Ages—specifically Albertus Magnus and Thomas
Aquinas—were responsible for the transfer of memory from rhetoric to
ethics. But even the pseudo-Ciceronian *Rhetorica ad Herennium* with its
division of rhetoric into *inventio, dispositio, elecutio, memoria,* and *pronuntio*
provides some distinctions that are significant for our present purposes.
Memory is there "the firm retention in the mind of the matter, words, and
arrangement" and "the treasure-house of the ideas supplied by Inven-
tion . . . the guardian of all the parts of rhetoric," a matter of art supple-
menting nature. The *Ad Herennium* distinguishes two kinds of memory
with lapsarian alignments: "The natural memory is that memory which is
imbedded in our minds, born simultaneously with thought. The artificial
memory is that memory which is strengthened by a kind of training and
system of discipline." The *Ad Herennium* is chiefly concerned with artificial
memory, a matter of images and of backgrounds (which are small, com-
plete, conspicuous, and serialized); it distinguishes between images of
subject matter and of words, the latter being a more bracing exercise to aid
the former; and it advises the choice of striking images, either positive or
negative, rather than ordinary ones for intensity and duration of impression
and for recollection in artificial memory. In view of our earlier consideration
of lapsarian imagery, the *Ad Herennium* example is telling: Solar eclipses are
more "marvellous" and therefore more memorable than sunrises or sunsets.
Summarizing, the treatise exhorts:

> Let art, then, imitate nature, find what she desires, and follow as she
> directs. For in invention nature is never last, education never first; rather the
> beginnings of things arise from natural talent, and the ends are reached by
> discipline.[7]

Insofar as memory operates before the fall it is primarily a matter of
Invention and of nature, not artifice; it is, as we have seen, a firm perception
of things. But after the fall what chiefly matters is discipline and what are to
be remembered are words, especially as Michael's lessons are secured in the
imagery of Adam's fallen world and as he presents his pupil with highly
striking images, morally positive and morally negative, precisely for their
intensity and memorial duration.

Memory before and Memory after the fall are implicit in the *Ad Heren-*

nium's distinction between the natural memory and the artifical memory. Ramus, according to Yates, equated not only Method but the whole of dialectic with what he considered the "true art" of memory, which retains and intensifies the principle of order from the traditional art of memory "but does away with . . . the side which cultivated the imagination as the chief instrument of memory." In Reformation fashion, he smashes the icons of imagination in favor of Ramistic dialectical order. "If Memory was the Mother of the Muses," Yates quips, "she was also to be the Mother of Method." Ramistic schematic diagrams descending from generals to specials replace topical artificial memory and in so doing eliminate the role of imagination as a natural and emotionally charged stimulus in favor of the abstract order of dialectical analysis, which was "natural" in Ramus's view of the correspondence between the internal and external reality. In Ramus's hands memory becomes based upon internal rather than external artificial signs. Michael is responsible for disciplining Adam's memorial capacity and exercising its art and method, replacing one meaning of *natural* with another. In view of the present lapsarian contrasts, it is not surprising that in general Yates finds Aristotle's views on memory are essential for the art of memory in the Middle Ages and Plato's views are essential for the art of memory in the Renaissance. Further, Yates describes a lively Elizabethan debate on the relationship between memory and imagination and on whether inner images were to be replaced by Ramistic Method or were to be magically developed into the sole instruments for the grasp of reality, a debate that is also a conflict between Protestantism and Roman Catholicism.[8]

In his full-length study of Ramus, Ong distinguishes between "simplification-for-understanding" and "simplification-for-recall" in formulations that neatly draw lines between what we have seen as the Raphaelean and the Michaelean procedures and intentions.

> "Things" are constituted not in opposition to the mind, but in opposition to the word. The word has an obvious vocal and auditory bearing, which tends to make the whole realm of "things" by contrast that which is apprehended visually, and to some extent tactually.

Visualist designs relate to Raphael as enunciations relate to Michael, and the visualist are the products of Invention—even such words as *place* and *discourse* have a spatial or visualist etymological base. Michael, on the other hand, is concerned with the process of hearing and enunciation. Ong traces this second component to Aristotle:

> Human knowledge for Aristotle exists in the full sense only in the enunciation, either interior or exteriorized in language; the *saying* of something about something, the *uttering* of a statement, the expression of a *judgment* (ultimately a declaring a "yes" or a "no").

There is, says Ong, "no adequate visualist equivalent for this act" of enunciation. Invention, with its backgrounds in classical concepts of knowledge and understanding, views cognition by analogy with vision and is marked by a high visual and spatial component. On the other hand, Disposition, with its backgrounds in the Hebraic concept of knowledge, views cognition by analogy with hearing and is connected with judicial procedure.[9]

Lapsarian contrasts between the Hellenic and the Hebraic and between Raphael's spatial uni-verse and Michael's judgmental presuppositions and procedures have been suggested through earlier evidence and commentary, but we may turn now to the contrasts between the visual and the aural in Raphael's central and Michael's final books of *Paradise Lost*. Raphael's materials and teaching operate in two visual modes. As we have seen, Raphael invents for Adam the immediate visual world before them, discovers its arguments to his pupil, and enhances Adam's "sudden apprehension" by articulating the meanings implicit in the cosmic and earthly evidence. Raphael's lectures on heavenly history, "th'*invisible* exploits / Of warring Spirits" (5.565–66) and "how this World / Of Heav'n and Earth *conspicuous* first began" (7.62–63; emphasis mine), are also highly visual storytelling. Raphael is the "Divine Interpreter" who reveals the unimaginable by creating and re-creating scenes that are speaking pictures. In his discourse, the medium—the hierarchical cosmos, angelic faith or apostasy in action, the relationship of sun and earth and Son and man—is the message.

Michael's content also occurs in two visual modes, but in both the visual serves primarily as a base to which are attached aural interpretations that are thereby stored for later retrieval by the memory. Michael leads Adam to the highest hill of paradise, which he calls "this top / Of Speculation" (12.588–89) and an ascent "In the Visions of God" (11.376–77)—the similar site in *Paradise Regained* is "this specular Mount" (4.236). Visually as medically, storing or nourishment gives way to re-storing or cure. On the mount of vision Michael removes the film to purge Adam's visual nerve that it may see "nobler sights" (11.411–15); Adam is medicined "Ev'n to the inmost seat of mental sight" (418), closes his eyes, is entranced, and is twice said to open his eyes again (423, 429) to look upon and to draw and hear conclusions about—that is, *to speculate* in both its senses—the pageants that are performed before the audience of pupil and teacher. In Michael's second visual mode—and the division approximately coincides with the division between Books 11 and 12—the balance of visual to aural shifts. As Michael says:

> but I perceive
> Thy mortal sight to fail; objects divine
> Must needs impair and weary human sense:
> Henceforth what is to come I will relate,
> Thou therefore give due audience, and attend. (12.8–12)

At the conclusion of their interview Adam calls Michael the "Seer blest" (553) who has measured for him "this transient World" against "Eternity, whose end no eye can reach" (554–56). Michael is an agent of the visionary, not the visual. What matters in his content is not the ostensible visual component but the aural interpretation, the discursive abstract analysis, the Christian theory that not only does not convey but even sometimes defies the sensual impression and the immediate reality. Michael may direct Adam's physical eyes toward a particular geographical site ("each place behold / In prospect, as I point them" [142–43]), but Michael himself perceives what is beyond the immediately sensory, saying of Abraham, for example, "I see him, but thou canst not" (128). Michael sees with the eyes of faith the suprasensual, the supramental, the supratemporal. Adam's perspective too is increasingly freed from confinement by the experiential. After Michael's account of Abraham's faithfulness, Adam calls the angel "Enlight'ner of my darkness" (271) and says of himself, "now first I find / Mine eyes true op'ning" (273–74). The differences in their vision, which began as differences between the angelic intuitive and the human discursive reason, are reconciled as reason gives way to revelation. Adam is awakened to "foresight" (11.368). As Barbara Lewalski's study of the symbolism of vision in the final books of the epic has shown, Adam's "spiritual myopia" is cured and his spiritual vision grows clearer as his bodily vision declines. Michael's prophecy is "structured so as to display the progressive manifestations of the Covenant of Grace operating throughout human history to create mankind anew, by means of Faith." [10]

Raphael's and Michael's contrasting uses of the visual are put into another kind of perspective by noting that for Milton as for Protestants and Puritans generally, Christianity was a religion of the ear rather than the eye. Reformation Protestantism emphasized the preaching of the Word, especially recalling Saint Paul's formulations that "Faith is by hearing" (Rom. 10:17) and that "we walk by faith, and not by sight" (2 Cor. 5:7). Because this tradition and Milton's relation to it have been traced in several recent fine studies, in particular Lewalski's *Protestant Poetics and the Seventeenth-Century Lyric* and Georgia Christopher's *Milton and the Science of the Saints*, we need not rehearse the matter here. Supplementing that tradition, however, Northrop Frye identifies Old Testament revelation as aural and attaches a New Testament transfer of the visual to the Second Coming in a provocative series of distinctions:

> The visual image is centripetal: it holds the body immobile in a pose of static obedience, and sets the sign of authority before it. The revelation by the Word is centrifugal: it is primarily a command, the starting-point of a course of action. In the Biblical view everything we can see is a creature of God: *fiat lux, et fuit lux*. Adam was surrounded with a visible paradise, but what the forbidden tree primarily forbids is idolatry, the taking of the visible object to be the source of creative power, as Eve does when after her fall she bows in homage to the tree. Since the fall, paradise has been an invisible inner state, to be brought into being by the revelation through the Word. [11]

Christian Doctrine may be invoked to conclude the point; there Milton states: "For the Word is both the Son and Christ, that is, as has been said, *the anointed*; and as he is the image, as it were, by which we see God, so is he the word by which we hear him" (Hughes, p. 972). After considering the Puritan traditions through which words alone give significance to physical objects and considering typology more generally, William Madsen explicates this Miltonic formulation:

> The word of classical philosophy was made flesh in order that the flesh might be made Word for Christians, that is, in order that the partial images and "shadowy Types" of Christ scattered throughout human history, and especially the history of the Chosen People, might be molded "into an immortal feature of loveliness and perfection," in order that the "unmeaning objects" upon which our senses gaze bewildered might be given the radiance of intelligibility through the mediation of language. [12]

In Raphael's visual mode, the Son is the "Divine Similitude," and in Michael's aural mode the Son is the Word. Michael is the angelic speaker "who future things canst represent / As present" (11.870–71) and who communicates the prospects of a "paradise within" to Adam within a mode of "new Speech" (12.5).

Many schemes of faculty psychology have been advanced through the ages, but we may take as our base the composite formulation of "our sage and serious poet Spenser," that "better teacher than Scotus or Aquinas" (Hughes, pp. 728–29). Characteristically, Spenser sets forward patterns of abstract ideas in combinations of agents and sites, and in the upper reaches of the castle of Alma in Book 2, canto 9, of *The Faerie Queene*, Guyon and Prince Arthur are thus introduced to embodiments of imagination, judgment, and memory, coinciding with human youth, maturity, and age and located serially in the front, center, and rear of the brain:

> The first of them could things to come foresee:
> The next could of things present best aduize;
> The third things past could keepe in memoree,
> So that no time, nor reason could arize,
> But that the same could one of these comprize.

As Spenser's recent editor points out, the first of these, Phantastes with his trappings of Saturnine melancholy, is not so much our modern *imagination* as he is "the power of the mind to put together image pictures from sense data"; "It is not restricted to things that exist and hence is associated with the future." [13] This figure is remarkable for "his quicke preiudize," "sharpe foresight," and "working wit, / That neuer idle was." His bailiwick is filled with buzzing flies and is colorfully decorated with:

> Infinite shapes of things dispersed thin;
> Some such as in the world were neuer yit,
> Ne can deuized be of mortall wit;
> Some daily seene, and knowen by their names.
> (2.9.50.3–6)

Imagination, in the words of Theseus in *A Midsummer Night's Dream*, is that faculty which "bodies forth / The forms of things unknown . . . and gives to airy nothing / A local habitation and a name" (5.1.14–17). Spenser's figuration of fancy gives way to the character and realm of Judgment, whose domain is

> painted faire with memorable gestes,
> Of famous Wisards, and with picturals
> Of Magistrates, of courts, of tribunals,
> Of commen wealthes, of states, of pollicy,
> Of lawes, of iudgements, and of decretals;
> All artes, all science, all Philosophy,
> And all that in the world was aye thought wittily.
> (2.9.53.3–9)

Judgment is "a man of ripe and perfect age, / Who did them meditate all his life long, / That through continuall practise and vsage, / He now was growne right wise, and wondrous sage" (54.2–5). As Judgment follows and completes Phantastes, so Judgment precedes and gives way to the final figure of Memory (Eumnestes = good memory), whose exercises (Anamnestes = memory in action or re-membering) illuminate the present by drawing upon the recorded past. Despite his bodily frailty, "Yet liuely vigour rested in his mind, / And recompenst him with a better scorse" (55.7–8). This figure, divided in its operations, has the advantage of "minds redoubled forse" (55.9). His "infinite remembrance" does not suffer the past to perish but keeps it "for euer incorrupted" (56.1, 4, 7). The act of remembering, like Anamnestes, is notably fresh and agile. The combination of aged faculty and youthful agency reflects the complexity, even the paradox, we have come to associate with the postlapsarian.

Although modified for his special purposes in "The Legend of Temperance," Spenser is here setting forth the basic pattern of faculty psychologies which, since Galen, have associated the *phantasia, cogitatio,* and *memoria* with the ventricles of the brain.[14] Aristotle, whose psychology is also biologically based, distinguishes likewise among perception, thinking, and judging and specifically recognizes two modes of imagination, a passive or receptive power of revived or residual sense impressions and an active and productive power of reconstructed or created images. His imagination mediates between sensation and thought and functions as a mental storehouse for absent objects and therefore as a kind of memory. Aristotle elsewhere recognizes memory as both perceptual and conceptual and distinguishes specifically between *memory*, which animals share, and *recollection* which is exclusively and definitively human.[15]

Avicenna, a mediator between ancient medical and philosophical traditions, builds his psychology directly on Aristotle but also endeavors to harmonize Aristotle with his teacher Plato's views on the soul. His psychol-

ogy is hierarchical as well as chronological. Avicenna expands the threefold,
ventricle scheme into five categories: common sense, fantasy (or representa-
tion), imagination, estimation (or opinion), and memory. The first two of
these, in the first ventricle, receive and preserve data from the five senses;
the next two, in the middle ventricle, bridge the gap between sensual data
and abstract forms, the imagination combining and separating them and
the estimative faculty "perceiv[ing] the non-sensible intentions that exist in
the individual sensible objects"; and finally, in the third ventricle the
retentive and recollective faculty is a storehouse of ideas or intentions as the
fantasy is a storehouse of images. Avicenna distinguishes between external
and internal senses, between active and passive faculties, between primary
and secondary perception, and between perception of forms and perception
of intentions.[16] These medically based views relate to the animal rather than
the rational soul, and thus to the prelapsarian basis on which the post-
lapsarian is also an overlay with regard—as, for example, in Augustine—to
such matters as the trinity of will, understanding, and memory.

Avicenna separates human reason from these animal faculties, and the
role he assigns to reason leads in a distinctly spiritual direction. When he
comes to discuss "How the Rational Soul Acquires Knowledge" (chapter
title), Avicenna's psychology wonderfully illuminates the nature of the pre-
lapsarian Adam. Avicenna speaks of the highest human faculty of the ra-
tional soul, indeed a "Divine Power," which he, like Raphael, calls Intui-
tion, or "potential intellect" (p. 35) or "prophetic inspiration" (p. 37), the
instantaneous acquisition of wide-ranging knowledge often apparently
from within the self rather than through instruction.

> In this state the material intelligence must be called "Divine spirit." It
> belongs to the genus of *intellectus in habitu*, but so lofty that not all people
> share it. It is not unlikely, indeed, that some of these actions attributed to the
> "Divine Intelligence" because of their powerful and lofty nature overflow
> into the imagination which symbolizes them in sense-imagery and words.
> (Pp. 35–36)

The capacity is so strong in certain people that they "do not need great
effort, or instruction and actualization, in order to make contact with the
active intelligence"; such minds instinctively perceive the middle terms of
syllogisms (p. 36).

Avicenna distinguishes two modes of cognition and two character types
that nicely capture the lapsarian categories. The first, as with Milton's

imaginative prelapsarian exercise, is posited as possibility rather than strict actuality:

> Thus there might be a man whose soul has such an intense purity and is so firmly linked to the rational principles that he blazes with intuition, i.e. with the receptivity of inspiration coming from the active intelligence concerning everything. So the forms of all things contained in the active intelligence are imprinted on his soul either all at once or nearly so, not that he accepts them merely on authority but on account of their logical order which encompasses all the middle terms. (P. 36)

Such a prelapsarian psychology, in Avicenna's view as in our examination of Ramistic categories above, contrasts with four discursive intellectual processes that directly address the postlapsarian psychology. In the first, through exercises of imagination and estimation the soul abstracts universals from particulars, essentials from accidents, to arrive at foundational principles. In the second, the soul sorts out negation from affirmation and accepts the self-evident or awaits the discovery of middle terms. In the third, through a series of logical procedures, it sorts out premises, necessary predications, contradictions, conjunction, and disjunction to arrive at necessary and universal conclusions in which "the soul acquiesces." Finally, having acquired these principles of conception and judgment with the help of the lower faculties, the soul progressively withdraws into itself and "becomes perfect and strong" and "isolates itself absolutely in its actions" (pp. 55–56). Thus, the Avicenna data lead us in a straight philosophical and chronological line from Adam's initial capacity for worship and for naming the animals to the plight and proper conduct of the "One Just Man" endeavoring through heroic patience to make his way through a fallen world with continuing spiritual growth and rewards.

It is not unusual for readers of *Paradise Lost* to read the natures of the first couple in terms of a physiologically based faculty psychology, aligning Eve with the fancy and Adam with reason, especially in order to find fault with Eve. Such a reading recognizes in the separation of Adam and Eve on the fateful morning an introduction of psychological imbalance to the composite human entity the first couple represent. Fredson Bowers reviews the issues compactly:

> It is thus possible to equate Eve, the female and so inferior element of the union, to passion (or emotion), the lower element of the soul, subject to the

governance of her superior, Adam. She is also matter and Adam the spirit; she the body, Adam the soul. . . . In that reason is the final arbiter of evidence which passion brings to its judgment, it is the superior; on the other hand, without the stimulus provided by emotion, reason remains passive and cannot institute a necessary action. Thus the question of superior and inferior rests on one narrow point; otherwise, reason and passion are each necessary to the other and may be said to fulfill the other in balanced action. [17]

Condemnatory equations of Eve with fancy may even be extended as far as Samuel Johnson's definition of imagination in *Rambler* 125 (28 May 1751) as "a licentious and vagrant faculty, unsusceptible of limitations, and impatient of restraint, [which] has always endeavoured to baffle the logician, to perplex the confines of distinction, and burst the inclosures of regularity." [18] It is overall easier to see that Eve has erred in separating her lesser faculty from Adam's reason, her "best prop" (9.433), than to acknowledge the analogous proposition that Adam's reason needs and is incomplete without Eve's fanciful nature, which is not precisely separable from the emotional tenor and curiosity that she also presents and represents. Without an Eve component to open up new territory and possibilities, Adam's stolid reason would stagnate; without her collecting of the representations of the senses, Adam could not exercise his reason in joining or disjoining data and generating knowledge or opinions. Without the supply of data from the first ventricle of the brain, his cogitative and estimative faculty could not operate to supply intentions for storage in the memory.

Early in Book 5 of *Paradise Lost*, Adam manifests his reasoning skills, his Spenserian Judgment, his cogitative and estimative capacities by presenting a theoretical review of faculty psychology. His discussion of intellectual hierarchy builds upon inherited tradition and presents the interrelations of the senses, the fancy, and the reason. For Adam the senses "represent" data; the fancy "forms" data; and the reason sorts data into dichotomous categories. It joins or separates, affirms or denies, and effects knowledge or opinion. Adam explicates the bases of Eve's toad-inspired dream in these terms:

> But know that in the Soul
> Are many lesser Faculties that serve
> Reason as chief; among these Fancy next
> Her office holds; of all external things,
> Which the five watchful Senses represent,
> She forms Imaginations, Aery shapes,

> Which Reason joining or disjoining, frames
> All what we affirm or what deny, and call
> Our knowledge or opinion; then retires
> Into her private Cell when Natures rests.
> Oft in her absence mimic Fancy wakes
> To imitate her; but misjoining shapes,
> Wild work produces oft, and most in dreams,
> Ill matching words and deeds long past or late. (5.100−13)

The hierarchy moves downward from soul to reason, to fancy, to the senses. What is especially striking about this formulation, however, is that it does not make provision for memory, except perhaps for implicit Ramistic "natural" memory. The fancy collects representations of the senses and submits them to reason, whose role it is to join or disjoin the components and to determine affirmation or denial, knowledge or opinion. Adam here employs the technical terms of Milton's *Art of Logic*, where likes are also joined to likes and where all knowledge consists of affirmations and one has knowledge (rather than opinion) when one knows the causes of the matter at hand. Milton's mimic fancy recalls Spenser's Phantastes. When the higher faculties are inoperative, mimic fancy undertakes the work of either fancy itself or reason (the "her" of line 111 is ambiguous) and puts together errant connections of sensory data. In Eve's account of her dream it is easy to recognize both the resemblances to their previous evening's conversation and the "addition strange" introduced by the Satanic interference. Adam's reasoned estimation of the operations of the "misjoining" and "ill-matching" faculty allays Eve's anxieties and clears her mind totally of the event. There is no residue of troublesome memory to burden her future or, as we see in retrospect, to aid her judgment at the moment of crisis: "So all was clear'd" (5.136). The matter has been referred or processed in only one direction, that is, downward. Dan S. Collins provides a careful explication of how "The normal flow of matter up to spirit requires both the irritants of mind and the expulsive or disciplining reaction by which the mind is purged or balanced." The perfection of Eden "implies a reliability of the mind to expel all thoughts and fancies which do not pertain to man's obedient love of God." Thus, he sees the clearing of Eve's bad dream as a "routine expulsion" of "the excrement of experience" borrowing the digestive imagery of which Raphael is so fond. [19] The irritants relate to fancy and Eve, the expulsive or balancing to reason and Adam. In this prelapsarian process, it is judgment not memory that performs the act of obedience. In terms of faculty psychology, the prelapsarian modus operandi is psychological simultaneity and is primarily apprehension, that is, imagination modulating into reason, rather than the full array of mental activity in which reason would then modulate into memory.

Raphael's visit, which follows almost immediately, may be described generally as laying a foundation of principles to be remembered and thus impinging upon what we have been viewing as Michael's territory. The goal is initially to reinforce and then to open up Adam's present judgment to expansive possibilities as well as to memory, to make memory less Aristotle's imaginationlike mental storehouse for absent objects and more Avicenna's storehouse of intentions, which leads to aspirational exercises of the soul. When Raphael arrives he rehearses the psychological hierarchy, distinguishing the angelic "pure / Intelligential substances" from humanity's "Rational" substance (5.407–9), and adds:

> And both contain
> Within them every lower faculty
> Of sense, whereby they hear, see, smell, touch, taste,
> Tasting concoct, digest, assimilate,
> And corporeal to incorporeal turn. (409–13)

Raphael then elaborates on the various forms and degrees of the creation and their spheres of activity and their shared and proportional tendency to work from body up to spirit. He articulates the levels of creation, distinguishing between "vital" (i.e., vegetational), animal, and intellectual spirits, as these

> give both life and sense
> Fancy and understanding, whence the Soul
> Reason receives, and reason is her being,
> Discursive or Intuitive; discourse
> Is oftest yours, the latter most is ours,
> Differing but in degree, of kind the same. (485–90)

Raphael reverses Adam's descendant hierarchy in offering his ascendant one and provides a continuum of substance that crosses over the threshold of transcendence at which Adam stands. Raphael's goal, described earlier as providing mediation between experience and faith, here may be described as broadening the human psychology in the direction of memory and thus reaching toward the completeness that in history, as opposed to ideality, becomes realized with the traumatic fall.

Although that reversal of direction may appear to be a minor matter, in fact here are addressed the two irreconcilable conceptions of the good that dominated Neoplatonism and medieval thought. According to A. O. Lovejoy, "The one was an apotheosis of unity, self-sufficiency, and quietude, the other of diversity, self-transcendence, and fecundity":

> The one God was the goal of the "way up," of that ascending process by which the finite soul, turning from all created things, took its way back to the immutable Perfection in which alone it could find rest. The other God was the source and the informing energy of that descending process by which being flows through all the levels of possibility down to the very lowest.[20]

In Milton's formulation, the latter is foundational to the former. Although the prelapsarian God may be said to be "the source" and to find his chief good by way of Adam's outlined descent, Raphael models also the direction of man's search for the good, the "way up." He initiates the pattern of postlapsarian relationship to deity (i.e., "*took its way back to* the immutable perfection"); in anticipation of Michael, he presents paradox and dynamism or return. Raphael is thus expanding upon the basic knowledge Adam possesses in his knowledge of the names of the animals with a new mode of evaluation; he shifts Adam's awareness from the creation to the Creator, from things to ideas, from apprehension to memory. Raphael introduces a process of gradual approach to the good, which Lovejoy again clarifies:

> At least a provisional and instrumental value might be recognized in things natural, even while all genuine good was declared to lie in a supersensible and supernatural order. Man might legitimately permit his mind to busy itself with the creatures and to find joy in them, so long as he used each of them as a means of passage to what lay above it on the vast slope of being.
> (P. 89)

As Adam's prelapsarian instructor, Raphael is guiding Adam above the physical levels of sense and imagination and toward the levels of reason and intellect, away from carnal sense and toward inner sense. In this evidence of faculty psychology as in such other kinds of evidence as the painless accumulation of knowledge, for example, Raphael is preparing for a human future that can grow toward perfection without the trauma of the fall. In the terms of the present argument, Raphael's materials overlap with Michael's to outline the full range of possibilities for the human condition, for what has been possible since his first appearance, that is, a traumaless working of body up to spirit rather than the crisis of felix culpa.

After Raphael's departure, Adam has occasion to recur to psychological schematizations in his recommendation against Eve's working alone. This time—and the difference is directly attributable to Raphael's discourse—the psychological hierarchy is apprehended in its relationship to the will and the memory. Adam "remembers" Raphael's lessons thus:

> Within himself
> The danger lies, yet lies within his power:
> Against his will he can receive no harm.
> But God left free the Will, for what obeys
> Reason, is free, and Reason he made right,
> But bid her well beware, and still erect,
> Lest by some fair appearing good surpris'd
> She dictate false, and misinform the Will
> To do what God expressly hath forbid. (9.348–56)

Adam is performing a proper prelapsarian exercise of memory in bringing to bear Raphael's stored lessons upon the present issue. Even in Eden the human faculties are subject to imbalance, and the imagination can supply "some fair appearing good," which is threatening, as well as provide a means for transcendence. As Collins has remarked, the high point of Adam's reply to Eve's request to work separately

> is his recognition that reason operates only as a function of God's providence. Whereas he had been content to deal with proximate cause in his earlier speech he now argues from the perspective of ultimate cause. Although one must remain watchful, he notes, reason can succeed only if the terms of trial are kept within the competence of the human understanding.[21]

With the fall, the ways God's providence and man's mind operate are changed, and the balance between reason and faith and between experience and faith, as among imagination, judgment, and memory, undergoes a radical shift.

To the Avicenna model of the human mind, the Church Fathers made a number of additions and modifications that illuminate that radical shift. In terms of faculty psychology, that evidence centers now not on the imagination but on the memory, and it is memory, as noted earlier, that has been moved from rhetoric to ethics. A selection of Patristic commentary will serve as a review of some postlapsarian evidence of *Paradise Lost*. More importantly, it serves in several suggestive ways to interlace the categories that have been dichotomized throughout the body of the present study.

The first half of Saint Augustine's tenth book of the *Confessions* is a paean for and meditation upon the memory as a way of knowing and especially as a way of knowing God; it equates the memory with the mind itself in an argument that also involves a redefinition of imagination.[22] Augustine promulgates three kinds of vision or fantasy: "the sensory-image, the phantasy proper, and the phantasy in the service of reason . . . a vision of sense, of imagination, and of intellect, or corporeal, spiritual, and intellectual." The first members here follow the Avicenna model, but the second and third diverge in spiritually interesting ways. The first is the capacity for receiving sense impressions; the second conceives of formerly experienced data now absent but available through the memory; and the third occurs where no imaginary likenesses are involved. In this Augustinian model as in earlier schemes, "Imagination has its essential role," as Murray W. Bundy has noted, "but a higher power must come in to give true understanding,"[23] and that higher power, as both revised imagination and memory, equates with Christ who is both *scientia* and *sapientia*.

In *The Paradise Within*, Louis L. Martz describes the Augustinian principles of interior illumination and the "indwelling teacher," summarizing in these terms:

> Augustine's incessant search for ultimate truth derives from a conviction that the intellect of man is an indestructible inner "light," which works toward knowledge through the guidance of a higher "Light" that is always present to the mind, even when the mind is not conscious of its presence. Discovery of truth consists in the operations of man's intellect, working within the "illumination" granted by divine power.[24]

Although he does not draw a lapsarian contrast, Martz finds that *Paradise Lost* includes both the optimism of the *Confessions* and "the less inclusive, darker view" of the later *City of God*. In the late Augustine:

> the power of the memory lies in his belief that the inner light comes from God, as Creator, Redeemer, and sustainer of life: creating man first with the natural light of reason, restoring that native light by grace through the sacrifice of Christ, and, beyond this, enlightening the mind by the rays of a supernatural light that shines within the human memory—memory conceived as a storehouse of potential forms. (P. xvii)

Put concisely, for Augustine the knowledge of God can be found within the memory and achieved by meditation. Memory is necessarily a time-defined category, but the memory also allows transcendence and what Marcia L.

Colish calls "artificial simultaneity."[25] Such formulations may be seen as a kind of theologizing of a number of Ramistic assumptions. In faculty psychology as in typology, Christ is the promise and fulfills the promises, and the faith of man living in a fallen situation is chiefly exercised in remembering the promises. In stressing the spiritual thrust of memory we may recall that for Augustine memory is one of the three powers of the soul along with understanding and will that are the image of the Trinity in man.[26]

As Augustine's scheme underscores the transcendent metaphysical awareness the postlapsarian Adam attains under Michael's tutelage, so Aquinas supplies a theory that clarifies the ways in which Michael attaches meaning for Adam's future remembrance to sites and characters from history and to the covenants of the Old Testament with their adumbrations of Christian antitypes. As Augustine's own proceeding is rhetorical, Aquinas's is decidedly logical. Aquinas sorts out and builds upon (or "answers," in his word) Aristotle, Avicenna, and Augustine, among others. For Aquinas, God is the source of all human understanding, and knowledge comes to the human soul either from above or through sense perceptions, either passively or actively; but even when constructing universals from sensible data, the mind remains dependent upon sense impression, abstracting universals from many particulars. Aquinas does away with Avicenna's distinction between two modes of the imagination and combines Avicenna's two storehouses of images and intentions, using the former as symbols of the latter, and the intentions are present in the images either by nature or because they have been placed there by the intellect. In Aquinas's words:

> Not only does the active intellect throw light on the phantasm; it does more; by its own power it abstracts the intelligible species from the phantasm. It throws light on the phantasm, because, just as the sensitive part acquires a greater power by its conjunction with the intellectual part, so by the power of the active intellect the phantasms are made more fit for the abstraction therefrom of intelligible intentions. Furthermore, the active intellect abstracts the intelligible species from the phantasm, forasmuch as by the power of the active intellect we are able to disregard the conditions of individuality, and to take into our consideration the specific nature, the image of which informs the passive intellect.

Man's source of knowledge is the material world to whose "innate species" his understanding responds.[27] Thus, to an Avicennan psychology, Aquinas adds the Augustinian concept of God as interior teacher. As Colish points out: "Thomas describes the active intellect, the mental faculty which abstracts the intelligible species from the phantasm and makes it possible for the mind to form a conceptual sign of its object, as a participation of God." [28]

Aquinas acknowledges the postlapsarianness of such procedure, saying: "In the present state of life in which the soul is united to a passible body, it is impossible for our intellect to understand anything actually, except by turning to the phantasms" (p. 177). Those phantasms are interrelated to inherited first principles and a prior knowledge of the divine. As Colish again remarks:

> God has expressly constructed the world to be more or less like Him, and to provide a set of signa Dei for man. Such signs are aids in the restoration of a correct relationship between man and God, a relationship which is obstructed by man's sin and lack of faith. (P. 182)

This is a process that provides epistemological foundations for reading experiential data as symbols, for a comparative process whose base is earthly data and whose goal is spiritually aspirational interpretation, what we have viewed earlier as postlapsarian literary criticism. In Aquinas's words,

> Incorporeal things, of which there are no phantasms, are known to us by comparison with sensible bodies of which there are phantasms. Thus we understand truth by considering a thing of which we possess the truth; and God . . . we know as cause, by way of excess and by way of remotion. Other incorporeal substances we know, in the present state of life, only by way of remotion or by some comparison to corporeal things. And, therefore, when we understand something about these things, we need to turn to phantasms of bodies, although there are no phantasms of the things themselves. (P. 179)

As E. Ruth Harvey summarizes, "By means of *phantasmata* the soul comes to know universals and is enabled to think on them; by means of the *phantasmata* stored in the memory, man can retain such *intelligibilia* in symbols." Because we learn to know the creation above us by means of the nature below and can express this knowledge of incorporeal things only in similitudes and likenesses drawn from material things, "Aquinas's theory allows the possibility of expressing the highest knowledge man can grasp in the guise of material things; it admits a whole world of symbolism as a process of knowledge which is both natural and necessary to human beings." [29]

Michael assists Adam's thinking to progress from a memory of things to a memory of words, drawing upon Aquinas's use of symbolic images and upon Augustine's intellectual transcendence. Moreover, when Adam discovers that he must leave Eden, he describes the change in terms that exactly, even technically, acknowledge the edenic terrain as a memory theater of the sort Frances Yates has explicated:

> This most afflicts me, that departing hence,
> As from his face I shall be hid, depriv'd
> His blessed count'nance; here I could frequent,
> With worship, *place by place* where he voutsaf'd
> Presence Divine, and to my Sons relate;
> On this Mount he appear'd, under this Tree
> Stood visible, among these Pines his voice
> I heard, here with him at this Fountain talk'd:
> So many grateful Altars I would rear
> Of grassy Turf, and pile up every Stone
> Of lustre from the brook, *in memory*,
> Or monument to Ages, and thereon
> Offer sweet smelling Gums and Fruits and Flow'rs:
> In yonder nether World where shall I seek
> His bright appearances, or footstep trace? (11.315–29; emphasis mine)

The concluding rhetorical question has its answer in the "paradise within" with which Michael's instruction ceases, having completed the reorientation of Adam's mode of thought as of the reader's from externals to internals and, in the terms of the *Ad Herennium*, from a memory for things to a memory for words, specifically the Word of Christian redemption, which is also a redemption of the imagination. Thus, psychological and spiritual strategies combine such theological principles as those of Augustine and Aquinas we have seen in an ethical overlay of what began as a physiological and rhetorical design. For the fallen, theological as well as psychological memory is the medium of one's relationship with the deity, and Christ is the mediator of the Word and the promises; he is the final cause and the energy and process through which man attains his end and his perfection, logically, psychologically, and theologically.

Finally, in Aquinas's contemporary, Saint Bonaventura, we find a combination of empirical psychology and mysticism. Bonaventura divides the psychological progress into three variously labeled stages: the external body, the spirit that looks inward, and the mind that looks above, linked with what he calls "the triple mode of theology—that is, the symbolic, the literal, and the mystical," with triple illuminations of the corporeal, the spiritual, and the divine, and with "the threefold existence of things, as in matter, in [creative] intelligence, and in eternal art." Each of these three phases is twofold, resulting in six powers of the soul and six stages of ascension into God, which correspond to the six days of creation and to the six wings of angelic form. The six psychological categories are sense, imagination, reason, intellect, intelligence, and the illumination of conscience or *synteresis*; the soul's nine sequential activities are perception, deliberation, self-impulsion, ordination, strengthening, command, reception, divine illumination, and union.[30]

Bonaventura's vision illuminates both the prelapsarian and the postlapsarian. The universe for him as for Raphael is regularly a mirror of God and a ladder on which to climb toward him. In created things shines forth

> the Creator's supreme power and wisdom and benevolence . . . as the carnal sense reports trebly to the inner sense. For the carnal sense serves him who either understands rationally or believes faithfully or contemplates intellectually. Contemplating, it considers the actual existence of things; believing, it considers the habitual course of things; reasoning, it considers the potential excellence of things. (P. 11)

The formulation effectively captures much of Raphael's procedure and goals, especially when we add to it the later view that "the external sensibles" enter the soul not through apprehension by the senses so much as through their similitudes (p. 16) and that the proceeding is variously governed by delight. For Bonaventura, "there is nothing higher than the human mind except Him Who made it." In addition, Bonaventura's account of the third phase of the apprehension/judgment/memory design captures much of Michael's proceeding and goals:

> The operation of memory is retention and representation, not only of things present, corporeal, and temporal, but also of past and future things, simple and eternal. For memory retains the past by recalling it, the present by receiving it, the future by foreseeing it. It retains the simple, as the principles of continuous and discrete quantities—the point, the instant, the unit—without which it is impossible to remember or to think about those things whose source is in these. Nonetheless it retains the eternal principles and the axioms of the sciences and retains them eternally. . . . It has an undying light present to itself in which it remembers unchangeable truths. And thus, through the operations of the memory, it appears that the soul

itself is the image of God and His likeness so present to itself and having Him present that it receives Him in actuality and is susceptible of receiving Him in potency, and that it can also participate in Him. (Pp. 22–23)

Michael's lessons are recalled also in Bonaventura's view of judgment that "reaches upward to divine laws if it solves its problems completely" (p. 25).

Like Michael's practice with his postlapsarian pupil, and like Augustine as viewed earlier, Bonaventura's theory of symbolic contemplation is decidedly Christocentric in its final stages. In a formulation that recalls Milton's *Of Education* as well as Ramistic pedagogical schemes, Bonaventura links Christ with the components of the trivium, with "grammar, which gives us the power of expression; logic, which gives us skill in argumentation; rhetoric, which makes us skillful in persuasion or stirring the emotions," as he links the first person of the Trinity to metaphysics, mathematics, and physics and the third person with the individual, family, and political problems, or what we might categorize as ethics, economics, and politics (p. 27). For Bonaventura as for Milton and the Ramists, reasoning is a lapsarian matter, and specifically "our soul has not been able to be raised perfectly from the things of sense to an intuition of itself and of the eternal Truth in itself unless the Truth, having assumed human form in Christ, should make itself into a ladder, repairing the first ladder which was broken in Adam" (p. 28). The mediating Christ is "as the tree of life in the middle of Paradise" (p. 29), and Bonaventura's view of Christ captures Michael's inclusive category of the paradoxical. Finally, in its combinatory theory and imagery, the following passage, though mystically expressed, draws together a variety of categories we have found descriptive of *Paradise Lost*:

> In this consideration is the perfection of the mind's illumination, when, as if on the sixth day, it sees man made in the image of God. If then the image is an express likeness when our mind contemplates in Christ the Son of God, Who is the natural image of the invisible God, our humanity now wonderfully exalted, now ineffably united, by seeing at once in one Being the first and the last, the highest and the lowest, the circumference and the center, the alpha and the omega, the caused and the cause, the creator and the creature, the book written within and without, [the mind] arrives at a perfect being in order that it may arrive with God at the perfection of His illuminations on the sixth level, as if on the sixth day; nor does anything more remain save the day of rest, on which, by the elevation of the mind, its insight rests from all work which he had done. (P. 42)

Notes

PREFACE

1 · Whiting, *Milton and This Pendant World*, passim; Hill, *John Milton: Poet, Priest, and Prophet*, p. 140; Mollenkott, "The Pervasive Influence of the Apocrypha in Milton's Thought and Art," in *Milton and the Art of Sacred Song*, ed. J. Max Patrick and Roger H. Sundell, pp. 34–43; Riggs, *The Christian Poet in "Paradise Lost,"* pp. 113–14; Entzminger, "Epistemology and the Tutelary Word in *Paradise Lost*," p. 94. Despite his title, "Before and After the Fall: Some Miltonic Patterns of Systasis," Frank A. Huntley does not explicate lapsarian dichotomies but rather considers such unions of complementary opposites as male and female and good and evil (in *Approaches to "Paradise Lost,"* ed. C. A. Patrides, pp. 1–14). He places the pattern of systasis in a context of backgrounds including Plato, Matthew Arnold's distinction between Hellenic and Hebraic, the Horatian ends of poetry to teach and delight, and Hegelian dialectic.

2 · Frye, "Agon and Logos: Revolution and Revelation," in *The Prison and the Pinnacle*, ed. Balachandra Rajan, p. 147.

3 · Hawkins, "Samson's Catharsis," p. 212.

4 · Samuel, *Dante and Milton: The "Commedia" and "Paradise Lost."*

5 · Madsen, *From Shadowy Types to Truth: Studies in Milton's Symbolism*, pp. 85–86, 86–87, 66–67, 83, 2. In these latter pages Madsen notes that Raphael is made to speak for the Neoplatonism in the epic—"He represents, as it were, the highest reach of the pagan intellectual." In general, however, Madsen feels that Neoplatonism like the classical, epical, and heroic in *Paradise Lost* is linked with the Satanic. He describes Milton as "anything but a Neoplatonist" and finds that in important ways *Paradise Lost* is in fact anti-Neoplatonic.

6 · Walter J. Ong, S.J., *Ramus, Method, and the Decay of Dialogue: From the Art of Discourse to the Art of Reason*, p. 23.

INTRODUCTION

1 · These and additional details may be found in footnotes to *John Milton: Complete Poems and Major Prose*, ed. Merritt Y. Hughes, pp. 307, 325 (hereafter cited as Hughes); in *A Milton Encyclopedia*, ed. William B. Hunter, Jr., et al., 7:93–95, 5:130–32; and in Gustav Davidson, *A Dictionary of Angels, Including the Fallen Angels*, pp. 240–42, 193–95. John

Peter—for whom Milton's angels, as servants of his "unprepossessing God," are "suspicious" and externally manipulated marionettes—finds a variety of faults with Raphael but judges Michael acceptable, integrated, and coherent (*A Critique of "Paradise Lost*," pp. 27–30). Stella P. Revard contrasts Milton's Michael with other Renaissance versions of the warrior angel in "The Renaissance Michael and the Son of God," in *Milton and the Art of Sacred Song*, ed. J. Max Patrick and Roger H. Sundell, pp. 121–35. For Renaissance analogues of the War in Heaven in which Michael replaces Christ as the concluding agent, see Revard, *The War in Heaven: "Paradise Lost" and the Tradition of Satan's Rebellion*, chaps. 5 and 7, pp. 109–10, and n. 5. She notes (p. 237) that the traditional Michael is never described without arms and armor. John T. Shawcross speaks of Michael as a Moses and "a Christianized form of Hermes as conductor of the dead to the Elysian fields" in *"Paradise Lost"* and the Theme of Exodus," pp. 13–14.

2 · Giovanni Pico della Mirandola, *On the Dignity of Man*, in *The Renaissance Philosophy of Man*, ed. Ernst Cassirer et al., p. 237.

3 · West, *Milton and the Angels*, pp. 142, 183–84. In the latter pages West identifies the Puritan bent of Milton's angelology in its general aim and atmosphere, conformity of doctrine, and manifest sympathy with the "science" of angelology.

4 · Greene, *The Descent from Heaven: A Study in Epic Continuity*, p. 7. Greene discusses Raphael but not Michael in *Paradise Lost* along these lines, noting that Raphael is sent "to expound the truth," not as with the descending messengers in other epics to prod or punish mortals (p. 405). For additional classical analogues to Raphael and the motifs of his visit (e.g., mission, journey, contrasts of the heavenly and the earthly, bird similes, warnings against uxoriousness), especially in Virgil, see Francis C. Blessington, *"Paradise Lost" and the Classical Epic*, pp. 25–34; on Michael, see pp. 66–72. In general, where Greene finds that Milton's epic "contained within itself, not accidentally but essentially, the seeds of the genre's destruction" (p. 407), Blessington finds "the classical world has not been destroyed, only extended and completed" in *Paradise Lost* and put in Christian perspective (p. 72). For John M. Steadman, in *Milton and the Renaissance Hero*, Milton "pushed to its logical conclusion the central emphasis of the heroic tradition—its stress on superlatives, its quest for excellence and 'highest worth,' its definition of heroism in terms of 'godlikeness' and 'excess of virtue'. Finding the true essence of heroic virtue in divine virtue, recognizing in God himself the heroic archetype of man, he tuned the epic lyre an octave higher than most of his predecessors. Instead of the praises of men, it sounds the honour of God. This transformation represents, in a sense, the death and resurrection of the heroic poem; the epic undergoes a humiliation and exaltation analogous to Christ's. Adam's defeat tolls the knell of heroic poetry; Christ's victory revives it" (pp. 200–201).

5 · In "Epic Address and Reference and the Principle of Decorum in *Paradise Lost*," Kester Svendsen collects and examines Raphael's and Michael's epithets for Adam (pp. 192–93) but curiously neglects epithets for these angels themselves.

6 · Greene, *Descent from Heaven*, p. 397.

7 · Svendsen, *Milton and Science*, p. 148. Riggs, in *The Christian Poet*, contrasts Raphael's arrival and phoenix simile with Satan's arrival in Eden and cormorant simile (pp. 106–9).

8 · Steadman, *Epic and Tragic Structures in "Paradise Lost*," p. 132. In *Sacred Discontent: The Bible and Western Tradition*, Herbert N. Schneidau outlines differing epistemological alternatives suggestively: "In the old world before the Hebrews and other demythologizers

disturbed it, the normal mode of knowledge was familiarization: to learn to make a flint knife, to recite oral epic, or to recognize the medicinal plants, you 'get to know them' as if they were people. . . . In this mainly oral world, knowledge is immediate, intuitive, empathetic, proprioceptive, an analogue of familial intimacy. But in the prophets' experiences we can see the incipient form of a new knowledge, involving dissociation of self: here new terms are needed; even the word *vision* is misleading because of its connotations of mystical union. These prophets know the truth because Yahweh's message reveals their fellow men in a new light of defamiliarization: a harsh glare in which the prophets, themselves separated from the communal life and the illusions of purpose it cherishes, see men as if they were ants, swarming and scurrying" (pp. 17–18).

9 · Lewalski, *Protestant Poetics and the Seventeenth-Century Lyric*, p. 160. For a discussion of Eve's relation to experience in comparable terms, see Georgia B. Christopher, *Milton and the Science of the Saints*, p. 160.

10 · Frye, *God, Man, and Satan: Patterns of Christian Thought and Life in "Paradise Lost," "Pilgrim's Progress," and the Great Theologians*, p. 81.

11 · Blackburn, "'Uncloister'd Virtue': Adam and Eve in Milton's Paradise," pp. 121–22, 123–24, 126–27. In *"Paradise Lost" and the Genesis Tradition*, J. M. Evans discovers two modes of innocence in the epic, one focused on Eve and the other on Adam, with Raphael bridging the gap between them. Educationally, Eve needs to be "propped" and Adam "lopped" (pp. 255–57, 268).

12 · Lewalski, "Innocence and Experience in Milton's Eden," in *New Essays on "Paradise Lost,"* ed. Thomas Kranidas, pp. 116, 88.

13 · Murray W. Bundy's discussion, in "Milton's View of Education in *Paradise Lost*," develops contrasts between Raphael and Michael as ideal teachers, although he attaches the evidence primarily to Adam's education in liberty and to controlling the passions by the reason.

14 · Ainsworth, *Milton on Education: The Tractate "Of Education" with Supplementary Extracts from Other Writings of Milton, Cornell Studies in English*, p. 45. See also Donald C. Dorian's notes to *Of Education* in *Complete Prose Works of John Milton*, ed. Don M. Wolfe et al., 2:366–67. In his preface Dorian assesses *Of Education* in these general terms: "The distinction of his tractate aside from its intellectual breadth and its frequent eloquence, consists not in Milton's solution to any specific educational problem of his time, but in the philosophical coherence of his educational principles both throughout the tractate and in relation to his more general views of virtue, liberty, and man's part in the divine scheme of being" (p. 359). In *Milton and Forbidden Knowledge*, Howard Schultz outlines the definitions and procedures of learning in *Of Education* in terms of the four logical causes, with "performing the offices" as formal cause and "repairing the ruins" as final cause. He also calls these two definitions modern and medieval (pp. 82–83).

15 · Rajan, "Simple, Sensuous, and Passionate," in *Milton: Modern Essays in Criticism*, ed. Arthur E. Barker, p. 6.

16 · Parker, "Education: Milton's Ideas and Ours," in *The Language Curtain and Other Essays on American Education*, p. 76. In "Milton's *Of Education* and the *Translatio Studii*," William Brennan examines *Of Education* as "an abstraction and idealization of those parts of his own education that Milton found most rewarding" (p. 56). In "Looking Back without Anger: Milton's *Of Education*," William Melczer places the tractate within the context of

Renaissance humanistic education (in *Milton and the Middle Ages*, ed. John Mulryan, pp. 91–102).

17 · Samuel, "Milton on Learning and Wisdom," p. 711. For her, the teaching of both Raphael and Michael is similarly based, and she outlines the principles on p. 713.

18 · Schultz, *Milton and Forbidden Knowledge*, p. 77. Schultz also finds the embryo form of Milton's lifelong notions of intellectual abuse in Prolusions 2, 3, and 7 (p. 75).

19 · Council, "*L'Allegro, Il Penseroso*, and 'The Cycle of Universal Knowledge,'" p. 204. In "Milton and Self-Knowledge," Albert W. Fields takes as his starting point the quotation from Prolusion 3 above and examines the relation of Milton's works to the *nosce teipsum* tradition. Kester Svendsen points out that the sweeping knowledge passages from Prolusions 3 and 7 and from *Vacation Exercise*, lines 33–46, can be "duplicated in content and scope from the title pages of dozens of medieval and Renaissance encyclopedias" (*Milton and Science*, p. 47).

20 · Rajan, "The Cunning Resemblance," in *Milton Studies VII: "Eyes Fast Fixt": Current Perspectives Methodology*, ed. Albert C. Labriola and Michael Lieb, pp. 36–37. In "*Areopagitica* as a Scenario for *Paradise Lost*," in *Achievements of the Left Hand: Essays on the Prose of John Milton*, ed. Michael Lieb and John T. Shawcross, pp. 121–41, Edward S. LeComte collects and discusses a number of conceptual issues shared by the two works and a remarkable array of verbal echoes between them.

21 · Rajan, "Osiris and Urania," p. 226.

I. LAPSARIAN STRUCTURES

1 · Samuel, *Dante and Milton*, p. 232.

2 · Charlton, "The Educational Background," in *The Age of Milton: Backgrounds to Seventeenth-Century Literature*, ed. C. A. Patrides and Raymond B. Waddington, pp. 102–37, esp. p. 119.

3 · Fish, *Surprised by Sin: The Reader in "Paradise Lost*," chap. 7.

4 · Clark, *John Milton at St. Paul's School: A Study of Ancient Rhetoric in English Renaissance Education*; the phrases in quotation marks are chapter titles in this book.

5 · Samuel, *Dante and Milton*, p. 222.

6 · Radzinowicz, "'Man as a Probationer of Immortality': *Paradise Lost* XI–XII," in *Approaches to "Paradise Lost*," ed. C. A. Patrides, p. 35. She draws the distinction generally in the terms I have borrowed: "improvement" and "amendment."

7 · For example, Lewalski, "Innocence and Experience in Milton's Eden," p. 110. Walter Clyde Curry also identifies Raphael as a metaphysician in *Milton's Ontology, Cosmogony, and Physics*, p. 113.

8 · Kaufmann, *"The Pilgrim's Progress" and Tradition in Puritan Meditation*; the terms in quotation marks are drawn from Kaufmann's chapter titles.

9 · Martz, *The Poetry of Meditation: A Study in English Religious Literature of the Seventeenth Century*, p. 13.

10 · Radzinowicz, "'Man as a Probationer of Immortality,'" pp. 36, 50.

11 · Samuel, *Dante and Milton*, pp. 231, 222.

12 · Smith, "Adam's Fall," in *Critical Essays on Milton from ELH*, pp. 183, 189, 190.

13 · Raymond B. Waddington has outlined the analogous units of Books 11 and 12 in these terms and pressed the comparison in "The Death of Adam: Vision and Voice in Books

XI and XII of *Paradise Lost*," pp. 12–15. Waddington is followed in this by Edward W. Tayler, *Milton's Poetry: Its Development in Time*, pp. 71 ff., who speaks of six "visions" in Book 11 and six "narrations" in Book 12.

14 · Summers, *The Muse's Method: An Introduction to "Paradise Lost,"* pp. 197, 208.

15 · Christopher, *Milton and the Science of the Saints*, p. 187; and Waddington, "Death of Adam," p. 10. Lewalski's description of Ecclesiastes as a two-part sermon, in *Protestant Poetics and the Seventeenth-Century Lyric*, p. 57, develops the distinction: The first sermon part discredits "all the goods (wealth, pleasure, honor, human wisdom) from which men seek happiness," and the second "demonstrates that happiness is to be found only in the fear of God and concern with heavenly things."

16 · MacCallum, "Milton and Sacred History: Books XI and XII of *Paradise Lost*," in *Essays in English Literature from the Renaissance to the Victorian Age Presented to A. S. P. Woodhouse*, ed. Millar MacLure and F. W. Watt, p. 159.

17 · Ibid., p. 161.

18 · Ibid., pp. 166–67. Jason P. Rosenblatt discusses one of these "loops," the double telling of the Exodus story at 12.163–96 and then again at lines 208–14. For him this instant replay of the Exodus climax momentarily defeats our expectation of sequential narration. "The approximation of simultaneity through the abrogation of chronological precedence is heightened by the image of Moses extending 'once more his potent Rod,' which takes us from the end to the beginning of the poem" ("Structural Unity and Temporal Concordance: The War in Heaven in *Paradise Lost*," p. 37). In *Process of Speech: Puritan Religious Writing and "Paradise Lost,"* Boyd M. Berry puts MacCallum's "loops of time" to good use in analyzing *Paradise Lost* against its Puritan background (pp. 209 ff.). For Berry the final three books of the epic are loops or epicycles within the larger loop of the entire poem; "lesser loops or cycles . . . mirror in microcosm the loop of all human history: time after time, an initial peace is broken by a fall, then restored by God" (p. 81). Berry examines Noah's story as "a loop of regeneration" (pp. 81–83).

19 · Kermode, "Adam Unparadised," in *The Living Milton: Essays by Various Hands*, ed. Frank Kermode, p. 99; and Berry, *Process of Speech*, passim.

20 · Christopher, *Milton and the Science of the Saints*, p. 181.

21 · Fish, *The Living Temple: George Herbert and Catechizing*, pp. 48, 44. Joseph H. Summers surveys Herbert's judgment that, although catechizing is better for informing parishioners, sermons are superior for inflaming them, in *George Herbert: His Religion and Art*, pp. 100–101, 109. Labeling Adam's encounter with Scripture "a catechetical exercise," Christopher likens it to Milton's own writing of *Christian Doctrine* (*Milton and the Science of the Saints*, p. 179); similarly, Fish notes that Calvin considered his *Institutes* a catechistic work (*Living Temple*, p. 60). In *Some Graver Subject: An Essay on "Paradise Lost,"* J. B. Broadbent looks at Michael as "preaching a 17th-century sermon of the plain Puritan kind recommended in William Perkins's *Art of Prophesying*. He takes a text, explains it, derives 'close and natural' doctrine from it, and applies the doctrine 'to the life and manners of men in a simple and plaine speech'" (p. 276).

22 · Hawkins, "Samson's Catharsis," p. 215.

23 · On the prelapsarian connection between and the postlapsarian divorce of pleasure and virtue, see Robert L. Entzminger, "Michael's Options and Milton's Poetry: *Paradise Lost* XI and XII," pp. 198–99, 204.

24 · McColley, *Milton's Eve*, pp. 188–89.

25 · Revard, *War in Heaven*, pp. 287–306; the quotations are from pp. 297, 296. Rosenblatt examines parallels between *Paradise Lost*, Book 6, and the Exodus and notes Michael's presentation of the Exodus in Book 12 as well as Exodus similes in Book 1 to "concord" the beginning, middle, and end of *Paradise Lost* and of temporal categories more generally, in "Structural Unity and Temporal Concordance," pp. 31–41. For a more general discussion of analogues between Raphael's and Michael's books of the epic, see John Reesing, *Milton's Poetic Art: "A Mask," "Lycidas," and "Paradise Lost,"* pp. 71–76, and nn. 3, 6, pp. 180–82.

26 · In what he calls one of Scripture's sublimest episodes, 1 Kings 18, Jack Goldman traces parallels between Abdiel and Elijah there surrounded by 450 priests of Baal and 400 priests of Ashtaroth ("Insight into Milton's Abdiel"). Mason Tung, in "The Abdiel Episode: A Contextual Reading," provides a thorough review of the various critical interpretations of the Abdiel episode (pp. 595–96). See also Revard, *War in Heaven*, passim; she stresses that Abdiel is enhanced as a model for Adam in being a member of the lower orders of angels.

27 · Berry, *Process of Speech*, p. 94; Levin, *The Myth of the Golden Age in the Renaissance*, p. 151; Frye, *The Return of Eden: Five Essays on Milton's Epics*, pp. 52–53; and Tayler, *Milton's Poetry*, p. 71. Tayler also cites Donne's formulation of a tripartite scheme with "'the two thousand yeares of nature, before the Law given by Moses, And the two thousand yeares of Law, before the Gospel given by Christ, And the two thousand of Grace, which are running now.'" He traces the tripartite, as does Levin, to Joachim de Fiore but also to Augustine.

28 · *The Geneva Bible: A Facsimile of the 1560 Edition*. On the Geneva Bible as a compact repository of Protestant thought in Renaissance England and on some uses Milton made of it, see Whiting, *Milton and This Pendant World*, pp. 129–47. Whiting was, I believe, the first to call attention to the Augustinian ages as an analogue of the hexaemeral creation and to note later variations of the scheme (in Isidore of Seville, the *Nuremberg Chronicle*, *Cursor Mundi*, DuBartas, and others) and to apply the design to *Paradise Lost*, Books 11–12 (chap. 6, "The Pattern of Time and Eternity," pp. 175–93). In "Milton and Sacred History," MacCallum builds on Whiting's foundation in Augustine and adds evidence from Samuel Mather and other Puritan commentaries. He notes that Augustine identified the present as the analogue of the sixth day and the seventh day as "the rest of the saints." Augustine draws this analogy in part thus: "'On the sixth day, in Genesis, man is formed after the image of God; in the sixth period of the world there is the clear discovery of our transformation in the renewing of our mind, according to the image of Him who created us'" (quoted in MacCallum, pp. 150–51). MacCallum notes also Mather's division of history into old and new dispensations, and his division of the old dispensation into two parts—from Adam to Moses' reception of the law, and from Moses to John the Baptist—and his division of the era before the law into three periods (Adam to Noah, Noah to Abraham, and Abraham to Moses) and the era after the law into four periods (pp. 151–52). As MacCallum describes the pattern of the Old Testament eras, each includes fall, judgment, regeneration, and renewal; in each a new world is born out of the ruins of the old through the man of faith; each is marked by covenants between God and his chosen individuals and nations; and each contains types of Christ. In the cumulative sequence MacCallum finds also an increasing urgency and an increase in typological suggestiveness (pp. 154, 152). See also Summers, *Muse's Method*, chap. 8, "The Final Vision"; Lewalski, "Structure and the Symbolism of Vision in Michael's Prophecy"; and Waddington, "Death of Adam," pp. 12 ff. Lewalski traces "six ages of restoration" to Hugo of St. Victor (p. 28). For a reading that extends the traditional ages to eight,

see Albert R. Cirillo, "Tasso's *Il Mondo Creato*: Providence and the Created Universe," esp. pp. 85, 91, 97.

29 · Radzinowicz, *Toward "Samson Agonistes": The Growth of Milton's Mind*, pp. 284–312, esp. pp. 289, 295, 301. Although the typical is more of a factor in the materials of Book 12, she stresses that in both 11 and 12 Milton is emphasizing the exemplary dimension of the histories, what is "normative and archetypal in them" (p. 294). Radzinowicz is one of the few commentators to review the text closely in relation to the so-called six eras of history (pp. 287 ff.), and she suggests a variety of genres for Michael's materials, especially "a six-act tragedy" in Book 11 but also "educative drama" more generally, "tragic masques," "unrolling pageant," and "dumb-show" (pp. 287, 285).

30 · Christopher, "The Verbal Gate to Paradise: Adam's 'Literary Experience' in Book X of *Paradise Lost*," pp. 72–73; and similarly, Christopher, *Milton and the Science of the Saints*, p. 141.

31 · John T. Shawcross treats the pattern we see in the careers of Abraham and Adam more generally in "*Paradise Lost* and the Theme of Exodus," noting the emphasis on trial and resistance when a type of Christ is involved and the emphasis on trial, fall, and repentance when a mere man is involved (p. 8). H. R. MacCallum also finds that with "the election of Abraham a new sense of direction and urgency enters the narrative," but he links it to "the angel's strategy in leading [Adam] from flesh to spirit" ("Milton and Sacred History," p. 164).

2. LAPSARIAN IMAGERY

1 · *The Divine Weeks and Works of Guillaume de Saluste Sieur du Bartas*, trans. Josuah Sylvester, ed. Susan Snyder, 1:115–16, lines 151–52, 157–58, 173–74.

2 · Tillyard, *Studies in Milton*, pp. 140, 138.

3 · Sims, *The Bible in Milton's Epics*, pp. 35–36. Raphael speaks similarly again at 8.100–103: "And for the Heav'n's wide Circuit, let it speak / The Maker's high magnificence, who built / So spacious, and his Line stretcht out so far; / That man may know he dwells not in his own."

4 · *The Book of Tobit*, in *The Apocrypha*, trans. Edgar J. Goodspeed, 12.6–7. Because Raphael does not appear in the canonical books, it is generally agreed by Milton editors and commentators that *The Book of Tobit* is an important source for Milton's use of the figure. Beverley Sherry reviews a half-dozen recent articles on Raphael's visit and stresses the *Tobit* link in "Not by Bread Alone: The Communication of Adam and Raphael." In "Celestial Entertainment in Eden: Book V of *Paradise Lost*," Jason P. Rosenblatt traces the parallels of Raphael's visit with the visit of the angels to Abraham at Mamre. Anthony Low, in "Angels and Food in *Paradise Lost*," develops a view of the meal in *Paradise Lost*, which he calls "a central symbol of the prelapsarian life," as "a kind of communion" contrasted with the pomp of the Roman Catholic mass (pp. 144, 140–42), and notes the absence of a shared meal with Michael (pp. 143–44).

5 · Madsen, *From Shadowy Types to Truth*, pp. 132, 142.

6 · Toliver, "Symbol-Making and the Labors of Milton's Eden," pp. 434–35.

7 · For an extended consideration of edenic language, especially the word/thing equation, in its philosophical context, see Fish, *Surprised by Sin*, chap. 3, pt. 2, esp. pp. 112–28.

Jackson I. Cope, in *The Metaphoric Structure of "Paradise Lost,"* observes that "Francis Bacon saw in paradisiacal knowledge the crucial symbol for the end sought by communication: 'The true end of knowledge . . . is a restitution and reinvesting (in great part) of man to the sovereignty and power (for whensoever he shall be able to call the creatures by their true names he shall again command them) which he had in his first state of creation'" (pp. 36–37). Ruth Wallerstein, in *Studies in Seventeenth-Century Poetic*, discusses Philo's conception of the Logos as a theory of language: "It conceives that speech issues concretely from the thought of man in a mode which parallels and reflects the creation of ideas and thence of particular things by the One, through the Word, or the divine wisdom. God, Philo says, brought the animals to man, to name, as Lord of all, in order as his teacher to test Adam; he kindled Adam's innate capacity to give them suitable names, bringing out clearly the traits of the creatures who bore them; 'for the native reasoning power . . . in the soul being still unalloyed, and no infirmity or disease or evil affection having intruded itself, he received the impressions made by bodies and objects in their sheer reality, and the titles he gave were fully apposite, for right well did he divine the character of the creatures he was describing, with the result that their natures were apprehended as soon as their names were uttered.' On this doctrine is grounded the symbolic interpretation of the names in the Bible through their etymologies" (pp. 38–39).

8 · MacCaffrey, *Spenser's Allegory: The Anatomy of Imagination*, p. 35.

9 · On the view that Hebrew was the original language, see Don Cameron Allen, "Some Theories of the Growth and Origin of Language in Milton's Age."

10 · Heninger, *Touches of Sweet Harmony: Pythagorean Cosmology and Renaissance Poetics*, passim.

11 · Arthur O. Lovejoy, *The Great Chain of Being: The Study of the History of an Idea*, pp. 58–59. With regard to the principles governing the Chain of Being in the tradition— qualitative continuity, unilinear gradation, plenitude, and sufficient reason—Lovejoy argues that Milton was antipathetic to the latter two (pp. 164–65).

12 · Nicolson, *The Breaking of the Circle: Studies in the Effect of the "New Science" on Seventeenth-Century Poetry*, p. 167; Curry, *Milton's Ontology, Cosmogony and Physics*, pp. 182, 177. In *From Shadowy Types to Truth*, Madsen traces Platonic and Neoplatonic backgrounds of the "scale of nature" and finds the present Milton passage "heavily charged with ambivalence, between Neoplatonic descent and return and emanationism and between dynamism and stasis" (p. 120). For him the inclusion of the process of moving upward through "contemplation of created things" adds a distinctly Hebraic and Christian note to the Neoplatonic ascent of the soul" (pp. 124–25). For a discussion of the sexual implications of the descent and ascent pattern in Raphael's speech at 5.469 ff., and of the creation and the descent of the spirit more generally, see O. B. Hardison, Jr., "Written Records and Truths of Spirit in *Paradise Lost*," esp. pp. 155–56.

13 · Gray, "Paradox in *Paradise Lost*," pp. 76, 81.

14 · McColley, *Milton's Eve*, p. 119. Similarly, elsewhere in this study McColley discusses Adam and Eve as cultivating the Amorous Life, the Active Life, and the Contemplative Life, or Ficino's *voluptas, imperium*, and *sapientia*, the first in their love for each other, the second in their care of the garden, and the third in their love of God (p. 73).

15 · Berry, *Process of Speech*, p. 245.

16 · Otten, "'My Native Element': Milton's Paradise and English Gardens." For an examination of the tradition within which Milton is working here, see A. Bartlett Giamatti,

The Earthly Paradise and the Renaissance Epic. The provision for work in Milton's garden protects our first parents from the spiritual dangers of delusiveness and idleness that define such gardens as Spenser's Bower of Bliss. On Eve's special relationship to the flowers of Eden, see John R. Knott, Jr., *Milton's Pastoral Vision: An Approach to "Paradise Lost,"* chap. 5, "Fairest of Creation," pp. 109–26. More generally, Knott observes, "To be attuned to nature in Eden is to be attuned to God, for the rhythm to which Adam and Eve respond is established by God and continuously glorifies him. Most visions of a delightful pastoral world are complete in themselves, but the dynamism of Milton's paradise forces one to recognize the source of all movement and its end" (p. 27). He notes also that the final books of the epic deal with "the adjustments that the Fall necessitates in man's ways of apprehending God" and that "Michael's instruction is in part a lesson in how to think metaphorically" (pp. 13–14).

17 · Svendsen, *Milton and Science*, p. 114; emphasis mine. For biblical backgrounds of this vegetation sequence (root, stalks, leaves), see Sims, *The Bible in Milton's Epics*, p. 31. In a close examination of this vegetative passage, in *"Virga Iesse,"* Goldberg finds here reflected both Neoplatonic cosmology and Christian history along with four different kinds of motion: "the movement around a central point on a single plane . . . the Neoplatonic movement of the *circuitus spiritualis*; the natural growth of the tree; the possibility of man's ascent"—to which he adds the motions of time (pp. 181–82). The lines combine both creation and re-creative history, with Christ as both root and flower, creative principle and re-creative force or seed (pp. 185–86). The image functions as analogy, typology, and anagogy and moves toward the ultimate identity of tenor and vehicle (p. 187).

18 · *Geneva Bible*, p. 2*v*.

19 · Christopher, "Verbal Gate to Paradise," p. 73. She examines the epic evidence against a background of data from Calvin and Luther especially dealing with the "perpetual sense of the scripture" or the "eternal new testament" (pp. 69–70), the mediational grace of verbal promise, and the doctrine of the Interior Teacher. She summarizes thus: "Once the Reformation had established scriptural promise as *the* sacramental reality and once the sacramental event depended upon the timing of the spirit, it thenceforth was often to be a lonely encounter with scripture—in short, a 'literary' experience. By the middle of the seventeenth century in England, differences of emphasis between Luther and Calvin tended to disappear in the experimental accounts of puritans, as *the* religious 'literary' experience became codified" (p. 73). On Gen. 3 : 15, see Milton's *Christian Doctrine* 1.14, in *The Works of John Milton*, ed. Frank A. Patterson et al., 15 : 253 (hereafter cited as CE). On Gen. 3 : 15 as messianic prophecy, see John M. Steadman, "Adam and the Prophesied Redeemer (*Paradise Lost*, XII, 359–623)"; C. A. Patrides, "The 'Protoevangelium' in Renaissance Theology and *Paradise Lost*"; and Christopher, *Milton and the Science of the Saints*. Christopher states that Milton's Protoevangelium of *seed/bruise* means that "Adam and Eve are presented as the first Christians, whose 'literary' experience with God's speech is of more importance than their role as first types" (p. 139, and see pp. 146, 167, 171). In "Blessed Are the Merciful: The Understanding of the Promise in *Paradise Lost*," J. Douglas Canfield considers the question of why the "mysterious terms" were considered "then best" and concludes that the device provides Adam and Eve an opportunity "to be merciful to one another so that they can then comprehend God's mercy" (p. 46).

20 · MacCallum, "Milton and Sacred History," pp. 160, 154. The mysterious term *seed* is recalled by Michael at 11.155 and 12.125, 148, 233, 327, 379, 395, 450, 543, 600–601;

by God at 11.116; and by Adam at 12.623. The passages have been reviewed by Dick Taylor, Jr., "Milton's Treatment of the Judgment and Expulsion in *Paradise Lost.*" See also Goldberg, "*Virga Iesse,*" pp. 184–86.

21 · Curry, *Milton's Ontology, Cosmogony, and Physics*, chap. 5, esp. pp. 121–23, 131, 139; see also his appendix, "Milton's Light Exhaling Darkness: A Study in Symbols." Dustin Griffin's "Milton's Moon" adds perspective to the discussion of Milton's solar imagery; note esp. pp. 158 ff., which link the moon with Christ. Svendsen, *Milton and Science*, pp. 65–72, 43, 84, 241. For backgrounds on the generative sun and a review of recent criticism on this Miltonic issue, see S. Viswanathan, "The Sun and the Creation of Adam: *Paradise Lost*, VIII.253–55."

22 · Cope addresses the question of analogues of Satan as light bringer and Christ as Morning Star and "dawning light" (10.423) in *The Metaphoric Structure of "Paradise Lost,"* pp. 122–28, esp. p. 123n.

23 · The fullest study of these issues is Lewalski, "Innocence and Experience in Milton's Eden."

24 · Chapter 3 of Summers' *Muse's Method*, "Grateful Vicissitude," pp. 71–86, provides a detailed and thoughtful examination of the morning hymn in *Paradise Lost*, Book 5; on the solar and cosmic evidence, see esp. pp. 80–81. Later, in explicating the opening line of Book 3 with its "offspring of Heav'n first-born," Summers notes that both light and Christ are that offspring in a metaphor that here goes undeveloped (pp. 92–93).

25 · The technique, according to Mollenkott, allowed Milton "to gain all the richness, familiarity, regularity, and formal structure of the Ptolemaic system without lending actual credence to it; and he has likewise allowed himself the luxury of speculation concerning the nature of various heavenly bodies and the possibility of their habitation by man" ("Milton's Technique of Multiple Choice," p. 102). More generally, she suggests that Milton used multiple choice to avoid committing himself to theological doctrines or details without concrete biblical support, that is, to "preserve biblical ambiguity without challenging biblical precision" (pp. 102–4). For seventeenth-century backgrounds of geocentricism and heliocentricism, see Lovejoy, *Great Chain of Being*, chap. 4. For more general and older backgrounds, see Grant McColley, "The Astronomy of *Paradise Lost*" and "Milton's Dialogue on Astronomy: The Principal Immediate Sources." After discussing Milton's and Raphael's passage on astronomy, Marjorie Nicolson concludes that Milton "denied the metaphysics of space," "yet he responded to the aesthetics of the new space as fully as any poet of his century" (*Breaking of the Circle*, pp. 183–88, esp. p. 187).

26 · Hill, *Milton: Poet, Priest, and Prophet*, p. 144.

3. LAPSARIAN LOGIC

1 · Milton's *Logic* has been recently edited and translated by Walter J. Ong, S.J., and Charles J. Ermatinger, in *Complete Prose Works of John Milton, Volume VIII, 1666–1682*, ed. Maurice Kelley (New Haven: Yale University Press, 1982). It appears also as volume 11 of *The Works of John Milton*, ed. Frank A. Patterson et al. (New York: Columbia University Press, 1935). Because the Columbia edition includes the Latin text, I have preferred it, but both editions are cited in my text: C = Columbia and Y = Yale. As Rosemond Tuve notes in

Elizabethan and Metaphysical Imagery: Renaissance Poetic and Twentieth-Century Critics, A. H. Gilbert's translation in the Columbia edition also has the advantage of preserving contemporary logical terminology (pp. 335–36n.). Both editions distinguish between Ramus's words in italic and Milton's words in roman typeface, but neither text accounts for the intermediary English Ramistic logic of George Downham from which Milton worked directly. That third dimension is established and analyzed by Francine Lusignan, "*L'Artis Logicae Plenior Institutio* de John Milton: Etat de la question et position." The first half of this study dates and otherwise places *The Art of Logic* in Milton's intellectual history; the second half examines its primary and secondary sources. For summary conclusions on Milton's debts to Downham's work, see pp. 351–59. Thomas S. K. Scott-Craig, in "The Craftsmanship and Theological Significance of Milton's *Art of Logic*," contrasts selected passages from the logic texts of Milton and Downham. For my purposes it is appropriate to assume Milton's agreement with Ramus's and Downham's points when he copies rather than quarrels with them, and I have thus not distinguished in my citations between these authors and typefaces. *The Logike of the Moste Excellent Philosopher P. Ramus, Martyr . . . per M. Roll. Makylmenaeum {Rolland M'Kilwein} . . . 1574* is conveniently available in a Scolar Press facsimile edition. This is the first English version of Ramus's *Artis Logicae*; it is #253 in Walter J. Ong's *Ramus and Talon Inventory*, a 558-page book whose subtitle clarifies the contents more fully: *A Short-Title Inventory of the Published Works of Peter Ramus (1515–1572) and of Omer Talon (ca. 1510–1562) in Their Original and in Their Variously Altered Forms with Related Material*. Ong (p. 2) counts 300 editions of Ramus's *Dialectic* in Latin or French as listed here. Editions of Milton's *Logic* are listed on pp. 277–84.

2 · Ong's fullest study is *Ramus, Method, and the Decay of Dialogue*, but of special interest for students of Milton's logic are Ong's introduction to the Yale edition cited in n. 1 above, along with an earlier version of some of that material published as "Logic and the Epic Muse: Reflections on Noetic Structures in Milton's Milieu," in *Achievements of the Left Hand: Essays on the Prose of John Milton*, ed. Michael Lieb and John T. Shawcross, pp. 239–68. The first of these places Ramus's logic against the backgrounds especially of the supposition logic of Peter de Spain and the place logic of Rudolph Agricola and against the background of the history of printing and therefore to some extent of verbal consciousness. Ramus differed from a number of his most prominent forebears in succeeding in coming out with a second half of logic to balance the first half of Invention (p. 115).

In *Metaphoric Structure of "Paradise Lost*," Jackson I. Cope deftly summarizes the argument of Ong's *Ramus, Method, and the Decay of Dialogue* in these terms: "Ramism was the Renaissance manifestation in which Europe saw the Scholastic revolution completed, the revolution converting the ancient aural world into the spatial world of the printed book, into the mechanistic Newtonian universe, into a pattern of dichotomizing diagrams depicting the structure of every science from rhetoric to biography, into—in short—'method,' as opposed to dialectic. 'Place' logic gradually evolved into diagrams, and it was the actual making physical of these dichotomies spawned of dichotomies which was the central aspect of the Ramist revolution of logic as it emerges from Ong's rich analysis" (pp. 32–33). Cope himself applies to *Paradise Lost* what he describes as the Ramist aesthetic: "the particular spatialized form of logic which reduced reality to a visual object, and supplanted dialogue by the monologue of the expositor pointing out the connections among parts" (pp. 33–34). For Cope, *Paradise Lost* "is a diagrammatic poem in which places cut across narrative to become interconnected into the image of this great argument, in which form emerges as continued metaphor" (p. 34).

My understanding of Ramism is also indebted to the following studies: Perry Miller, *The New England Mind: The Seventeenth Century*; Wilbur S. Howell, *Logic and Rhetoric in England, 1500–1700*; and Tuve, *Elizabethan and Metaphysical Imagery*. For a concise account of the career and guiding principles of Ramus, see Pierre A. Duhamel, "The Logic and Rhetoric of Peter Ramus." I have most often cited Miller in what follows because his phrasing is often so effective and also because my argument calls for the kind of generalized context that his study establishes, the more so because Ramus's own logic text remained in something of a fluid state during his lifetime, evolving variously as Ramus's mind changed, especially in response to contemporary accusations of superficiality. Like Ong, Tuve sees the chief Ramistic novelty as the new light in which older principles are reenvisioned: The differences between Ramistic and traditional logic, she says, "are both less remarkable and more important than they look" (p. 331).

Works targeted more specifically on Milton's Ramism include: Leon Howard, "'The Invention' of Milton's 'Great Argument': A Study of the Logic of 'God's Ways to Men'"; P. Albert Duhamel, "Milton's Alleged Ramism"; Peter F. Fisher, "Milton's Logic"; and Lee A. Jacobus, *Sudden Apprehension: Aspects of Knowledge in "Paradise Lost."* Both Howard and Fisher provide descriptive summaries of the content of Milton's *Logic* and thus a helpful initiation into its vocabulary. Duhamel's contrast between Milton's and Ramus's *Logics* is limited by its failure to take into account the intermediary logic text of Downham. In the terms I have been employing, Duhamel links Ramus himself with the prelapsarian and Milton with the postlapsarian. For him "Milton was never a Ramist except superficially" (p. 1043). Jacobus calls attention to Ramus's fusion or confusion of rhetoric and logic, literature and philosophy (p. 126). In the first half of chapter 6, "Logic in the Garden," Jacobus provides convenient background on Ramus and his place in the history of logic and discusses the Ramistic general principles he judges most significant for Milton study. He notes, for example, that the emphasis on causes is a Ramistic feature (p. 134) and that Ramus does away with Aristotelian emphasis on the forms, moods, and memorization of syllogistic study and stresses aspects of Ramistic Judgment (p. 136). In the second half of this chapter, Jacobus specifically examines *Paradise Lost*'s Ramism only in the Adam and Eve discussion of separation in Book 9 and in Eve's Book 9 conversation with Satan. On the latter, for Jacobus Satan proceeds with the temptation largely on the grounds of inartificial argument. For a supplementary consideration of Milton's edenic knowledge and the seventeenth-century context of literature and biblical commentary, see Joseph E. Duncan, *Milton's Earthly Paradise: A Historical Study of Eden*, chap. 6, esp. pp. 147–58. In "'Go': Milton's Antinomianism and the Separation Scene in *Paradise Lost*, Book 9," Joan S. Bennett notes that, in the earlier discussion about separating, "Adam reasons largely noetically by arranging axioms in their natural hierarchy" whereas Eve "resorts to the more tedious method of syllogism"; he proceeds intuitively, she discursively (pp. 398–99). Although his title suggests pertinence to my argument, in fact the point of Dennis H. Burden's *Logical Epic: A Study of the Argument of "Paradise Lost"* is not that Milton's epic is a technically "logical" product but that it is a reasonable, self-consistent, closely discriminated justification of God's ways in line with the authority of the Bible and that Milton has here done a lot of alert, systematic, hard thinking about his data and issues.

In *Of Education* Milton speaks of the three "organic arts which enable men to discourse and write perspicuously, elegantly, and according to the fitted style of lofty, mean, or lowly" in these terms: Logic, "with all her well-couched heads and topics," is cited for its usefulness; Rhetoric is "graceful and ornate"; and poetry "would be made subsequent, or indeed rather precedent, as being less subtle and fine, but more simple, sensuous, and passionate" (Hughes, pp. 636–37). For an examination of the implications for poetry in Ramus's logic, see Robert Daly, *God's Altar: The World and the Flesh in Puritan Poetry*, pp. 50–56. Irene Samuel, in "Milton on the Province of Rhetoric," discusses *Of Education* against a background of Milton's *Art of Logic*. She judges the chief Ramistic influence on Milton as the interrelation of logic and rhetoric and says that the study of logic must precede the study of rhetoric and poetics (p. 181); on Milton's distrust of inartificial arguments, see pp. 183–87. In "Logic and the Epic Muse," Ong examines the curriculum recommended in *Of Education* as proceeding Ramistically from the general to the particular (p. 258); and, similarly, Rajan, "Simple, Sensuous, and Passionate," p. 7; and Christopher Grose, *Milton's Epic Process: "Paradise Lost" and Its Miltonic Background*, pp. 29–36, 123–39. For a brief discussion of the alignment of the poetical with the logical argument and especially Milton's emphasis on logical causality and disjunctive structures and his uses of paradox and juxtaposition of different cognitive levels, see Steadman, *Epic and Tragic Structure in "Paradise Lost,"* pp. 129–33; see n. 19, p. 183, for an extensive bibliography on various modes of paradox in *Paradise Lost*.

3 · Ong, *Ramus, Method, and the Decay of Dialogue*, pp. 7, 197, 198, 204, 187–88, 270, 184, and cf. p. 243, where *definition* is defined as "single terms broken down into their constituent elements"; and Miller, *New England Mind*, p. 151. Of the initial version of Ramus's logic, Ong comments: "Since the only kind of organization for discourse which Ramus imagines is the 'collocation' of thought-corpuscles or arguments, or of clusters of such corpuscles, the only kind of variation he can imagine is that which arises as the result of the suppression of an argument or argument cluster where it should normally be found. This outlook governs his explanation of induction, enthymeme, and example. . . . all merely syllogisms for Ramus, with one or another part suppressed or understood" (p. 186). And, similarly, "This dialectic which terminates in 'method' ends where it began, in an approach to knowledge limited by what is implied originally in the metaphor of the topics" (p. 247); and "All 'teaching' is, to Ramus' mind, a movement from the generic to the 'specific.' Definition itself is subservient to this movement, and so is syllogism, for syllogism operates by definition and distribution or division" (p. 204).

4 · *The Complete Works of Christopher Marlowe*, ed. Fredson Bowers, 1:376; Craig, *The Enchanted Glass: The Elizabethan Mind in Literature*, p. 143. The longer quotation records Ong's précis of the argument of Perry Miller's *New England Mind*, in *Ramus, Method, and the Decay of Dialogue*, pp. 3–4. Ong speaks elsewhere in this study of "Ramist mono-methodology" (p. 256) and of Ramist dialectic as "the most recklessly applied [quantification system] that the world has ever seen" (p. 203). On these same issues, Boyd M. Berry has observed: "The Puritans, who were the religious innovators of their age, did not so much innovate as methodize and solidify and elaborate upon a few great intellectual breakthroughs of the early Reformers. . . . Indeed, it was that systematic elaboration which they themselves defined as intellectual progress" (*Process of Speech*, p. 86). Among the "inkhorn terms"

against which Marlowe's contemporary George Puttenham inveighs in *The Arte of English Poesie*, ed. Gladys Doidge Willcock and Alice Walker, p. 147, are *Methode* and *methodicall*, although he himself uses "methodes" on p. 306 and "methodically" on p. 159.

5 · See *Christian Doctrine*, 1.1, in Hughes, pp. 900–904 and CE 14:3–25. On the Ramistic organization of *De Doctrina Christiana*, see Gordon Campbell, "*De Doctrina Christiana*: Its Structural Principles and Its Unfinished State," esp. pp. 243–49, and note the charts on pp. 247–49. In appendixes to her *Toward "Samson Agonistes,"* Radzinowicz provides Ramistic diagrams, including "A Topical Synopsis of *De Doctrina Christiana*, Book I" (p. 386) and "A Schematic Outline of *De Doctrina Christiana*, Book II" (pp. 384–85). Although she does not label it as Ramistic, Sister Mary Irma Corcoran provides a Ramistic diagram of "Milton's Analysis of the Virtues (CD, XVII)" in Appendix 3 of her *Milton's Paradise with Reference to the Hexaemeral Background*, p. 136. In "Milton's *Accedence Commenc't Grammar*," Gordon Campbell finds an analogously Ramistic organization: As *Christian Doctrine* divides between the knowledge and the love of God, between faith and worship, or between data and use, so Milton's grammar divides between "Right-wording, usually call'd *Etymologie*; and right-joyning of words, or *Syntaxis*." Ramists normally bifurcated grammars into etymology and syntax (see Ong, *Ramus, Method, and the Decay of Dialogue*, p. 260). On Milton's use of Ramistic reasoning regarding divorce, see Theodore L. Hugelet, "The Rule of Charity in Milton's Divorce Tracts." In *Sudden Apprehension*, Jacobus finds Ramistic dichotomization characteristic of Milton's *Art of Logic* but "not a particularly noticeable feature of other works by Milton" (p. 20).

6 · Miller, *New England Mind*, pp. 111, 133.

7 · *Re-* words predominate in these glances at the phrasing of *Of Education* as they do in the following passages from Milton's *Christian Doctrine*, which address similar issues within a distinction between natural and supernatural renovation of human faculties: "The change which takes place in man . . . is that whereby the natural mind and will of man being partially renewed by a divine impulse, are led to seek knowledge of God, and for the time, at least, undergo an alteration for the better"; "The intent of *Supernatural Renovation* is not only to restore man more completely than before to the use of his natural faculties, as regards his power to form right judgment, and to exercise free will; but to create afresh, as it were, the inward man, and infuse from above new and supernatural faculties into the minds of the renovated"; and "Regeneration is that change operated by the Word and the Spirit, whereby the old man being destroyed, the inward man is regenerated by God after his own image, in all the faculties of his mind, insomuch that he becomes as it were a new creature, and the whole man is sanctified both in body and soul, for the service of God, and the performance of good works" (CE 15:353–55, 367).

8 · For a collection of seventeenth-century theological and philosophical comments on naming, see Cope, *Metaphoric Structure of "Paradise Lost,"* pp. 35–49. Cope summarizes: "My larger historical point has been that this wanton objectifying movement in European thought—so conveniently focused around the flourishing of Ramism and its aftermath—produced an unexpected result when it moved men to objectify words. For with that attempt the most antipoetical, from one point of view, of pedagogical systems, became from another, the impetus for renewed attempts to liberate language in the ways poets liberate it. That is, Ramism and the forces which fed into it in the seventeenth century induced men to leap the

aural structures of syntactical discursion in search of an objective, 'corporeal' status for the word itself, a status in which it would not be a dependent sign but an immediate creative entity" (p. 178). In "Epistemology and the Tutelary Word," Entzminger notes: "In paradise, words have no real etymology, just as Adam has no real history, and so even when speaking 'sacred metaphor,' Adam's use of language is unself-conscious, unaware of the dualism which makes the expressed unity all the more striking to Milton's readers. After the fall, words, like man, acquire a history, making them ambiguous" (p. 106). In "Speech in *Paradise Lost*," Beverley Sherry traces the Renaissance tradition of a corruption of human speech occurring not with Babel but with the fall and notes the belief in Milton's prose (in *The History of Britain, Colasterion,* and *The First Defense*) "that whenever there is a fall from virtue there is a decay of eloquence, that a lack of truth is betrayed by ineptitude in words" (p. 250).

9 · Ong, "Logic and the Epic Muse," p. 250.

10 · Miller, *New England Mind*, pp. 149–50.

11 · Howell, *Logic and Rhetoric*, p. 368, cites Bacon for this definition. Cf. Walter J. Ong: "Ramus belongs to the strictly amateur school of logicians who picture induction and deduction simply as reciprocal movements, not as radically different kinds of psychological performances irreducible to one another" (*Ramus, Method, and the Decay of Dialogue*, p. 258).

12 · C33, 35; Y223, 224. For a consideration of causes in *Christian Doctrine*, see Radzinowicz, *Toward "Samson Agonistes*," p. 318, and Jacobus, *Sudden Apprehension*, p. 19. Adam identifies his own causes in the conversation with deity in Book 8; he recounts his history when he manifested his form, creation, and rational soul and when he distinguished himself in terms of both essence and number from the efficient deity. It may be said that Raphael's review of the Chain of Being account, Book 5.469–90, imposes logical or causal structure on Adam's Chain of Being account in the morning hymn earlier in Book 5.

13 · Ong, *Ramus, Method, and the Decay of Dialogue*, passim; Miller, *New England Mind*, p. 124. Ong notes the looseness of such Ramistic usage: "Thus the 'things,' or 'arguments,' which crop up in Ramism are not bits of the physical world transferred to the intellectual realm, nor bits of the intellectual realm slipped into the physical; they are noncommital terms with an extraphilosophical, legal and rhetorical history which admirably conditions them for spreading out indifferently into both realms" (p. 66). Milton calls his fellow students "arguments" in Prolusion 7 (Hughes, p. 629). On Ramistic arguments more generally, see Ong, *Ramus, Method, and the Decay of Dialogue*, pp. 199–205; Duhamel, "Milton's Alleged Ramism," pp. 1042–43; and Tuve, *Elizabethan and Metaphysical Imagery*, pp. 344–45. Tuve emphasizes that for Ramists to invent was simultaneously to argue (p. 334) and that a Ramistic argument shows "a fitness to be related to another" argument (p. 344). In an earlier study, Tuve defines a Ramistic "argument" with special clarity as follows: "In dialectic, each concept is an 'argument,' through which we reach to greater and greater concepts, also "arguments'; in turn, each concept is built up of lesser 'arguments,' down to the very words which compose it, in an unbroken *crescendo* and *decrescendo*. Every object in nature is (not only 'is the basis for') an 'argument,' say of order, of God; the qualities of anything are the 'arguments' of that subject. A single word may be an 'argument,' in that it 'hath a fitness to argue something.' . . . The argument is the relatableness of a word or a thing, its 'reference' or 'relation' . . . by which it is ready to hook into other arguments, and by an infinite progression build up into the whole structure of truth." And she adds: "It is

clear that to a Ramist the world was full of arguments; the moment you utilize anything for its significance, it becomes one" ("Imagery and Logic: Ramus and Metaphysical Poetics," pp. 383, 384).

14 · Miller, *New England Mind*, p. 149; and cf. Howell, in *Logic and Rhetoric*, p. 24, who calls Invention "a process in which an author found subject matter by connecting his mind with the traditional wisdom of his race and by allowing that contact to induce a flow of ideas from the general store to himself."

15 · Ong, *Ramus, Method, and the Decay of Dialogue*, p. 208.

16 · A Ramist approaching Genesis 1 would find there confirmed his predisposition to conceive the deity as also a Ramist and the created universe as Ramistically ordered. The first or efficient cause appears in verse 1: "In the beginning God created the heaven and the earth"; the material cause derives from "Let there be light" (3); the formal from "Let there be firmament" (6); and the final cause acknowledges each event by affirming "that it was good"; "for the sake of which" is a multiplying of divine goodness. The deity provides a radical notation in naming the light *day*, the darkness *night*, the firmament *heaven*, the dry land *earth*, and the waters *seas*. The deity of Genesis 1 is most radically a Ramist in his distribution procedures and his thorough commitment to dichotomy: he bifurcates light/darkness, waters under firmament/waters above firmament, waters/dry land, day/night, greater light/ lesser light, and male/female. There are distributions by subject/adjunct as well as by cause/ effect: fish/fowl/beasts, water/air/earth. Verse 25 ("And God made the beast of the earth after his kind, and cattle after their kind, and every thing that creepeth upon the earth after his kind") shows both a distribution process and a genus/species format, as does verse 28. The deity offers comparisons of equals in these genera and of greaters/lessers in the creation of man in his likeness and image (form) and dominion (end). In "Milton's Paraphrase of Genesis: A Stylistic Reading of *Paradise Lost*, Book VII," Ernst Haublein presents a minutely detailed comparison of the two texts, emphasizing representative selective passages. His note 45 discusses Raphael's (rare) direct address to Adam (pp. 109–10). For another consideration of the relation of Book 7 to the Bible, see Sims, *The Bible in Milton's Epics*, pp. 33–35. Jason Rosenblatt places several key portions of *Paradise Lost*, Book 7, against a background of patristic, medieval, Rabbinic, and Reformation commentaries on Genesis, in "Angelic Tact: Raphael on Creation," in *Milton and the Middle Ages*, ed. John Mulryan, pp. 21–31. Contrasting *Paradise Lost*, Book 7, with Genesis in *Process of Speech*, Berry notes that only in Gen. 1 : 12 does God not control the action of every sentence, whereas Book 7 of Milton's epic delineates "not what God did but what his creatures did, of themselves, in response to the initial creative impulse" (p. 234). Berry adds, "The profusion of verbs which Milton's muse employs in book seven and the cosmic dance they spell out enable the creatures to follow the divine lead, to respond to his gestures on their own"; Book 7 "embodies syntactically a *mutuality* of effort in a circular movement. The creator begins, the creation responds, and the creator completes as action returns to him, both within the individual days and through the story as a whole"; God acts on the first two days, creation begins to act in response on the third day, especially as is seen in the incidence of verbs of emerging upward (pp. 234–35). For Helen Gardner, in *A Reading of "Paradise Lost,"* "The seventh is the one purely happy book of *Paradise Lost* and shows Milton's genius at its most genial and delightful, filling out the bare narrative of Genesis with a wealth of knowledge and imagination, with constant touches of observation, of beauty, humour, delicacy, and grotesqueness. It is inspired by

Milton's passionate belief in the goodness of the natural world as it was created and his delight in the principle of life, in all its manifestations" (p. 75). On the procreative representation of creation in Book 7, see Edward LeComte, *Milton and Sex*, pp. 85–88. Balachandra Rajan comments: "For Milton, the creation is the perfect poem. He mentions it first among his poetic intentions, he returns to it as the matrix of his utterance. All of his eloquence is shaped by its activity. Paradise is perfected by its plenitude. Hell is its parody, the causeway from Hell its burlesque. The reverberating overtones of the Fall are Chaos. The atonement is a new creation, a bringing of good out of evil. Everything that the epic says and does is suffused and controlled by this central efflorescence" ("Simple, Sensuous, and Passionate," p. 14). As O. B. Hardison points out in "Written Records and Truths of Spirit," p. 153, Plato's *Timaeus* also treats creation as the imposition of form, originating in God, upon matter.

17 · Milton discusses the biblical names for Satan in *Christian Doctrine* 1.9 (Hughes, p. 992; CE 15 : 111). *Satan*, from the Hebrew, means *adversary*, and in *Paradise Lost* Satan is so labeled in the Father's first speech to the Son in Book 3, line 81, again by the Son at 3.156, and more largely by the narrator at 2.629, "the Adversary of God and Man."

18 · Miller, *New England Mind*, p. 151. In "Logic and Rhetoric of Peter Ramus," Pierre A. Duhamel speaks similarly: "The art can be discovered by searching three books: the characters imprinted in the individual soul by God, nature, and the natural functions of the hand and the tongue. The natural power to reason, the image of the parent of all things, God, is born with man. It is here that he is in closest agreement with several affirmations of Puritan scholasticism, and one can easily understand how his thought became closely tied to theirs. Like the Puritans, Ramus assumed an intimate concurrence of God in nature and with them indicated that the power of reason was the image of God in men. The use of the syllogism was proper to the regenerate for the Puritans, whereas for Ramus it was common to all men" (p. 168). The linguistic link between *logic* and *logos* (cf. John 1 : 1) makes an equation between the two inevitable. Peter F. Fisher provides an expansive technical comparison of the syllogisms of Milton, Ramus, and Aristotle, in "Milton's Logic," pp. 53–59.

19 · Ong, *Ramus, Method, and the Decay of Dialogue*, p. 259; for further discussion, see pp. 258–62.

20 · Gayle Edward Wilson considers several aspects of rhetoric and logic in the first of Michael's tableaux in "'His Eyes He Op'n'd': The Abel–Cain Vision, *Paradise Lost*, XI.427–448." Of special interest to the present study is the listing of dissentany arguments on p. 8.

21 · Christopher, *Milton and the Science of the Saints*, p. 193.

22 · Ong, *Ramus, Method, and the Decay of Dialogue*, p. 242. Ong points out: "Thus in Ramus's age and even much earlier, *specialization in syllogisms is regularly evidence less of a scientific mind*, well or misled, *than of a basically didactic mind and a didactic framework for thought*" (p. 243; emphasis his).

23 · Howell, *Logic and Rhetoric*, pp. 156, 160; Miller, *New England Mind*, p. 111. Although he does not specify the disjunctive syllogism, in *Milton's Use of Du Bartas*, George Coffin Taylor treats the *whether . . . or* construction in the two poets, calling it "the *formula of scientific doubt*" (pp. 77–78; emphasis his); he also cites the inquiry into causes (p. 101) and the checking of curiosity (p. 102) in the two poets.

24 · Neal W. Gilbert, *Renaissance Concepts of Method*, p. 131; and Ong, *Ramus, Method, and the Decay of Dialogue*, pp. 184, 224, 189, 192. Speaking similarly of this early version of

Ramus's logic, Ong observes: "Although he does not yet have the term 'methodized,' the nature of the transformation he looks forward to is evident. It is a tidying up, an elimination of *commentitia* or unstable structures in the curriculum. For it is somehow through a flawless summary or *summa* of all the curriculum subjects that the mind ultimately arrives at God" (p. 189). And, again, "The peculiar role which 'genus' plays in Ramus's thought makes it difficult for him to keep God from being a kind of universal genus for all things, or, even worse, the summary of all curriculum subjects" (p. 189).

25 · On Natural vs. Prudential Method in relation to the postlapsarian, see Howell, *Logic and Rhetoric*, pp. 164–65. In *Ramus, Method, and the Decay of Dialogue*, Ong links Prudential Method with crypsis (pp. 253, 281).

26 · A number of critical studies have devoted considerable attention to *death* in *Paradise Lost*. Most recently, in *Milton and the Science of the Saints*, Christopher has combined the literary with the religious in pointing out that Michael "mentions the death of Christ at least fourteen times between lines 398 and 430 of Book XII, all of which amounts to considerable rhetorical emphasis, but his interest is to explain the metaphysical mechanics that make his death promissory." And, again, "The verbal formulations are varied and inconsequential, but these undistinguished lines are all presumed to have enormous epiphanic potential. In the event that the word 'life' is understood as metonymic to the quality of life promised, a sacramental transaction will have taken place" (pp. 129, 130). In *Milton's Poetic Art*, John Reesing observes: "Thus by the end of Book II the word 'death' has been made so polysemantic that it can serve thenceforth as one of the most complexly evocative of all the words in the special vocabulary of the poem. Milton will be using it to signify either a character in the story; or a mode of penal existence characterized by loss and eternal misery, pain, and frustration; or—as Adam and Eve imagine will be their fate—an event or experience that simply ends existence by an act of final destruction" (p. 57).

For a discussion of the word and theme of death, see Reesing, *Milton's Poetic Art*, pp. 55–68; Tayler, *Milton's Poetry*, pp. 73–88; and Waddington, "Death of Adam," pp. 15–21. Waddington argues that Adam is "dead" throughout Book 11 until the equivalent of baptism with Noah's flood and that this accounts for the shift from vision to narration. In "'If Shape It Might Be Call'd That Shape Had None': Aspects of Death in Milton" (esp. pp. 48–49, 51–53), Cherrell Guilfoyle examines the character and theme of death in *Paradise Lost*, and death in Milton's works more generally, against the background of the four degrees of death in *Christian Doctrine*. Milton's thinking on spiritual death is encapsulated, Guilfoyle says, in *Paradise Lost* 9.901, "Defac't, deflow'r'd, and now to Death devote" (p. 50). Within his larger argument of antimetabolic structures governing *Paradise Lost*, Galbraith Miller Crump suggests parallels between the allegorization of Death in Book 2 and the visions of death Michael provides in Book 11 (*The Mystical Design of "Paradise Lost,"* pp. 128–29); for structural parallels more generally between Books 2 and 11 and between Books 1 and 12, see pp. 123–47.

27 · Clark, *Milton at St. Paul's School*, passim; Gilbert, *Renaissance Concepts of Method*, p. 143, and see p. 203; and Ong, *Ramus, Method, and the Decay of Dialogue*, pp. 191, 176, 190, 193, 264. John M. Steadman broadens the inquiry into Invention and Disposition from Logic toward poetry and painting in chapter 7 of *The Lamb and the Elephant: Ideal Imitation and the Context of Renaissance Allegory*.

4. LAPSARIAN POETICS

1 · The distinction is developed by Georgia B. Christopher in *Milton and the Science of the Saints*, specifically on p. 126 and more generally passim: "Puritan writing is much more figurative than often supposed because discursive language treating divine matters may be metonymy. Puritan texts therefore become very fluid, their shape shifting as metonymy is discovered in verbiage seemingly barren of figuration, or as metaphor is suddenly seen in its metonymic aspect. The coincidence of metaphor and metonymy often makes alternate routes available by which to arrive at a 'correct' reading; everything depends upon whether the Spirit chooses to move along the metaphoric or metonymic axis. Milton, in *Paradise Lost*, takes pains to ensure the hermeneutic fluidity, now leaning heavily toward one axis, now toward the other, but committing himself absolutely to neither" (p. 126). "To puritan cognoscenti . . . the power of both metaphor and metonymy depends upon an ingrained knowledge of the matter treated. . . . It will help if [the reader] is familiar with the biblical vocabulary available for metaphoric substitution. In like manner, the power of metonymy depends upon knowing the whole story very well—upon knowing what is next to what" (p. 132). Raphael's metaphors align men and angels, but the metonyms invite "us to see the connection between the language of promise, heaven, and a particular human existence" (p. 126). Christopher is principally concerned with the literary dimension of Protestant religious experience; her fine argument, along with Barbara K. Lewalski's *Protestant Poetics and the Seventeenth-Century Lyric*, on which it builds, variously lies behind the present study. Foundationally, for Christopher, Luther addresses "the moment when the *viva vox Christi* flames forth from some human presentation of God's promise" in a "literary experience" that is "a *de facto* sacrament" (p. 120); and "Calvin's brilliant achievement is to invoke the almost subliminal experience of figurative transfer as a sudden leap and to use it to describe the motions of faith," thus joining Heaven and earth by metonymy and making sacramental action a tropological event (p. 122). See also pp. 127, 142–44, 175, 180. In *Biblical Criticism and Heresy in Milton*, George N. Conklin has outlined Milton's own exegetical techniques against the background of the "Renaissance stimulus to the linguistic aspects of Reformation exegesis" and distinguished between the quite different theological questions raised by the Renaissance "grammatical analysis *of* the passage" and "the medieval inter-pretative gloss *on* a passage of Scripture" (pp. 11, 1, and esp. chap. 2).

Although Michael Lieb's purposes and views of *Paradise Lost* differ greatly from my own, his *Poetics of the Holy: A Reading of "Paradise Lost"* touches variously on a number of matters discussed in the present chapter. Especially helpful is his chapter 3, "Sacral Poetics," in which Lieb examines a wide array of traditional and Miltonic evidence on what he calls "Milton's hierophantic poetics" (p. 45), his link of the poet with prophet and priest, the interchangeability for Milton of sacerdos and vates (p. 46), of the cultic and the oracular. Moses is the consummate model of prophet, priest, and poet (p. 50), and Christ is the ultimate oracle (p. 52). More generally, Lieb dismisses *Paradise Lost*'s Protestantism or Puri-tanism (pp. 328–29) and its "complex logical superstructure of doctrinal exploration and rational discourse" (p. 100) in favor of *Paradise Lost* as numinous and as radiating outward from the theocentric and the Christocentric (p. 80). For him *Paradise Lost* in part "conceive[s] of itself as a verbal representation of the sanctuary": "One enters *Paradise Lost* with the same feeling of what Milton in *Christian Doctrine* defined as 'adoratio' and 'sanctificatio' (CM, 17:81). One enters with a knowledge that here is worship ('cultus,' to use Milton's term) of the highest sort, where the poem itself becomes sacrament, the symbol of things sacred, and where one becomes a participant 'in an extraordinary act' of 'liturgical service' that is 'ceremonially sacramental'" (p. 84).

2 · Lewalski, *Protestant Poetics and the Seventeenth-Century Lyric*, pp. 3, 6, 4. Elsewhere Lewalski speaks of Moses and David as poetic role models ("Typological Symbolism and the 'Progress of the Soul' in Seventeenth-Century Literature," in *Literary Uses of Typology from the Late Middle Ages to the Present*, ed. Earl Miner, pp. 107–10).

3 · Rajan, "Osiris and Urania," pp. 227, 225.

4 · Madsen, *From Shadowy Types to Truth*, pp. 100–101, and see pp. 88–89, 78. For his different purposes Madsen judges even Raphael's "shadow of Heav'n" as typological rather than Platonic.

5 · Allen, "Milton and the Descent to Light," in *Milton Studies in Honor of Harris Francis Fletcher*, p. 8.

6 · Dante, *Convivio*, in *Literary Criticism of Dante Alighieri*, trans. Robert S. Haller, pp. 112–14, liii.

7 · Murrin, *The Veil of Allegory: Some Notes toward a Theory of Allegorical Rhetoric in the English Renaissance*, pp. 70, 115–16, 121, 55. Isabel G. MacCaffrey draws the distinction in lapsarian terms attaching "synthetic allegory" to the transcendent world and "analytical allegory" to the fallen world (*Spenser's Allegory: The Anatomy of Imagination*, pp. 33, 60). See also chapter 4 of Steadman, *The Lamb and the Elephant*, on allegory, esp. pp. 72–73, and on Milton, esp. pp. 89–95.

8 · Madsen, *From Shadowy Types to Truth*, pp. 75–77. Elsewhere (p. 100) Madsen distinguishes between philosophical allegory and predictive allegory.

9 · The cited assessment is from C. A. Patrides, "*Paradise Lost* and the Theory of Accommodation," p. 59. Patrides examines a number of contemporary statements on the theory of accommodation and distinguishes interestingly between anthropomorphic and anthropopathetic conceptions of the deity (p. 62); and see Patrides, *Milton and the Christian Tradition*, chap. 1, pt. 1. On accommodation, see also Frye, *God, Man, and Satan*, pp. 7–13.

10 · For an extended discussion of Milton's comments on accommodation in *Christian Doctrine*, see Leland Ryken, *The Apocalyptic Vision in "Paradise Lost,"* pp. 7–33. Ryken concludes that Milton's theory of accommodation emphasizes the literal interpretation or the physical aspects (pp. 17–18), that Milton regarded accommodation as equally applicable to biblical interpretation and poetic theory and technique (p. 19), and that accommodation could be used to support either a literal or an allegorical method of biblical interpretation (p. 30). Lee A. Jacobus, in *Sudden Apprehension*, distinguishes between prelapsarian and postlapsarian revelations, saying that Raphael "accommodates slightly" but Michael does so "mightily" (p. 90); and see p. 100 where Michael's accommodation is described as medically based.

11 · Hartman, "Adam on the Grass with Balsamum," in *Beyond Formalism: Literary Essays, 1958–1970*, p. 136. Later in the essay Hartman speaks of the opposite of accommodation as "conflagration, a burning up of restrictive mystery, an opening up of man, a cleansing of the doors of perception," in sum an apocalypse (p. 137).

12 · MacCallum, "Milton and Figurative Interpretation of the Bible," pp. 402–3. In *The Motives of Eloquence: Rhetoric in the Renaissance*, Richard A. Lanham distinguishes two modes of Western literature—the serious and the rhetorical with their contrasting theories of style, motive, identity, and knowledge. The former category, our prelapsarian, stresses a central self, a serious motive, "a scientific, measurable reality independent of man," and narrative form; the latter category, our postlapsarian, stresses a social self, acting "from role-sustaining motives in a dramatic reality." The problem he identifies as facing the mystic serious speaker is that "He can soar beyond language only if we agree beforehand to overlook his language. His chronic problem, as a poet, is to fabricate a structure which will encourage this act of oblivion. Stylistic self-consciousness for him means disaster. . . . he must create a context which does not notice words as words." But for the alternate mode, our postlapsarian and Michael's province and practice, the word and the presentation of the word become the dominant fact. The emphasis is between the two shifts from monad to system, from object to process, from the known to the knower, and this is precisely the altered world and humanity Michael must address. See esp. pp. 18, 210, 34–35, 38, 219.

13 · Allen, *The Harmonious Vision: Studies in Milton's Poetry*, pp. 102, 101. In "Milton and the Symbol of Light," in *Ten Perspectives on Milton*, Merritt Y. Hughes traces the Augustinian background of the equation of God with uncreated light and distinguishes it from created light, either incorporeal or corporeal, "found only in the consciousness of creatures and physically available to them" (p. 89).

14 · Ferry, *Milton's Epic Voice: The Narrator in "Paradise Lost,"* p. 28. Ferry describes Milton's exploitation of metaphorical blindness in Book 3, lines 40–55, as "one of his most dazzling achievements" (p. 28). She traces in lines 21–36 "the pattern of descent and reascent, of loss and restoration, of departure and return" (pp. 26–27), and she links the lines with the encompassing theme of loss of paradise (pp. 28–34).

15 · In "'Most Perfect Hero': The Role of the Son in Milton's Theodicy," in *Paradise Lost: A Tercentenary Tribute*, ed. Balachandra Rajan, Hugh MacCallum examines the extraordinary variety and richness of the Son's roles in *Paradise Lost* within the context of contemporary theological dogma and speculation. See esp. pp. 102–4 on the unknowable God and the Son's mediatorial roles. MacCallum finds that at several points in the epic Christ's office is presented "in terms of two main functions, one external, the other internal, one the priestly work of satisfaction, the other the prophetic work of illumination" (p. 103). As its title suggests, this issue is explored in Marilyn Arnold, "Milton's Accessible God: The Role of the Son in *Paradise Lost*."

16 · Berry, *Process of Speech*, title of chap. 15. See also Joan Webber's review of the role and relationship of Father and Son in *Milton and His Epic Tradition*, pp. 113–14. Later Webber takes a distancing perspective on this complex issue: "The more time I spend thinking about Milton's God, the more difficult it seems to me to take any kind of exclusive approach to his definition. Simply, God cannot be defined. Neither a strictly historical, orthodox theological context, nor one, like mine, which comes from the style of the poem and its poet and muse, can wholly satisfy. Although that is hard on the critic, it seems right that if Milton has succeeded, then his God should defy language" (p. 224).

17 · Recurrent diction and images align the theology of Book 3 and the created cosmos of Book 7. Book 3, for example, speaks of "a cloud / Drawn round about thee like a radiant

Shrine" (378–79); the first day's light in Book 7 is similarly "Spher'd in a radiant Cloud" (247), and on the fourth day light is "Transplanted from her cloudy Shrine" (360). God is the "Fountain of Light" at 3.375; in Book 7 the sun itself is "made porous to receive / And drink the liquid Light" (361–62) and is itself a "Fountain" (364) from which "other Stars / Repairing, in thir gold'n Urns draw Light" (364–65).

18 · See Griffin, "Milton's Moon," p. 163. Lewalski reviews the varied New Testament vocabulary of signification in *Protestant Poetics and the Seventeenth-Century Lyric*, pp. 111–12; and see Paul J. Korshin, "The Development of Abstracted Typology in England, 1650–1820," in *Literary Uses of Typology*, ed. Miner, pp. 148–49, 163. In establishing the framework for her stylistic analysis in "The Limbs of Truth: Milton's Use of Simile in *Paradise Lost*," Linda Gregerson supports the view of the coherence of Raphaelean learning by contrast with postlapsarian discontinuities. She finds that "Raphael's analogical method of instruction is presumably endorsed by the underlying coherence and continuity of creation" and notes that "Adam is to curb his inquiry into the motions of the stars, but only that he may better address his steps to the course which will lead him by degrees to God. . . . The boundaries he discovers are the boundaries of ordered progress, not the pattern of stasis" (pp. 136–37).

19 · Milton's "what surmounts the reach" lines have been the target of a variety of provocative commentary; see, e.g., Madsen, *From Shadowy Types to Truth*, pp. 87 ff. Jacobus, in *Sudden Apprehension*, notes that although Adam's senses may be surmounted his understanding is not (p. 92); Ryken, in *Apocalyptic Vision in "Pardise Lost*," divides the speech in half, viewing the first portion in relation to accommodation and the second supplementary portion in relation to the Platonic theory of Ideas (pp. 7–33); he stresses that Milton "asserts that the earthly copy is an accurate analogue of divine reality, not a vague image to be penetrated and transcended," and generalizes: "Just as the doctrine of accommodation could be used to support either a literal or an allegorical method of biblical interpretation, the Platonic theory of Ideas is capable of leading either to an acceptance of the visible image or an attempt to dissolve the image and go beyond it" (p. 30). Jon S. Lawry's full-length study, *The Shadow of Heaven: Matter and Stance in Milton's Poetry*, is variously illuminating; but specifically of Raphael's poetic and "tutelary narrative" of the Satanic rebellion, Lawry remarks: "We must allow Raphael's interior epic narrative at least a symbolic or figurative truth as it involves actions entirely apart from man," but "also, we are to receive the narrative individually as divine story reflects the truth that involves the life of each man"; "the theory of accommodation therefore works in both directions" (p. 199). In *Milton and the Science of the Saints*, Christopher remarks on Christ's characteristic "what if" constructions in *Paradise Regained* (p. 207).

20 · R. H. West says there is no precedent for Milton's "ultimate analogy of angelic to human," i.e., the lovemaking of angels, in *Milton Encyclopedia*, 7:95; and see also 1:49–50, on angelic lovemaking.

21 · Milton, *Art of Logic*, Book 1, chaps. 18–22. Chapter 5 of Isabel G. MacCaffrey's *"Paradise Lost" as "Myth"* examines some interesting evidence of the imagery and theme of likeness. Studies of Miltonic comparison generally concern themselves with the six books of *Paradise Lost* that are not the focus of the present study, that is, Books 1–4 and 9 and 10. The concern, in other words, is with the epic device of simile rather than with intentions and procedures within the poem's narrative categories. Such studies include James Whaler,

"Compounding and Distribution of Similes in *Paradise Lost*," "Grammatical *Nexus* of the Miltonic Simile," and "The Miltonic Simile." More recent discussions include Sims, *The Bible in Milton's Epics*, pp. 219–37, and see p. 28; Christopher Ricks, *Milton's Grand Style*, chap. 4; and Grose, *Milton's Epic Process*, chap. 6. In a general way Grose's chapter 5 places Milton's use of metaphors against the background of Milton's *Art of Logic*. He does briefly consider what he labels "Raphael's great similitude" (p. 147), i.e., the Battle in Heaven, in its rhetorical context; elsewhere he calls the same material "a simile *involving* the poem's primary metaphor" (p. 138; emphasis his). See also Grose, "Milton on Ramist Similitude," in *Seventeenth-Century Imagery: Essays on Uses of Figurative Language from Donne to Farquhar*, ed. Earl Miner, pp. 112–13, where Grose notes the lapsarian bases of Ramism. Ryken's *Apocalyptic Vision in "Paradise Lost"* is one of the rare Milton commentaries to consider Raphael's small comparisons between Heaven and earth (pp. 21–22, 32–33, and passim). Ryken also collects contrasts (chaps. 3, 4, 5), comparisons via negation (chap. 4), and "generic imagery" (pp. 212–19). For him *apocalyptic* means something like *transcendent*, that is, remote from fallen reality, related to a higher truth, and portraying an ideal state (p. 4).

22 · These commonplaces are warnings Milton added to the given texts of Ramus himself and Downham. The more usual Ramistic assumption, as expressed by Rosemond Tuve, for example, is that Ramistic specials have the capacity to state generals, and thus specific images have the power to convey or make manifest universals: "The influential part of the notion is that which receives emphasis elsewhere in Ramist doctrine—that the tiniest unit functions in a structure of thought by virtue of something in *its* nature; that, since the tie is essential, the special cannot help but 'mean' the general" (*Elizabethan and Metaphysical Imagery*, chap. 12, passim, esp. pp. 347, 349).

23 · *The Complete Works of Sir Philip Sidney*, ed. Albert Feuillerat, 3 : 17.

24 · Rajan, "Osiris and Urania," pp. 222–23.

25 · Frye, *God, Man, and Satan*, pp. 9, 13.

26 · Sidney, *Works*, 3 : 33, 28, 29.

27 · Plato, *The Republic*, trans. Paul Shorey, 1 : 179, 183, 197; 2 : 465; 1 : 181, 183. For a review of criticism supporting Raphael as Platonic and Michael as typological, see Radzinowicz, *Toward "Samson Agonistes,"* pp. 308–11. Northrop Frye supplies this Platonic perspective: "The colloquy of Raphael and Adam is a Socratic dialogue without irony, a symposium with unfermented wine, a description of an ideal commonwealth ending with the expulsion of undesirables, and (for Adam is the king of men) a cyropaedia, or manual of royal discipline" (*Return of Eden*, p. 12).

28 · Samuel, *Plato and Milton*, pp. 46, 43, and chap. 3. For a selection of Milton's comments on Plato, see "On the Platonic Idea as Understood by Aristotle" (Hughes, pp. 56–58); *Il Penseroso*, lines 89–92; *Doctrine and Discipline of Divorce* 3.2.398; and *Apology for . . . Smectymnuus* 3.1.293.

29 · Patrides, "*Paradise Lost* and the Theory of Accommodation," p. 58; Martz, *The Paradise Within*, pp. 123–24; Riggs, *The Christian Poet*, p. 59; Empson, *Milton's God*, p. 54; Johnson, *Lives of the English Poets*, ed. George Birkbeck Hill, 1 : 185; and Revard, *War in Heaven*. Revard's introduction reviews three centuries of criticism of Book 6, esp. pp. 16–19, 21–22; chapter 3 tellingly places Milton's War in Heaven against a background of sermons on the Gunpowder Plot and Milton's Gunpowder poems; on backgrounds of the war as psycho-

mythia see pp. 174–75; "for his seventeenth-century readers the 'warring angels' of Revelation symbolized Christians engaged in present struggles against evil" (pp. 127–28). As Revard shows, Milton's format for the Battle in Heaven differs from Renaissance norms; of these Milton's first day is typical, but his second day (and indeed his division of the battle into three stages) is thoroughly innovative (pp. 182–86; but cf. Spenser, *The Faerie Queene*, 1.11).

30 · St. George, "Psychomachia in Books V and VI of *Paradise Lost*," p. 186. St. George has found that "a longing to rewrite Milton's narrative seems to haunt every serious discussion of the War in Heaven" (p. 185). She reads the war as an analogy of "the conversion struggle of the human spirit" (p. 193), with good angels aligning with divine tendencies in the human mind, bad angels with demonic tendencies, and God with reality (p. 187). Thus, "reality will, by the revelation of itself, define the outcome of the contest, but only after that contest has reached its logical apogee, which is inconclusiveness" (p. 188). But see also James G. Mengert, "Styling the Strife of Glory: The War in Heaven"; Mengert argues for an artistic mode opposite to allegory "in order to minimize what would seem to be the obvious spiritual significance of the battle" and suggests that "Milton depreciates the *spiritual* level by putting greater pressure on the *literal*" (p. 100).

31 · In *The War in Heaven*, Stella Revard describes the analogous lessons that the battle teaches Adam and Eve in similar terms, but for her the lessons to those two pupils differ. For Eve the narrative illustrates Satanic subtlety and provides Abdiel as a practical example of resistance to temptation (pp. 278–79); Adam, however, faces a different challenge on the model of Michael or Gabriel, that is, "how to keep faith in a seemingly impossible situation" (p. 281). "Will he, like those angels he saw embattled against Satan, strive on, even though the strife seems hopeless, the situation remediless: Facing apparent defeat, can he, like them, keep heart? Will he think that God has deserted his creature? The lesson of the war in Heaven is that God *does* keep faith with those who keep faith with him. The loyal angels who abide by God despite the fury of their Satanic adversaries see the apparently hopeless war reversed, see the Messiah come to rescue" (pp. 282–83, and see pp. 116–17, 122). Adam has the choice between Satan and Messiah as Eve has the choice between Satan and Abdiel. "From the lowly Abdiel to the majestic Michael," Revard continues, "the loyal angels testify for truth and advance the kingdom, and as such they exemplify the Puritan ideal of soldiership" (p. 122). Such militancy is neatly captured in Boyd M. Berry's chapter title: "Adam and Eve: The Hero as Gardening Soldier" (*Process of Speech*, chap. 17).

32 · Berry, *Process of Speech*, p. 234. *Standing*, according to Berry, is "the perfect verb to represent this Puritan mode of heroism": "The faithful must and they do rejoice to maintain an erect physical posture, to rest, to witness God's glorious triumph, and to keep the faith" (p. 185, also p. 242, and cf. *Paradise Lost*, 6.801–2). Berry also labels Milton's militant God in Book 6 "the Arch-Puritan in the way he repeatedly sends his creatures on missions which are strategically impossible and eventuate in no conclusion" (p. 179).

33 · Note the pun on *arm/harm* at 6.656. Spenser plays with the same homonym in *The Faerie Queene* 1.11.27, and there is a pun on *arms/harm(less)* in Prolusion 7 (Hughes, p. 623). On this pun, see Johnson, *Lives*, 1:185.

34 · Christopher, *Milton and the Science of the Saints*, pp. 89, 92, 93, 108.

35 · *The Complete Works of Walter Savage Landor*, ed. T. Earle Welby, 5:258. On Satanic wordplay, see also Revard, *War in Heaven*, pp. 18, 105–6; Stephen Wigner, "Outrageous Noise and the Sovereign Voice: Satan, Sin, and Syntax in Sonnet XIX and Book VI of *Paradise*

Lost," esp. pp. 155–56, 159–60; and in "Styling the Strife of Glory," pp. 111–12, Mengert discusses analogies of verbal and physical debate and of physical martial encounter with intellectual and social analogues in the diabolical punning. He theorizes thus: "The effect, however [of Satan's use of multisignificant language], is actually to reduce the utility of language as a vehicle of genuine communication. The exaggerated, self-conscious nature of the punning display undercuts the genuine associative capacity of language by making the process so patent and mechanical. And notice how the association with physical combat reduces the corresponding types of verbal encounter to formalized, aggressive modes of contact: debates, transactions, arguments, interviews. Communication becomes merely another form of attack" (p. 112). In " 'Plain' and 'Ornate' Styles and the Structure of *Paradise Lost*," Peter Berek neatly defines God's contrasting verbal repetitions, which "remove the least shade of ambiguity from the terms, isolating once and for all their single precise meaning. The effect of the repetition is to treat word and doctrine as though they were identical; to treat language not as an imperfect, man-made medium for trying to get as close as one can to expressing the essence of ideas which have an existence independent of words, but instead as an exact set of counters for ideas, having no value or even existence apart from these ideas. Language is stripped of emotion, stripped of connotations, and used as though it were as abstract and precise as mathematical notation" (p. 241). On God's speech as *verbum reale*, see Christopher, *Milton and the Science of the Saints*, pp. 101–19. Christopher reviews in passing the most prominent recent criticism on this issue.

36 · Hesiod, *Theogony*, trans. Norman O. Brown, p. 56. On the bases and tradition of the Muses, see Ernst Robert Curtius, *European Literature and the Latin Middle Ages*, trans. Willard Trask, chap. 13, especially on Urania as Milton's way of handling the "embarrassing predicament" of Christian epic (pp. 243–44). On Urania as Christian Muse, especially by way of DuBartas's *L'Uranie*, see Lewalski, *Protestant Poetics and the Seventeenth-Century Lyric*, pp. 9, 231.

37 · On identifications of Milton with Orpheus, see Douglas Bush, *Mythology and the Renaissance Tradition in English Poetry*, p. 296, and Caroline W. Mayerson, "The Orpheus Image in *Lycidas*," in *Milton's "Lycidas": The Tradition and the Poem*, ed. C. A. Patrides, pp. 119–20. Riggs, in *The Christian Poet*, discusses prelapsarian Adam as a poet in the modes of Orpheus and David (pp. 71–82), speaks of Raphael's "two major poems, the War in Heaven [an "epic within an epic," p. 123] and the song of creation" (p. 111), and notes the absence of complex simile in Michael's books (p. 137). Riggs quotes from Alexander Ross's *Mystagogus Poeticus* as follows: "Christ is the true *Orpheus*, who by the sweetness and force of his Evangelical musick caused the Gentiles, who before were stocks and stones in knowledge, and no better than beasts in Religion, to follow after him: It was he only who went down to hell to recover the church his Spouse, who had lost her self" (p. 78n.).

38 · Rajan, "Osiris and Urania," pp. 229, 224, 220. Rajan adds: "Metaphor may be a betrayal; it is also the thin screen of a necessary safeguarding" (p. 230).

39 · Samuel Taylor Coleridge, *Biographica Literaria: or, Biographical Sketches of My Literary Life and Opinions*, in *The Collected Works of Samuel Taylor Coleridge*, ed. James Engell and W. Jackson Bate, 1:304.

40 · MacCaffrey, *"Paradise Lost" as "Myth*," pp. 142, 143, 177. She illustrates the mythic layering of *Paradise Lost* in these inclusive terms: "The Fall of Man can be interpreted physically as the encroachment of Chaos on Creation, psychologically as the descent of the

conscious mind into the unconscious, or spiritually as the dislocation of God's natural hierarchy of sense, will, and reason. The same images can accommodate all three" (p. 168).

41 · Ferry, *Milton's Epic Voice*, chaps. 3, 4, 5, esp. pp. 108, 113, 115, 117, 92. Ferry contrasts sacred metaphors not only with the epic similes through which the narrator is able to re-create unity because he has been illuminated by divine inner light but also with what she calls "allegory." She sees *Paradise Lost* as generally "anti-allegorical" and Satan as "the father of allegory," by which she means that he falsifies images: "By refusing to recognize the spiritual realities of God's creation he destroys the distinctions of language which express the hierarchy of being." For Ferry, in allegory "meaning is not *identified* with physical reality . . . but is *represented* by physical reality"; "We are at once made to see the scene and to feel that what we see must be transcended, or translated into an abstract meaning" (pp. 107, 133, 144, 122).

42 · Nicolson, *Breaking of the Circle*, pp. 2, 7, 126. Rosemond Tuve has taught the same lesson in several complex arguments, but this comment on Herbert's practice, in *A Reading of George Herbert*, may be taken as a concise summary: "He writes not of events and facts, but of meanings and values, and he uncovers rather than creates these meanings. . . . He not only respects the world of meanings thus presented as real, but in turn, like all poets, he embodies in metaphor these values he cannot say otherwise. . . . This perception of all things in their metaphorical dimension is the greatest single discovery we can make concerning the quality of life by reading the poetry of the sixteenth and seventeenth centuries. It was far from new then; for these centuries it was not a discovery but a habit. It is a mode of approach to truth which Western culture has slighted for some centuries, with bitter results" (pp. 103–4).

43 · Collett, "Milton's Use of Classical Mythology in *Paradise Lost*," p. 95; Frye, *Return of Eden*, p. 118; Lewis, *A Preface to "Paradise Lost*," pp. 129–30; Martz, *The Paradise Within*, pp. 142, 159; and Peter, *A Critique of "Paradise Lost*," p. 140. See also *Addison: Criticisms on "Paradise Lost*," ed. Albert S. Cook, p. 148. Addison complains further in *Spectator* 369: "He has devised a very handsome Reason for the Angel's proceeding with *Adam* after this manner; though, doubtless, the true Reason was the difficulty which the poet would have found to have shadowed out so mixed and complicated a story in visible objects. I could wish, however, that the author had done it, whatever pains it might have cost him. To give my opinion freely, I think that the exhibiting part of the history of mankind in vision, and part in narrative, is as if an history-painter should put in colors one half of his subject, and write down the remaining part of it" (p. 148). See also E. M. W. Tillyard, *Milton*, p. 256. William Riggs cautions, "Yet while Books XI and XII—particularly XII—seem at times little more than biblical paraphrase it is certainly not true that the material they contain is 'untransmuted'" (*The Christian Poet*, pp. 97–98). Arnold Stein finds the artistic "presence" "almost entirely missing" during Michael's narrations or after the penitence of Book 10: "There are no calculated interruptions, no moments of engaging reticence, no art of encouraging the reader to anticipate the poet and rewarding such failures, no art of surprise." Nor, says Stein, is the poet himself any longer felt to be on trial (*The Art of Presence: The Poet and "Paradise Lost*," pp. 160–61).

44 · Frye, *Return of Eden*, p. 118; Prince, "On the Last Two Books of *Paradise Lost*," in *Milton's Epic Poetry: Essays on "Paradise Lost" and "Paradise Regained*," ed. C. A. Patrides, p. 245; and *Paradise Lost: A Poem in Twelve Books*, ed. Thomas Newton, 2:446–47. Prince defends his feelings of "a loss of interest, a slight weariness, almost a sense of disappoint-

ment" on the grounds that Milton has artistically calculated such a mood of "imagination satisfied" as part of his great epic design ("Last Two Books," p. 245). For Dennis Burden, in *The Logical Epic*, p. 180, the climax of Book 12 "is not reached with any notable growth or development" and arouses only a "lacklustre response" in most of its readers. For an extensive bibliography of both negative and positive critical commentary on Books 11 and 12, see Radzinowicz, "Man as a Probationer of Immortality," pp. 31–32, nn. 1 and 2. For further bibliography critical and supportive of the artistry of the final books, see Sister Mary Brian Durkin, "Iterative Figures and Images in *Paradise Lost*, XI–XII," p. 157, n.1. Her study traces the rhetorical and prosodic techniques Milton uses "to intensify the instructional impact of the poem and to heighten the visual and auditory beauty of countless lines" (p. 140). Several criticisms of the style of *Paradise Lost* more generally may here be acknowledged. Thus, in *Milton and Science*, Svendsen comments from his special point of view: "One reason for the failure of *Paradise Lost* with respectful readers in every generation is the apparent breakdown of communication within the poem of what seems aesthetically intractable fact (free will, anti-Trinitarianism, astronomical debate) and the genuine human condition, imaginatively presented" (p. 246); and in *Milton and the Christian Tradition*, Patrides states, "Nearly every time God appears in *Paradise Lost* the poetry responds adversely, becoming flat, dull, monotonous" (pp. 141–42).

45 · Johnson, "Life of Cowley," in *Lives*, 1 : 20.

46 · Ong, "Logic and Rhetoric," in *Milton Encyclopedia*, 5 : 32. In *Ramus, Method, and the Decay of Dialogue*, Ong has said of the "plain style": "This style is certainly not the high or grand style, nor is it the low or the middle style. It is the phoenix which rises from the holocaust of all three styles, the verbal counterpart of the coming visualist universe of 'objects,' voiceless and by that very fact depersonalized, which would soon recommend to the Royal Society, as Thomas Sprat records in his history, 'a close, naked, natural way of speaking,' as near the 'mathematical' as possible" (p. 213).

47 · Berek, "'Plain' and 'Ornate' Styles," pp. 237–46; Entzminger, "Michael's Options and Milton's Poetry," p. 208, citing William Haller, *The Rise of Puritanism* (New York, 1957), pp. 108, 101; Lewalski, *Milton's Brief Epic: The Genre, Meaning, and Art of "Paradise Regained,"* p. 325; Herbert, *The Works of George Herbert*, ed. F. E. Hutchinson; and Christopher, *Milton and the Science of the Saints*, p. 19.

48 · Rajan, "Osiris and Urania," pp. 225–26, 228, 230. On Osiris, see also Rajan, "The Cunning Resemblance," pp. 36–37.

49 · Jean Danielou, S.J., *From Shadows to Reality: Studies in the Biblical Typology of the Fathers*, pp. 11, 28, 30. Reformation and Puritan views of and emphases within typology are thoroughly examined in Lewalski, *Protestant Poetics and the Seventeenth-Century Lyric*, chap. 4; in "Typological Symbolism," in *Literary Uses of Typology*, Lewalski speaks of Milton's Adam in the epic's final books as a reader of future types (p. 82). The editor of that volume, Earl Miner, notes in his preface that all its essays include efforts to define typology. Very helpful for the study of general and historical backgrounds of typology are the first fifty pages of Sacvan Bercovitch's "Annotated Bibliography," in *Typology and American Literature*, ed. Bercovitch. In *From Shadows to Reality*, Danielou distinguishes usefully between eschatological typology and Christian typology on p. 77; notes that "the theological sense controls the illustrative one" (p. 85); and calls prophecy "the typological interpretation of history" (p. 157). Danielou offers suggestively: "The Old Testament is both a memory and a prophecy. We can

go further, and say that it is the prophecy which makes it a memory: the mighty works of the past are recalled only as the foundation of future hope. For it is very noticeable that the Prophets foretell events to come as the recovery of what has passed" (p. 154). For more on the relation of the Old to the New Testament, see p. 190. William W. Kerrigan, in *The Prophetic Milton*, traces to Luther a substitution of *sensus historicus* and *sensus propheticus* for the traditional "letter" and "spirit," thus reemphasizing an earlier connection between prophecy and exegesis (p. 92). He also quotes Donne that "*Prophecy* is but antidated *Gospell*, and *Gospell* but postdated *prophecy*" (p. 104). On typology, see also D. W. Robertson, Jr., *A Preface to Chaucer: Studies in Medieval Perspectives*, chap. 4, esp. pp. 290–94.

50 · See Auerbach, *Mimesis: The Representation of Reality in Western Literature*, p. 171; and Lewalski, *Milton's Brief Epic*, pp. 167–68; for a summation of the typological tradition as available to Milton, see pp. 168–69.

51 · Frye, *God, Man, and Satan*, pp. 8–9; Christopher, *Milton and the Science of the Saints*, pp. 6–7, 178; and Lewalski, *Protestant Poetics and the Seventeenth-Century Lyric*, p. 72. Lewalski summarizes further: "I suggest that the Bible became the treasury of images and symbols for English Protestants generally in the sixteenth and seventeenth centuries, and that ecclesiastical ceremonies and sacraments, nature itself, and personal experiences of all sorts came to be interpreted through the language of scripture, recognized as radically figurative. This process offered biblical imagery and poetic figures to the Christian poets as vehicles of charged significance, presenting universal religious meanings against which particular observations and experiences might be measured and analyzed" (pp. 72–73). Christopher's supporting citation from Luther can be matched closely by Milton's *Christian Doctrine*, CE 16:273–75. On literary categories in *Christian Doctrine*, see Christopher, *Milton and the Science of the Saints*, p. 92, and on literary categories more generally see chap. 4, pt. 3.

52 · *Summa Theologica*, trans. Fathers of the English Dominican Province, 1:7. For advice to sermon writers on expanding their sermons through fourfold allegory and other devices, see Harry Caplan, *Of Eloquence: Studies in Ancient and Mediaeval Rhetoric*, ed. Anne King and Helen North, pp. 64–66, 143–45.

53 · Gregory, quoted in Caplan, *Of Eloquence*, p. 95, and Dante, "Letter to Can Grande," *Literary Criticism*, p. 99. For a useful array of backgrounds on fourfold medieval allegory, including as many as eightfold interpretations, see Caplan, *Of Eloquence*, pp. 97–102; pp. 123–26 list and summarize various recommended sermon structures.

54 · The phrasing cited is from Caplan, *Of Eloquence*, p. 95, but the example occurs frequently, as in Lewalski, *Milton's Brief Epic*, p. 95.

55 · Dante, "Letter to Can Grande," p. 99, and see *Literary Criticism*, pp. 112–14, for a secular analogue. For an expansive consideration of the typology of the Exodus, see Danielou, *From Shadows to Reality*, Book 4, esp. chap 1. The Old Testament interpretation was eschatological; the New Testament proclaimed the Exodus typology fulfilled in Christ; and the Church Fathers were chiefly concerned to demonstrate the Exodus in relation to the sacraments and more generally the day-to-day life of the Church (p. 175). Christ invokes a type of Moses, the Red Sea, and the Promised Land, in *Paradise Regained* 3.433–40, in which Abraham modulates into Moses as the whole into Christ as antitype. Northrop Frye, in *Return of Eden*, points to the combination of quest theme and settlement theme in the Exodus story as paralleling the *Odyssey* and the *Aeneid* (p. 3).

56 · Madsen, *From Shadowy Types to Truth*, p. 6; and Berry, *Process of Speech*, the title of chap. 8. According to James H. Sims, *The Bible in Milton's Epics*, in Books 11 and 12 "hardly a line is without one [biblical] reference and in many lines the references are multiplied" (p. 47). For a review of Gospel (as opposed to Pauline) passages backgrounding typology, see Lewalski, *Protestant Poetics and the Seventeenth-Century Lyric*, p. 111. In *"Paradise Lost": An Account of Its Growth and Major Origins*, Grant McColley has indicated that the proportions of lines Milton devotes to the various biblical data—490 from fall to flood, 163 to the rest of Genesis, 97 to Exodus, and so forth—accurately reflect the proportional interest shown in contemporary biblical commentaries, literary paraphrases, and incidental biblical references (pp. 185–86).

57 · MacCallum, "Milton and Figurative Interpretation of the Bible," pp, 405, 407, 409. In *The Enclosed Garden: The Tradition and the Image in Seventeenth-Century Poetry*, Stanley Stewart cites Weemes in a tidy formulation of the levels of allegory: "Here we come upon what seems, perhaps, a confusing use of language. For while Weemes has already argued that allegory is identical to the 'mysticall' meaning of Scripture, he now insists that the 'mysticall' dimension is divided into levels, the allegorical, tropological, and anagogical. His explanation is interesting in that it shows the way in which the commentator could hold the various levels to be, simultaneously, both different and the same: 'These are not properly divers senses, but divers applications of one sense to our instruction, faith, and manners.' The levels of Scripture, in other words, corresponded in their application to different aspects of the spiritual life. The allegorical implications of allegory were the typological relations between the Old and New Testaments. The tropological understanding of Scripture concerned the relation between biblical metaphor and human conduct. The anagogical level (preeminently the domain of the finest seventeenth-century poets) applied 'when things literally expressed, doe signifie something in heavens blisse'" (pp. 18–19).

58 · Allen, "Milton and the Descent to Light," pp. 178, 177. Allen suggests that Milton presents Moses as "a master typologist" instructed by Jehovah himself in order to instruct humanity in typology" (p. 178).

59 · Ulreich, "The Typological Structure of Milton's Imagery," pp. 78, 72. More generally, Ulreich observes: "Typology, the analysis of the literal type and its subsequent recreation by the antitype of the Word *made flesh*, is a paradigm of the imaginative process in Milton's poetry. The letter of his imagery is destroyed in order to be reborn in the spirit of his symbolic intention; his imagination works first to abstract meaning from the letter (in effect to destroy images) and then to reembody that meaning. He interprets a sign and then re-presents it as inseparable from the significance which he has developed discursively; he re-creates concrete meaning. Perhaps the most explicit embodiment of this process—a kind of imaginative self-illustration—occurs in Raphael's ode on Creation (PL V, 469–505)" (p. 72).

60 · MacCallum, "Milton and Sacred History," p. 154.

61 · Radzinowicz, *Toward "Samson Agonistes,"* p. 301.

62 · Bush, *"Paradise Lost" in Our Time*, p. 36. The "Pisgah vision" of Jason Rosenblatt's title, "Adam's Pisgah Vision: *Paradise Lost*, XI and XII," refers to Moses' glimpse of but exclusion from the Promised Land in a context where Canaan thus equates with typological fulfillments generally (pp. 68–69).

63 · Rosenblatt, "The Mosaic Voice in *Paradise Lost*," pp. 207, 226. Rosenblatt describes a Neoplatonic Moses in the prelapsarian books of *Paradise Lost* and a typological Moses in the

final books and relates this to narration and style, as for example: "The development in the reader of an awareness of incompleteness and a desire for fulfillment is part of a strategy in the later books of *Paradise Lost* which translates principles of mediation, of redemption and intercession, into a poetic technique" (p. 221). For Moses as a model of the narrative poet as David is a model of the lyric poet, see also Lewalski, "Typological Symbolism," pp. 107–10.

64 · Danielou, *From Shadows to Reality*, Book 5, chap. 1, and esp. pp. 229–30, 263, 269, 286; on the importance of Origen to this type, see pp. 276 ff.

65 · MacCallum, "Milton and Sacred History," p. 160, quoting *Tetrachordon*.

66 · Caplan, *Of Eloquence*, pp. 54, 124, 55–56, quoting an anonymous medieval sermon manual. On Protestant sermon theory, see Lewalski, *Protestant Poetics and the Seventeenth-Century Lyric*, pp. 214–26.

67 · Broadbent, *Some Graver Subject*, p. 276. And see Entzminger, "Michael's Options and Milton's Poetry," p. 201.

68 · Lewalski, *Protestant Poetics and the Seventeenth-Century Lyric*, chap. 5 passim, and esp. pp. 148, 154–55, 149.

69 · Basil Willey, *The Seventeenth Century Background: Studies in the Thought of the Age in Relation to Poetry and Religion*, pp. 77–78.

5. WIDENING PERSPECTIVES

1 · Ong, "Logic and the Epic Muse," pp. 264–65. In *Ramus, Method, and the Decay of Dialogue*, pp. 113–14, Ong offers a caveat against overapplication of binary schemes.

2 · Fisch, "Hebraic Style and Motifs in *Paradise Lost*," in *Language and Style in Milton: A Symposium in Honor of the Tercentenary of "Paradise Lost,"* ed. Ronald D. Emma and John T. Shawcross, pp. 49, 42.

3 · On indicative and commemorative languages, see Marcia L. Colish, *The Mirror of Language: A Study in the Medieval Theory of Knowledge*, p. 5; Greene, *Descent from Heaven*, passim; Entzminger, "Epistemology and the Tutelary Word," p. 94.

4 · Bundy, "'Invention' and 'Imagination' in the Renaissance," pp. 541–42; and similarly, William O. Scott, "Ramism and Milton's Concept of Poetic Fancy," p. 185. He labels logic "an important propaedeutic for the inspired poet" (p. 187). Tuve, "Imagery and Logic," p. 372; and see Puttenham, *The Arte of English Poesie*, p. 307. See also Steadman, *The Lamb and the Elephant*, pp. 111–12.

5 · Puttenham, *The Arte of English Poesie*, pp. 3, 18, 19.

6 · Milton, *The Art of Logic*, C471, 269, 11–13, 321; and see Y390, 313, 213–14, 333.

7 · Yates, *The Art of Memory*, pp. 298, 57, 8–10, 5; and {Cicero} *ad C. Herennium de ratione dicendi*, trans. Harry Caplan, pp. 7, 205, 207, 215, 223–25, 219, 221. For another widely varied documentation of the nature and history of the study of the memory, see Harry Caplan, "Memoria: Treasure-House of Eloquence," in *Of Eloquence*, pp. 196–246. In the same volume, Caplan notes that Francis Bacon divides "human learning into the realms of philosophy, guided by the faculty of reason; poetry, ruled by the imagination; and history, presided over by the memory" (p. 201). History, à la John Aubrey, records that Milton himself had an excellent memory (Hughes, p. 1022).

8 · Yates, *Art of Memory*, pp. 236, chap. 12, and esp. pp. 286, 306, 234. According to Walter J. Ong in *Ramus, Method, and the Decay of Dialogue*, "The memorization process for

Ramus is virtually synonomous with understanding itself, to the extent that the success of the Ramist dialectic as a memory device proves the validity of the dialectic as a true interpretation of reality" (p. 194; and see p. 280). For further comment on the relationship of Ramus and memory, see Ong, "Logic and the Epic Muse," p. 247, and Gilbert, *Renaissance Concepts of Method*, p. 142.

9 · Ong, *Ramus, Method, and the Decay of Dialogue*, pp. 89, 129, 108, 110, 114.

10 · Lewalski, "Structure and the Symbolism of Vision," pp. 32, 28.

11 · Frye, "Agon and Logos," pp. 146–47; and see Christopher, *Milton and the Science of the Saints*, chap. 1, pt. 1. "Whenever God spoke to man by signs, he always added an accompanying word," as Christopher points out later; and specifically in *Paradise Lost*, "Adam does not really 'see' the dumb shows until the Angel's verbal account has been interposed, like a theatrical scrim, between his pupil and the visible vision" (pp. 176–77, and similarly, pp. 177–78).

12 · Madsen, *From Shadowy Types to Truth*, pp. 178–79.

13 · Spenser, *Faerie Queene*, ed. Roche, 2.9.49.1–5, and notes, p. 1128. Useful contextual backgrounds are available in William Rossky's "Imagination in the English Renaissance: Psychology and Poetic," which examines what Renaissance English popular psychology and varied literary works have to say on the operation, disrepute, and defense of the imagination. Against complaints about imagination as passionate, uncontrollable, distorting, and the like, in essence "Poetic imagination is good imagination" (p. 69) because it provides emotional control as well as moral persuasion.

14 · On the threefold Galenic or medical tradition, see E. Ruth Harvey, *The Inward Wits: Psychological Theory in the Middle Ages and the Renaissance*, pp. 10, 17, and esp. 35 and 69, n. 111. Harvey considers "the inward wits" to be mediators between body and soul (p. 2), and her study thus divides between a medical and a philosophical tradition. I should make clear that at present I am concerned only with such "inward wits" or what Aristotle and Avicenna identify as the faculties of the animal soul rather than the rational soul or spiritual self. Svendsen, in *Milton and Science*, examines contemporary encyclopedic backgrounds for Adam's faculty psychology of Book 5.100–16 (pp. 36–38). For an overview of Ramistic views of faculty psychology, see Miller, *New England Mind*, pp. 240–41.

15 · *Aristotle: On the Soul, Parva Naturalia, On Breath*, trans. W. S. Hett. On the threefold division, see, e.g., "On the Soul," p. 155; on Imagination, see "On the Soul" 3.3–8; and on Memory, see "On Memory and Recollection" 1–2, esp. pp. 305, 283, in *Parva Naturalia*. For a more continuous and inclusive account, see William A. Hammond, *Aristotle's Psychology: A Treatise on the Principle of Life*, pp. lvi–lxiii, lxxxi–lxxxv; and Murray W. Bundy, *The Theory of Imagination in Classical and Mediaeval Thought*, chap. 3, esp. pp. 71–74. In *Sudden Apprehension*, Jacobus discusses *Paradise Lost* 5.100–15 as applying Aristotelian faculty psychology (pp. 120–21), and he takes a positive view of Milton's presentation of fancy (pp. 76, 98–99). In a discussion of *Samson Agonistes*, Albert R. Cirillo distinguishes between creative and responsive memories ("Time, Light, and the Phoenix: The Design of *Samson Agonistes*," in *Calm of Mind: Tercentenary Essays on "Paradise Regained" and "Samson Agonistes" in Honor of John S. Diekhoff*, ed. Joseph A. Wittreich, Jr., p. 210).

16 · *Avicenna's Psychology: An English Translation of Kitab al-najat, Book II, Chapter VI . . .*, by F. Rahman, pp. 30–31; and see Harvey, *Inward Wits*, pp. 23–24, 41–47, 52–53, and Bundy, *Theory of Imagination*, pp. 179–80, 182–83, 185, 191–92.

17 · Bowers, "Adam, Eve, and the Fall in *Paradise Lost*," p. 265. Bowers stresses the point (p. 268) that the fancy and Eve are themselves uncorrupted, that the evil comes from outside in both the dream and the temptation of Book 9. For Russell E. Smith, Jr., Adam is a split personality—split between the Adam in him and the Eve in him—and this split coincides with his internal theoretical knowledge or obedience and the externalization in Eve ("Adam's Fall," pp. 194, 193). For backgrounds describing and allegorizing male and female components, see Corcoran, *Milton's Paradise*, pp. 62–69, and Evans, *"Paradise Lost" and the Genesis Tradition*, pp. 71–77, 99, 268. Joseph E. Duncan argues for the allegorization of Adam and Eve as a Renaissance commonplace with supporting citations from Erasmus, Sir Thomas Browne, and Sir Henry Vane, as well as Philo (*Milton's Earthly Paradise*, p. 258, and see pp. 265–66). According to Harry Levin, in *Myth of the Golden Age*, "When the fable was allegorized by Saint Ambrose . . . Eden stood for the soul; Adam symbolized the understanding and Eve the senses, with the serpent as delectation" (p. 176).

18 · Johnson, *The Rambler*, 2 : 300, in vol. 4 of *The Yale Edition of the Works of Samuel Johnson*, ed. W. J. Bate and Albrecht B. Strauss.

19 · Collins, "The Buoyant Mind in Milton's Eden," pp. 243, 235. In "Eve's Dream," Diane K. McColley examines some contemporary backgrounds for the faculty psychology, especially the fancy, behind the dream (esp. pp. 26–28, 39). For the appetite as a parody of revelation and other commentary on faculty psychology, see Frye, *Return of Eden*, pp. 74–75, 97–98. And see Sharon Cumberland and Lynn Veach Sadler, "Phantasia: A Pattern in Milton's Early Poems." For further discussion of Milton's faculty psychology, see Radzinowicz, *Toward "Samson Agonistes,"* pp. 57–60, and Donald M. Friedman, *"Lycidas*: The Swain's Paideia," p. 7.

20 · Lovejoy, *Great Chain of Being*, pp. 82–83. Lovejoy adds: "It was the Idea of the Good, not the conception of a self-transcending and generative Goodness, that determined the ethical teaching of the Church (at least in her counsels of perfection) and shaped the assumptions concerning man's chief end which dominated European thought down to the Renaissance, and in orthodox theology, Protestant as well as Catholic, beyond it. The 'way up' alone was the direction in which man was to look for the good, even though the God who had from all eternity perfectly possessed the good which is the object of man's quest was held to have found, so to say, *his* chief good in the 'way down'—had, in the curious and significant phrase of the Areopagite, been 'cozened by goodness and affection and love, and led down from his eminence above all and surpassing all, to being in all.' The consummation towards which all finite things yearn, and towards which men were to strive consciously, was to return to and remain in the Unity which yet did not, and by its essence could not, remain within itself" (p. 84).

21 · Collins, "The Buoyant Mind," p. 244.

22 · *The Confessions of St. Augustine, Bishop of Hippo*, trans. E. B. Pusey, pp. 230 ff., esp. p. 237.

23 · Bundy, *Theory of Imagination*, pp. 167–69.

24 · Martz, *The Paradise Within*, pp. xiii, xix, xiv. See also Jacobus, *Sudden Apprehension*, pp. 105–6, 197, 204.

25 · Colish, *Mirror of Language*, pp. 50–53. Her chapter title and subtitle here are telling: "St. Augustine: The Expression of the Word" and "Functions of Redeemed Speech." On Christ as *scientia* and *sapientia*, see p. 78.

26 · See St. Augustine, *The Trinity* 10.11, trans. Stephen McKenna, in *The Fathers of the Church*, 45:310–12; and Colish, *Mirror of Language*, pp. 74–79.

27 · Aquinas, *Summa Theologica*, 4:99–101, 88–89, 107, 187, 160–63, 164. In a nice distinction, Aquinas makes the point that whereas human intellect understands material things by abstracting from the phantasms, and through material things acquires some knowledge of immaterial things, the angelic nature knows material things through the immaterial (p. 184). On Augustinian and Thomistic views of thing/word relationships and of allegory as Protestant background, see Lewalski, *Protestant Poetics and the Seventeenth-Century Lyric*, pp. 73 ff., 113 ff. Georgia Christopher's distinction between "Thomistic man" and "Reformation man" aligns with our prelapsarian and postlapsarian categories (*Milton and the Science of the Saints*, p. 148).

28 · Colish, *Mirror of Language*, p. 179, and see pp. 172–83.

29 · Harvey, *Inward Wits*, p. 60, and see also pp. 54–55, 58–59.

30 · St. Bonaventura, *The Mind's Road to God*, a translation of *Itinerarium Mentis ad Deum* by George Boas, pp. 8, 10, 43, 4, 9, 30. See also Bundy, *Theory of the Imagination*, pp. 207–9, and Madsen, *From Shadowy Types to Truth*, pp. 132–35. In Bonaventura, according to Boas, is found a fusion of the hierarchies of logical classes, values, and reality (p. x), which we may compare with Ramism. Although the Columbia index to *The Works of John Milton* shows nearly a full page of references to Augustine, there are none to Bonaventura and only one to Aquinas, the famous contrast to Spenser as teacher.

Bibliography of Works Cited

Addison, Joseph. *Addison: Criticisms on "Paradise Lost."* Edited by Albert S. Cook. Reprint. New York: Phaeton Press, 1968.

Ainsworth, Oliver M. *Milton on Education: The Tractate "Of Education" with Supplementary Extracts from Other Writings of Milton.* Cornell Studies in English, vol. 12. New Haven: Yale University Press, 1928.

Allen, Don Cameron. *The Harmonious Vision: Studies in Milton's Poetry.* Baltimore: Johns Hopkins University Press, 1954.

―――. "Milton and the Descent to Light." In *Milton Studies in Honor of Harris Francis Fletcher,* pp. 614–30. Urbana: University of Illinois Press, 1961.

―――. "Some Theories of the Growth and Origin of Language in Milton's Age." *Philological Quarterly* 28 (1949): 5–16.

Aquinas, St. Thomas. *The Summa Theologica of St. Thomas Aquinas.* Translated by the Fathers of the English Dominican Province. 22 vols. 2nd ed. London: Burns, Oates & Washbourne, 1922.

Aristotle. *On the Soul, Parva Naturalia, On Breath.* Translated by W. S. Hett. Loeb Classical Library. Cambridge: Harvard University Press, 1935.

Arnold, Marilyn. "Milton's Accessible God: The Role of the Son in *Paradise Lost.*" *Milton Quarterly* 7 (1973): 65–72.

Auerbach, Erich. *Mimesis: The Representation of Reality in Western Literature.* Reprint. Garden City, N.Y.: Doubleday (Anchor Books), 1957.

Augustine, St. *The Confessions of St. Augustine, Bishop of Hippo.* Translated by E. B. Pusey. New York: Dutton, 1951.

―――. *The Trinity.* Translated by Stephen McKenna. Vol. 45 of *The Fathers of the Church.* Washington, D.C.: Catholic University of America Press, 1963.

Avicenna. *Avicenna's Psychology: An English Translation of Kitab al-najat, Book II, Chapter VI . . . ,* by F. Rahman. London: Oxford University Press, 1952.

Bennett, Joan S. "'Go': Milton's Antinomianism and the Separation Scene in *Paradise Lost,* Book 9." *PMLA* 98 (1983): 388–404.

Bercovitch, Sacvan. "Annotated Bibliography." In *Typology and American Literature*, ed. Bercovitch, pp. 245–337. Amherst: University of Massachusetts Press, 1972.

Berek, Peter. "'Plain' and 'Ornate' Styles and the Structure of *Paradise Lost*." *PMLA* 85 (1970): 237–46.

Berry, Boyd M. *Process of Speech: Puritan Religious Writing and "Paradise Lost."* Baltimore: Johns Hopkins University Press, 1976.

Blackburn, Thomas H. "'Uncloister'd Virtue': Adam and Eve in Milton's Paradise." *Milton Studies* III (1971): 119–37.

Blessington, Francis C. *"Paradise Lost" and the Classical Epic*. Boston: Routledge & Kegan Paul, 1979.

Bonaventura, St. *The Mind's Road to God*. Translation by George Boas of *Itinerarium Mentis ad Deum*. New York: Liberal Arts Press, 1953.

The Book of Tobit. In *The Apocrypha*, trans. Edgar J. Goodspeed. Chicago: University of Chicago Press, 1939.

Bowers, Fredson. "Adam, Eve, and the Fall in *Paradise Lost*." *PMLA* 84 (1969): 264–73.

Brennan, William. "Milton's *Of Education* and the *Translatio Studii*." *Milton Quarterly* 15 (1981): 55–59.

Broadbent, J. B. *Some Graver Subject: An Essay on "Paradise Lost."* London: Chatto & Windus, 1960.

Bundy, Murray W. "'Invention' and 'Imagination' in the Renaissance." *Journal of English and Germanic Philology* 29 (1930): 535–45.

———. "Milton's View of Education in *Paradise Lost*." *Journal of English and Germanic Philology* 21 (1922): 127–52.

———. *The Theory of Imagination in Classical and Mediaeval Thought*. Illinois Studies in Language and Literature, vol. 12 (1927). Reprint. Ann Arbor, Mich.: University Microfilms, 1966.

Burden, Dennis. *The Logical Epic: A Study of the Argument of "Paradise Lost."* Cambridge: Harvard University Press, 1967.

Bush, Douglas. *Mythology and the Renaissance Tradition in English Poetry*. Rev. ed. New York: Norton, 1963.

———. *"Paradise Lost" in Our Time*. Reprint. Gloucester, Mass.: Peter Smith, 1945.

Campbell, Gordon. "*De Doctrina Christiana*: Its Structural Principles and Its Unfinished State." *Milton Studies* IX (1976): 243–60.

———. "Milton's *Accedence Commenc't Grammar*." *Milton Quarterly* 10 (1976): 39–48.

Canfield, J. Douglas. "Blessed Are the Merciful: The Understanding of the Promise in *Paradise Lost*." *Milton Quarterly* 7 (1973): 43–46.

Caplan, Harry. *Of Eloquence: Studies in Ancient and Mediaeval Rhetoric*. Edited by Anne King and Helen North. Ithaca, N.Y.: Cornell University Press, 1970.

Charlton, Kenneth. "The Educational Background." In *The Age of Milton: Backgrounds to Seventeenth-Century Literature*, ed. C. A. Patrides and Raymond B. Waddington, pp. 102–37. Manchester: Manchester University Press, 1980.

Christopher, Georgia B. *Milton and the Science of the Saints*. Princeton: Princeton University Press, 1982.

————. "The Verbal Gate to Paradise: Adam's 'Literary Experience' in Book X of *Paradise Lost*." *PMLA* 90 (1975): 69–77.

{Cicero} *ad C. Herennium de ratione dicendi*. Translated by Harry Caplan. Loeb Classical Library. Cambridge: Harvard University Press, 1954.

Cirillo, Albert R. "Tasso's *Il Mondo Creato*: Providence and the Created Universe." *Milton Studies* III (1971): 83–102.

————. "Time, Light, and the Phoenix: The Design of *Samson Agonistes*." In *Calm of Mind: Tercentenary Essays on "Paradise Regained" and "Samson Agonistes" in Honor of John S. Diekhoff*, ed. Joseph A. Wittreich, Jr., pp. 209–33. Cleveland: Press of Case Western Reserve University, 1971.

Clark, Donald L. *John Milton at St. Paul's School: A Study of Ancient Rhetoric in English Renaissance Education*. New York: Columbia University Press, 1948.

Coleridge, Samuel Taylor. *Biographica Literaria: or, Biographical Sketches of My Literary Life and Opinions*. Vol. 7, pts. 1 and 2, of *The Collected Works of Samuel Taylor Coleridge*, ed. James Engell and W. Jackson Bate. Bollingen Series, no. 75. London: Routledge & Kegan Paul, 1983.

Colish, Marcia L. *The Mirror of Language: A Study in the Medieval Theory of Knowledge*. New Haven: Yale University Press, 1968.

Collett, Jonathan H. "Milton's Use of Classical Mythology in *Paradise Lost*." *PMLA* 85 (1970): 88–96.

Collins, Dan S. "The Buoyant Mind in Milton's Eden." *Milton Studies* V (1973): 229–48.

Conklin, George N. *Biblical Criticism and Heresy in Milton*. New York: King's Crown Press, 1949.

Cope, Jackson I. *The Metaphoric Structure of "Paradise Lost"*. Baltimore: Johns Hopkins University Press, 1962.

Corcoran, Sister Mary Irma. *Milton's Paradise with Reference to the Hexaemeral Background*. Washington, D.C.: Catholic University of America Press, 1945.

Council, Norman B. "*L'Allegro, Il Penseroso*, and 'The Cycle of Universal Knowledge.'" *Milton Studies* IX (1976): 203–19.

Craig, Hardin. *The Enchanted Glass: The Elizabethan Mind in Literature*. New York: Oxford University Press, 1936.

Crump, Galbraith Miller. *The Mystical Design of "Paradise Lost"*. Lewisburg, Pa.: Bucknell University Press, 1975.

Cumberland, Sharon, and Lynn Veach Sadler. "Phantasia: A Pattern in Milton's Early Poems." *Milton Quarterly* 8 (1974): 50–55.

Curry, Walter Clyde. *Milton's Ontology, Cosmogony, and Physics*. Lexington: University of Kentucky Press, 1966.

Curtius, Ernst Robert. *European Literature and the Latin Middle Ages*. Translated by Willard Trask. Reprint. New York: Harper Torchbooks, 1963.

Daly, Robert. *God's Altar: The World and the Flesh in Puritan Poetry*. Berkeley: University of California Press, 1978.

Danielou, Jean, S.J. *From Shadows to Reality: Studies in the Biblical Typology of the Fathers*. Westminster, Md.: Newman Press, 1960.

Dante Alighieri. *Literary Criticism of Dante Alighieri*. Translated by Robert S. Haller. Lincoln: University of Nebraska Press, 1973.

Davidson, Gustav. *A Dictionary of Angels, Including the Fallen Angels*. New York: Free Press, 1967.

DuBartas. Guillaume de Saluste. *The Divine Weeks and Works of Guillaume de Saluste Sieur du Bartas*. Translated by Josuah Sylvester; edited by Susan Snyder. Oxford: Oxford University Press (Clarendon Press), 1979.

Duhamel, Pierre Albert. "The Logic and Rhetoric of Peter Ramus." *Modern Philology* 46 (1949): 163–71.

———. "Milton's Alleged Ramism." *PMLA* 67 (1952): 1035–53.

Duncan, Joseph E. *Milton's Earthly Paradise: A Historical Study of Eden*. Minneapolis: University of Minnesota Press, 1972.

Durkin, Sister Mary Brian. "Iterative Figures and Images in *Paradise Lost*, XI–XII." *Milton Studies* III (1971): 139–58.

Empson, William. *Milton's God*. Rev. ed. London: Chatto & Windus, 1965.

Entzminger, Robert L. "Epistemology and the Tutelary Word in *Paradise Lost*." *Milton Studies* X (1977): 93–109.

———. "Michael's Options and Milton's Poetry: *Paradise Lost* XI and XII." *English Literary Renaissance* 8 (1978): 197–211.

Evans, J. M. *"Paradise Lost" and the Genesis Tradition*. Oxford: Oxford University Press (Clarendon Press), 1968.

Ferry, Anne Davidson. *Milton's Epic Voice: The Narrator in "Paradise Lost."* Cambridge: Harvard University Press, 1963.

Fields, Albert W. "Milton and Self-Knowledge." *PMLA* 83 (1968): 392–99.

Fisch, Harold. "Hebraic Style and Motifs in *Paradise Lost*." In *Language and Style in Milton: A Symposium in Honor of the Tercentenary of "Paradise Lost,"* ed. Ronald D. Emma and John T. Shawcross, pp. 30–64. New York: Ungar, 1967.

Fish, Stanley E. *The Living Temple: George Herbert and Catechizing*. Berkeley: University of California Press, 1978.

———. *Surprised by Sin: The Reader in "Paradise Lost."* Berkeley: University of California Press, 1971.

Fisher, Peter F. "Milton's Logic." *Journal of the History of Ideas* 23 (1962): 37–60.

Friedman, Donald M. "*Lycidas*: The Swain's Paideia." *Milton Studies* III (1971): 3–34.

Frye, Northrop. "Agon and Logos: Revolution and Revelation." In *The Prison and the Pinnacle: Papers to Commemorate the Tercentenary of "Paradise Regained" and "Samson Agonistes" Read at the University of Western Ontario March-April 1971*, ed. Balachandra Rajan, pp. 135–63. Toronto: University of Toronto Press, 1973.

———. *The Return of Eden: Five Essays on Milton's Epics*. Toronto: University of Toronto Press, 1965.

Frye, Roland M. *God, Man, and Satan: Patterns of Christian Thought and Life in "Paradise Lost," "Pilgrim's Progress," and the Great Theologians*. Princeton: Princeton University Press, 1960.

Gardner, Helen. *A Reading of "Paradise Lost."* Oxford: Oxford University Press (Clarendon Press), 1965.

The Geneva Bible: A Facsimile of the 1560 Edition. Introduction by Lloyd E. Berry. Madison: University of Wisconsin Press, 1969.

Giamatti, A. Bartlett. *The Earthly Paradise and the Renaissance Epic*. Princeton: Princeton University Press, 1966.

Gilbert, Neal W. *Renaissance Concepts of Method*. New York: Columbia University Press, 1960.

Goldberg, Jonathan. "*Virga Iesse*: Analogy, Typology, and Anagogy in a Miltonic Simile." *Milton Studies* V (1973): 177–90.

Goldman, Jack. "Insight into Milton's Abdiel." *Philological Quarterly* 69 (1970): 249–54.

Gray, J. C. "Paradox in *Paradise Lost*." *Milton Quarterly* 7 (1973): 76–84.

Greene, Thomas M. *The Descent from Heaven: A Study in Epic Continuity*. New Haven: Yale University Press, 1963.

Gregerson, Linda. "The Limbs of Truth: Milton's Use of Simile in *Paradise Lost*." *Milton Studies* XIV (1980): 135–52.

Griffin, Dustin. "Milton's Moon." *Milton Studies* IX (1976): 151–67.

Grose, Christopher. *Milton's Epic Process: "Paradise Lost" and Its Miltonic Background*. New Haven: Yale University Press, 1973.

———. "Milton on Ramist Similitude." In *Seventeenth-Century Imagery: Essays on Uses of Figurative Language from Donne to Farquhar*, ed. Earl Miner, pp. 103–16. Berkeley: University of California Press, 1971.

Guilfoyle, Cherrell. "'If Shape It Might Be Call'd That Shape Had None': Aspects of Death in Milton." *Milton Studies* XIII (1979): 35–57.

Hammond, William A. *Aristotle's Psychology: A Treatise on the Principle of Life*. London: George Allen, 1902.

Hardison, O. B., Jr. "Written Records and Truths of Spirit in *Paradise Lost*." *Milton Studies* I (1969): 147–65.

Hartman, Geoffrey. "Adam on the Grass with Balsamum." *ELH* 36 (1969): 168–92. Reprinted in *Beyond Formalism: Literary Essays 1958–1970*, pp. 124–50. New Haven: Yale University Press, 1970.

Harvey, E. Ruth. *The Inward Wits: Psychological Theory in the Middle Ages and the Renaissance*. Warburg Institute Surveys, vol. 6. London: Warburg Institute, University of London, 1975.

Haublein, Ernst. "Milton's Paraphrase of Genesis: A Stylistic Reading of *Paradise Lost*, Book VII." *Milton Studies* VII: *"Eyes Fast Fixt": Current Perspectives in Milton Methodology*, ed. Albert C. Labriola and Michael Lieb (1975), pp. 101–25.

Hawkins, Sherman. "Samson's Catharsis." *Milton Studies* II (1970): 211–30.

Heninger, S. K., Jr. *Touches of Sweet Harmony: Pythagorean Cosmology and Renaissance Poetics*. San Marino, Calif.: Huntington Library, 1974.

Herbert, George. *The Works of George Herbert*. Edited by F. E. Hutchinson. Oxford: Oxford University Press (Clarendon Press), 1941.

Hesiod, *Theogony*. Translated by Norman O. Brown. Indianapolis: Bobbs-Merrill, 1953.

Hill, John Spencer. *John Milton: Poet, Priest, and Prophet: A Study of Divine Vocation in Milton's Poetry*. Totowa, N. J.: Rowman & Littlefield, 1979.

Howard, Leon. "'The Invention' of Milton's 'Great Argument': A Study of the Logic of 'God's Ways to Men.'" *Huntington Library Quarterly* 9 (1945–46): 149–73.

Howell, Wilbur S. *Logic and Rhetoric in England, 1500–1700*. Princeton: Princeton University Press, 1956.

Hugelet, Theodore L. "The Rule of Charity in Milton's Divorce Tracts." *Milton Studies* VI (1975): 199–214.

Hughes, Merritt Y. "Milton and the Symbol of Light." In *Ten Perspectives on Milton*, pp. 63–103. New Haven: Yale University Press, 1965.

Huntley, Frank A. "Before and after the Fall: Some Miltonic Patterns of Systasis." In *Approaches to "Paradise Lost": The York Tercentenary Lectures*, ed. C. A. Patrides, pp. 1–14. London: Edward Arnold, 1968.

Jacobus, Lee A. *Sudden Apprehension: Aspects of Knowledge in "Paradise Lost."* The Hague: Mouton, 1976.

Johnson, Samuel. *Lives of the English Poets*. Edited by George Birkbeck Hill. 3 vols. Oxford: Oxford University Press (Clarendon Press), 1905.

———. *The Rambler*. Vol. 4 of *The Yale Edition of the Works of Samuel Johnson*, ed. W. J. Bate and Albrecht B. Strauss. New Haven: Yale University Press, 1969.

Kaufmann, U. Milo. *"The Pilgrim's Progress" and Tradition in Puritan Meditation*. New Haven: Yale University Press, 1966.

Kermode, Frank. "Adam Unparadised." In *The Living Milton: Essays by Various Hands*, ed. Frank Kermode, pp. 85–123. London: Routledge & Kegan Paul, 1962.

Kerrigan, William W. *The Prophetic Milton*. Charlottesville: University Press of Virginia, 1974.

Knott, John R., Jr. *Milton's Pastoral Vision: An Approach to "Paradise Lost."* Chicago: University of Chicago Press, 1971.

Korshin, Paul J. "The Development of Abstracted Typology in England, 1650–1820." In *Literary Uses of Typology from the Late Middle Ages to the Present*, ed. Earl Miner, pp. 147–203. Princeton: Princeton University Press, 1977.

Landor, Walter Savage. *The Complete Works of Walter Savage Landor.* Edited by T. Earle Welby. 16 vols. London: Chapman & Hall, 1927.

Lanham, Richard A. *The Motives of Eloquence: Rhetoric in the Renaissance.* New Haven: Yale University Press, 1976.

Lawry, Jon S. *The Shadow of Heaven: Matter and Stance in Milton's Poetry.* Ithaca, N.Y.: Cornell University Press, 1968.

LeComte, Edward S. "*Areopagitica* as a Scenario for *Paradise Lost.*" In *Achievements of the Left Hand: Essays on the Prose of John Milton*, ed. Michael Lieb and John T. Shawcross, pp. 121–41. Amherst: University of Massachusetts Press, 1974.

———. *Milton and Sex.* New York: Columbia University Press, 1978.

Levin, Harry. *The Myth of the Golden Age in the Renaissance.* New York: Oxford University Press, 1964.

Lewalski, Barbara K. "Innocence and Experience in Milton's Eden." In *New Essays on "Paradise Lost,"* ed. Thomas Kranidas, pp. 86–117. Berkeley: University of California Press, 1971.

———. *Milton's Brief Epic: The Genre, Meaning, and Art of "Paradise Regained."* Providence: Brown University Press, 1966.

———. *Protestant Poetics and the Seventeenth-Century Lyric.* Princeton: Princeton University Press, 1979.

———. "Structure and the Symbolism of Vision in Michael's Prophecy, *Paradise Lost*, Books XI–XII." *Philological Quarterly* 42 (1963): 25–35.

———. "Typological Symbolism and the 'Progress of the Soul' in Seventeenth-Century Literature." In *Literary Uses of Typology from the Late Middle Ages to the Present*, ed. Earl Miner, pp. 79–114. Princeton: Princeton University Press, 1977.

Lewis, C. S. *The Discarded Image: An Introduction to Medieval and Renaissance Literature.* Cambridge: Cambridge University Press, 1970.

———. *A Preface to "Paradise Lost."* London: Oxford University Press, 1942.

Lieb, Michael. *Poetics of the Holy: A Reading of "Paradise Lost."* Chapel Hill: University of North Carolina Press, 1981.

Lovejoy, Arthur O. *The Great Chain of Being: A Study of the History of an Idea.* Reprint. New York: Harper Torchbooks, 1960.

Low, Anthony. "Angels and Food in *Paradise Lost.*" *Milton Studies* I (1969): 135–45.

Lusignan, Francine. "*L'Artis Logicae Plenior Institutio* de John Milton: Etat de la question et position." Ph.D. dissertation, University of Montreal, 1974.

MacCaffrey, Isabel G. *"Paradise Lost" as "Myth."* Cambridge: Harvard University Press, 1959.

————. *Spenser's Allegory: The Anatomy of Imagination*. Princeton: Princeton University Press, 1976.

MacCallum, H. R. "Milton and Figurative Interpretation of the Bible." *University of Toronto Quarterly* 31 (1962): 397–415.

————. "Milton and Sacred History: Books XI and XII of *Paradise Lost*." In *Essays in English Literature from the Renaissance to the Victorian Age Presented to A. S. P. Woodhouse*, ed. Millar MacLure and F. W. Watt, pp. 149–68. Toronto: University of Toronto Press, 1964.

————. "'Most Perfect Hero': The Role of the Son in Milton's Theodicy." In *"Paradise Lost": A Tercentenary Tribute*, ed. Balachandra Rajan, pp. 79–105. Toronto: University of Toronto Press, 1969.

McColley, Diane K. "Eve's Dream." *Milton Studies* XII (1978): 25–45.

————. *Milton's Eve*. Urbana: University of Illinois Press, 1983.

McColley, Grant. "The Astronomy of *Paradise Lost*." *Studies in Philology* 34 (1937): 209–47.

————. "Milton's Dialogue on Astronomy: The Principal Immediate Sources." *PMLA* 52 (1937): 728–62.

————. *Paradise Lost: An Account of its Growth and Major Origins*. . . . Chicago: Packard, 1940.

Madsen, William G. *From Shadowy Types to Truth: Studies in Milton's Symbolism*. New Haven: Yale University Press, 1968.

Marlowe, Christopher. *The Complete Works of Christopher Marlowe*. Edited by Fredson Bowers. 2 vols. Cambridge: Cambridge University Press, 1973.

Martz, Louis L. *The Paradise Within: Studies in Vaughan, Traherne, and Milton*. New Haven: Yale University Press, 1964.

————. *The Poetry of Meditation: A Study in English Religious Literature of the Seventeenth Century*. New Haven: Yale University Press, 1954.

Mayerson, Caroline W. "The Orpheus Image in *Lycidas*." *PMLA* 64 (1949). Reprinted in *Milton's "Lycidas": The Tradition and the Poem*, ed. C. A. Patrides, pp. 116–28. Rev. ed. Columbia: University of Missouri Press, 1983.

Melczer, William. "Looking Back without Anger: Milton's *Of Education*." In *Milton and the Middle Ages*, ed. John Mulryan, pp. 91–102. Lewisburg, Pa.: Bucknell University Press, 1982.

Mengert, James G. "Styling the Strife of Glory: The War in Heaven." *Milton Studies* XIV (1980): 95–115.

Miller, Perry. *The New England Mind: The Seventeenth Century*. Reprint. Boston: Beacon Press, 1961.

Milton, John. *John Milton: Complete Poems and Major Prose*. Edited by Merritt Y. Hughes. New York: Odyssey Press, 1957.

————. *Complete Prose Works of John Milton*. Edited by Don M. Wolfe et al. 8 vols. New Haven: Yale University Press, 1953–82.

————. *Paradise Lost: A Poem in Twelve Books.* Edited by Thomas Newton. 2 vols. 4th ed. London, 1757.

————. *The Works of John Milton.* Edited by Frank A. Patterson et al. 20 vols. New York: Columbia University Press, 1931–42.

A Milton Encyclopedia. Edited by William B. Hunter, Jr., et al. 9 vols. Lewisburg, Pa.: Bucknell University Press, 1979.

Mollenkott, Virginia R. "Milton's Technique of Multiple Choice." *Milton Studies* VI (1975): 101–11.

————. "The Pervasive Influence of the Apocrypha in Milton's Thought and Art." In *Milton and the Art of Sacred Song,* ed. J. Max Patrick and Roger H. Sundell, pp. 23–43. Madison: University of Wisconsin Press, 1979.

Murrin, Michael. *The Veil of Allegory: Some Notes toward a Theory of Allegorical Rhetoric in the English Renaissance.* Chicago: University of Chicago Press, 1969.

Nicolson, Marjorie. *The Breaking of the Circle: Studies in the Effect of the "New Science" on Seventeenth-Century Poetry.* Rev. ed. New York: Columbia University Press, 1962.

Norford, Don Parry. "The Sacred Head: Milton's Solar Mysticism." *Milton Studies* IX (1976): 37–75.

Ong, Walter J., S.J. "Logic and the Epic Muse: Reflections on Noetic Structures in Milton's Milieu." In *Achievements of the Left Hand: Essays on the Prose of John Milton,* ed. Michael Lieb and John T. Shawcross, pp. 239–68. Amherst: University of Massachusetts Press, 1974.

————. *Ramus and Talon Inventory: A Short-Title Inventory of the Published Works of Peter Ramus (1515–1572) and of Omer Talon (ca. 1510–1562) in Their Original and in Their Variously Altered Forms with Related Material.* Cambridge: Harvard University Press, 1958.

————. *Ramus, Method, and the Decay of Dialogue: From the Art of Discourse to the Art of Reason.* Cambridge: Harvard University Press, 1958.

Otten, Charlotte F. "'My Native Element': Milton's Paradise and English Gardens." *Milton Studies* V (1973): 249–67.

Parker, William R. "Education: Milton's Ideas and Ours." In *The Language Curtain and Other Essays on American Education.* New York: Modern Language Association of America, 1966.

Patrides, C. A. *Milton and the Christian Tradition.* Reprint. Hamden, Conn.: Archon Books, 1979.

————. "*Paradise Lost* and the Theory of Accommodation." *Texas Studies in Literature and Language* 5 (1963): 58–63.

————. "The 'Protoevangelium' in Renaissance Theology and *Paradise Lost.*" *Studies in English Literature* 3 (1963): 19–30.

Peter, John. *A Critique of "Paradise Lost."* New York: Columbia University Press, 1960.

Pico della Mirandola, Giovanni. *On the Dignity of Man.* In *The Renaissance Philosophy of Man*, ed. Ernst Cassirer et al., pp. 215–54. Chicago: University of Chicago Press, 1948.

Plato. *The Republic*. Translated by Paul Shorey. 2 vols. Loeb Classical Library. London: Heinemann, 1930.

Prince, F. T. "On the Last Two Books of *Paradise Lost*." *Essays and Studies*, n.s. 11 (1958): 38–52. Reprinted in *Milton's Epic Poetry: Essays on "Paradise Lost" and "Paradise Regained*," ed. C. A. Patrides, pp. 233–48. Baltimore: Penguin Books, 1967.

Puttenham, George. *The Arte of English Poesie*. Edited by Gladys Doidge Willcock and Alice Walker. Cambridge: Cambridge University Press, 1936.

Radzinowicz, Mary Ann. "'Man as a Probationer of Immortality': *Paradise Lost* XI–XII." In *Approaches to "Paradise Lost": The York Tercentenary Lectures*, ed. C. A. Patrides, pp. 31–51. London: Arnold, 1968.

———. *Toward "Samson Agonistes": The Growth of Milton's Mind*. Princeton: Princeton University Press, 1978.

Rajan, Balachandra. "The Cunning Resemblance." *Milton Studies VII: "Eyes Fast Fixt": Current Perspectives in Milton Methodology*, ed. Albert C. Labriola and Michael Lieb (1975), pp. 29–48.

———. "Osiris and Urania." *Milton Studies* XIII (1979): 221–35.

———. "Simple, Sensuous, and Passionate." *Review of English Studies* 21 (1945): 289–301. Reprinted in *Milton: Modern Essays in Criticism*, ed. Arthur E. Barker, pp. 3–20. New York: Oxford University Press, 1965.

Ramus, Peter. *The Logike of the Moste Excellent Philosopher P. Ramus, Martyr . . . per M. Roll. Makylmenaeum {Rolland M'Kilwein} . . . 1574*. Scolar Press facsimile ed. Menston, England, 1970.

Reesing, John. *Milton's Poetic Art: "A Mask," "Lycidas," and "Paradise Lost*." Cambridge: Harvard University Press, 1968.

Revard, Stella P. "The Renaissance Michael and the Son of God." In *Milton and the Art of Sacred Song*, ed. J. Max Patrick and Roger H. Sundell, pp. 121–35. Madison: University of Wisconsin Press, 1979.

———. *The War in Heaven: "Paradise Lost" and the Tradition of Satan's Rebellion*. Ithaca, N.Y.: Cornell University Press, 1980.

Ricks, Christopher. *Milton's Grand Style*. Oxford: Oxford University Press (Clarendon Press), 1963.

Riggs, William G. *The Christian Poet in "Paradise Lost*." Berkeley: University of California·Press, 1972.

Robertson, D. W., Jr. *A Preface to Chaucer: Studies in Medieval Perspectives*. Reprint. Princeton: Princeton University Press, 1969.

Rosenblatt, Jason P. "Adam's Pisgah Vision: *Paradise Lost*, XI and XII." *ELH* 39 (1972): 66–86.

———. "Angelic Tact: Raphael on Creation." In *Milton and the Middle Ages*, ed.

John Mulryan, pp. 21–31. Lewisburg, Pa.: Bucknell University Press, 1982.

————. "Celestial Entertainment in Eden: Book V of *Paradise Lost.*" *Harvard Theological Review* 62 (1969): 411–27.

————. "The Mosaic Voice in *Paradise Lost.*" *Milton Studies* VII: *"Eyes Fast Fixt": Current Perspectives in Milton Methodology,* ed. Albert C. Labriola and Michael Lieb (1975), pp. 207–32.

————. "Structural Unity and Temporal Concordance: The War in Heaven in *Paradise Lost.*" *PMLA* 87 (1972): 31–41.

Rossky, William. "Imagination in the English Renaissance: Psychology and Poetic." *Studies in the Renaissance* 5 (1958): 49–73.

Ryken, Leland. *The Apocalyptic Vision in "Paradise Lost."* Ithaca, N.Y.: Cornell University Press, 1970.

St. George, Priscilla P. "Psychomachia in Books V and VI of *Paradise Lost.*" *Modern Language Quarterly* 27 (1966): 185–96.

Samuel, Irene. *Dante and Milton: The "Commedia" and "Paradise Lost."* Ithaca, N.Y.: Cornell University Press, 1966.

————. "Milton on Learning and Wisdom." *PMLA* 64 (1949): 708–23.

————. "Milton on the Province of Rhetoric." *Milton Studies* X (1977): 177–93.

————. *Plato and Milton.* Ithaca, N.Y.: Cornell University Press, 1947.

Schneidau, Herbert N. *Sacred Discontent: The Bible and Western Tradition.* Baton Rouge: Louisiana State University Press, 1976.

Schultz, Howard. *Milton and Forbidden Knowledge.* New York: Modern Language Association of America, 1955.

Scott, William O. "Ramism and Milton's Concept of Poetic Fancy." *Philological Quarterly* 42 (1963): 183–89.

Scott-Craig, Thomas S. K. "The Craftsmanship and Theological Significance of Milton's *Art of Logic.*" *Huntington Library Quarterly* 17 (1953): 1–16.

Shawcross, John T. "*Paradise Lost* and the Theme of Exodus." *Milton Studies* II (1970): 3–26.

Sherry, Beverley. "Not by Bread Alone: The Communication of Adam and Raphael." *Milton Quarterly* 13 (1979): 111–14.

————. "Speech in *Paradise Lost.*" *Milton Studies* VIII (1975): 247–66.

Sidney, Sir Philip. *The Complete Works of Sir Philip Sidney.* Edited by Albert Feuillerat. 3 vols. Cambridge: Cambridge University Press, 1923.

Sims, James H. *The Bible in Milton's Epics.* Gainesville: University of Florida Press, 1962.

Smith, Russell E., Jr. "Adam's Fall." *ELH* 35 (1968). Reprinted in *Critical Essays on Milton from ELH,* pp. 182–94. Baltimore: Johns Hopkins University Press, 1969.

Spenser, Edmund. *The Faerie Queene.* Edited by Thomas P. Roche, Jr. Harmondsworth: Penguin Books, 1978.

Steadman, John M. "Adam and the Prophesied Redeemer (*Paradise Lost*, XII, 359–623)." *Studies in Philology* 56 (1959): 214–25.

————. *Epic and Tragic Structures in "Paradise Lost."* Chicago: University of Chicago Press, 1976.

————. *The Lamb and the Elephant: Ideal Imitation and the Context of Renaissance Allegory.* San Marino, Calif.: Huntington Library, 1974.

————. *Milton and the Renaissance Hero.* Oxford: Oxford University Press (Clarendon Press), 1967.

Stein, Arnold. *The Art of Presence: The Poet and "Paradise Lost."* Berkeley: University of California Press, 1977.

Stewart, Stanley. *The Enclosed Garden: The Tradition and the Image in Seventeenth-Century Poetry.* Madison: University of Wisconsin Press, 1966.

Summers, Joseph H. *George Herbert: His Religion and Art.* Reprint. Binghamton: Medieval & Renaissance Texts & Studies, 1981.

————. *The Muse's Method: An Introduction to "Paradise Lost."* New York: Norton, 1962.

Svendsen, Kester. "Epic Address and Reference and the Principle of Decorum in *Paradise Lost.*" *Philological Quarterly* 28 (1949): 185–210.

————. *Milton and Science.* Cambridge: Harvard University Press, 1956.

Tayler, Edward W. *Milton's Poetry: Its Development in Time.* Pittsburgh: Duquesne University Press, 1979.

Taylor, Dick, Jr. "Milton's Treatment of the Judgment and Expulsion in *Paradise Lost.*" *Tulane Studies in English* 10 (1960): 51–82.

Taylor, George Coffin. *Milton's Use of DuBartas.* Cambridge: Harvard University Press, 1934.

Tillyard, E. M. W. *The Elizabethan World Picture.* Reprint. New York: Random House, n.d.

————. *Milton.* London: Chatto & Windus, 1930.

————. *Studies in Milton.* London: Chatto & Windus, 1964.

Toliver, Harold. "Symbol-Making and the Labors of Milton's Eden." *Texas Studies in Literature and Language* 18 (1976): 433–50.

Tung, Mason. "The Abdiel Episode: A Contextual Reading." *Studies in Philology* 62 (1965): 595–609.

Tuve, Rosemond. *Elizabethan and Metaphysical Imagery: Renaissance Poetic and Twentieth-Century Critics.* Reprint. Chicago: University of Chicago Press, 1961.

————. "Imagery and Logic: Ramus and Metaphysical Poetics." *Journal of the History of Ideas* 3 (1942): 365–400.

————. *A Reading of George Herbert.* Chicago: University of Chicago Press, 1952.

Ulreich, John C., Jr. "The Typological Structure of Milton's Imagery." *Milton Studies* V (1973): 67–85.

Viswanathan, S. "The Sun and the Creation of Adam: *Paradise Lost*, VIII. 253–55." *Milton Quarterly* 8 (1974): 80–82.

Waddington, Raymond B. "The Death of Adam: Vision and Voice in Books XI and XII of *Paradise Lost*." *Modern Philology* 70 (1972): 9–21.

Wallerstein, Ruth. *Studies in Seventeenth-Century Poetic*. Madison: University of Wisconsin Press, 1965.

Webber, Joan M. *Milton and His Epic Tradition*. Seattle: University of Washington Press, 1979.

West, Robert H. *Milton and the Angels*. Athens: University of Georgia Press, 1955.

Whaler, James. "Compounding and Distribution of Similes in *Paradise Lost*." *Modern Philology* 28 (1931): 313–27.

———. "Grammatical *Nexus* of the Miltonic Simile." *Journal of English and Germanic Philology* 30 (1931): 327–34.

———. "The Miltonic Simile." *PMLA* 46 (1931): 1034–74.

Whiting, George W. *Milton and This Pendant World*. Austin: University of Texas Press, 1958.

Wigner, Stephen. "Outrageous Noise and the Sovereign Voice: Satan, Sin, and Syntax in Sonnet XIX and Book VI of *Paradise Lost*." *Milton Studies* X (1977): 155–65.

Willey, Basil. *The Seventeenth Century Background: Studies in the Thought of the Age in Relation to Poetry and Religion*. Reprint. Garden City, N. Y.: Doubleday (Anchor Books), 1955.

Wilson, Gayle Edward. "'His Eyes He Op'n'd': The Abel-Cain Vision, *Paradise Lost*, XI. 427–448." *Milton Quarterly* 14 (1980): 6–12.

Yates, Frances A. *The Art of Memory*. Chicago: University of Chicago Press, 1966.

Index